Why Literature Matters
in the 21st Century

Dec. 17, 2004

For Jeff,

With gratitude for his

support of scholarship at

Notre Dame,

Mark

Why Literature Matters in the 21st Century

Mark William Roche

Yale University Press

New Haven and London

Set in Adobe Garamond and Stone Sans types by The Composing Room of Michigan, Inc.
Printed in the United States of America.

Library of Congress Cataloging-in-Publication Data

Roche, Mark W.
      Why literature matters in the 21st century / Mark W. Roche.
            p.   cm.
      Includes bibliographical references and index.
      ISBN 0-300-10449-9 (cloth : alk. paper)
          1. Literature and morals.   2. Literature and technology.   3. Criticism.
      4. Canon (Literature).   I. Title.

PN49.R63 2004
801′.3—dc22

                                                                                          2004043535

A catalogue record for this book is available from the British Library.

The paper in this book meets the guidelines for permanence and durability
of the Committee on Production Guidelines for Book Longevity of the
Council on Library Resources.

10 9 8 7 6 5 4 3 2 1

For Vittorio Hösle,
a genial philosopher
and even more genial friend

Contents

Acknowledgments

For institutional assistance I am grateful to the University of Notre Dame, which has generously supported my research with time and funding. Few institutions hold so consistently to the idea of the scholar-administrator that they grant leaves to deans. In particular, I should like to thank President Edward A. Malloy, C.S.C., and Provost Nathan O. Hatch for granting me a partial leave in 1999 and 2000. The Humboldt Foundation generously funded my work with a research fellowship during the first half of 1997.

During my Humboldt stay at the University of Essen my host was Vittorio Hösle, and I owe him thanks in at least two respects: first, as an interlocutor he has helped me sharpen my thinking on many occasions; second, his writings on metaphysics, ethics, aesthetics, and the philosophy of technology have given me a richness of categories with which to approach some of the problems I address in this work; the substance, clarity, and range of Hösle's writings, his critiques of important thinkers, such as Hegel and Heidegger, and his reformulations of objective idealism and concrete suggestions for modernity have earned him a distinguished place among contemporary philosophers.

Long before I put pen to paper, I discussed some of these ideas with students at the Ohio State University in two graduate seminars, the first, "Objective Idealism and the Study of Literature," in the spring of 1988 and the second, "Literature in the Age of Technology," in the spring of 1993. During my stay in Essen I was able to present the ideas in a series of colloquia to faculty and students of philosophy and literature. For comments and questions during these sessions, which were arranged by Christian Illies and Dietrich Koch, I am grateful. Also, Dirk Hohnsträter (Berlin) made helpful comments on that early draft. Similarly rewarding was a discussion of chapter 1 and part of chapter 2 with the 1999–2000 fellows of the Erasmus Institute of the University of Notre Dame, which was arranged by William Donahue (Rutgers University) and Roger Lundin (Wheaton College). The comments of Gary Gutting (Notre Dame) and Rev. Robert Sullivan (Notre Dame) were especially important for the further development of my manuscript. Scholars from whom I have learned in discussing aspects of technology include especially Alan Beyerchen (Ohio State) and John Hampshire (Broad Reach Communications). I am also grateful to the two readers for Yale University Press and to Otto Bohlmann and John Kulka of Yale University Press. In addition, I would like to thank Nancy Moore of Yale University Press for overseeing the production of the book and Linda Webster for preparing the index.

Barbara Roche's emphasis on ideas that might reach a broader readership has been an inspiration, as has been her exceptional work as a gardener and an artist. Duncan and Gabriel awakened in me a greater awareness of the spirituality of nature than I would have thought possible. So, too, if in different ways, am I grateful to Banquo, Bridget, Iona, Karma, Kizmet, Leoni, Lexicon, Macbeth, and Wacondo.

Sources and Translations

Throughout this book I draw on various traditions and debates in developing a new perspective on the opportunities and challenges facing literature and literary criticism in the technological age. I focus to a considerable degree on the German intellectual tradition, ranging from late eighteenth- and early nineteenth-century philosophers working within an idealist paradigm to more modern and contemporary thinkers. Also, many of my cross-cultural comparisons are devoted to Germany and to contemporary literary-critical studies in Germany. This orientation enables me to draw on a rich cultural tradition and to offer cross-cultural comparisons for an American audience while still addressing concerns that have broader resonance and animate literary criticism in America today. One of the book's goals is to make this tradition of thought, as well as other selected thinkers from different and primarily European traditions, relevant for contemporary concerns of a universal nature and in a way that is accessible to a wider audience.

For most of the foreign sources, I have drawn on published translations, as is evident from the list of works cited. Foreign sources are listed in the case of passages for which no published translation exists or simple passages for which consulting a published translation would have been superfluous; in these cases I translated the texts myself. In a few cases I benefited from consulting published translations but chose to deviate from them; these passages are always indicated with the phrase, "translation modified."

Chapter 1 Introduction

The arts and humanities, including literature and literary criticism, concern themselves with the fate and prospects of humankind. These fields have been placed under increasing pressure to give an account of themselves—partly because unlike science and technology the value of the arts and the humanities is not immediately apparent, partly because states and universities have suffered harshly competitive fiscal demands, and partly because increased criticism has been lodged against the arts and humanities from both within and beyond the academy. Any attempt to justify the arts and humanities must account for their universal purpose and their specific role in a given age. Today the fate and prospects of humanity are under the influence of technology—the technological transformation of the world was *the* defining feature of the twentieth century, both in the strict sense of the harnessing and transformation of nature and the creation and application of tools, machines, and information and in the broad sense of an elevation of means-ends rationality.

THE CHALLENGE OF TECHNOLOGY
AND THE CRISIS OF LEGITIMACY

Technology represents a mode of means-ends thinking that allows us to ma-nipulate material for a given end. We can be said to live in an age of technology when four conditions have been met: first, our daily living presupposes con-stant interaction with the products of technology, such that we have as steady a relation to these products as we do to nature or to other persons; second, the most dramatic events of our era are defined by technology, in this case new in-ventions that change our lives dramatically, for better and for worse; third, our mode of thinking is very much driven by the paradigm of technology, by which I mean above all technical rationality; and fourth, technology takes on a life of its own, becoming not just a means to a higher goal but its own end—such that, for example, the products of technology elicit new needs as much as sat-isfy intrinsic needs. These conditions apply to the contemporary age and have increasingly defined the modern world since the first industrial revolution. In the words of the Swiss dramatist Friedrich Dürrenmatt, "Technology is the thought of our age in visible, pictorial terms" (26.63).

The influence of technology on modernity places new tasks before both lit-erature and literary criticism, and a legitimation of these spheres must reflect on these new tasks. Accordingly, I analyze the moral aspects of literature and liter-ary criticism in general, discuss prominent categories of the technological age and the influence of technology on literature, and address what great literature and literary criticism should be specifically in this age. The topic is innovative in at least two respects. First, the question of a moral justification of literature and literary criticism tends to be neglected—both by philosophers, who have increasingly retreated into the narrow confines of their own subdisciplines, and by literary critics, who despite their attention to issues of self-reflection have fo-cused more on historical and sociological issues, pragmatic concerns, and ques-tions of ideology or interpretation than on the fundamental principles of their profession, including the value of literature and literary criticism. Exceptions, such as Sven Birkerts, are few and far between and surface for the most part out-side the mainstream of the academy. Conferences on the profession of literary criticism tend to address its history and sociology, the descriptive not the nor-mative sphere. When the future is thematized, one tends to speak of pragmatic concerns, such as there being either too many students (in graduate programs) or too few students (in undergraduate programs) and in the latter case, how we might enroll more students. Sometimes the suggestion made is to become more interdisciplinary, which need not mean—but unfortunately often does mean—that beyond expanding our horizon, we should also abandon the teaching of literature as literature. We rarely ask why we should read literature and why we should pursue literary criticism, nor generally is the question asked, What are our specific obligations as literary scholars in an age marked by technology and increasingly threatened by ecological crisis?[1] This inattention to the ethical challenges of modernity is one of the central reasons for the contemporary crisis in literary criticism, and the emphasis on the *how* at the expense of the *why* is—as we shall see below—simply another expression of technological consciousness.

Second, although the philosophy of technology is a burgeoning field, few philosophers of technology reflect at any length on art, even those, such as Hans Jonas and Karl-Otto Apel, who address ethics and technology. Here, too, the exceptions are few; one thinks above all of Walter Benjamin's well-known contribution *The Work of Art in the Age of Mechanical Reproduction.* Although philosophers of technology have tended to neglect literature and literary criticism, one can integrate their insights by asking not only what arguments and categories these thinkers introduce and to what extent they are valid but also what relevance their ideas have for the study of literature in the technological age. In this sense I attempt to extend such thinkers as Jonas and Apel beyond their immediate claims. Some attention has been given by literary critics to the thematic study of technology in literature, and much can be gained from the few analyses available. Nonetheless, literature seems to be ahead of literary criticism, as there are seemingly more works, including anthologies of literary works, that thematize technology than literary-critical studies of the topic.[2]

In contrast to the modern tendency to place in opposition to one another two dominant spheres of knowledge, science and technology over against the humanities and the arts, the Greek notion of *techne* suggests that technique and art need not be viewed as exclusive poles. *Techne* means both art (e.g., literature) and craft (i.e., technique). As such it differs from *episteme,* which signifies pure knowledge or science. For the Greeks the artist was a craftsman, shoemaking was an art, and sculpture was a technique. For Plato no distinction existed between the fine and the mechanical arts. This connection between technique and art is widely characteristic of the premodern world. It is prominent, for example, in drawing and painting, where perspective, anatomy, and geometrical proportions assumed great significance; thus, for Leonardo da Vinci art and science were one and the same. Nonetheless, a shift occurs beginning in isolated cases already in the sixteenth century and, bolstered by the scientific revolution of the seventeenth, becoming widespread by the end of the eighteenth (Kris-teller 507–27). Art and technique no longer serve the same purpose but develop independently and autonomously. The *artes liberales* and *artes mechanicae* di-verge, and technology becomes aligned with science and industry, while art de-velops stronger ties to the humanities.

In *Man in the Age of Technology* Arnold Gehlen, one of Germany's earliest philosophers of technology, recognized that the emergence of the technological age was sped by the congruence of science, technology, and capitalism (11–13). Rapid scientific advances accelerate the development of new technologies, both of which require the investment of capital. Also, technical inventions make the market that much more efficient, improving infrastructure, commerce, and the number of desirable goods. In turn, the competitive nature of the market econ-omy hastens the already quick developments of science and industry.[3] Science and technique have become so intertwined that systematic reflection on tech-nique has become integral to the techniques themselves, and so many diverse techniques function in such close cooperation that today one speaks simply of "technology" even when describing the object sphere. Technical breakthroughs in the modern era were not isolated phenomena but "came in clusters, interact-ing with each other in a process of increasing returns" (Castells 1.37). In this way isolated techniques were transformed into the mass phenomenon of tech-nology. Today, with so many technical innovations converging into shared en-terprises and cooperative endeavors, the sense of technology as a single entity is accentuated daily. The complexity of modern technology, in its intersection with science and capitalism, represents not simply a quantitative break from the techniques of earlier eras, it is qualitatively different. In the premodern era, the poet frequently drew metaphors from the world of technique; Homer, like the medieval poets after him, was still close to the life worlds in which tech-niques, such as plowing or weaving, played roles. In contrast, the modern poet rarely employs metaphors from today's technology, the jet engine or the nuclear reactor, for example. The complexity of modern technology and our distance from its inner workings further this break and its effect on poetics. Not surpris-ingly, Dürrenmatt speaks of "the technology that has become impenetrable" ("Ich bin" 34).

Given the complexity of modern technology, literature and technology seem to have become separate and unbridgeable spheres. Half a century ago C. P. Snow advanced the thesis that natural scientists and literary intellectuals live in separate worlds. With increasing specialization in both realms, along with post-modern critiques of reason arising in the humanities and the prestige of traditional humanistic study diminishing among many scientists, Snow's claim has lost little of its relevance. Rare is the person who crosses these borders. Yet such crossings are to be encouraged, and the connections between literature and technology may be greater in principle than they appear at first glance. Technology is creative, and literature follows certain laws. Commonalities exist between them, as ancient and medieval thinkers believed, and the spheres are enriched when interaction and reflection surface in both directions. Certainly the differences between traditional techniques and modern technology will render any contemporary crossing of these spheres qualitatively different from, and immensely more difficult than, those of earlier eras.

Nonetheless, already with the emergence of photography and later with film, we again see both the need and the opportunity to bridge art and technique. Some of today's most avant-garde artists have returned to this original union by using technology to create great art, as, for example, in the computer graphic art of Charles Csuri. One is also reminded of Edgar Allen Poe's description of the poetic craft as involving, in his metaphor, "wheels and pinions" (289) or of his construction of "The Raven" as proceeding "step by step, to its completion with the precision and rigid consequence of a mathematical problem" (290). One thinks as well of Gottfried Benn's statement that "a poem very rarely comes into being—a poem is made" (1059) or Dürrenmatt's description of himself as a "craftsman" (Bienek 108). So, too, can we consider the integration of art and technology in such spheres as sculpture, graphics, and film, or the architect's necessary engagement with both spheres, which reached a high point in the integrative efforts of the Bauhaus. Not only do we see occasional integration, we see actual inversions, whereby a bridge, for example, may evidence a certain beauty and elegance, and a painting may be distinguished by its jarring negation of beauty.[4] In any age the artist must execute well in his or her chosen medium. A goal of this book is to suggest that on many levels art can respond to technology's positive and negative moments in as yet unexplored ways. Technology is an imaginative enterprise, and much of the wisdom contained in it has a poetic dimension, but it nonetheless seems to lack certain aspects privileged when we speak of art as opposed to technology. This book attempts to define these features.

Not only does a scientific technology emerge that differs from the techniques of art, both art and technology become autonomous vis-à-vis morality. For centuries art was created within an overarching moral universe. The link between art and the sacred is obvious to anyone who reflects on the history of the visual arts or music. Carl Dahlhaus has shown in *The Idea of Absolute Mu-*

sic that the connection between music and text and the development of music within a functional context, a paradigm that was prominent from antiquity to the seventeenth century, dissolved in the modern era. Music increasingly developed what was unique to itself, a purely independent instrumental music without concept, object, or purpose, which became known as absolute music. Also in literature we see the dissolution of a tradition that encompassed virtually all literary activity through the end of the eighteenth century and viewed literature as serving a moral purpose and as embedded within a broader moral frame.

The catalysts for the disassociation of art from morality were multiple. First, modernity increasingly lost its belief in a religious or even simply a moral frame. The distinction between *is* and *ought* that Kant had emphasized and that elevated morality in the wake of the modern dissolution of religion loses all effectiveness if the normative sphere cannot be adequately grounded, and skepticism toward such grounds has consistently increased since the nineteenth century. Second, if the normative realm cannot be grounded, one turns to being, though no longer a realm of being that has implicit in it a normative claim, but sheer facticity. The social sciences, which emerge at this time, approach the descriptive sphere with new methodologies, and literature in some ways does the same, though with different means, analyzing the complexity of the modern psyche, our human relations, and our social world, including modern humanity's lament over a loss of orientation. Analyses of this broad and increasingly complex realm of reality become further and further divorced from the kind of thinking that focused on transcendental claims and, indeed, more and more removed from any moral sphere of evaluation. The recognition that many spheres of social reality had not been included in previous claims of synthesis and the discovery of alternative paradigms, bolstered by the emergence of historicism, also contributed to this erosion of the transcendental. Third, a central idea of modernity is that each sphere of life is fully autonomous. Art, business, law, politics, science—each develops according to the logic of its own subsystem, and each sphere is divorced from the moral realm.

This idea is imaginatively expressed in Hermann Broch's *The Sleepwalkers,* to which I return below, and has been prominent in the analyses of sociologists from Max Weber to Niklas Luhmann. The artist is slowly freed of having to work in harmony with other spheres. A concept of originality replaces the idea of contributing to our understanding of the cosmos, of God, or of human potential. This freedom unleashed an incredible range of options and led to some extraordinary aesthetic works. It also precipitated not only a divergence in spheres and a rejection of the ideal of holistic knowledge but also in some thinkers, such as Kierkegaard, who reflects on the aesthetic, ethical, and religious modes, a theoretical sharpening and an embrace of the distinctions, and in some writers, Oscar Wilde, for example, a deep antagonism between the aesthetic and the ethical: "The sphere of Art and the sphere of Ethics are absolutely distinct and separate" (1048; cf. 17). Indeed, in "The Decay of Lying" Wilde argues not only that art has intrinsic value and need not be viewed as subordinate to external ends but also that art cannot serve any external ends; if it does, it is no longer art (976).

We find ourselves today in a complex position. Artists and critics tend to bracket moral questions. Art increasingly becomes a sophisticated game devoid of moral value, or it is reduced to commercial entertainment and kitsch. In a climate in which the value of art is not part of a broader sphere and the dominant subsystem of modernity, the economic, determines value through an elevation of instrumental reason, not only society's but also the artist's recognition of the value of art begins to wane. We become further and further estranged from the questions of why art is legitimate and valuable and which art should be preferred. The predicament of the artist in such an age is difficult. Artists working in earlier eras knew to what ends they might develop their talents. They knew what themes were privileged and what higher purpose their creativity might serve. In a sense the artist's optimism was still evident during the early stages of aesthetic autonomy; charting new territory gave the artist an enabling sense of opportunity. Even in Dahlhaus's account of absolute music we recognize not only the development of music's autonomy but also the idea that music is expressive of the absolute, an idea that today seems entirely foreign. We have now reached a point where the modern artists who seek to articulate a vision cannot imitate the models of the past, which seem no longer to hold; yet if they continue simply to innovate, primarily by way of a negation of tradition, the public may remain cold to their work. Even the artist's bold sense of resistance to the status quo is dissolved when recognized in its fuller context. Insofar as art participates in the historical development of autonomous subsystems, the autonomous artist does not resist his or her age as much as participate in the general subsplintering of values: just as other spheres call for experts, so now are there specialists in art, removed from the broader sphere of life. The artist's would-be distance from society only fulfills the expectation that the artist operate within his or her autonomous sphere and have no impact on the larger world.

People are driven to become artists by their talents and their desire to develop and express them, but in an age when art no longer seems to serve a moral purpose, the question of the artist's role becomes increasingly unclear. The number of modern artists who suffer difficult lives and crises of identity increases, and these problems are related not only to the stresses of creation and the difficulties of reception but also to the unsettling idea that the artist's path may be devoid of higher purpose. We must have respect and compassion for artists who find themselves in this unenviable situation. Few authors have portrayed this complex predicament more insightfully than Thomas Mann in *Doktor Faustus.* Mann's hero, Adrian Leverkühn, is so eager to find a viable path that will allow his extraordinary talents to be fulfilled that he is willing to negotiate with the devil. The despair of isolation, intensified by his disengagement from the burden of tradition, which he can only mock, and his eventual capacity for expression, which presupposes a break with morality, leads to ruin. Leverkühn's plight shows the tragedy of the modern artist, who is overburdened with tradition and unable to work within a moral frame. Upon abandoning love and the moral sphere in order to break through as an artist, Leverkühn becomes a murderer and is damned. Nonetheless, we empathize with him even as we condemn him.

We understand how art has developed so as to have been divorced from morality and we sense the incredible burdens of being an artist in an age that tends no longer to see the value of art beyond its status as a commercial product or an idle game. Nonetheless, the idea that art has nothing or little to do with truth or goodness, that it must operate independently of a moral universe, is distinctly modern and may need to be viewed as a tendentious ideology, which after a short period of release may now actually be hindering the value and self-consciousness of the contemporary artist. What ultimately is wrong with this separation of art and morality? To suggest that art has only a formal value and that a determination of its quality is not subject to an evaluation of its content, which can be accomplished only from within a moral frame, not only leads to the artist's despair, it is also philosophically untenable. Morality is not one subsystem among the others, such that there is art, science, religion, business, politics, and so forth, *alongside* morality. Instead, morality is the guiding principle for all human endeavors.[5] This is not to say that great art cannot arise out of a culture in which art has become an autonomous subsystem, or that freedom from ethical considerations doesn't allow poets to create with a greater sense of experimentation and focus on form, but it does suggest that the modern autonomy of art is not in every respect welcome. This critique of autonomy has its analogy among those who argue, contrary to modern developments, that the economy cannot be fully divorced from ethics, or that science is subject to higher claims of moral legitimacy.

In modernity art has increasingly freed itself not only from artistic precepts but also from any reflection on its morality or relation to truth. I do not question the facticity of this development, which is simply a manifestation of the modern emergence of discrete subsystems of culture and leads to new insights and opportunities even as it gives rise to other problems. I do, however, problematize this development insofar as the *quaestio iuris* is concerned, and in doing so I do not differ from writers—from E. T. A. Hoffmann to Thomas Mann and beyond—who question their own artistic paradigms. To render art entirely autonomous is to say that morality, too, is only one sphere among many, and so would free one to remove morality from other spheres, such as religion or politics, which few advocates of aesthetic autonomy would likely endorse. Any reprehensible action could be justified by way of its autonomous sphere: it was for art, it was for war, it was for religion, it was for love, and so forth. Certainly, reprehensible actions also arise when individuals commit acts for allegedly moral purposes, but our recognition of an action as reprehensible presupposes that higher moral norms allow us to measure an allegedly moral stance as immoral. In this sense the superiority of the moral is not brought into question.

Every enterprise, especially those that receive public funding, should have moral legitimacy. One can legitimate the value of an activity either by pointing to its intrinsic value or by stressing its value for society. The question of the moral legitimacy of art should not be relegated to a nonquestion (which is in many ways the dominant liberal position) or a simplistic response (which is in many ways the dominant conservative stance). Several ambiguities lie in the term *morality*. Most commonly, it refers to questions of conduct and behavior. In this context moral art might be viewed as art that does not violate the moral customs of the age, for example, that it not contain frank depictions of sexuality. I mean something entirely different. My concern is the moral value of literature, whether it is worthy of our investment of time and if so, what it can and should be. To distinguish between "moral conventions," that is, the moral claims and customs of a certain society at a given point in history, and "morality," that is, the moral claims legitimated by reason after measuring and evaluating specific moral conventions, is important. Keeping this distinction in mind, we can recognize that the morality of some literary works might consist in breaking free of the moral conventions of a given age, which from a higher perspective are to be viewed as less than ideal.

IDEALISM AS A RESOURCE

Philosophy and the individual disciplines can intersect in either of two directions. On the one hand, philosophy can reach out to other disciplines and address the claims of those sciences instead of being simply philosophy for the sake of philosophy; and it is indeed imperative that philosophy do so if it is to remain relevant. On the other hand, philosophical questions can be raised from within the specific disciplines, whenever these disciplines address the fundamental questions of their enterprise. What is art? Why should we read literature, and which literature should we read? How might literary criticism enhance our experience of literature? One sign of the crisis of literary criticism is that such questions have for the most part been neglected or become taboo. To answer them presupposes a normative level, and we live in an age of normative paralysis.

Several ironies surface in this development. First, literature and literary criticism have never been doubted by the general public as much as they are today, and so the question of legitimacy is central to the future health of the discipline. Second, literary criticism has never been as self-reflective as it is today, yet the most central normative questions are consistently neglected. Third, even as literary critics have abandoned the idea of grounding any normative claims, literary criticism has itself become increasingly dogmatic, splintering into schools and subschools that speak their own language and criticize one another, often without addressing overarching questions of legitimacy. Fourth, and most ironic, in the past thirty to forty years literary critics have undertaken a desperate search for relevance. Relevance is indeed desirable, but in this search extra-aesthetic and ideological considerations have so fully replaced aesthetic ones that the question of why we should study literature has remained unanswered precisely by those who have sought to give moral relevance to the study of literature.

Many persons looking for orientation from the field of literary criticism are skeptical about its current state and are looking for alternative perspectives. Undoubtedly very few contemporaries would expect to find viable answers in the tradition of objective idealism, which argues that synthetic a priori knowledge exists and that this knowledge has ontological valence. Held by Plato and Hegel and currently given its strongest defense in the diverse writings of Vittorio Hösle,[6] the view that there is an ideal sphere that transcends nature and consciousness is foreign to what Stanley Fish would call "the *going* argument," namely, that there are no foundational positions and that the only norms to which one can legitimately appeal are the professional norms practiced at any given time ("Anti-Foundationalism" 68; cf. Culler 45). When the distinction between *is* and *ought* is leveled, the power of the professions increases. Professional consensus is in principle no longer accountable to a higher purpose, and criticism of the reigning paradigm becomes increasingly difficult, as people have professional stakes in the status quo, which itself becomes the standard of judgment. Nonetheless, in a climate that fails to excite both practitioners and observers, alternative perspectives may be both welcome and invigorating.

At least two ways exist to show the validity of a position—to argue from first principles that are proven or to demonstrate a position's heuristic value. Since this book is not an effort to develop first principles and since few contemporaries would find an objective idealist framework a natural choice for the present age, I pursue the second path, attempting to present a framework that allows us to see the sphere of literary studies in unexpected ways. While many of my positions can be grounded within the book itself, others draw on a tradition of thought that is presupposed, and not proven, in this study. While presuppositions exist for all works of literary criticism, this book's presuppositions are not part of the consensus of the age. For many centuries the strongest defense of the arts and humanities derived from the idealist tradition. This tradition has vanished for the most part, and our contemporaries have considerable difficulties convincing others of the value of the arts and humanities. Certainly, insights into their value may derive from diverse complementary sources, and one writer, among others, might well draw on this tradition. If we are in agreement that the humanities, literary criticism in particular, are suffering from a crisis of legitimacy, we must be flexible and open in seeking solutions. Skeptics of a more traditional stance may wish to begin with my analyses of culture studies and deconstruction in chapter 4. If the evaluation of contemporary currents seems sound, then the skeptical reader might return to the book's more logical opening and read the development of normative principles that motivate the later evaluation.

Suppose then, for the sake of argument, that even though few would accept the premises of idealism, we experiment with some of its positions and weigh whether or not it might allow us to see values and perspectives that might otherwise be hidden. In drawing on this tradition, I do not follow all of its claims; the reader will recognize specific points of disagreement with Plato and Hegel, which are highlighted in my reflections. In addition, any effort to reawaken some of the forgotten arguments of objective idealism needs to draw on the diverse advances in the individual sciences and arts since the last system of idealism was developed. Hösle, for example, employs the rich resources of the social sciences in developing his arguments on morals and politics, and in an earlier study, in which I developed Hegel's theories of tragedy and comedy for the contemporary age, I sought to integrate advances in the arts since the time of Hegel. In this book, I not only attempt to integrate post-Hegelian advances in literary criticism, I seek to bring the tradition of objective idealism into conversation with the challenges of the technological age.

The idealist thinker who engaged the moral value of literature more fervently than any other is Friedrich Schiller. Schiller takes his initial cues from Kant. Among Kant's main achievements in aesthetics are not only a rich account of aesthetic judgment but also a recognition of the intrinsic value of art and its relation to morality and an articulation of the connections between art and nature. Schiller, both poet and Kantian, challenges the philosopher in various ways, arguing, for example, that our motivations for moral action need not derive only from reason. But Schiller also develops a Kantian perspective; indeed, his importance in the history of aesthetics derives from his extraordinary ability to explore the seemingly contradictory path of art as autonomous and as moral. Schiller links the autonomy of art with its wholeness and harmony, which represent a counterimage to the fragmentation of reality; the experience of harmony has an effect on our souls and is viewed as a prerequisite for the moral regeneration of society. I return to this insight, but seek to supplement it in diverse ways. First, Schiller's efforts, not unlike Kant's, are highly formal, and an aesthetics that seeks to deepen Schiller's claims about the moral value of literature will need to integrate the historical perspective and concrete content characteristic of Hegel's aesthetics, even if on diverse points (such as whether philosophy makes art superfluous, I side with Schiller against Hegel). Second, any effort to return to a thinker like Schiller, whose aesthetic works are now two centuries old, must also be enriched by reflections on the developments of modernity—both in the object world, ranging from technology to politics and art, and in the scholarly world, encompassing advances in the natural sciences and the emergence of the social sciences. Above all, the ugly, which dominated aesthetic discussion immediately after the idealist period, needs to be fully integrated into art. Schiller can be valuable for the present, but we cannot be Schillerians.

My analysis of why literature matters in the twenty-first century has three parts. The book begins with a normative discussion of the value of literature and literary criticism. Despite my focus in this first part on more traditional questions and a more traditional aesthetics, I do not ignore contemporary developments: chapter 4, for example, outlines strengths and weaknesses in contemporary literary criticism. Recent developments offer us new ways of viewing art, and these valuable horizons should not be lost. However, the question also arises of whether some valid questions have been forgotten. The historical transcendence of a theory is not one and the same as its philosophical refutation. A return to certain questions that have been neglected in modernity may in fact be the best way to open up new vistas for modernity. In the book's second part I turn to a descriptive account of the dominant categories of the technological age and their impact on aesthetics. I consider some of the intellectual-historical prerequisites of the technological age, especially those with a direct or indirect impact on aesthetics, and their manifestation in society and culture. I also reflect on the ways in which the specific technical innovations of the age have influenced not only society in general but also art and especially literature. Combining the normative and descriptive parts, I then turn in the third section to constructive suggestions concerning the possibilities of literature and literary criticism in the technological age, that is, a discussion of what great art and literary criticism should be today and the ways in which art can address some of the central categories and problems of the technological age. This triadic structure gives us insight into the universal value of literature and literary criticism and their specific possibilities and challenges in the twenty-first century.

Part One **Moral Principles of Literature and Literary Criticism**

.

Chapter 2 The Value
of Literature

In our age of normative crisis, such terms as "art" and "literature" tend to be reduced to current usage. Art is whatever a certain group deems it to be. To suggest otherwise is to risk being viewed as a censor of others' perspectives, instead of a critic seeking the best truth claims. In contrast to this reigning sociological view, the definition of art I develop is normative: I do not describe what various persons, institutions, or cultures consider art to be, I ask what art should and can be if it has moral value. Why can artistic, and in particular literary, activity be morally excellent, and how can it realize this ideal? In order to answer these questions, two issues must be addressed. First, in what ways is beauty compatible with, and related to, truth and goodness? Second, in what ways is beauty unique and different from the true and the good?

THE MOMENT OF TRUTH

Art deals with the basic structures of being, nature, and spirit. In the *Republic* Plato disparages the artist as an imitator twice removed from reality (595–608). According to Plato, the poet imitates not the original form or idea but its real manifestation in the world.[1] Although some poets can be characterized in this way, the essence of great poetry is not the imitation of an imitation. Already Plotinus suggests, in contrast to Plato, that the object of imitation is not nature but the ideal. The artist does not simply reproduce what is but goes back to "the Reason-Principles from which Nature itself derives" (para. V.8.1). Schelling and Hegel argue more fully that art does not merely imitate what is, it reflects on a reality that is higher than so-called reality itself; in Schelling's words, "the *ideal* is the real and is much more real than the so-called real itself" (*Philosophy* 35; cf. Hegel 13.22). Art can be viewed as higher than everyday reality insofar as it is closer to expressing truth. What we call everyday reality may have more aspects of deception, insofar as it shields us—by way of the capriciousness of situations and events, the clutter of external and superficial objects, and the immediacy of sensuous impressions—from a more essential meaning, a more genuine reality. Everyday reality is not free of this higher spirit and essence, but art, unlike everyday reality, with its multiple contingencies, emphasizes and reveals this higher reality. In this sense art has a profound metaphysical dimension; it does not imitate the external world, it makes visible for us the absolute. In one sense, to be elaborated more fully below, art is higher than the original of which it is a copy, for it brings that original to semblance. Poetry, then, is a semblance of the ideal or an "idealization" of reality that conveys truths that are timeless and transferable to other cultures and ages and truths that address and derive from the particular and often unique challenges of a given age. Even when art fails to give us satisfactory answers to complex questions, it still takes our gaze from the inessential to the essential.

Fidelity to external reality is, therefore, not a criterion of great art. Already Aristotle recognized that art evokes a higher reality; in exhibiting the basic structures of being, it is superior to history: "The distinction between historian and poet . . . consists really in this, that the one describes the thing that has been, and the other a kind of thing that might be. Hence poetry is something more philosophic and of graver import than history, since its statements are of the nature rather of universals, whereas those of history are singulars" (1451b). The poet seeks the higher laws of possibility and necessity and is thereby not restricted to what already exists. Art need not be accurate, in the sense of being correct in its depiction of a person or event, if indeed historical events have triggered the poet's imagination, but it must be true in the sense of revealing through its expression a higher essence.[2] Thus, Hegel cogently argues that a portrait that abstracts from the contingent and reveals the essence of a person's character can be "more like the individual than the real individual himself" (15.104). An aesthetic capacity allows us to see not simply the externality already present to us but the essence behind externality. Paul Klee writes in this spirit: "Art does not reproduce the visible, but rather renders visible [Kunst gibt nicht das Sichtbare wieder, sondern macht sichtbar]" (118). Our reception of Macbeth, Othello, and Lear gives us great insight into psychological truth, more insight than we find in newspaper reports about "real" stories of ambition, jealousy, and suffering. Goethe's Faust captures more of what life means than may a "real" scholar or lover. In a sense he is the original; we may appear to be like or unlike him, not he like or unlike us.

In claiming that art makes visible a higher reality, I do not in the least want to suggest that idealist aesthetics is incompatible with the value of everyday reality. Eric Auerbach profoundly elaborates the ways in which the Marcan account ennobles St. Peter, a mere servant, to tragic stature (40–47). The modern era, inspired by Christianity, has had a strong democratizing potential, which might at first glance seem to be at odds with an idealist account of art as ascending spirituality, but the greatness of the idealist account is that the recipient of beauty does not simply ascend above the finite and the everyday, he recognizes the extent to which the finite itself is capable of revealing and embodying a higher truth. From the perspective of beauty the finite becomes more vivid in itself and more evocative of transcendence. The connection is not dualistic but dialectical, and idealist art, in its highest sense, does not take us away from the everyday as much as illuminate the higher meaning implicit in the everyday.

Useful in this context would be to distinguish between two types of ideals. Certainly art will sometimes portray the kinds of ideals that Plato elevates as having normative value and transcending what is present in everyday reality, but in many cases art will, instead of transcending reality, simply render it more visible. Here we could still say that art portrays an ideal, though it is analogous not to Plato's ideal good but to Max Weber's concept of the ideal type. Weber suggests that beyond the multiple phenomena and variations of reality, ideal types give us a heuristic lens to understand reality and a vocabulary to describe it. These ideal types are not always distinguished on an evaluative level: "There are ideal types of brothels, just as there are of religions" (200). In terms of literature, we may recognize something akin to ideal types in evil figures, such as Shakespeare's Edmund or Iago, or we may reflect in this way on figures who are much more difficult to evaluate, such as Cervantes's Don Quixote or Molière's Alceste. Art is capable of uncovering ideal-typical norms in Weber's sense; these acts of unveiling give us great insight into the logic of human behavior and the consequences of given positions. Of course art portrays these insights into the essential structures of reality by way of particular stories and images and not by way of abstractions, and art gives greater voice to the complex juxtaposition of characteristics prominent in reality than the abstract purity of Weber's ideal types would allow; in addition, in art, unlike in the social sciences, we are fascinated not only by the content but also by the manner of presentation, which gives distinct shape and definition to the content. Nonetheless, the effort to render the essential structures and forms of reality more visible is common.

Art, then, unveils aspects of reality (if it were only to mirror visible reality, it would lack independent justification). We can readily embrace the idea that art makes visible those parts of reality that are otherwise veiled to us, especially in a technological age, where many of our actions are mediated and many of the consequences of our action not readily visible. The relationship between art and hidden reality surfaced as prominent in the writings of Georg Lukács, the most influential Marxist literary critic of the twentieth century, who saw in critical realism a privileged form of art (459–603). In the realism of such writers as Balzac, Tolstoy, and Mann, Lukács recognized a critical portrayal of social, economic, and historical reality. Thus, Lukács privileged more realistic authors, such as Mann, over more avant-garde and experimental artists, such as Franz Kafka. The paradox of the progressive critic favoring the more conservative authors arises, on the one hand, because Lukács was able to recognize the extraordinarily complex and in some ways unintentionally forward-looking insights that lay embedded in complex realist texts and, on the other hand, because his sense of realism was not sufficiently broad as to include what Kafka and others were able to recognize in the reality of their day.

I would propose that so long as we reflect on art as making reality visible, we must include authors like Kafka. Fantastic and disharmonic art render visible what tends to be neglected in our everyday relationship to reality or our everyday use of categories. Such art arouses awareness of what might superficially be overlooked; it draws our attention to the marginal, the less readily apparent, the forgotten. Recognition of these essential aspects of reality, rendered invisible or unclear in the complexity of our everyday lives, including a variety of individual and collective denial mechanisms, has great value. Not all problems can be traced back to social, economic, or historical causes, and not all realistic portrayals in this broad sense need be subsumed under a more superficial concept of reality. We needn't be constrained by a more restrictive definition of realism if we recognize that also superficially unrealistic authors make visible essential aspects of reality. This embrace of a broader concept of realism derives from an objective idealist frame that recognizes reason in the world and so seeks to make sense of all positions, including those that may seem aberrant, even as it measures them against a higher form of reason.

Beyond rendering reality visible in a form that may not be overtly evaluative or that may be highly ambiguous, but whose main purpose is simply to disclose reality, art can also evoke a higher reality. It may do so in either of two ways. On the one hand, by showing what is less than is ideal, art may criticize the negativity of reality, measuring it as deficient against a higher moral standard; in such a relationship, an ideal is implied, and satire in the Schillerian sense is operative. In making conscious the errors of an age, subversive art increases the likelihood that these errors will be overcome. On the other hand, art may more directly evoke a normative ideal. In such a case art is neither a lens onto the hidden aspects of reality nor directly critical of it; instead, it sketches an ideal to counter reality. Art need not only offer insight into the structures of what is, it may also render the ideal real.

The ideal evoked in art may be simply formal. Organic unity may counter the chaos of the age purely on the level of form. But one often sees also on the level of content a thematization of moral positions. When we read literature, we discover stories of prudence, justice, fortitude, and temperance, tales of faith, hope, and charity as well as narratives that depict pride, envy, anger, sloth, avarice, gluttony, and lust. Not only the medieval Dante shows us the horrors of vice and the harmony of virtue. Virtually every substantial work of literature engages moral questions, and through these encounters with fictional characters we gain a subtler sense of virtue and vice. The reader encounters imaginative and compelling situations that he has yet to experience, and these literary encounters are capable of giving him a more differentiated grasp of life as well as a wider and more nuanced moral compass. Even Plato recognizes that stories of good and great men inspire the young "to imitate them and long to be like them" (*Protagoras* 326a). Artworks are one means of portraying the dignity and wretchedness of humanity. If literature had no ethical value, it would be a mere diversion that we needn't take seriously. Kant, who recognized the significance of the moral sphere for the essence of humanity, rightly argues that if we immerse ourselves in art that does not engage questions of value, we shall reduce art to "a diversion, of which one continually feels an increasing need in proportion as one has availed oneself of it as a means of dispelling the mind's dissatisfaction with itself, with the result that one makes oneself ever more and more wasteful and dissatisfied" (*Critique of Judgment* B 214, translation modified).

Even those who see literature as devoid of ethical models tend to believe that its undermining of ethical models serves a higher moral purpose.

Character is developed and formed not only by way of philosophical categories and theoretical knowledge. Models, including literary models, are very important and are available through literature, whether as fictional depictions of historical figures or as imaginative portrayals of invented figures. Not surprisingly, a central point in the development of Friedrich Hölderlin's Hyperion is his encounter with Adamas, who both exemplifies what Hyperion should become and points him toward the models of antiquity. Important in the mediation of such models is the encounter with figures in one's own tradition or era and persons of great moral value from a variety of traditions, cultures, and ages. Such reading experiences give us new moral perspectives, deepen our sensibilities, and expand our emotional richness.

Frequently our experience of the ethical dimensions of an artwork does not so much expand our knowledge of ethics as deepen our understanding of the implications of our ethical positions. Noël Carroll articulates this position when he defends a *"clarificationist view"* of the relationship between art and moral understanding (142). Art clarifies, through specific narratives, our moral beliefs and their applicability to new spheres. Instead of learning new propositions, we grasp through art more subtle connections between general moral precepts and previously overlooked aspects of life. Art brings our abstract concepts into play with concrete situations and vivid examples. This richness of examples is no less important than the validity of our abstract moral rules. As a result we may extend our sympathies to persons or groups whose claims for justice may previously have been less visible to us.

Another ideational moment of art is that thinking guided by imagination leads to an abundance of philosophical prolepses—art anticipates the problems of philosophy. Many issues of substance exist in the technological age that philosophers have not yet fully grasped as problems or for which they know of no solutions. Art anticipates problems, and it sketches, however unconsciously, however elliptically, answers to these problems. That psychology was first introduced through literature, not philosophy, that technology was first thematized in literature, not philosophy, that great artworks by Thomas Mann, Robert Musil, and Hermann Broch seek solutions to problems that still remain unsolved speaks for this idea. Great literature is able to draw our attention to still unresolved problems without elevating the dissonance of nonresolution as an end in itself. Through imagination and sensuous embodiment art reveals truths that would otherwise not be accessible to us, or at least not yet accessible.

Artists discover and portray truths without fully grasping all that their images and narratives imply. In this sense the artist may be earlier than the philosopher, even when the artist is in less conceptual command of the material. Moreover, artists, working as they do within the realm of possibilities, are able to experiment with positions that are as yet unclear and untested, and they can do so without causing direct harm. John Gardner alludes to this possibility: "True moral fiction is a laboratory experiment too difficult and dangerous to try in the world but safe and important in the mirror image of reality in the writer's mind" (115–16). Whereas some works advance a doctrine already clear to the writer, other works pursue unfinished thoughts. Thinking through options via the imagination brings us closer to truth, even if the positions adopted contain an unwitting account of their own untenability. Literature allows us to anticipate positions we have not yet encountered. This proleptic function works both for society as a whole, as a writer engages new issues, and for the younger individual, whose literary experiences open up personalities and worlds that are for the reader as yet unexplored.

Finally, art contributes not only to an individual's search for edification; it contributes as well to the collective identity of a culture. Through art we learn to recognize, confront, and overcome our past and contemporary crises. We also learn to articulate our ideals for the future. Virgil's *Aeneid* performed this function for the age of Augustus. For other eras, the works of Dante, Shakespeare, Schiller, Dostoevsky, and Brecht performed similar functions. Today film contributes significantly to the formation of a culture's collective identity. This collective aspect takes us to art's second moment, its sensuousness, for the collective power of art depends on its sensuous aspects, its stories, its symbols, its emotional appeal.

THE MOMENT OF SENSUOUSNESS

Beauty contains a moment of truth, but the distinguishing feature of beauty vis-à-vis philosophical truth is its sensuousness. Where Plato and Plotinus see beauty as highest when it is free of sensuousness and where Hegel believes that philosophy is higher than art because of its freedom from the senses, I argue— with Schiller and Hölderlin—that precisely this sensuous moment gives art an edge over the purely cerebral realm of philosophy. Artistic truth, in its particularity and concreteness, is more readily visible and accessible than philosophical truth.

Artistic masterpieces are possible in various kinds and from various traditions—where one philosophical truth excludes competing truths, one sensuous representation does not exclude another. There are infinite ways of instantiating the ideal through beautiful expression. Therefore a variety of works can address a multiplicity of needs without limiting one another in an exclusive competition. The universal principles of art are not only compatible with a diversity of expression, they are enriched by this diversity. Each age will seek newer, more diverse manifestations of beauty, which harmonize universal principles with the particular needs of the age. Similarly, our experience of beauty can be analogous to our experience of the diversity of expression of different cultures, which seek to realize in different ways some of the highest ideals of humanity. Literature opens up for us the value of diversity, the richness of different stories, multiple traditions, various virtues, even as we recognize through these works certain common aesthetic principles. Through its variety literature covers a range of models and addresses the personal orientations of multiple readers. As such it is an especially welcome feature of a democracy; its citizens may find through literature a range of engaging experiences and alternative perspectives that stretch and refine the imagination. Artworks are not only unique, they also evolve from diverse traditions. This plurality is appealing insofar as the more voices that are present, the likelier is the possibility that good voices, which might otherwise not be represented, will be heard and appreciated.

A work of literature interests us not because it was written by person X or Y but because person X or Y was able to write something of general interest that provides a vision, a critique, an epiphany, a mood, something of value to a broader consciousness—and yet in a style that belongs uniquely to person X or Y. The sensuous dimension gives a work the unique shape of its creator, but its belonging to the realm of art constitutes its broader interest. The work and its style have both universal and particular elements. On the more individualistic level, within the range of works that one can argue are objectively great, some works will speak to one person more, some to another, some at one stage of life, others at another stage. In this respect taste has both a universal and a particular dimension. Though art has universal requirements for its excellence, these can be fulfilled in such a way as to appeal to different people at various times in manifold ways. Art is a unity of unity and multiplicity, unified in its essence but complex enough to appeal to diverse temperaments and sentiments and to elicit a variety of intellectual, emotional, and physiological responses. Art's universality precludes a merely subjective evaluation; its particularity encompasses the diverse ways in which, even objectively speaking, such criteria might be met. One may prefer the simple or the ornamental, the serious or the comic, but common in all such judgments is the elevation of content, form, and their relation. The claim that universal standards exist for great literature is fully compatible with the idea that different persons and different cultures will be drawn to one kind of work or another. In other words, universal evaluation does not exclude personal taste, and personal taste does not preclude universal evaluation, a point that is at the center of Ronald Peacock's study of literary evaluation. Our response to sensuous stimuli allows for a great range; so, too, our ability to process certain kinds of more intellectual literature varies; finally, our needs vary as well—by time period, culture, age, and personal disposition and need. If we agree that beauty manifests itself in diverse ways and that the artist will find a pattern fitting to his or her talents, then it seems also to follow that readers will find a corpus of works, which may change over time, that will do at least two things: reinforce their preferences, tastes, and identity—not just in literature but in general; and expand their preferences, tastes, and identity—not just in literature but in general.

The sensuous moment of art is located above all in its form. We recognize a variety of artforms, from architecture and sculpture to painting, music, literature, and film. Within literature form includes genre, structure, style, and manner, each of which can be studied from diachronic and synchronic perspectives as well as by way of the individuality of the author and the uniqueness of the work itself. Different forms lend themselves to different contents, although at times the connections may be extraordinary, unexpected, and ingenious. In addition, diverse forms may be stretched in a variety of directions, such that artworks of the same form or genre may embody brevity or fullness, lightness or weight, clarity or depth. Just as we gain emotional richness through our encounters with literature, so do we develop a greater appreciation for the range and subtlety of language and the artful combination of words. Diction, syntax, imagery, metaphor, rhythm, sound—all these and related features contribute to the sensuous structure and reception of the work.

Whereas insight into overarching and specific ethical issues follows from art's moment of truth, the primary ethical consequence of art's moment of sensuousness is its power of motivation. Art addresses the imaginative, emotional, and subliminal parts of the self that motivate the soul more than mere argument does. Where reason sometimes falls short of motivating persons, art often succeeds—because of its examples and models, its sensuous patterns, and its imagery as well as its resulting appeal to the emotions.[3] Art gives us an intensity often lacking in merely conceptual experience. Art is more of a bridge than philosophy, particularly insofar as it conveys concrete truths that grip the imagination, particular expressions and images that say more and awaken more sympathy than any argument or citation of statistics. Plato banished the poets precisely because he recognized their power to motivate.

One reason for the power of art is its combination of universality and particularity: art conveys insights of universal significance by way of particular stories, and we better relate to and sympathize with the particular. This power to grip the imagination through form, language, and the particular is common to all literature. Art fills us with enthusiasm and disgust, sympathy and dislike, and infinite shades inbetween. Martha Nussbaum suggests that in reading literature, we gain "the ability to imagine what it is like to live the life of another person who might, given changes in circumstance, be oneself or one of one's loved ones" (5). Among the moral categories that tend to be neglected in a Kantian framework are precisely those cultivated through art and the imagination—empathy with troubled individuals, sensitivity to the needs and challenges of others, and admiration for characters who embody virtues. That stories and parables, in mediating between the particular and the universal, help elicit such moral categories is illustrated symbolically by a passage in chapter 9 of Erich Maria Remarque's *All Quiet on the Western Front* where Paul's relationship to the enemy is completely shaken by his one-on-one encounter with a Frenchman in no-man's-land. Instinctively, Paul stabs him, but as Paul slowly begins to see him not as an idea or an abstraction or the anonymous enemy but as a particular person, a man like himself, he sympathizes with him, identifies with him, and only later is able to see this caring as madness.[4] One might also think of the German reception of the Holocaust television series in the late 1970s. Facts and statistics on the Holocaust had been known for decades, but a particular story altered the German relationship to the past and set off a furious debate and a stronger attempt at mastering the past.

If one wanted to argue that contemporaries are too immersed in their more primitive selves, as advertising all too well knows, then art would have to be viewed as a more likely path to lead us to our higher selves than, say, philosophy, for the extraordinary gift of art is to mediate, as Plato's Diotima tells us, like *eros,* from the material to the spiritual. Art grabs our senses, but it raises us beyond them, giving us an emotional attachment to goodness. Schiller was very much cognizant of this impulse, not only in his theoretical writings but also in his dramas, where frequently noble action is motivated by love for a particular person—the sensuous awakens the spiritual. We see this, for example, in *Don Carlos,* where the titular hero is inspired, in turn, by his love for Elisabeth and Marquis Posa.

We bring moral judgments to literature. One character may be noble, another cowardly. But our experience of literature in turn brings aesthetic judgments to bear on our intuitive moral judgments. My desire is not to challenge Kant by grounding ethics in art but to supplement Kant by recognizing aesthetic experience as a motivating force in ethical action. Thus the reverse of bringing moral judgments to literature is to bring aesthetic judgments to morality. We feel an instinctive disgust at the absence of courage or integrity, instinctive pleasure at acts of benevolence, and these instincts are healthy; in this way literature educates to values. If beauty is the manifestation of truth in the sensuous world, then it follows that beauty exists outside literature, in life—in loftiness of spirit, noble action, courage, and other virtues. As Plotinus notes, there is a beauty in character and in conduct of life, a beauty of the virtues (para. I.6.1). Virtue can be laborious, but it can also be instinctive; good literature assists in our attaining to the latter.

A common image from antiquity to modernity is that we are filled by the radiance of that in which we are immersed. Plotinus relates that "it will often happen that persons climbing heights where the soil has taken a yellow glow will themselves appear so, borrowing color from the place on which they move" (para. V.8.10, translation modified). According to Feuerbach, to contemplate the infinite is to confirm in ourselves the infinitude of thought (26). So, too, with art. Those who are immersed in great works by Cervantes, Molière, or Lessing will learn from them certain virtues, will become in a way the image of those works, and those whose experience of "beauty" is restricted to what often passes for such in contemporary letters will reflect to the same degree the level of virtue and beauty that these works embody. Not only do we need a certain glimmer of substance in ourselves to grasp substance, the more we partake of the substantial, the more it fills us.

Finally, though accessible to conceptual analysis, the sensuous dimension gives art a complexity that, much like the human subject, is not exhausted by conceptual analysis. This inexhaustibility is true of all great intellectual works—Plato's *Republic*, Boethius's *Consolation of Philosophy*, or Weber's *Economy and Society*, for example. Literature, however, is especially privileged here because it attends specifically to its own form, which includes the integration of gaps or "Leerstellen," whose purpose is to invite the reader to fill in connections and meanings (Iser, "Die Appellstruktur"). Because the literary work does not refer to an external reality that could be explored independently of the text, we must use our imagination and our attentiveness to its many layers to see hidden connections, project meaning, draw conclusions, and understand the work's full implications for ourselves as readers. Moreover, even the most conscious authors of literary works are frequently unaware of the full complexity of their linguistic creations; immersed in sensuousness, literary works are often ambiguous and multivalent. Most important, in our reception of art our conceptual categories must give way, as Kant suggests, to the free play of imagination, which mediates between the sensuous and rational spheres.

The two dominant models of truth in the tradition are coherence and correspondence. Coherence is a necessary, but not sufficient, condition of truth: truth cannot be self-contradictory. Correspondence has traditionally been understood to mean that a theory is true if it corresponds to reality, but Hegel gives correspondence an inverse spin, arguing that truth arises when objectivity is in conformity with its concept, when the descriptive realm matches the normative sphere (e.g., 8.86 and 8.323). We speak in this way, for example, when we say that someone is a true friend or that the *Iliad* is a true work of art. In contrast to a modern view which asserts that truth lies only in propositions (Rescher 1), I find Hegel's view of truth as a self-accord of reality with its concept or ideal to be a powerful, if often forgotten, resource. According to this view, something is true when it is as it should be. My theory of art tries to integrate both of these models, suggesting that great art coheres internally and fulfills art's normative criteria. A third theory of truth, which has won over many adherents in recent decades, is the consensus theory. Though significant insofar as it integrates the claims that our discovery of truth depends on our listening to diverse perspectives and that to realize truth in society we need a critical mass of support, it nonetheless suffers from several weaknesses, the most fundamental of which are its empty formalism and its possibility of leading to positions that may gain a majority but that nonetheless violate transcendental principles.

A fourth theory of truth is particularly important for art and has been advanced by Heidegger, truth as unconcealment (*Unverborgenheit*) or revealedness (*Entbergen*). The true (*alethes*) is the unhidden, what has emerged from the hidden into the open, what has been removed from the sphere of forgetfulness. What Heidegger means with this idea of truth as *aletheia* or unconcealment has at least three moments. First, poetic truth is not something that we can will or force. Instead, it happens to us. It finds us; we do not find it. As with grace, our primary action toward it must be openness of comportment.[5] Second, because this concept of truth arises not from our intentions but from our alertness, our listening for it, we must be especially attentive as recipients. We must listen to the otherness of the other, quietly, patiently. And, according to Heidegger, we are listening not for the intentions or subjectivity of the author but for the participation of the work itself in opening up the truth of art. Third, the artwork not only reveals, it also conceals. The artwork cannot be exhausted by our conceptual analysis. This third aspect has its dangers (as Plato would no doubt remind us), but it would be silly to ignore it as a moment in all great art. We might even be tempted to capture it with Benjamin's concept of "aura" (222), to which I return below: no matter how close we may come to analyzing and exhausting the meaning of a literary work, some moments that affix, transform, and captivate us simultaneously elude us. One aspect of literary criticism is the search to discover what in an artwork resists discovery and does not easily yield to universal and conceptual thought. This element of resistance is not to suggest that the greatness of art lies in its incomprehensibility; instead, an important moment of art eludes conceptual thought and appeals to our imagination, though also to our unconscious. We may be able to receive and be influenced by aspects of a work that we are as yet unable to recognize or articulate. This moment is at play when we recognize that even after reading a work several times, even after writing about it extensively, the work still attracts us and can sustain rereadings that generate in our mind new connections, new affects, and renewed delight in ways that we cannot fully formulate. *Aletheia* is a moment of all great art, and one of the critic's tasks is to reflect not only on what he or she understands of a work but also on what resists interpretation and cannot be fully named. Sometimes literature attracts us precisely for those reasons we do not comprehend, which is both its danger and its joy. By affixing us in a part of the soul that is removed from clear comprehension, literature is able not only to confuse us but also to bring us into areas that our mind, limited by conventional categories and expectations, might not otherwise take us. In this sense the truth of art is very much linked to its sensuousness.

The sensuous dimension of literature reinforces the value of the literary experience as an end in itself. When we read nonliterary works, we tend to focus solely, or at least primarily, on the information we take from them, reading such works for practical purposes. Louise Rosenblatt draws a helpful distinction between what she calls a nonaesthetic or efferent reading, deriving from the Latin *efferre* (to carry away), and an aesthetic reading. The efferent reading stresses the common and pragmatic effects of reading, "what will remain as the residue *after* the reading—the information to be acquired, the logical solution to a problem, the actions to be carried out" (*The Reader* 23). The aesthetic reading, in contrast, focuses on the personal experience of reading itself, including the affective response triggered by the work's sensuous structures and components, which are not reducible to what we carry away from the work on the level of information. The aesthetic reading places great emphasis on what occurs, what the reader lives through during the reading process itself. The intensity of the aesthetic experience, its evocation of the sensuous and emotional, as well as the intellectual, is triggered by the work's linguistic structures and nuances.

INTERCONNECTEDNESS

Beauty has two moments, truth and sensuousness, content and form. In its moment of truth art imitates not reality but the ideal. The essence of its form is not simply to be grasped within the rubric of form but must be taken to mean an appropriateness in the relation of content and form. Great art integrates these two moments organically, that is, in such a way that to separate the universal meaning and the concrete shape would be to violate the integrity of the whole. An insightful work that has no sensuous dimension fails to be beautiful, and a sensuously attractive work that has no substantive ideational moment also fails to satisfy the conditions of beauty. Art has the privileged structure of communicating universality by giving it a sensuous form and at the same time rescuing particularity from arbitrariness by investing it with meaning. We might therefore call the artwork a *coincidentia oppositorum,* or, to use Hegel's vocabulary, concrete universal (13.100–101). Any work that fails to integrate the two moments will suffer. This is not meant to exclude complex interconnections; in the epic theater of Brecht, for example, form and content are at odds with one another, but this very disjunction is an element of form that serves what one might call its metacontent. The diction with which Benn's "Lost I" opens is not superficially organic but heterogenic, yet this disrupture serves, on a metalevel, the poem's theme of unconnectedness and alienation. All great artworks have an organic connection, be it simple or complex, between the two moments. If the sensuous aspect of an artwork is not organically linked to its concept, then one loses nothing by substituting for the artwork simple philosophical articulation. The organic artwork does more: it interlaces the ideal and the material, such that, though independently interesting, their full meaning arises only through their interconnection. Interconnectedness is an important dimension of aesthetics, though a tendency exists in the tradition to isolate either content or form.[6] Not only is one-sidedness to be avoided, we must reflect on the complex interaction of both moments.

Just as the two major elements of form and content belong together, so do the various parts stand in an organic relation to one another. First, all the parts have a certain autonomy, which renders them interesting in and of themselves.

When we read, the individual characters and sections of a work have intrinsic value and contain diverse features. The idea that every part has autonomous value is fully compatible with the idea that some parts will have greater value. The value of diverse parts differs by work, with lyric and drama, especially tragedy, being for the most part more compact, whereas the novel more readily allows for what E. M. Forster calls "round" and "flat" characters, those who engage us more fully in their complex individuality and those who are more recognizable as formulaic or typical (46–54). Flat characters are often integrated for humor or appropriateness, and their role is more supportive. According to Forster, "the test of a round character is whether it is capable of surprising in a convincing way. If it never surprises, it is flat" (54). The use of predictable figures and less central passages helps via contrast to highlight a work's most important flourishes. Although one or two crucial characters or passages may form the keystone of a work and are thus elevated above the others in prominence, this elevation should not imply that the other parts lose their independent interest; in a great work every part garners interest.

Second, each part is connected to the others; they fit or belong together such that no part is not expressive of the whole. Everything needed is present, everything superfluous is absent, and all the parts cohere. Third, and this brings together the truth of the first two moments, the artwork has in common with the mechanical that it is a set of relations, but unlike the mechanical, it is more than the sum of its parts; every part belongs to the whole and contributes to the whole such that, despite the relative interest they garner as parts, their full meaning evolves only from their position within the totality of the artwork and slowly becomes recognizable in this way (Hegel 13.156–57). The partial dimensions of the artwork are interesting in and of themselves; they appear completely independent and contingent, but in the process of exploration and interpretation, they assume an element of connectedness and necessity, such that they gain a richer identity in the whole. What at first appears to be simple chance and externality reveals itself for the interpreter to be organically related; thus, the alteration of any part would imply a transformation of the whole (cf. Aristotle, *Poetics,* ch. 7). Or as Coleridge suggests, the parts "mutually support and explain each other" (2.13). For Coleridge a poem is a composition that proposes "to itself such delight from the *whole,* as is compatible with a distinct gratification from each component *part*" (2.13). Both the parts and the journey of their unfolding into a harmonic whole give pleasure to the activity of the mind. Coleridge adds in support of what Rosenblatt was later to call the aesthetic reading: "The reader should be carried forward, not merely or chiefly by the mechanical impulse of curiosity, or by a restless desire to arrive at the final solution; but by the pleasureable [*sic*] activity of mind excited by the attractions of the journey itself" (2.14).

This organic relationship of part and whole is reminiscent of living biological structures; in this sense it suggests vitality and dynamism, although unlike biological structures, which have a telos of reproduction, artworks are ends in themselves. The elevation of the organic also relates to the sequential structure of a work. Aristotle privileges organic over episodic plots (1451b). His argument is simple but compelling: what is probable or necessary has a more privileged status than what is arbitrary, which is not to say that art must be predictable. On the contrary, Aristotle elevates those plots that surprise us even as they follow the law of cause and effect. He privileges an action that is whole and complete and resembles "a living organism in all its unity" (1459a, translation modified). The connection between art and the organic is also visible etymologically: *ars* or art is related to *artus* or joint and *armus* or shoulder. The concept implies the act of putting together, joining, or fitting diverse parts in order to create a whole. This connection between art and the organic begins already with Plato and extends onward to the classical literary criticism of Horace and Pseudo-Longinus and into the period of German idealism. It fades, however, or is directly countered, in the modern era, and its few adherents, Leo Spitzer, for example, stand out as exceptions. Modernity tends to elevate the arbitrary or contingent. Ideally, it would do so in order to show to what extent the contingent must be seen as a necessary ingredient of the whole and to exhibit to what extent the contingent plays a role in life. In truth, the contingent gains aesthetic value only when it is sublated, when the seemingly contingent relates to a work's overarching principle.

In tragedy the organic expresses itself in the structure whereby greatness leads inexorably to suffering; the two are not accidentally related. In modernity, this bond is often severed, such that suffering has no intrinsic connection to greatness. This freedom from the organic did lead to some extraordinary innovations in drama, including the development of greater sociological and psychological insight into the causes and effects of suffering, as I have argued elsewhere (*Tragedy* 100–102). Compensation for the lack of the formal connection between greatness and suffering also elicited in many cases wonderful rhetorical advances. Nonetheless, these modern developments are not in every case gains. The severing of greatness from suffering weakens the organic and thus the aesthetic dimension. In many cases, we recognize a movement of the aesthetic away from the organic, as in open drama, which has its place within the variety of aesthetic expressions but lacks a requisite element of great art. However, the hermeneutic process sometimes leads us to recognize common themes and motifs in the individual scenes, such that the organic remains, if initially hidden and ultimately looser. One of the tasks of the critic is to show how the various parts of an artwork relate to one another, if often in very complex ways. The endeavor of the literary critic is in this sense not unrelated to the modern scientist who seeks in nature the hidden order and veiled patterns behind the seemingly arbitrary and chaotic.

The modern critique of the classical dictum that all elements should relate to one another in such a way as to be "like a living being" (Plato, *Phaedrus* 264c, translation modified) or to form "an organic whole" (Pseudo-Longinus, ch. 10) has intensified in the wake of the national socialist elevation of organic art, to which at least five arguments may be countered.[7] First, the abuse of a theory cannot be taken as an argument against the theory itself, unless a necessary connection exists between the two, which is lacking in this case: not all organic art stems from cultures that revoke human rights, as is evident by the importance of the organic both for the literature of German *Klassik,* with its elevation of humanity and cosmopolitanism, and in the revival of classical architecture in the early American republic; and not all fascist regimes privilege classical art, as is clear from the connections between the avant garde and fascism in Italy.

Second, advocates of organic art have often failed to recognize that many seemingly dissonant and negative works are in fact organic, but organic in a complex way and on a metalevel, insofar as dissonance serves a higher meaning or insofar as an artwork may be the negation of a negation; in short, such critics often fail to grasp the complex beauty of much of modern art. This failure of perception does not mean that the works of modern art rejected by the National Socialists are not in a complex way organic.

Third, the particular manifestation of organicism in national socialist art tends to involve an elevation of the whole at the expense of the integrity of the particular: the creation of types rather than individuals mirrors the political effort to submerge, rather than sublate, the individual within the whole; in this sense national socialist art lacks the balance of a desirable organicism. This lack of balance between part and whole is sometimes reinforced by a lack of measure; one thinks of the elevation of the monumental.

Fourth, two uses of organic must be distinguished: the first, which I have emphasized, concerns itself with artwork aesthetics; the second belongs in the realm of production aesthetics and has to do with the idea that art is generated through an organic process of growth, of ripening. This second form of the organic is not a necessary corollary to the first (a work can integrate form and content and part and whole and have been developed by any number of means), and it is truly unimportant from the perspective of artwork aesthetics. Yet precisely this concept of the organic, as defined by the sphere of production, developed into the vague idea of a privileged destiny for the German nation. The organic in the sphere of production is not equivalent to the organic in the artwork, nor is it necessary to recognize the organic in production. The separation between production and artwork aesthetics is reaffirmed by the fact that the National Socialists virtually ignored the organic in the autonomous artwork and stressed instead the organic in the historical development of the German nation.

Fifth, art includes among its possibilities the creation of models with which one can identify and which contribute to the formation and cultivation of a collective identity; there may be a valid human urge toward a more affirmative art of this kind, and it would be both morally irresponsible and strategically unwise to leave the creation and appreciation of such art solely in the hands of those whose worldview violates universal principles of justice. We can dismiss the additional argument that because the modern world is full of arbitrary and chance events as well as contradictions, any organic art must fail to do justice to these complexities. The claim presupposes that art only imitates superficial reality: art does not capture reality's higher essence, does not negate its negativity, and does not offer a counterimage. Such a claim is itself an arbitrary limitation of the possibilities of art.[8]

Our concept of unity must be complex. The mixture of genres is not an argument against the harmony of form and content, especially as unity presupposes, rather than precludes, difference. Tragicomedy, for example, can be an appropriately complex way to address an intricate subject. Also, an element of formal dissonance may serve a higher unity. Heinrich Heine uses dissonance to great effect in his poetry when he breaks from romanticism to realism and disillusionment; we laugh or think about the vagaries of the romantic. Similarly, in the opening of the *Harz Journey* we are alerted to the lack of coherence in the modern world; in each case, the moment of dissonance serves the work's higher meaning. The episodic form of Arthur Schnitzler's *Anatol* formally reinforces the protagonist's lack of progress and enlightenment and is in this way organic. The one time toward the end of Theodor Fontane's *Effi Briest* when the narrator addresses the character directly, this rupture of narrative distance is a grand example of foregrounding (ch. 36). It does not disturb, it heightens, the effects of Effi's fall and our sympathy for her. We recognize a higher purpose as well when Kafka tells bizarre tales in the most straightforward of all prose styles; the sense of tension is organically heightened by the dissonance of form and content. We can include within our higher, dialectical concept of unity also the gaps that surface in many modern texts. Such ruptures of meaning may in fact serve on a formal level the higher insight of the work, as seems evident, for example, in a masterpiece like Kafka's *The Trial.* These examples are not meant to expand the concept infinitely. In his study of literary evaluation, Walter Müller-Seidel gives several detailed examples of dissonance that does not serve the purposes of the works in question and forces us to question their aesthetic value (70–74 and 100–104).

The more original the work, the more difficult it is to recognize the constituent moments and their meaningful interconnections. This difficulty is especially intense in postclassical eras, where the artistic desire to be innovative may oblige authors to experiment with forms that appear to be, at least superficially, inorganic. To create great art after an era defined by great art is a burdensome challenge. In our capacity to see the hidden logic of seemingly inorganic forms, to grasp new and surprising interconnections, we must be very broad. Nonetheless, we needn't endorse every new work. Indeed, the greatness of the organic model lies in mediating between what one might call the arbitrarily mechanical and the arbitrarily autonomous. The abandonment of the organic has been reinforced by the mistaken sense that the organic involves a constraining and mechanical concept of art. The mechanical, which is to be distinguished from the organic, does prescribe certain formulas for an artwork, which may involve precepts concerning plot, diction, length, character types, or number of acts. The artist is expected to fulfill these criteria and is thereby beholden to the false notion that the parts of a work are primary to the whole, to the transformation of parts into a greater whole. Such a model allows little room for the artist's creativity and modulation of convention. A second model moves to the extreme opposite end, elevating the autonomy of each work and bracketing its relation to any and all aesthetic principles. The autonomous model rejects even the idea of the interconnection of parts; art is free of constitutive elements and of the integration of parts into a meaningful whole. Not only does this theory eliminate any possibility of evaluation, in an age of overproduction it steals our attention from truly great works and makes us slaves to whatever is produced or thrust before us. Its transformation of a given model into infinite, arbitrary possibilities is characteristic of a negative or an antithetical stance. Justly recognizing that some poetic constraints are arbitrary and that to compete with the weight of tradition one must innovate, the autonomous mode mistakenly fails to recognize anything that transcends the arbitrary. The organic, in contrast, suggests that the constituent elements of a great artwork—from language and manner to theme and structure—are variable, but what remains common is the transformation of the elements into a meaningful whole. In this sense it allows for the freedom of creativity but guards against the arbitrariness of absolute autonomy. Our reception and evaluation of works should eschew mechanical expectations and seek to uncover the organic behind the seemingly arbitrary. By recognizing Shakespeare's works as transcending the mechanical prescription of the three dramatic unities and yet as being neither arbitrary nor without a higher unity, August Wilhelm Schlegel, for example, was able to reevaluate Shakespeare for the modern era.

One can divide aesthetic tendencies in many different ways. If we accept the idea that art contains two moments—thought or content and sensuousness or form—then we can view aesthetics as having three possibilities: one may isolate content at the expense of form, one may stress form at the expense of content, or one may view both moments in their simultaneity. Taking content for a moment, one can view art as expressing simple truths in an affirmative way, as negating false positions, or as integrating complex truths by attending to both moments, including the overcoming of the antithetical in the synthetic. Traditional religious art might be viewed as affirmative, satiric art might be viewed as negating false positions, and a more complex art may integrate both moments. We can also view art from the perspective of form. One perspective recognizes in art the execution of traditional forms; another sees in art the mockery of traditional forms; a third discerns in art the creation of new forms by virtue of the act of thinking through the inadequacies of previous forms. One can also view the interrelation of form and content. One position says that they must be in perfect harmony; another perceives the need for dissonance and clash, an ironic tension between form and content; a third sees more complex interplay between the two. The problem of translation, in which something is always lost, confirms the need for our attention to the often implicit connections between form and content. Essential to beauty is the harmony of form and content, and harmony is another way of expressing noncontradiction. Whereas untruth in its multiple forms is ugly, beauty and truth are ultimately intertwined. Surprisingly, consciousness of this connection between truth and beauty, or truth and elegance, may be more prominent today in the sciences than in the humanities (cf. Farmelo).

Not only are truth and beauty related, so too is goodness. All three are defined by the compatibility of form and content. We have already proposed that beauty is the complex harmony of form and content. Truth, like the good and the beautiful, presupposes an accord of form and content. This Hegelian insight has two dimensions. First, as I have suggested, truth is an appearance in harmony with its idea, that is, the particular content must be in accord with its higher concept or form, as in the example above of a true friend. Second, truth presupposes that the content of a statement be compatible with the mode of its expression, that no performative contradiction occur. Whereas a semantic contradiction functions entirely on the propositional level, deriving from the two parts of a single statement, *a* and *non-a,* a performative contradiction arises not within the level of content but between content and form, between what is said and what is presupposed in the act of saying what is said. For example, in the statement "I am modest," no immediate contradiction is recognizable on the level of content. However, modesty is the virtue of not drawing attention to one's virtues, so as soon as I say that I am modest I am no longer modest; the contradiction arises between form and content. In truth, I am allowed to say that I am modest only when I do not say it.

Goodness is likewise to be recognized as the combination of form (the Kantian principles of autonomy and noncontradiction) and content (the filling in of Kantian ethics with specific ethical claims and a differentiated, nonformal ethics of values, that is, a hierarchy of goods, as Hegel saw and Max Scheler argued in the twentieth century). In another respect we can see the good as mediating between form and content. One of the challenges of ethics is to discover which local traditions, which contents, are compatible with a universalist ethics. This process is designed not only to help us discover what is universal but also to allow what does not contradict the universal, and is central to a particular culture, to enrich the totality of cultures, much as art serves the function of creating a diversity that still satisfies the formal demands of beauty.

While Kant rigorously separates the ethical concept of the good from the aesthetic experience of beauty, the two spheres are, even for him, not without connections.[9] Aesthetic judgment mediates between understanding and reason, and both the good and the beautiful, unlike the pleasant, are universal. In addition, aesthetic judgment, in its freedom from empirical laws, intersects with the transcendent, like the moral law itself. The freedom of imagination parallels the moral freedom of the will. Most important, as Kant argues in the *Critique of Judgment,* aesthetic experience can help us esteem ethical goodness. Our experience of beauty teaches us to appreciate nature in a disinterested fashion, viewing it not simply as a means but as an end in itself, which complements and supplements the moral imperative to view all rational beings as

ends. Through aesthetic experience, we also recognize a correspondence between our disinterested pleasure of nature and nature itself, which reinforces,
by analogy, our sense that (moral) ideas have objective reality (B 169). When
this aesthetic appreciation of nature is habitual, it creates "a mental attunement
favorable to moral feeling" (B 166). Moreover, our experience of the sublime, in
the form of the vastness or power of nature, which transcends our sensuous capacities, triggers awareness of the morally good, which alone is truly sublime,
insofar as everything else, including nature, pales before it (B 74–131). The
ideas of reason transcend all sensuous intuition, according to Kant, but we can
conceive of these ideas indirectly and analogically, through symbols, and for
Kant, given the connections described above, "the symbol of the morally good"
is "the beautiful" (B 258). Insofar as beautiful objects awaken sensations that
have analogies to moral judgments, Kant notes, not surprisingly, that popular
consciousness ascribes moral terms to aesthetic objects. One could take this
point further, in a direction beyond Kant, and argue that our experience of
those aesthetic objects to which we intuitively attach moral terms may help refine our awareness of the moral sphere, if not in terms of grounds, then at least
in terms of inclination, motivation, and our intuitive grasp of the unity of all
knowledge.

By combining the ideal and the sensuous, the beautiful shows us that the
ideal can be made real. Art functions as proof of the possibility of the ideal—an
insight endorsed by thinkers as diverse as Hegel (15.244 and 15.437) and Santayana (164). Art's reconciliation of the ideal and the concrete anticipates the
broader telos of history. In this sense art is both complete within itself, autonomous, and part of a higher whole, itself an organic part of what transcends
it. Earlier I suggested that art has a proleptic dimension: thinking guided by
imagination helps us anticipate positions that have yet to be philosophically articulated. Here we see a second sense in which art is a prolepsis. If art realizes a
symmetry of the ideal and the material within the realm of the aesthetic, it gives
us confidence that the ideal can yet be realized in the wider material world. The
ultimate telos of philosophy is its realization in the world; art anticipates this telos by showing us that the idea can be made real—at least within the aesthetic
sphere.

THE ISSUE OF AUTONOMY

In his *Critique of Judgment* Kant recognized that aesthetic experience is characterized by disinterestedness (B 14–16). In viewing a painting of a mountain

stream, we are not awakened to thirst. In viewing the sculpture of a beautiful body, we do not desire to possess it. Santayana has added to Kant's analysis the suggestion that beyond any immediate postponement of utility other pleasures are suspended as well: "We do not mix up the satisfactions of vanity and proprietorship with the delight of contemplation" (25). In this sense art takes us beyond our immediate selves, beyond calculation and ulterior motives. Our disinterested contemplation is not an indifference but an openness to the otherness of the artwork as other, as that which is not reduced to utility. I do not want to suggest, thereby, that emotions or desire fade from aesthetic experience; instead, a mechanical means-end thinking disappears, and various vital impulses that are their own intrinsic end remain.

Art, we have suggested, differs from everyday reality insofar as everyday reality is tied up with needs and desires and is not often orchestrated in such a way as to allow its higher meaning to emerge. In contrast, art lifts us to a realm free of desire and instinct and beyond the haphazardness and arbitrariness of everyday life. In this sense art has autonomy. Art is also potentially autonomous vis-à-vis everyday reality insofar as it can, through imagination, take us to other times and places, even to the unreal. Art is removed from the merely temporal and is potentially of supertemporal significance. Earlier we introduced the idea that the truth of art does not lie in its accuracy. And though art contains a sensuous dimension, it sheds mere externality as its sole defining characteristic, revealing thereby a higher essence.

Precisely in its autonomy, however, art has a moral dimension. First, a work may perform an edifying function based on its integrity as an artwork. The harmony of the artwork, a harmony derived in part by its being self-contained, serves as a countermodel to a reality defined by fragmentation and disorder. What is thereby self-contained and autonomous is nonetheless capable of meaningfully affecting its recipients. Second, "autonomous" in its highest sense means "in accordance with reason," an insight that was especially clear to the German idealists. The demand that art contain a moment of truth, a moment compatible with the tenets of reason, guarantees for art both a moment of morality and a moment of autonomy in this higher sense of the word. Here, too, the autonomy of art is paradoxically one and the same with its morality. Certainly, an art that no longer believes in objective values has difficulties inspiring its audience and eliciting emotional attachment; it leaves us cold. An artist who displays objective values gives us more orientation, both morally and emotionally. If true freedom consists not in arbitrariness but in being at one with what is other, as Hegel suggests (e.g., 8.84), then art is a model freedom, for it combines the spiritual with nature, and as such works in harmony with, not against, nature and the cosmos. Indeed, it not only integrates the material sphere, it embodies the structure of a microcosm. Finally, art's freedom from reality and from the instrumental sphere gives it an identity that permits authors, as Gardner has noted, to experiment with ideas, to test them, to consider them in ways that are nonthreatening but that may in the long run be useful—also for moral questions.

The elevation of autonomy, defined more as a negative *freedom from,* has led in modernity to a gradual freeing of art from any moral dimension, but this concept of freedom from morality is partly ill-founded (there is a paradoxical utility to art's apparent lack of utility, as we have just seen) and partly an aberrant development (the principle of art for art's sake, no less than analogous truisms like "business is business" and "war is war," suggests a lack of overarching legitimacy). Art should free itself of the particular, often ungrounded morality of its age, just as science advances when it is not encumbered by unnecessary ideological restrictions. Art should experiment and not be constrained by poetic principles that lack a higher justification than mere convention, much as religion is strengthened when it successfully distinguishes between its essential and historically contingent dimensions. Undoubtedly, the liberating effect of art's freedom, first, from religion and, second, from reason, led to the generation over time of an extraordinary number of interesting aesthetic innovations as well as new and great artworks. However, something was also lost in this development. Although art has an autonomy vis-à-vis the world, if it is to have legitimacy, it must, like science, subscribe to a higher morality. Hoffmann showed the dangers of aesthetic autonomy by portraying certain artist figures as criminals, even murderers, as in *Mademoiselle Scuderi.* New forms give us new ways of viewing the world, but not all vistas bring us closer to truth. Great art, however, accomplishes this, if often in unexpected and paradoxical ways.

To differentiate three forms of autonomy may be useful at this point. First is the autonomy that is constitutive of an artwork as an artwork. This "aesthetic autonomy" consists of the artwork's intrinsic value, its transcendence of everyday reality, and its freedom from the sphere of desire. Second is the autonomy that relates to the idealist sense of freedom: the artwork is constituted in accordance with a higher reason, not haphazardly or arbitrarily. This "autonomy of reason" can be set against a modern definition of autonomy as something following its own laws even if these should violate reason. To follow laws that are arbitrary and not in accordance with reason is to be not autonomous but heteronomous, beholden to arbitrariness. In this sense we must protect art's true

autonomy against those advocates of autonomy who see no contradiction between autonomy and arbitrariness. We may recall here that the autonomy of
reason is not unique to the sphere of aesthetics but is manifest in other areas as
well, for example, in ethics, where true freedom consists of action in accordance
with the moral law, whatever the external causes of this action may be. Third,
the artwork should be autonomous in the sense that it be free of any false dependence on contingent and historical conventions, a form of autonomy we
might call "autonomy vis-à-vis contingency." Certainly, multiple, contingent
factors will influence the author's creation; these are unavoidable. Without
such factors no artworks could ever be created, but the author should be free to
overlook those that have no higher authority. The work need not be bound by
rules that can claim only historical validity. To take one example, the idea of the
three unities has only historical validity not because some eras did not follow it
but because some dramas that disregard the three unities are great works.

Kant affirms the artist's autonomy in a different, but compatible, way when
he suggests that the genius creates works that evoke a harmony of form and a
richness of meaning as well as a harmony of form and content, but without following rules. The artwork should not be determined by external forces, be these
poetic, political, or didactic, that carry no substantive weight, that do not contribute to the higher design of the work. This is the autonomy to which we refer when we criticize the arbitrariness of convention and the subjugation of art
to religious or political ends. At the same time, the artist must remain true to
the essence of art. In the history of aesthetics various conventions have been
falsely put forth as essential, but this abuse is not an argument against such distinctions in principle, merely a cautionary lesson for us to be as flexible and
hermeneutically adept as possible in seeking to grasp the hidden logic of newer
works. At the same time, not all new works that break free of conventions embody the autonomy of reason, for just as conventions have been falsely raised to
absolute status, so have many artworks falsely laid claim to, or falsely been credited with, having fulfilled the higher concepts of aesthetic autonomy and autonomy of reason. Vigilance is needed in both directions.

Insofar as moral legitimacy derives from intrinsic value or value for society,
we should consider the way in which these two moments relate to individual
artworks. If we grant the intrinsic value of literature, we can elevate literature
independently of its ability to realize social or political goals. A poem that is free
of a specifically religious or political content may have value simply as an instantiation of beauty, as a harmony within itself. Some works, on the other
hand, will attend directly to social and political problems and shed light on is-

sues confronting a particular culture. Such works have value for society independently of their aesthetic dimensions. However, their value as literature depends not only on their content but also on their ability to harmonize form and
content. One might, for example, want to argue that Heinrich Mann's *The
Subject* does a superior job of capturing the many layers of its society, Wil-
helmine Germany, in comparison with Thomas Mann's *Doktor Faustus,* which
seeks to uncover diverse aspects of emerging national socialism. This evaluation
may be just, but it does not exhaust our aesthetic evaluation of the two works,
which must also attend to form and those aspects of content that transcend the
social and political spheres. Those literary works with the greatest value satisfy
both moments: Hölderlin's *Hyperion,* for example, can compete with virtually
any other German novel on the level of form—with its complex structure, its
layered narrative levels, its rich intertextuality, and its beautiful rhetoric—but
it also has great extrinsic value, as it presents insights of both existential significance (in its reflections on how to wrestle with pain, suffering, and loss) and sociopolitical significance (in its articulation of the relation of art, religion, and
philosophy to the state). Here intrinsic value and value for society are intertwined, even if in such a great work we may find weaknesses, for example, in the
development of minor characters.

   A work contains its own inner logic, which the reader must attempt to uncover, and if the work expands our expectations, even as it remains within the
most fundamental tenets of good art, then it successfully influences our aesthetics. However, the idea, supported by some proponents of autonomy, that
the only norm by which a text can be measured is its own inner logic entails
abandoning serious evaluation, for a text could in fact be a simple scribble or its
content could be unsublated evil, and if we apply the proposed maxim, then
the text must be judged against its intention as a scribble or as unsublated evil.
If the measure of evaluation is defined in this way, then the work cannot be
judged as poor for having failed to reach normative expectations. This is value-
free science at its most destructive level. What is left is merely the hermeneutic
act of understanding, not also the aesthetic act of evaluation. In contrast, the
objective idealist model introduces and defends the characteristics of great art,
and works are judged to fulfill them or not, just as we might say that these are
the characteristics of meaningful friendship, and certain relationships may or
may not fulfill them. Independently of the intention of a work, we can say that
good art fulfills certain norms in general and that specific themes and subjects
demand particular forms and levels of complexity. We must be general in these
claims, so as to recognize works that test and expand our previous judgments,

but without such claims, we are at a loss to judge works and unable to defend the enterprise of literary criticism and the production of art, the endeavor on which the first enterprise depends. If there are no public norms to define good art, little reason exists for the public to support art—how could it reasonably support one artist and not another, one taste and not another?

Schiller claims that an analogy can be drawn between beauty and the ideal state. In its ideal form, the state does not simply represent the abstract structure of Kantian morality; ideas are given material shape in rules or laws and in the dynamic ethical life or *Sittlichkeit* of a people. Important is the coherence of abstract justice with the concrete legal system and ethical life. Moreover, the state is not simply a social contract of use to its citizens but an institution that has intrinsic value, as an instantiation of the ideal sphere. The state has a level of autonomy vis-à-vis the citizens and politicians who give it life. In this sense the state is analogous to the artwork, understood not as an arbitrary construct but as a concrete and harmonious instantiation of the ideal sphere. When the state fails to reach this dimension, art may provide a counterinstance, either on the level of content or by the simple intrinsic value of its beautiful mediation of the ideal and the material. Its autonomy is, paradoxically, not without a connection to the broader sphere, and so it contributes to a higher concept of coherence and of moral value, to which every state is likewise subservient.

THE ROLE OF THE UGLY

To embrace any concept of the organic that does not account for the marginal, the dissonant, and the ugly would be unwise, for the ugly is a prominent dimension of reality. The ugly can relate to aesthetics in, seemingly, three ways.[10] An initial position might suggest that the ugly does not belong in art at all and should be excluded. A second position might argue that the ugly is equal with, or even superior to, the beautiful. A third position would argue that art must account for, and even portray, the ugly, but that it should be recognized as subordinate to beauty, which is accomplished neither by ignoring the ugly nor by glorifying it but by integrating and overcoming it. The ugly has importance as a part within the whole of a work, which must in its entirety be recognized as beautiful. I side with the synthetic view: spirit is sufficiently strong to immerse itself in, and survive in, negativity. A simple condemnation of the ugly is anti-intellectual and overlooks the aesthetic principle that the meaning of each part derives from the whole, from which follows that the parts may be transformed in the whole. Important in this context is to distinguish at least two definitions of beauty. One definition suggests that the beautiful artwork is superficially harmonic and pleasing to the senses. This very limited definition captures certain forms of art but is hardly exhaustive. It excludes, for example, the tragic and the sublime. A merely pleasing work can easily become empty of substantive meaning and devoid of struggle. A higher form of beauty allows for struggle, pain, and dissonance. It requires only the correspondence of part and whole and of form and content. Some content simply cannot be subsumed under the first, more superficial definition of beauty, which indicates its limits.

Beauty deals not only with the pure and the superficially harmonic; it must—if not in each instance at least in its full range—also attend to the ugly. It must reflect in itself the negative—evil, contempt, weariness of life, cynicism, isolation, hunger, death. In the words of Plotinus, the ugly soul is "dissolute, unrighteous; teeming with all the lusts; torn by internal discord; beset by the fears of its cowardice and the envies of its pettiness; thinking, in the little thought it has, only of the perishable and the base; perverse in all its impulses; the friend of unclean pleasures; living the life of abandonment to bodily sensation and delighting in its deformity" (par. I.6.5). This is the ugly—in life and in art. It can assume many different guises: the boring, the dissonant, the brutal, the obscene, the self-indulgent, the monotonous, the grotesque, the malicious, the vain, the envious, the formless, the frivolous, the repulsive, the senseless, the purely negative, and so forth. Art has the task, among others, of looking evil right in the eye, which means that much of art will contain the ugly, the aesthetic counterpart of evil. One must allow a great deal of space for artists to wrestle with evil and the ugly without condemning their works as somehow falling short of an aesthetic and moral ideal. Indeed, this is particularly true in modernity, for, as Hegel has argued (10.316–17), evil is related to subjectivity, or the dissolution of inherent order, and in an age of subjectivity evil will play a greater role and is thus that much more central to the artist's vision. The role of evil in metaphysics and ethics is analogous to the role of the ugly in art, including not only the subject matter but also the artist's abandonment of traditional aesthetic norms. (For Hegel evil and progress are intertwined with subjectivity and the negation of tradition.)

The portrayal of the ugly in art was not new in the nineteenth or twentieth century, as the works of Hieronymus Bosch, Mathis Grünewald, Pieter Bruegel, and Francisco Goya indicate, but it has intensified in modernity. One catalyst for this interest in the ugly was fascination with evil, which increased in the nineteenth century, first, as attention was drawn to what was ignored in idealist claims to synthesis and, second, as sociology and psychology uncovered more of the complexities of humanity. As a result, aesthetic portrayals of negativity and oppression increased. Loveliness and harmony gave way to truth and attentiveness to the deficiencies of the real. Some such presentations were descriptive, even clinical, and not at all overtly evaluative. However, the reader is generally encouraged through such portrayals to recognize the often latent origins and consequences of evil. If fascination with evil, however, gains the upper hand in relation to evaluation, or if contrasting images are absent, evil can destroy art. We are reminded of Pope's lines: "Vice is a monster of so frightful mien, / As, to be hated, needs but to be seen; / Yet seen too oft, familiar with her face, / We must endure, then pity, then embrace" (523).[11] Two stronger arguments for presenting evil in literature can, however, be found. The first suggests that to show life in its full range, we cannot exclude evil. The second, which is more evaluative, argues that the truly good presupposes the negation of evil, and so evil must be presented as an option worthy of being overcome.

The reasons, then, for the inclusion of the ugly are analogous: first, art deals with the universality of existence, and within the universal, the ugly cannot be excluded; second, all complex art requires the ugly as a moment within a more overarching whole. Much that is not beautiful can and should be presented, but it must be superseded in one fashion or another in the course of the work— negativity, for example, that is negated, as in comedy, or evil that is combined with an element of greatness, as in tragedy. More important, beauty is the appropriateness of form to content, such that in an interpretation of life the form may require great asymmetries and perversions of what is traditionally called beautiful, but the metasymmetry of form and content, along with the specific rhetoric of the work, its style if you will, may render the work beautiful.

Hegel elevates contradiction as a path to truth. The sphere of contradiction within art is occupied by the ugly. In *Art and the Absolute*, one of the more interesting recent books in aesthetics, William Desmond endeavors to suggest, with Hegel, that art is a privileged window onto the absolute, and he seeks to show that Hegel's reflections on art, as the sensuous appearance of truth, can address modern as well as traditional art. He focuses thereby also on the ugly (150–59). A sign of the times, however, is that even as astute a critic as Desmond does not recognize that the ugly was the dominant category of the post-Hegelian era. This development begins with Weiße and continues above all with Ruge, Vischer, and eventually Rosenkranz, who devotes an entire study to the aesthetics of the ugly. For the post-Hegelians the category most frequently linked with the ugly is the comic. Rosenkranz, for example, writes: "The comic is the *dissolution* of the ugly insofar as it *destroys itself*" (*System*, par.

831). In another passage he suggests: "In the comic, ugliness is posited as the negation of the beautiful, which, however, it negates in turn" (*Aesthetik* 53). Comedy is built on the structure of portraying what is inadequate, untenable, deviant, and, showing its inner contradiction and self-cancellation, the self-destruction of what is untenable. Thus, the ugly is invited into art but only insofar as it is transformed or overcome. The figure by which this is accomplished is frequently the *reductio ad absurdum*. Obscenities and the grotesque as forms of the ugly are presented only in order to be mocked, displaced, relativized.

Art can transform the ugly in various ways: by portraying pain as sublime or noble (as in tragedy); by mocking insufficiency and error (as in satire or comedy); or by immersing itself in, and overcoming, evil (as in speculative art). Great artists who portray the ugly—one thinks, for example, of Franz Kafka or George Grosz—normally portray the ugly in order to undermine it or uncover it as negative. The art of Bernd Löbach, to take an example of a contemporary artist concerned with technology, draws our attention to our careless exploitation of the environment.[12] Through symbolic language he wants his viewers to see a deeper reality that our everyday activity veils. He shows an aquarium filled not with water and fish but with batteries, or he creates towers out of trash, which he calls "Refuse Forest." Löbach does not elevate the ugly to the level of the beautiful; instead, he forms the ugly in such a way as to elevate our level of insight through what he calls "ecologically critical art." Critical and didactic, his works form a legitimate element within the diversity of art, even if they lack complexity, multivalence, and a speculative structure.

As Löbach rightly tells us, a problem associated with the technological age is waste. Good literature, however, can sharpen our eyes to the issue of waste in far more indirect ways than we find in Löbach, for in the great artwork we see that no element is not expressive of the whole; every part is interrelated and in some sense necessary. Waste is not easily located in the great works of Sophocles or Shakespeare. Great literature sensitizes us to the issue of how to experience pleasure free of the visible manifestation of waste. The economy of the great artwork is a model for a larger economy. Not only in its form but also in its thematic dimensions, art deals with waste: to note one example, tragedy thematizes greatness that is wasted, thus enhancing in our recognition of this loss our appreciation of transcendent values.[13] Finally, in an overarching sense, great art sensitizes us to the value of goods that endure and are not simply throwaway productions.

Modern criticism is primarily attracted to negative categories: rupture, asymmetry, chaos, imbalance, above all, dissonance. Ancient wisdom suggests that only the eye that is itself sunlike can see the sun, only the soul that is itself beautiful can envisage true beauty (*Republic* 508–9; Plotinus, para. I.6.9). We might invert this image and suggest that only those whose sense of beauty is so dimmed can view as beautiful what lacks the essential qualities of beauty, and yet this seems to be the tendency of the age. What rationale lies behind this abandonment of the beautiful? At least three reasons suggest themselves. First, art should serve the purpose, we are told, of undermining tradition and stability; it should question what is. This ideology privileges rupture and disruption, art that is fleeting, not permanent, abrasive, not harmonic. Second, dissonant art is seen as the appropriate art form for our age, which is itself out of balance and confused. Third, critics argue that any harmony is somehow feigned and inappropriate.

Against these reasons I would counter, first, that there is no reason why art cannot embrace, as well as modify, tradition. Artistic excellence does not call for an either-or mentality. Indeed, if we only undermine the old without creating and establishing the new, we shall lack alternatives and fail to realize them. Second, the most appropriate art form for an age of imbalance, especially if art is a counterforce to reality, may be balance. Note, by the way, the hidden contradiction between the first rationale (art as resistance) and the second rationale (art as imitation). Third, it does not follow—either logically or experientially—that works of balance and harmony are necessarily superficial and weak. Often poets are driven to focus, perhaps unknown to themselves, on precisely those elements that need to be addressed before a greater whole can be viewed as truly harmonic. In a larger frame the coherence of the whole requires attention to fragmentation and dissonance. The very turn to the ugly in nineteenth- and twentieth-century art may thus be indicative of a higher logic— the attempt to seek out those moments that were neglected in earlier attempts at synthesis.[14]

That modern art tends to be more critical than idealizing may be said to serve an important societal function in an age where much invites critical reflection, but mere critique, mere negation of negativity, prevents us from achieving and recognizing the full range of artistic possibilities that other generations have enjoyed more abundantly than we have. If the modern world is dissonant, and dominant art mirrors this dissonance, then a nonmimetic, avant-garde art would portray what is counter to dissonance, an ideal world. We might reformulate a phrase of Hegel's and propose that art is its age captured in sensuous presentation. This would explain the very strong desire toward negativity and the ugly in contemporary art, and it would reconfirm the idea that art can be understood partly in terms analogous to the Weberian ideal. But just as Hegel's definition of philosophy as its age captured in thought has been justly criticized as quietistic, so too is this definition of art inadequate. One must also show alternatives, and the literary critic is right to expect of contemporary art both immersion in what is and reflection on what should be. In an age that lacks manifestations of synthesis, this higher task is not easy, but it remains desirable. Moreover, to portray mere hints of synthesis, gestures toward the ideal, thematizing possible but fragile efforts in an age of fragmentation may be a viable path.

Chapter 3 The Value
of Literary Criticism

Under aesthetics we traditionally consider three subfields: production aesthetics, artwork aesthetics, and reception aesthetics. All art can be studied from these three perspectives, which might be viewed along a spectrum, as there is natural overlap in many areas. In production aesthetics we deal with those forces that contribute to the generation of a work, such as the formal prerequisites of artistry, including the relationship between *physis* and *techne* or *ingenium* and *ars;* the concepts of creation dominant in an age, including the level of originality desired and expected; biography, including family and other influences and issues related to the author's gender, ethnicity, and sexual orientation; the social status and economic position of the artist, including questions of patronage and market; the psychology of the artist and of the creative process; the diverse presuppositions of a particular artist's creative work; source studies, including the writer's schooling and reading and other intellectual influences; the author's geographical background and the influence of place, region, and environment on his or her writing; the writer's politics; the genesis of a work, including earlier versions, related manuscripts, and alterations; the broader sociohistoric context; the position of the artist within the development of a national literature or within a dialogue with other cultures; and the precise means of production available to the artist, from oral tradition to computers.

Artwork aesthetics analyzes and evaluates the form of art, "form" being understood both in a micro-sense (the rhetoric, stylistics, and structure of the work) and in a macro-sense (the genre to which the work belongs and the literary period of which it may be characteristic); the content of the work, including the story, theme, argument, and broader ideas; and the interrelation of form and content and of parts to the whole.

Reception aesthetics encompasses publication history, including censorship, distribution mechanisms, and sales; performance, where appropriate; audience expectations and the ways in which artworks may expand or transform a reader's expectations; translation as a form of interpretation; the emotions evoked by certain genres and by individual works; the ways in which one's position—as defined by period, class, gender, ethnicity, sexuality, or ideology—influences one's reading; the level of a work's openness to diverse interpretations; links between general hermeneutic principles and the phenomenology of reading; cognitive-psychological and neurobiological analyses of the reading process; the history of a work's reception, including empirical questions, such as readership and changes in literary-critical interpretations and evaluations and influence on other works; the norms and conventions of interpretive communities as they shift over time; and reflection on the social system of literature, including the functions of literature for readers.

THE PRIORITY OF ARTWORK AESTHETICS

While every intellectual product has a sphere of production and reception, not every intellectual product is an artwork. From this distinction follows the superiority of artwork aesthetics, for only here is the artwork analyzed as a work of art. Psychological, sociological, and historical methodologies are limited insofar as they focus on the external dimensions of an artwork, not its essence, not what makes it an artwork. If literary criticism is to be attentive to what makes art uniquely art, it must attend primarily not to production or reception but to artwork aesthetics, focusing thereby on the content and form of art, their interrelation, and the connection of the parts to the whole. The excellence of an artwork depends on the quality of its idea and its form, not on its having been created by someone who lived in a given era or who had a particular background, traits common to many individuals whose intellectual products do not interest us in the least; nor does it depend on a given culture's reception of the work, as not all cultures have approached works with cogent categories. To elevate production over the work would be to find oneself arguing that a work is good because it was created by a certain genius or a person with particular characteristics or because the work emerged during a certain era. To elevate reception over the work would be to find oneself arguing that a work is good because people say that it is good instead of making the more rational claim that people find a work good because it is good.

The prominence of artwork aesthetics can be briefly illustrated by way of tragedy and comedy, theories of which have often suffered from a focus on reception at the expense of the artwork itself. While many theories of tragedy, including Aristotle's in central parts of the *Poetics,* focus on reception, Schelling, Hölderlin, Hegel, and Szondi address the structure of tragedy in the artwork itself and come thereby to differentiated assessments of which tragic structures are excellent as well as which fail to embody a truly tragic dimension. In another work I attempted to draw on these thinkers to outline a normative theory of the tragic that accounts for the diversity of individual works. This distinction between the normative and descriptive spheres is essential for the question of evaluation, to which I return below. Also with regard to comedy, various theories of laughter have been explored. D. H. Monro summarizes these as superiority, incongruity, release from restraint, and ambivalence. As Hösle has shown in a recent study of Woody Allen, only the theory of incongruity refers to the object, whereas the other theories refer to subjective processes. Therefore, only the incongruity theory, which is compatible with the other theories insofar as they address different dimensions, can be the basis of a normative theory of the comic. Only it can suggest why we should or should not laugh. Only an analysis of the object can tell us whether our laughter is intelligent and whether our feelings of superiority or ambivalence are justified.

Artwork aesthetics has been relegated to secondary status in recent years. This devaluation followed a certain historical logic. The New Critics often took as a presupposition that every artwork was a successful unity, and the interpreter's task was to unravel this unity. More sociohistorically minded critics not only justly recognized that the ideal unity of an artwork often could not be uncovered without attending to the work's broader contextual references, they also unveiled, partly by drawing attention to the historical referents in the work, the many ways in which aesthetic unity was fragile or counterfeit. Unfortunately, just criticisms of weak instantiations of artwork aesthetics have been supplemented by more tendentious arguments. In devaluing the autonomy of the artwork, many critics assume, first, that the artwork necessarily serves the values of those for whom it was produced and, second, that ideas are to be weighed not for their intrinsic validity but in the light of their origins or the interests they serve. Instead of focusing on the artwork, such critics argue, we should attend to the conditions of its genesis and its extrinsic purpose. But ideas are valid or invalid based not on their genesis or purpose but on their level of coherence. To argue otherwise is to commit the performative contradiction of arguing for the substitution of power for argument and to open the sinister door that screens ideas based on categories of person. When validity is viewed as equivalent with interests, critics are free to argue with opponents not by demonstrating that their views are internally incoherent, or that they fail to capture the essence of what they describe, but by appealing to origin and motive.

The emphasis on reception has been reinforced by the further development of hermeneutics and the just idea that we must be sensitive to the openness of the text. We want to avoid all reductionism and be receptive to new meaning. One of the values of literary criticism is reinforced by an insight of reception theory, the idea that the meaning of a work is codetermined by the object under study and the observer of that object. Thus, meaning depends not only on the quality of the artwork but also on the quality of the imagination with which one approaches it. The more schooled the imagination is in reading, the more one can take from a literary work; the more intelligent the reader, the more the work has to say. Thus, reception aesthetics teaches us the value of asking good questions, including attending to those elements that are especially prominent in artwork aesthetics. However, reception aesthetics has also elicited positions that give insufficient attention to the work itself or that overemphasize the subjectivity of the reading process.

In recent years systematic and normative categories have for the most part been abandoned; therefore, the searching question, What is art? has given way to the unwittingly dogmatic claim, If someone calls it art, it's art. This statement itself makes a claim about art, namely, that there is nothing distinctive about art. Without a rational dimension, however, art and the study of art are reduced to sociology and psychology. The increasing subjectivity of our culture is reflected in the fact that artworks and interest in them were once focused on the object represented, then on the producer of the object, and now on the recipient. Our values have shifted from the object to the genial creator and now to ourselves. With this shift the distinguishing features of the aesthetic object and the aesthetic experience are increasingly ignored or openly denied, as, for example, by Barbara Smith (34).

The priority of artwork aesthetics does not exclude the limited value of reception and production aesthetics. Hegel showed in his grand survey of art the important interrelations between artwork and historical context, and several classics of modern literary study are oriented toward this contextual sphere. One thinks, for example, of Arnold Hauser's *Social History of Art and Literature.* My own stress on the technological age has led me to integrate historical context (production and reception) into my reflections. In an age that ignores production and reception, we benefit by recognizing their value. However, the pendulum appears to have swung in the opposite direction: today we need more reflection on the philosophical and sensuous dimensions of artworks. Given the priority of artwork aesthetics, inattention to these is a graver error than neglect of their contextual surroundings.

HERMENEUTIC PRINCIPLES

The meaning and significance of literary works very much depend on the concepts, categories, and questions we bring to them. The hermeneutic process makes clear that our horizon of expectations influences the meaning we derive from an object. The stronger our concepts and categories, the better the questions will be that we ask of literary works; the greater our imagination and the more flexible our minds, the more we discover. At the same time, the more we attend to the unique patterns and structures of the work under question, the more grounded our insights will be. Although art often makes understandable and accessible what might be incomprehensible and inaccessible in the form of reasoning, art is also complex and in need of interpretation. Meaning is not self evident; it must be ascertained through interpretation. This endeavor is often difficult because, among other reasons, an array of differences—historical, cultural, and evaluative—exist between the creator and the recipient that must be at least partially bridged. The interpreter's task is to be schooled in the categories of interpretation, the history of art, and the specific diachronic and synchronic dimensions affecting the particular work under analysis, all of which are prerequisites for a meaningful bridge.

A basic principle of hermeneutics, therefore, is to bring to the work those categories and accompanying knowledge that will yield the most interesting results.[1] We want to take out of any aesthetic engagement the best that the work has to offer. One category of the highest order is unity, which has three dimensions. First, hermeneutics seeks the principles by which we bridge subject and object, interpreter and work. Second, the critic attempts to integrate part and whole and seeks thereby also the overarching unity of the artwork. Third, the critic must attend to the unity of the two distinguishing features of the artwork, its form and its content. I turn now to these three aspects in greater detail.

Interpretation has a circular dimension. One approaches the text with certain expectations, which are revised through interpretive work; in turn, these revised expectations open up ever newer facets of the work, which elicit refinement after refinement of our assessment of the work and revision after revision of our preconceived understanding. Though we cannot approach a text without categories, we can bring stronger or weaker categories and questions to a text, and we can attend more or less carefully to the specificity of the text, to the ways in which it sparks our sense of its complex interconnections. Heidegger suggests of this hermeneutic circle: "What is decisive is not to get out of the circle, but to get in it in the right way" (*Being and Time* 143). We must recognize with Heidegger and his student Hans-Georg Gadamer that we always approach texts with a certain pre-understanding that evolves in the course of exegesis, such that our horizon of understanding expands. The circle is inescapable, but potentially productive. Wrestling with interpretive problems sheds light on the work and on the interpreter as well.

To supplement Gadamer by attending to historical differences and levels of validity is important. Our interpretations should not be unduly limited by authorial intentions or earlier interpretations, but when visible differences exist between our readings and the meanings assigned to them by authors or earlier critics, we should acknowledge these differences. If, for example, we transform what was meant literally in the Bible into something symbolic, we should recognize and acknowledge this historical divide. A positivistic moment is necessary to help us distinguish the many historical contingencies and idiosyncracies on the level of intention and tradition from the ideal or systematic sphere of meaning we seek in our interpretations. In the tradition it was widespread to attempt symbolic readings of works, overlooking their original, literal meanings or *sensus litteralis* and focusing on their broader significance or coherence for the present, the *sensus spiritualis,* without, however, acknowledging this difference. We owe an effective critique of this strategy to Spinoza's evaluation of Maimonides in the *Tractatus theologico-politicus,* where Spinoza criticizes Maimonides and others for ignoring this objective difference. Gadamer seeks to overcome the historicist restriction Spinoza and later thinkers impose on hermeneutics, whereby the intended meaning is viewed as the true meaning of the work. Gadamer would overcome this restriction by letting interpretation emerge from historical tradition, which means that intentional meaning, the meaning of tradition, and our meaning have equal value; they are simply different.

Two serious problems follow, however, from Gadamer's position. First, despite his theoretical elevation of the otherness of the other, Gadamer cannot in practice recognize or articulate historical distinctions. Historical accuracy, which is the value of the positivistic, historicist model introduced by Spinoza, is foreign to Gadamer. Good arguments exist for reading the Bible and other works symbolically, in the light of their ideal meaning, but when we do so, to recognize that we are reading the works differently from the way the writers intended is useful. Recognition of such difference has a certain hermeneutic value in itself and is, more important, a useful tool on the path to systematic reflection, which brings us to Gadamer's second weakness. Gadamer cannot distinguish between interpretive and evaluative levels. In other words, by seeking to fuse his horizon with the historical horizon, he not only misses the specific difference of the historical other, he is unable to evaluate the validity of the historical other and take it seriously as an alternative position; it is simply another path in the tradition. Gadamer suggests that in reception we are interested in solutions to common problems (e.g., 299, 373, 392), but this alleged interest is hardly supported by Gadamer's nonevaluative elevation of difference (302). An ideal sphere of meaning, which presupposes the question of evaluation, the validity or lack of validity of earlier thoughts when translated into a systematic perspective, is foreign to him. For Gadamer each period and each interpretation has its own validity; we understand differently, not better. In short, Gadamer has no means by which to reject the prejudices of tradition as untenable; here, as frequently elsewhere in modernity, truth is reduced to what survives and has power; a normative moment is absent, and the proximity of Gadamer's theory to legal positivism becomes clear. A consequence of his metatheory is that it prevents Gadamer from defending his theory against misunderstandings and rejection. He cannot be understood objectively—either in terms of intentions or validity—only variously, which means that Gadamer can be said to mean any number of things, and his readers are free to evaluate him in any number of ways—without recourse to intention or truth.

In contrast to Gadamer, I would argue that the optimal hermeneutic strategy seeks to grasp the ideal sphere of meaning. This involves, first, what is implied but not stated in certain works, by which I mean not only an esoteric meaning that may be intended, yet veiled, but also the meaning that follows from a just interpretation of the work, even if this meaning was not consciously intended. Gadamer would of course grant this initial principle, and his effectiveness in underscoring it represents one of his great achievements on behalf of modern hermeneutics. Nonetheless, the theory that the meaning of an artwork cannot be reduced to the consciousness that created it was already introduced by Plato, who suggests in the *Apology* (22b–c) and argues more fully in *Ion* that poets are poor interpreters of their works; they write not so much out of wisdom as out of instinct or inspiration. Although great artists may often have an unconscious sense of what is right, as when they step back to view a canvas before continuing to paint or make revisions after rereading some lines of a poem, they less commonly have the categorical apparatus to describe the value of their works or their meanings. To decipher the meaning of a work, one must relate image to thought; one must mediate the work with reflection—in this realm of mediation and abstraction the poet may be found wanting. Many works of literature have a life of their own. The artist intends one thing, but the words, the images, the structures magically relate to convey something else. Given the organic dimensions of artworks, this vitality is hardly surprising.

Beyond the elevation of work over consciousness, a second moment is required, which Gadamer neglects. The ideal critic also seeks, as far as is compatible with the work itself, an interpretation that allows the work to fulfill the highest aesthetic principles, including not only the integration of form and content and of part and whole, but also the embodiment of a content that is compatible with the true and the good. The ideal reading not only does the most justice to the work as an artwork, but, other things being equal, makes the work as eloquent, truthful, and coherent as it can be. The meaning of a work partly depends on the agility of the interpreter and the coherence of his or her thought, so as to bring out of the work the most meaningful interpretation, and this interpretation, to return to the first point, may well be something else and something grander than the artist ever intended. Gadamer, with his emphasis on tradition, does not recognize any higher principles, any ideal sphere, against which artworks are to be measured. Meaning is not weighed in its relation to truth.

The reader who wants to grasp only what the writer wanted to say is a historian of ideas, not a true scholar of literature. The critic who in elevating tradition reads the work without attending to its participation in an ideal discourse that has stronger and weaker arguments falls prey to the historicist thinking that says we understand only differently, never better or worse. Even more problematic, though in some ways merely a consequence of this, is the subjectivist critic who reads into a text whatever seems of interest to him or her, without attending to differences between text and interpretation, without engaging in a dialogue that recognizes the difference that makes present an other worldview as other. As we seek to uncover the ideal meaning that corresponds both to the work and to our highest expectations of art, we must endeavor to understand the work's historical emergence or specificity, recognizing what was said at the time and in the tradition and the extent to which these earlier interpretations have only historical validity. The ideal sphere can benefit from, but cannot be reduced to, a recognition of authorial intention or tradition. However, just as we might improve our grasp of the ideal sphere, so might we lose it; what was thought earlier, whether as original intention or as interpreted earlier in the tradition, may have more validity than what is generally thought today. Only by attending to this historical difference are we aware of the systematic level and, therefore, in a position to learn from the past as different, instead of falling prey to the temptations to describe a work without evaluating the legitimacy of its arguments or to make the work say whatever we want it to say. A meaningful unity of work and recipient does not exclude moments of difference, both historical and evaluative, or moments of new insight. In sum, we must seek to grasp the work, by revising our initial understanding, as the work becomes more present to us and as we recognize to what extent it does or does not contribute to higher truth claims.

My position might be clarified by comparison with the analogous sphere of legal hermeneutics. One model of legal hermeneutics elevates authorial intention (what Hirsch calls "meaning" instead of "significance"). In the United States this interpretive practice is associated with those who focus on the *mens auctoris*, seeking to grasp the intentions of the founding fathers when they drafted the Constitution. The limits of this paradigm are several: discerning original intentions is not always possible; the intentions may not always be reasonable or just; they may appear empty vis-à-vis new issues that have arisen in the meantime; and any text may have implications—positive or negative— that were not foreseen by its authors. Although the intentionalist paradigm has several weaknesses, in a culture that cannot reach a consensus on normative questions this method of interpretation has a certain pragmatic value. A second hermeneutic strategy is to turn to tradition: the equivalent within jurisprudence of Gadamer's elevation of tradition would be the technique of ruling by precedent and tradition, which likewise has no normative instance but, depending on the culture, great common sense. Unfortunately, German legal

positivism did not fare as well as did its British counterpart in the twentieth century; in Germany the philosophical weakness manifested itself as a historical
problem. Without recourse to a concept of justice beyond legality, aberrant legal
developments cannot be criticized, and they may gain, through mere historicity,
a false legitimacy. A third hermeneutic strategy recognizes in all legal judgments
the wielding of ungrounded power, as in critical legal studies. The analogue in
literary criticism encompasses the theories of deconstruction and culture studies, which I address below. The model I am proposing here includes a normative
dimension, measuring texts against an ideal sphere of meaning, and so it is
closest to natural-law theory, which, unlike the other paradigms, draws a strict
distinction between justice and legality, as in the civil rights rhetoric of Martin
Luther King Jr. Like its equivalent in literary criticism, natural-law theory seeks
an ideal, normative sphere. As privileged hermeneutic practice I propose reflection on the ideal meaning of a literary work, which is not reducible to intention, tradition, or power and which is best elicited by a combination of interpretive sensibility and philosophical reflection. The ideal hermeneutic unity of
subject and object necessarily leads to normative questions.

The second way in which the critic seeks unity is in the relation of part and
whole, whereby the critic also seeks to define the overarching unity of the work.
Any good critic knows that the meanings of the individual parts cannot be fully
determined except by their relationship to the whole. At the same time, the
whole cannot be grasped until the many parts are understood in their autonomy. This does not mean that understanding does not occur; instead, it means
that understanding is continuously enhanced and revised. Leo Spitzer calls this
almost simultaneous movement from part to whole and back again to the parts
"the philological circle" (20). In the great artwork, as I have suggested, every
moment is related to every other. Such an artwork has an economy whereby
every part contributes to the meaning of the whole; no one part is unnecessary
or inexpressive of the higher meaning. This economy of style is common to
great works—whether they be simple couplets or massive novels. Therefore, an
important interpretive set of questions becomes, how to divide the work into
parts and how to relate the parts to one another. One of the critic's primary
tasks is to illuminate both these interrelations and the necessity of individual
parts that may at first blush seem superfluous or not integral.

Beyond relating part and whole, the critic seeks the overarching principle or
unity of the entire work. Every great work has a unifying dimension, and all
readers ideally seek that unifying principle which manifests itself in every facet
of the work. Indeed, the parts must be understood—not in their genesis, but in

their validity—as being determined by the overarching idea or whole. We may recognize this unity in a character or event or in a metaphor, theme, category, or insight. The overarching principle may even lie in a highly complex and ambiguous statement, which nonetheless unifies all the parts of the work. Owing to the great variability of artworks, no mechanical formula exists for discovering a work's unifying dimension. We must read carefully and allow ourselves the patience to be struck by the details of a work, we must ask probing and suggestive questions, and we must bring our experience to bear on the work's unique structures.

The third and final moment of unity to which the critic must attend is the unity of the two distinguishing features of the artwork, its sensuousness or form, which differentiates it from other nonartistic intellectual endeavors, and its intellectual meaning or content, which distinguishes it from simple matter. Most important, the critic must attend to the often complex relationship between the two spheres, isolating now one, now the other, but ultimately reflecting on their interconnection, even if it be ironic or visible only on a metalevel.

One value of the study of literature is its cultivation of intellectual virtues. The complex or subtle work of literature that requires careful reading and interpretation challenges the spontaneity, imagination, and intelligence of the reader. Some literary works have visible gaps that require the reader to think through various interpretive possibilities. In this sense readers must adopt a Socratic or Brechtian frame, whereby they are not seeking a ready-made solution as much as using their imagination and entering into active dialogue with the work. One thinks, for example, of the philosophical and literary genre of the dialogue or of the unresolved quandary presented to the reader at the conclusion of Brecht's *The Good Person of Sezuan*. Through the interpretive process the reader gains greater sensibility and gives new life to the work. By teaching students the content and form of literary works, by confronting them with great and different traditions, but also by teaching them the mode of thinking associated with this process, they are better able to analyze problems in the world as well. Because we must receive complex artworks with greater care and effort than much of what otherwise occupies our consciousness, the reception of art sharpens our cognitive capacities. We learn a sensibility or sensitivity to subtle differences. At the same time, the study of literature teaches us to look at the whole and not just at parts, to synthesize the parts into a whole. It allows us to recognize that meaning may unfold slowly and that the whole may be disclosed to us only as we recollect diverse parts and begin to discern patterns. It teaches us to weigh the significance of an event or occurrence or an encounter and to imagine alternatives. It teaches us how to synthesize evidence, articulate a complex view, and draw appropriate conclusions. It teaches us to respond to life with emotion and sympathy as well as analysis and judgment, and it teaches us the importance of reason and evidence in an emotionally charged arena. To understand ever new facets of a work contributes to flexibility of mind and an awareness of the need for breadth and balance. The study of literature can enhance what Robert Lane calls "mental clarity" and "citizen education" (*The Liberties* 5 and 84). In this sense the study of literature is an important element of liberal education.

Students who argue for or against a particular interpretation learn the formal skills of weighing and marshaling evidence. They learn to understand the types of evidence one can employ and their strengths and limitations. This process develops the students' aesthetic sensibilities and eristic capacities. It also cultivates an awareness of the need to be ever open to new perspectives and arguments. Ideally, interpreters look for counterevidence to the reading they have developed, integrating the evidence proleptically, clearly demarcating the limits of the reading, or developing a complex metareading that emerges from a series of possible interpretations. Attention to contrasting moments is a privileged dimension of interpretation. We don't want oversimplistic readings, inattentive to the work's many layers, or one-sided readings, neglectful of those moments not easily assimilated into the primary reading. The critic might therefore be encouraged to develop what might be called a strong reading (for which there is dominant evidence) and a weak reading (for which there is some evidence to counter the strong reading, yet not enough to overturn it). This results in an honest relationship to the work and has the side benefit of helping us guard against dogmatism. The best criticism approaches a work with complex categories but lets the work enrich those categories; it does not come to the work to prove a doctrine already developed. Recognizing the sensuous as resistant to mere conceptualization, the literary critic must attend to the complexity of the individual work, including its paradoxes, ambiguities, and moments that resist conceptualization or seem counterintuitive; he or she must recognize *aletheia* as a moment of art.

EVALUATION

The critic must also evaluate a work's excellence. It is difficult to imagine more fundamental questions in literary study than, What does the work mean, and

how do I know what it means? and, Is this a good work, and how might I justify my evaluation to others? All literature is capable of interesting us in one
sense or another, but this claim does not imply that all literature interests us
equally or should interest us equally, which brings us to the first reason for evaluation. Literary works vary immensely in their capacity to engage us, and they
differ in their ability to animate us on various levels; some are more worthy of
our investment of time than others. If we agree that literature has moral relevance, then the question is not only how shall we spend our hours but also what
influence various works will have on our spirit and character, our development
and aspirations, and our responsibilities to ourselves and others. The need for
selection and the need for guidance speak for the informed practice of literary
evaluation.

Moreover, evaluation is inevitable. Hierarchies are ever present, simply by
the choices a reader or critic makes, and value judgments should be as well-
grounded as possible. In nonscholarly debates we tend to evaluate art in emotive—which is to say, subjective—terms: a work is exciting or boring, interesting or dull. In these instances the stress is not on the work but on the
individual's relation to the work, which should not be excluded but rather be
integrated into a higher level of reflection. To remain within the emotive sphere
and to claim that every view is colored by subjectivity frees us, first, from our responsibility to the work itself and, second, from systematic reflection and evaluative questions. Our senses and our emotions tell us to what extent a book has
gripped our soul, but it is best to test these against more fundamental aesthetic
and hermeneutic reflections, as the senses and emotions are notoriously ma-
nipulable and deceptive. Especially literary critics should be able to articulate
more than their intuitive preferences; they must seek principles of evaluation
and strive to develop an appreciation of the full range of literary excellence,
even beyond those works that engender a more personal satisfaction.

Taking evaluation to the level of the concept tests not only our emotions.
The question of evaluation forces us to ask hermeneutic questions in a deeper
sense than if we simply interpret and do not ask about value; evaluation gives us
greater understanding and a richer aesthetic experience. Some great works require such effort on our part that we are less the judge of them than they are the
judge of us: we measure ourselves against such works, testing our historical
knowledge and hermeneutic skill, in short our capacity to appreciate what others have seen before us, which is not to say that we cannot also criticize the
works previously considered great, but to do so requires both hermeneutic and
aesthetic competence. Whereas the question of interpretation (hermeneutics)

has in recent years become divorced from, and has tended to supersede, the question of evaluation (aesthetics), they are related. Evaluation is at least a three-step process: delineating the standards of excellence (aesthetics); defining the characteristics of the particular work of art (hermeneutics); and judging whether the particular case meets the standards delineated, whereby the individual case may push us to reconsider our initial standards (the synthesis of aesthetics and hermeneutics). The question of evaluation allows us to understand much not only about the individual work but also about the general purposes and techniques of art, insights of general value that allow us to be our own critics of works as we read them. The practice of evaluation is beneficial to all readers of literature, not just specialists.

Having established the desirability of evaluation, we must ask whether it is possible to defend our evaluations. Without clear standards by which to distinguish good art from bad art, literary critics are of little use to others. If we accept the arguments above concerning the priority of artwork aesthetics, then unless our interest is not essential, not primarily literary, but extrinsic, then artwork aesthetics will determine which works are most excellent as literature. And if literature scholars do not choose works by this criterion, who will? Müller-Seidel rightly recognizes that evaluation is one of the last products of a long hermeneutic process: one must first understand before one can judge (35–36). But the complexity of evaluation is precisely why we need guidance and why the literary critic must attend to this task and to the reasoned judgments of earlier thinkers, even if they may be in need of revision: individuals who want to address this task themselves would in principle need to read and study all of world literature before they would be in a position to say which of it was most worth reading. The literary critic has thereby obligations both to contemporaries and to future generations, for the decisions of the present will decide not only which works are preserved but also which will be consulted as possibly worthy of further preservation.

A judgment about beauty is a value judgment. Therefore, no number of facts will allow us to determine whether or not a work of art is beautiful. This limitation does not excuse the literary historian—who may be more versed in collecting information than the more aesthetically oriented critic—from making value judgments, for the very questions of how much space to devote to a given writer and which facts and connections are significant must be informed—at least partly—by value judgments about literary works. If the facts alone don't suffice, and other categories must apply, the question arises, which ones? And whence are they derived? We determine the beauty of an object, I would argue, in the light of its truth, its sensuous form, the relation of the two, and the relation of part to whole and vice versa. In short, what we have established above about the qualities of an artwork should guide us in the question of its evaluation. Is there an overarching truth in the work? Is the form aesthetically appealing and does it match the content? Do the work's various parts agree or are they in disarray, and are they necessary or superfluous?

Bad art fails in at least one of three ways. First, the ideas may be corrupt, harmful, misleading, mediocre, or in some other way untrue. Second, the form may be uneconomical, artificial, haphazard, unnecessarily obscure, pedestrian, or in some other way deficient. Third, the two sides, the meaning and the shape, may be unrelated, at odds with one another, such that even a metaharmony cannot be deciphered. Untrue content may range from the mistaken, as when a poet's description of nature is inaccurate without thereby serving a higher poetic purpose, to the immoral in its various guises. Not only Plato but also Aristotle criticize untrue content of this kind (1460b).[2] Harmful content embedded in clever form only invites imitation even as it debases the ideal. Leni Riefenstahl may represent for modern audiences an elevation of grandiose form that masks immoral content. Content can be weak in a less spurious way: consider works whose content is exhausted by the concerns of the age and so fails to address subsequent generations or, weaker still, works whose content is so banal or so without general interest that it cannot reward the attention even of contemporaries. Weak art might also be art that permits of no interpretation whatsoever because the work is so hermetic or so formless as to be beyond meaningful communication.

In both cases we see the connection between hermeneutic and aesthetic principles: a work that resists interpretation because it has little to say or seemingly nothing to say does not justify our investment of time; such a work can hardly claim moral value. This weakness is merely a stylistic analogue of a greater demand we place on art—that it be of intersubjective interest. In criticizing such art, I do not of course include richly ambiguous art that is not meaningless but simply unusually difficult to interpret.

The second danger, that of defective form, is at first blush relatively harmless. We may think that it simply wastes our time, but the danger is deeper. Kitsch is also morally bad, for it lowers our expectations and choices with regard to the possibilities of art. A failure in form allows for a range of possibilities, from ineffective diction and stylistic flaws, such as bad rhymes, mixed metaphors, or unmotivated breaks in style, to a plot that has no justifiable or organic structure or a text that is full of sentimentality and clichés. Weaker literature from a formal perspective does not have the textured form or richness characteristic of great literature: it does not commend a second reading or a detailed interpretation but quickly exhausts itself as being of only ephemeral interest. Its parts are not rich enough to sustain further examination or closer scrutiny.

Before we turn to the third form of bad art, it may be useful to ask the question, Which is worse, bad content or bad form? Our answer parallels our earlier reflections on good art. While we can say that there are objective factors for calling art good or bad, our own choices as to which works will speak most fully to us at any given time will be colored by contingent factors. Similarly, our answer to the question of which form of objectively bad art is worse might best be guided by further reflection on the recipient. Some persons will be misled by bad content, in which case the first kind of bad art may be more dangerous. Others will see through the content and not be led astray as easily, even as they enjoy its outstanding form.

The third form of bad art violates the interrelation of content and form, and so contributes to undermining our sense of what beauty is, unless of course we use our concept of beauty to recognize the work's deficiencies. Here a clever content and a remarkable form may simply not intersect in such a way as to support one another and create a meaningful whole. For example, a work may integrate clever formal elements that do not serve the content, or an interesting content may not fill the possibilities of a given form.

It is time to rethink the idea of harmful art without immediately associating such endeavors with authoritarianism, antiquarianism, or arbitrariness. A lack of reflection on what distinguishes good art from bad art renders us slaves to traditional evaluations, interest-driven evaluations, or arbitrary evaluations. Tolstoy's discussion of art has many weaknesses, including his definition of art, which is certainly not sufficient (according to Tolstoy art conveys feelings from one person to another); the argument that all art is equally accessible to everyone; or his condemnations of Dante, Shakespeare, Goethe, and Beethoven. But Tolstoy makes at least one good point, namely, that some art is harmful. Tolstoy criticizes, for example, artificiality and forced originality, unnecessary obscurity, and fine phrasemaking without content. He praises sincerity that seeks to convey moral values, along with clarity, simplicity, and economy. Whether one agrees or disagrees with Tolstoy's definition of good art, one can only admire his honesty and the high value he places on art. As Tolstoy says, art cannot be a mere diversion, saving people from their boring lives. Bad art, seeking to substitute beauty for morality instead of integrating morality into beauty, is a waste of labor on what is useless or even harmful; it confuses children and others, is contrary to the highest principles of humanity, and exerts a corrupting influence on society. No artist or critic since Plato has so clearly outlined the dangers of bad art or what Tolstoy calls "counterfeit art" (93).

When we forget the legitimacy of art (when we can only laugh at Plato and Tolstoy), we simultaneously renounce its higher possibilities (which Schiller, for example, evoked). Not to question some art is to level all art. Good art has a substantial idea that is expressed well and in such a way that the idea and the expression reinforce one another. The best art also addresses the new challenges of an age, though it is more than simply ephemeral. Works that fulfill these conditions will have a certain reception, as Pseudo-Longinus suggests in a memorable passage in chapter 7 of *On the Sublime.* First, such works will appeal to persons from diverse cultures and eras, precisely because of their universality; these works are impossible, or at least difficult, to resist, as they work so profoundly on our minds and senses. Works will not be great because they have appealed through the ages; instead, works appeal through the ages because they are great. While this should free us to make our own judgments, we may also want to be guided, initially, by the judgment of the ages, for it may contain a certain wisdom that we should at least consider. Second, the richness of an immortal work is not only difficult to resist in its initial appeal, it will also both invite and withstand rereading and reexamination; readers may return to such works to discover again and again new facets of meaning and significance. Third, such works will leave an unforgettable impression of the intensity of the reading experience and of its meaning and significance for the reader beyond the immediate reception. Great works remain firmly and ineffaceably in memory.

Evaluation does have aspects of historical situatedness, which is appropriate. Our evaluation of older works will partly depend on their compatibility with certain needs and expectations of the present. Different literary works address diverse needs; this follows from the historical development of humanity and the variety of ways in which aesthetic excellence can be formed and appreciated. This historical moment does not, however, mean that one cannot discuss both what in principle constitutes good literature and which forms of literature seem to be most important for the needs of a given age. Despite this attention to the historical moment, we should recognize that the greatest works of art are of value not only for one time period; they have a broader appeal that transcends their time. Otherwise, we would have an existential engagement only with contemporary literature, and works of earlier eras would be of merely historical interest. Art, however, is more than art history. The other historical moment in aesthetic evaluation has to do with the emergence of new art forms that test and may expand our sense of the realm of the aesthetic. We need to let new works raise legitimate questions about our previous concepts of aesthetic excellence.

Just as the political philosopher must ask what constitutes the good state, so must the literary critic ask what constitutes good literature. If we only describe different kinds of literature without evaluating works, then our value as critics is diminished. In order to evaluate, then, the literary critic needs judgment, a sense of what good art is and what it is not. But something else is needed as well, and Plato raises this point in the second book of the *Laws*: the good literary critic must "be equipped not only with wisdom, but particularly with courage" (659a–b). Literary critics must not learn their verdicts from the audience, letting themselves be intimidated into them by the multitude and their own incompetence, nor can they defer out of cowardice to the consensus, giving voice to positions that belie their innermost convictions. Literary critics, much though they want to learn from other voices, ultimately occupy their positions because they are to teach others, which includes clearly stating a position when it contradicts the majority view. The task of the literary critic is to make judgments and, by arguing openly for them, to improve the aesthetic judgment of listeners. In a climate where literary critics are often attacked with ad hominem arguments or where the majority is moving in another direction, the literary critic must evidence courage.

Truth can be achieved—to employ here a still useful Platonic distinction— by either knowledge or right opinion. Those who have knowledge understand the arguments that lead to truth. Knowledge makes them better able to apply truth in its often complex ramifications and arms them against attacks on truth, as they are not swayed by misleading arguments. Right opinion is not so secure. For this reason, Plato questioned the poets, who give us not arguments but appearances, not knowledge but opinion, and just as easily harmful opinion as right opinion. Over time these harmful opinions can become habits. Although Plato has been justly criticized for his censorship of poetry, we can draw two lessons from his position, both of which are in a sense arguments for literary criticism. The first consequence we can draw from Plato's analysis is the need for the literary critic to evaluate literary works, including their truth claims and moral value. Any state that protects freedom of speech without thereby falling apart at the core is to be privileged over a society that suppresses opinion, however objectionable, in order to survive. But the illegitimacy of censorship says nothing about the literary critic's obligation to praise artworks that satisfy our highest expectations and to criticize artworks that delight in unworthiness. This is not censorship, an issue of legality, but evaluation and critique, an issue of judgment. As Gardner suggests, "Bad art should be revealed for what it is" (106). The critic should weigh not only the formal merits of literary works but also their moral content, whether they offer the semblance of good character and the undermining of evil disposition or the elevation of evil disposition and the undermining of the good, and with this the true and the beautiful. To praise the worthy and rebuke the harmful is the literary critic's moral charge.

Two cautionary moments must be raised here. On the one hand, literary critics attend primarily to the beautiful. They should not praise moral works that lack good form, nor neglect the formal virtues in works that they must criticize for their content. The literary critic must attend always to both moments of art. On the other hand, the literary critic must recognize that the moral value of an artwork is not always easily decipherable; demanding art requires interpretation, and the critic can propose an interpretation of a work that gives it a moral dimension, recognizing perhaps a more complex critique of the immoral hero or narrator than other, more superficial interpretations might suggest. The good critic may consider it necessary to provide more than one reading of a work in order to determine which reading is both more coherent vis-à-vis the work and more coherent vis-à-vis the ideal of beauty to which the work aspires.[3] Similarly, artists may be testing and weighing several different principles and options in their characters or plots, and we must attend to the complexity of imaginative presentation, with its inclusion of alternative possibilities.

Such complexity is especially visible in modernity, which likes to play with unreliable narrators whose views of the world may differ from those espoused by the work as a whole, as in Mann's *Doktor Faustus* or Günter Grass's *The Tin Drum*. We cannot always expect the simple principle of poetic justice. In violating this principle, the poet may be drawing our attention to the inability of society to uncover corruption, as in Gerhart Hauptmann's *The Beaver Coat*. The principle may be only subtly presented, such that the character does not suffer superficially but is deprived of realizing his higher being, as is the case with Judah in Woody Allen's *Crimes and Misdemeanors*. Always the critic must attend to the complexity of the text and the multiplicity of possible interpretations. Just as the hero of a fiction may wrestle with confusion and error, so must the reader. Nonetheless, a simple lingering in cynicism without a struggle against it is not good art, for it contradicts one of art's tenets: either one must reinterpret the work to see cynicism as a moment that is subordinate in the whole or one must question its greatness.

Because of the superiority of artwork aesthetics, we must view as excellent a work that lends itself to a complexly positive interpretation. We can say that the best reading accounts for the most parts of the text and relates these parts to the work's overarching principle and simultaneously defends a reading of the work that preserves its moral value. In some cases a reading that is truest to the work in terms of correspondence, i.e., interpreting its structures and meaning, may be unable to elevate it in terms of coherence, i.e., in terms of its compatibility with truth and beauty. A difficult question arises when one can coherently defend as a strong reading a moral interpretation of a work, but most contemporary readers are unable or disinclined to read the work this way. Instead of seeing, for example, the negation of an untenable position, readers see and identify with the untenable position.

Two responses to this situation strike me as important. First, one can recognize that works of this kind may lead audiences astray, such that they are drawn to identify with immoral actions or themes. This is a danger of art, and one can ask whether works that are so elusive as not to make their negation of negativity clear are ideal for an age that seeks orientation in the moral realm. But any such critique must be directed at the recipients, for the issue of reception is subordinate to the quality of the artwork as such. Second, one can make a strong argument for the value of an education in hermeneutics and evaluation, precisely so that on the level of reception some readings are less frequent. Literary critics have an obligation to mediate such capacities in their writings or classes by dealing with ambiguous works of this kind, and they have a responsibility to comment on works that receive such an interpretation among the public. It would, however, be a mistake to criticize the works themselves—if indeed we elevate artwork aesthetics over reception aesthetics.

It may be added here as a corollary that also the issue of form has two dimensions: some forms are truly weak and must be recognized as such. However, in some cases the weakness may lie not in the form but in the interpreter of the form, who is unable to recognize its appropriateness. Such an interpretive failure may occur when new forms develop, and the critic lacks the categorical apparatus to recognize their emerging greatness. T. S. Eliot comments: "The rudiment of criticism is the ability to select a good poem and reject a bad poem; and its most severe test is of its ability to select a good *new* poem, to respond properly to a new situation" (*The Use of Poetry* 18). An interpretive failure may also arise with older forms, where the critic is simply not capable of rec-

ognizing their beauty, which may indeed require imagination and great hermeneutic skill. Schelling criticizes Gothic architecture as being a mere imitation of
nature, and indeed a less privileged element of nature, a forest (*Philosophie,* par.
112). Hegel, in contrast, recognizes in Gothic art, via comparison with the
Greek temple, profound elements of Christian transcendence: it is an appropriate form for what he calls romantic art (14.332–46).

Sextus Empiricus argues quite well that poets do not prove their sayings but
do offer them, and they are part of their messages and the effect of art; thus, the
critic who merely offers exegesis, without evaluating the work and its claims,
without moving into philosophy, is lacking; indeed, such critics are positively
dangerous, for the poets say much that is "ruinous for practical life" (1.279).
The critic's task is to recognize such statements, not to seek the chimera of
value-free criticism or to impose on the text whatever views he or she happens
to have developed. If the value of the literary critic resides in interpreting and
evaluating literature, and an evaluation of literature presupposes weighing the
tenability of the ideas and the success of their execution, how can the literary
critic flourish without a knowledge of philosophy? The critic must have a wide
knowledge of the spheres addressed in a work for purposes of detailed under
standing, but interpretation does not exhaust literary criticism; it encompasses
evaluation and therefore knowledge of the good and the true as well. I would
thus consider philosophy a central ancillary discipline to literature, more important even than history and sociology, which tend to be more highly valued
but which tell us more about production and reception than about artwork aesthetics.

When we consider the interpretive practices of critics, we do not find a great
deal of criticism in the sense of evaluation.[4] Those who interpret the classics
tend simply to understand the meanings at play instead of also asking the questions, Which of the works under consideration are better than the others and
why? Which of the ideas have only historical interest and which speak to universal concerns? A moment of literary criticism rightly expected by the public
beyond the sifting of works already created is an articulation of those principles
that distinguish a great work in general and for the age. In this sense literary
criticism could in principle influence the further development of literature: to
lessen contemporary weaknesses and point the path toward the realization of
higher ideals in literature.

The second lesson we can draw from Plato's analysis is that, even if we believe, in contrast to Plato, that the state should not censor any works, the state
should make an effort to cultivate the best literature and the best literary criti-

cism, those works that serve the higher ends of literature. Just as the state modifies the market with policies of social assistance, so should it support works (both of the past and of the present) that serve the higher ends that mere market forces might not foster. The state need not supplant the marketplace of ideas, but it should also not sit idly by and refrain from contributing to this marketplace—via public television, public universities, and state-sponsored workshops, symposia, and grants.

In a democratic culture, the state's support of the arts would seem to have at least three reasonable possibilities. First is support of high culture that has steep presuppositions for its reception and thus appeals primarily to an educated and often wealthier public. Although the state should support works of high aesthetic value and should recognize the value of reaching persons who may, because of their education, be highly influential, taxing the entire populace to subsidize art that may not be accessible to the vast majority and that has its own wealthy patrons should probably not be one of the state's highest priorities. Second would be support of innovative programs to increase the aesthetic education of those persons, frequently less educated and thus often financially less advantaged, whose appreciation of high culture is diminished because of their experience and education in aesthetic matters. This support would seem to have great value; it would not only expose persons to great art but also develop their long-term capacity to appreciate such art, thereby widening the future recipient base for such art. Third would be support of cultural products of high aesthetic value that appeal to a broader public, including those who may have less formal education or experience in the arts. While the second possibility may have greater long-term value for those who choose to participate in such programs, the legitimate desire to reach persons based on their current backgrounds and interests and the immediate benefits of such an effort also elevates the third possibility.

Ironically, we see in the United States the following problem. The state justifies its support of the arts because they fulfill a moral and social function, but this function is seemingly absent in many works that critics would like to see better nourished. But instead of giving concrete arguments for the value of the art, one speaks only of prudishness or censorship on the part of the state or its agencies. Why should the state fund works that destroy the moral and social stature of art? Certainly the state cannot and should not tell an artist what to create or a critic what to think, but it can expect of the artists and critics it funds something of intrinsic value or something useful for society, and it has every right to expect that an artist or critic it is supporting who cannot fulfill such a function (or indeed is counterproductive to such a function) should turn to the market for his or her support. The state has an interest in letting our natural distaste for bad literature merge with strong arguments in support of this evaluation. For those who are certain that this should not be a goal of the state, I ask, Doesn't the state require among its citizens industry and integrity, justice and moderation, courage and temperance, as well as identification with its highest purpose, if the state is to survive and flourish? Doesn't the state's schooling, therefore, not only educate us in practical matters but also seek to cultivate civic virtues and excellence of mind? Don't the actions of the state—from the orchestrated celebration of certain holidays to the enactment of laws against discrimination—imply that the state is involved in fostering shared traditions and collective values? Such efforts relate to the highest duty of the state, according to John Stuart Mill, who writes: "The first element of good government, therefore, being the virtue and intelligence of the human beings composing the community, the most important point of excellence which any form of government can possess is to promote the virtue and intelligence of the people themselves" (19.390). If the state, with this ideal of virtue and intelligence in mind, already contributes funding for arts and humanities projects, shouldn't it do so wisely?

UNIVERSALITY AND PARTICULARITY

A work has a greater claim to eminence when it addresses the problems specific to its age even as it conveys insights of universal significance. Literature may render visible hidden aspects of the present, it may rebuke the present in its limitations, or it may embrace it in its emerging possibilities. But great works not only address the themes of the age, they also invite repeated readings by subsequent generations, which is only possible if their themes resonate universally and are not exhausted by the passing fancies and interests of the time of their origin. Thus, the concept of universality and particularity of art can be seen not only in Aristotle's idea that art imitates a particular action of universal significance or Hegel's idea that art gives particular form to the universal, but also in the idea that great art has qualities that give it supertemporal value even as it has elements that distinguish it as addressing and embodying the particularities of an age.

The literary critic must seek the transhistorical truth of the artwork. Yet the best literary critics fulfill not only this universal requirement, they also address the needs of their culture and their age. Because all great art has both transhistorical and historical moments, the critic who wants to address the age will also know its needs and the ways in which a contemporary author does or does not address those needs. Some critics attend only to the universal and thereby fail to elicit any connection with an audience preoccupied with its own legitimate concerns. Some critics attend only to those moments that do connect with the present or study only those works that address contemporary topics, and they fail to write criticism for the ages. Still worse, some critics do neither, treating works as museum artifacts and reading them only in the light of a past age, with interest neither in their universal dimension nor in their status as relevant, by way of contrast, to the present.

For a tradition to have meaning two presuppositions must be met. On the one hand, the tradition must be a reservoir of insights that transcends our day. On the other hand, it must be a living and developing entity that resonates in the present and is transformed by the present. In this spirit, Eliot speaks of the writer who works meaningfully within a tradition as having a "historical sense, which is a sense of the timeless as well as of the temporal and of the timeless and the temporal together" ("Tradition" 14). The critic's task is not only to interpret and evaluate literature but also to comprehend it, to grasp it in its systematic and historical order. The critic should recognize when significant new works modify that order and give it new scope and direction. In this sense not only does tradition shape the present, the present alters tradition and thereby the meaning of the past. The transhistorical and the historical affect one another reciprocally.

The good critic seeks to recognize in works from other eras or cultures points of broad human interest but will also ask in what ways works of the past address the most pressing contemporary interests and concerns—whether via parallel or contrast. One wants simultaneously to transmit the value of great works from a variety of traditions and be engaged in contemporary societal concerns. Clearly, one of the most pressing concerns of the current era is the influence of technology on our environment, psychology, and social intercourse. Critics have been quick to address those concerns that apply to them in their specificity within their own culture, ethnicity studies, gender studies, and gay and lesbian studies, for example, but they have been slower to address this concern, which seemingly relates to all and thus to no one group more than to another.

Aesthetic reception has an element of particularity as well as universality. Some needs and concerns are greater in one era than another. Weimar film, for example, resonated with its age partly because it addressed chaos, false authority, instability, panic, and other concerns of the age. Its appeal today has much to do with these continuing concerns. Just as we can reflect on which literature, past or present, best speaks to our age, so too can we ask which methodologies best address our age. We may supplement our supertemporal concerns with specific questions of the day, but critics fail if they attend only to the works of one period, for knowledge of any period or author requires a level of general competence. So, for example, the specialist in the literature of German *Klassik* must know tragedy and comedy, and not just the tragedy and comedy of that era. He or she must know something about the thematic portrayal of friendship and the mediation of tradition.

Finally, the ideal critic's ability to synthesize the universal and the particular is not exhausted by attention to what is both enduring and timely. Just as the artist must attend to both the particular and the universal, so does the ideal critic address both the specificity of artworks in their many details and the broader questions implied by such works. One must mediate between the importance of details and their broader significance, avoiding thereby a criticism that is so focused as to be irrelevant and so flighty as to be inattentive to the particularities of art and of specific artworks. Overspecialization obscures reflection on universality and on the justification of one's studies. At the same time, the contemporary emphasis on theory engenders critics who say little about what is the ultimate focus of the discipline, the individual literary work in all its beauty and complexity.

I have thus far named the most essential requisites of good literary criticism: priority given to artwork aesthetics over production and reception aesthetics; mastery of the hermeneutic principles of interpretation; the development of clear and coherent principles of evaluation; and attentiveness to the transhistorical and historical moments of the artwork.

Just as the practice of literary criticism must be attentive to the specific needs of the day, so must it be mindful in its self-reflection of contemporary concerns. The final three topics to which I turn are particularly significant today. The first is theory, which has become another catalyst for our moving further and further away from artwork aesthetics, but which is ultimately valuable, when practiced sensibly, as an education to freedom, which is not to be equated with arbitrariness. However, instead of freeing us, much of contemporary theory binds us in two illicit ways: first, it makes us a slave to the methodology introduced, partly because we do not see alternative models presented, partly because we find it difficult to criticize a position that, despite all its rhetoric, eschews any identity; and second, it sometimes narrows our horizon by laying on works specific questions that yield less than the text has to offer. The second characteristic of literary criticism neglected today is simple intelligibility, which seems to have been left behind as a necessary principle of literary criticism some years back, when theory caught the imagination of many scholars. The third is existential interest, which appears to have disappeared in the wake of several different developments: scholarly historicism; the artificiality of twice removed theorizing; and movement away from the artwork, which alone can inspire us, toward the historical conditions of production and reception. In certain cases we encounter quarry workers, who produce reams of positivistic information or ideological criticism but who don't seem even to like literature. Whereas my discussion of the value of theory is elicited by its contemporary prominence and in some quarters its controversial nature, in many ways what I say here is simply an addendum to my concern with basic questions of aesthetics and hermeneutics. While my comments on intelligibility and existential interest are likewise elicited by the contemporary scene, each is not the unique concern of literary criticism but a universal prerequisite of superior scholarly inquiry in any field.

THEORY AS FREEDOM

An emphasis on theory at the expense of the study of great works of literature is one reason for the drop in student interest in literature at many universities, especially when one considers that "theory" is often not even theory about literature. Students who enter the classroom and are met with a faculty member's ideological perspective and jargon-driven works of theory rather than efforts to interpret great works of literature may turn to other disciplines. Nonetheless, theory can be a positive force, and in an age when the value of literature is no longer a given, theory is necessary. In principle reflexivity is higher than nonreflexivity, as it brings us insight into the grounds for action. Reflexivity permits us to consider the questions of why and how we undertake a particular task. In this sense theory should be a welcome dimension of every literary critic's work.[5] The best literary critics can defend their approaches within the range of options available; only in this way is the critic free. Freedom consists in knowing alternatives, weighing options, and making a rational selection among them. Not to reflect on diverse methods is to be the slave of whatever method one learned at the university, that procedure which one in a sense inherited, or to be beholden to whatever procedures gain ascendancy in the discipline. Thus, the best literary critic knows of alternatives and integrates into his or her approach whatever is of value in alternative approaches. Precisely for this reason this work attends also to some of the strengths and weaknesses of competing models of literary criticism. Insofar as literature is defined by its mediation of the intellectual and the sensuous spheres, one must seek an integrative approach, which should not be confused with an additive approach.

In a second sense as well theory educates to freedom, for good theory guides our attention to what is most important, thus freeing us from narrow or aberrant predispositions. A coherent theoretical frame frees us from asking ancillary questions that lead us away from, rather than toward, the artwork, and it guards us from being taken in by whatever approaches and alternative readings may increasingly find publication without their having satisfied principles of good literary criticism. The moment of freedom applies not only to the implementation and sifting of specific methodologies or interpretive strategies but also to the very question of why we should pursue literary criticism. Nonreflection means we have not chosen our profession freely.

As I mentioned in the introduction, a method can be defended in two ways. First, one can give a philosophical defense, arguing that competing theories suffer because of internal contradictions or inattention to the essential aspects of the object of study; one counters with arguments for the consistency of one's approach and its compatibility with first principles. Second, one can defend one's approach heuristically, offering as evidence the results of one's inquiry, persuading the reader that the questions one has chosen to ask of a literary work have made it more interesting than it had previously appeared or that these questions have opened up new dimensions of the work or even a new interpretation that calls into question previous readings. Whether one pursues the one or the other, to reflect on the value of one's approach is ideal, so that one is at home in it—not only intuitively but also consciously, as a form of knowledge and not opinion.

INTELLIGIBILITY

Great literary criticism seeks to be understood; consensus is not a condition of truth but a condition of its realization, which is the telos of truth. One of our moral tasks is to be just to the artwork, to allow its greatness to emerge in the hands of the critic who renders transparent its aesthetic moments. Another principal task is to help the reader or student find value in artworks and to grasp why and in what ways works that speak to him or her intuitively are worthy of further reflection, in short, to elucidate and illuminate the characteristics of great works. This second moment is rarely acknowledged. Most literary criticism is written not for the general cultivated public but for the few scholars who are themselves involved in intricate debates; it is not directed to a broader audience of intelligent readers. Those persons in a privileged position have a moral obligation to share their insights with others. Literature is written not for the scholar but for the general public, and so the critic should speak not only to the scholar but also to the intelligent layperson. Most literary criticism, however, does not satisfy the moral value of enhancing the reader's understanding of the work. This certainly applies to the overemphasis on literary history, which interests the scholar dramatically more than the layperson. Literary criticism is written for other literary critics. Indeed, many publications are written in such a way that the style would preclude an undergraduate in the field or a broadly interested scholar beyond the humanities from understanding the thrust of the inquiry.

The situation in Germany is slightly better than in America, though not without exceptions. The ability of the German literary critic to write for a broader audience stems partly from the cultural emphasis in the German-speaking countries on the educated layperson and the higher value given to the arts among laypersons. This audience in turn elicits from scholars a number of readable prefaces to literary works, addresses to the general public, accessible interpretations of major works, and newspaper reviews. In Germany the middle class is well educated and is naturally interested in the literature of its own language, so there is an attractive market force at play precisely within the field of literary criticism. The number of teachers at the Gymnasium who teach German literature is very high, and certain works of criticism seek this broader audience as well. In addition, German scholars have for the most part resisted the inroads of deconstruction and been skeptical of culture studies. The consequences include a majority of criticism still being written about major works of the tradition and less criticism invaded by jargon.

The success of the German literary critic is ironic, for precisely the British and the Americans have in many fields managed to develop a tradition of writing scholarly works that are both substantial and accessible. In English one often finds the best general introductions to authors, even German ones. German scholarship, on the other hand, with the exception of its successful forays into a more journalistic mode, faces several challenges. First, with some notable exceptions, it tends to be overspecialized, taking very narrow topics as the focus of its studies. Second, its scholarship tends to be laced with so many erudite notes that it often becomes less than readable. Third, in Germany the dominant paradigm is more historical than hermeneutic, which is not what the reader of a literary work necessarily desires. A fascinating publication like Hans-Jürgen Schings's work on Schiller's wrestling with the Freemasons when he wrote *Don Carlos* says, for all its historical acumen, very little about how we might in the light of this knowledge better interpret *Don Carlos*. A similar lament might be sounded about highly detailed historical studies published in recent decades, as, for example, in the *Georg Büchner Jahrbuch*. Finally, and this is related to the historicist emphasis just noted, the scholarliness and historicity of the German critic tend to work against an existential engagement with literature. One asks, How did a given age define tragedy? One doesn't ask, What is tragedy universally or why is tragedy a topic worthy of engaging us today? Ironically, the very givenness of the value of the tradition works against the critics' need to justify the existential value of their enterprise.

To return to America, the development there is ironic as well, for the tradition of broader, accessible studies for the general public has tended to give way, in the humanities and especially in literary criticism, to the idea that one writes for other critics in a language that only they can comprehend. The desire to write like more prestigious critics in a form that is accessible only to the select few and to claim the distinction of being able to understand such obtuse writing may serve the need of certain scholars and students for a sense of belonging, but it effectively reveals the irrelevance of literary criticism for the broadly educated public. That these stylistic tendencies arise within a frame that is unable to justify the value of the humanities and so only contributes to its crisis is clear to anyone looking in from the outside and seeking genuine orientation from the humanities. Instead of providing that orientation in accessible language, one simply denounces the critics of the humanities as having misinterpreted the trends or having abstracted from them singular anecdotes in the interests of a conservative cultural and political agenda. Were all of this accurate, it would remain an ad hominem argument and still not address the vacuum of orientation in the contemporary humanities.

Also contributing to the lack of intelligibility is the elevation of research at the American university. Accessible writing is a form of teaching. Inaccessible writing is valued as research. The shift in favor of research works more in the direction of the German model, where professors have not traditionally been evaluated in any serious or responsible way for their teaching, leaving this dimension of their work to the individual conscience and abilities of the instructor. This lack of attention to teaching has not been without its effect on scholarship, as the greatest teachers are often the clearest writers. The elevation of graduate education at the expense of undergraduate education at many American universities is related to this inability to reach out beyond one's subdiscipline. How many of America's literary critics are focusing their energies on students from other disciplines, the social sciences, science, and engineering, showing them the value of literature in understanding the world, in developing one's character, or in appreciating the richness and diversity of language? With the contemporary devaluation of the study of rhetoric and its ideals, communication among disciplines has become less and less frequent, not to mention communication to those outside the academy. This is unfortunate, and one cannot but ask why support for such an enterprise remains strong among those who are not addressed by such publications.

The problem of intelligibility is internal to much of contemporary theory, that is, it is not accidental, for two models of communication seem to exist. First, we may believe that a common language allows us to speak with one another across disciplines. In this case we are motivated to converse with others— both to test our ideas and to communicate the value of our insights. This option seems not to be open to certain contemporary schools of criticism, for their doctrine is that of a second model of communication: any discussion within a so-called common sphere of disinterested rationality is not possible, and any appeal to such a sphere is a shield to disguise specific political interests. From this perspective truth and lucidity are viewed as naive. The critic has the following options: first, opt not to be intelligible, so as to avoid complicity with those in power; second, write intelligibly about various issues but presuppose the second model, and so commit a pragmatic contradiction; third, espouse the first model but fall back into disciplinary discourse, which is remarkably easier to speak, and become as irrelevant as if one did not believe in intelligibility; and fourth, accept the first model and speak intelligibly to the wider audience, which offers one the responsibility of testing one's ideas against those who do not share the same presuppositions and of communicating to others the insights one has garnered.

Poor writing also has several contingent, but nonetheless common, origins. First, unintelligible writing is often the result of inadequate thinking. Unless we have thought through an issue clearly, we cannot write about it lucidly. Simply because a thought is complex, we needn't conclude that we cannot write about it clearly. Second, poor writing sometimes stems from a desire not to be understood; to write in such a way as not to be understood—either because one writes sloppily or because one writes in the language of the in-group—is to render oneself immune to criticism. This is especially unfortunate when critics

consider themselves to be engaged in important historical, political, or sociological analyses that transcend the bounds of literature. Only when one writes
clearly can one's thoughts really be analyzed and evaluated. Certainly, we can
recognize the value of esoteric writing, but this must be attractive and meaningful at some level and is ideally integrated with an exoteric meaning, as in
Plato's dialogues, so that diverse readers are addressed, if in different ways.

Third, when an evaluation of the aesthetic merits of an artwork is deemed
unworthy and elitist by literary critics, the effect on one's rhetoric is not negli-
gible, and the ironic result is that unintelligibility is the worst form of elitism,
for it is based not on a standard of excellence but on arbitrary exclusion. This
exclusion is all the more unappealing when it is tinged with high moral rhetoric
about breaking down categories between insiders and outsiders. The explanation John Ellis gives for this combination of arcane language and moral appeal
may have some merit: according to Ellis, one of the reasons for the increasing
use of impenetrable, seemingly profound, language, whether conscious or not,
is that it allows one to make strong moral judgments without sounding naive,
unsophisticated, or priggish (*Literature Lost* 10).

Fourth, a related reason for impenetrable prose is that when well-known
views are disguised in bold and unusual rhetoric, they seem new; to relinquish
this rhetoric is to forfeit the claim of originality, so one desires by all means to
hold on to the mirage of novelty, whether consciously or not, and one persists
with a vocabulary not familiar to others and which seemingly represents innovative thinking. Fifth, in analogy to the previous point and related to the first
claim above, one finds among critics the desire to embrace for oneself the claim
of deep and rigorous thought, which seems to imply unwieldy diction and inaccessible syntax. Unfortunately, this is more often the veil of vanity than of
profundity. Finally, the inflation of jargon also stems from a callous indifference to one's audience; one focuses on thinking through problems that may
have only parochial interest and does not see a moral imperative to communicate thoughts of broader interest in intelligible language.

The situation is aggravated insofar as much of what we learn we learn from
example; certainly, we think, if X and Y write unintelligibly, then I needn't aspire to the naive ideal of clarity either. Consider this sentence of the much-
admired Fredric Jameson, which is not quoted out of context, for his book *Signatures of the Visible* begins with this sentence: "The visual is *essentially* porno-
graphic, which is to say that it has its end in rapt, mindless fascination; thinking about its attributes becomes an adjunct to that, if it is unwilling to betray its

object; while the most austere films necessarily draw their energy from the attempt to repress their own excess (rather than from the more thankless effort to discipline the viewer)" (1).[6]

One of the greatest ironies in the contemporary academy is the emerging loss of intelligibility and the simultaneous call for more interdisciplinary work, which is frequently evoked by the very scholars whose writing suffers from a lack of clarity. Certainly, one presupposition of meaningful interdisciplinary work is making one's contributions intelligible to persons in other disciplines. But much of what would count as contributions to knowledge by contemporary literary and cultural critics can be deciphered only by others who share not only their discipline but also their subschool of criticism. The problem of unintelligible and nonsensical prose was dramatized in the 1990s when Alan Sokal, a physicist, published an article in *Social Text* that was deliberately written as drivel and designed as a hoax. In an era when ideology and unintelligibility often triumph over argument and clarity, the parody fitted in perfectly well with the other published articles.

Having said all of this, I do not want to deny the value of specialist contributions. New knowledge most frequently arises when researchers focus on narrower areas. In addition, we cannot deny that some contributions may be less understandable not because they contain unnecessary jargon but because they presuppose a certain intellectual expertise on the part of the reader.[7] If every study were made accessible to all, every work of literary criticism would need to introduce some of the basic information of the field, but this is neither practical nor efficient. Certain works of literary criticism will simply presuppose knowledge of certain terms, be they genre terms, e.g., sonnet, comedy of manners, or *Bildungsroman,* or rhetorical terms, such as polyptoton, anaphora, or aposiopesis, period terms, such as Biedermeier, poetic realism, or Expressionism, or theoretical terms, such as hermeneutics, artwork aesthetics, or performance studies. A language exists for each field of study, which represents less the jargon of the day than the classical presuppositions of inquiry. To build on a certain level of common knowledge permits one to advance more quickly to substantive insights.

Nonetheless, we must guard against only specialist contributions being written and against contributions being written that contain not the intellectual prerequisites of the discipline but the jargon-driven language of ephemeral literary-theoretical tendencies. Also, one must weigh very carefully what kind of specialist study is chosen. A critical edition of a major author is work for the ages, but a specialized study of a minor writer, best forgotten, is difficult to justify. Certainly when we choose to work on minor authors, we should be expected to give arguments legitimating the study. Simply to state that no one has investigated the author, without simultaneously making a strong claim as to why the author should be studied, is to fish for a topic on which one can claim originality, hardly a sufficient criterion for study, let alone for publication. When critics spend much of their time searching for marginal topics that lend themselves to an original thesis (because little attention has been given to them) or discussing other contemporary critics instead of analyzing literary works or engaging thinkers who deserve our attention, it is easy to see why these critics fail to capture the imagination of those standing on the sidelines. Debate becomes a matter of internal, indeed hermetic, dialogue.

The topic of literature in the technological age should have greater appeal than such internal discourse, a surprisingly large segment of which debates what the profession should be doing without doing what it should be doing—which is certainly not to debate endlessly within itself about itself. Indeed, courses on literature in the technological age should have the advantage of reaching out to students in other disciplines, just as artworks that treat this theme will interest more than just literary critics. Literary critics should write about the literature of technology so as to interest others as well. The questions evoked by such a field of inquiry are interdisciplinary, and where this interdisciplinary interest exists, we have a moral obligation to communicate our insights with economy and clarity. Readers want literary criticism to help them understand the latent meanings of works, but this enterprise will succeed only if we make our knowledge accessible.

EXISTENTIAL INTEREST

Two reasons exist for the study of literature: because it has intrinsic value and because literary categories are relevant for life. The scholar of literature should be able to convey both the appreciation of literature as literature and the relevance of literary works for our comprehension of the world and development of character. When one or the other or even both are lacking, the student of literature tends to lose interest, and the value of literary criticism becomes bankrupt. Indifference, not enthusiasm, is the result.

Plato identifies enthusiasm as one of the defining features of poetic inspiration (*Ion* 533ff.; *Phaedrus* 245a). It is as if one were possessed by a god, or a god were within one. Similarly, the lover of literature is enraptured—enthusiastic for the experience of beauty and its transferability to life. This concept of divine possession appears to have been lost in the scholarly development of literary criticism. Plato criticizes enthusiasm when it comes at the expense of reason, and rightly so, but the existential interest that motivates literary criticism should not disappear in the face of mere sobriety. The idea behind Plato's discussion of the poet's being enraptured is that the truth of the poet is not the poet's alone, that the gods speak through the poet. In a more secular context, we might reformulate the matter thus: we as readers are not interested in what the individual poet said for the sake of the individual poet; instead, we are interested in what the poet says that has value beyond the particularity of the poet. We are interested in the beauty of the poet's statement as such, but also in the transferability of the poet's insight and rhetoric beyond the poet's private situation. This broader dimension presupposes an existential interest in art.

There is a tendency among scholars to study literature in an antiquarian way. One explicates the works and relates them to their context, but the scholar does not learn from them. Such historical scholarship is not literary scholarship in the highest mode. Another practice that only hastens the demise of literary studies is the effort to demonstrate a theory, already conceived, in the work. The critic does not discover new dimensions of the theory through reading; he or she merely proves what is already presupposed. In this way there is little love of literature, little reason even to discuss the work. True scholars of literature let the literary work perplex them; they think through its various facets and ask what the work tells them about life. This elevation of perplexity and thought, of imagination and meaning, of excitement and wonder, distinguishes such a scholar from the antiquarian historian or the dogmatic ideologue.

The great literary critic is not to be reduced to the specialist who knows how to debate the minutiae of an age or the methodologist who knows how to make every text conform to a given doctrine; such critics experience moments of awe at the beauty of literature and let the spirit of the text work on them. Their minds take risks with a text, for the critics let it influence them, indeed encourage it to work on them, for they are not yet fully formed and seek to develop their minds through this engagement. Their primary concern is not the display of the specialist's knowledge, the vanity of being recognized as encyclopedic in the field, or the gross manipulation of literature for a particular agenda, however just that agenda might be; it is, instead, the astonishment, wonder, and impact of new and meaningful insight, the kind of relationship to a work of art evoked in Rainer Maria Rilke's "Archaic Torso of Apollo": "For every part of this commanding form / holds you in its gaze. Henceforth, your life must change" (91). The great literary critic seeks an aesthetic experience, a dialogue with a grand work, a meaningful encounter. Such critics see their enterprise as a way of life, not as a way of making a living. They are excited by the varieties of literary works and enriched by the breadth of perspective the works grant them. Literary criticism is no longer a value-free discipline if the works we study have more than merely historical interest, if the poems of Hölderlin or of Heine speak to us directly and not only as historical-cultural artifacts. When transferred to the classroom, this existential moment means that as much as the teacher may prepare for eventual discussion, the teacher must be absolutely present in the classroom to engage the interpretations and arguments as they emerge from students. Such teachers act maieutically toward both the text and other interpreters, frequently discovering new insights and complexities themselves in the process of an intense engagement with the artwork.

Among our literary critics are those who pursue their enterprise without courage, first asking what other interpreters will say about a particular method, interpretation, or claim, and then plying their trade with neither enthusiasm nor conviction. To see students excited about literature enter graduate school and within several years grow to hate the enterprise to which they have committed themselves is devastating. How can they not develop in this way if their teachers and potential mentors are themselves uncommitted to the study of literature as literature? Much of what goes on in the classroom is an exercise. We do not take the past seriously for the present. We collect data and relate them to other data, exhibiting our knowledge of the material, or we measure the past against today's ideological standards. But if we learn only about the past and not also from the past, if we avoid a genuine dialogue that seeks the meaning and value of other models, why do we bother to teach and study the past? What is the inner imperative to do so? Pedantry will not suffice to excite students or justify the field to its critics. Heidegger argues, rightly, that this antiquarian view of the past is a symptom of the technological age—a view we shall consider anon. The resulting loss of models among teachers of literature is a great disservice to our youth. Some critics may fear that scholarly precision will somehow be compromised if evaluations are made or an existential moment of interest is unveiled. However, precisely these are needed; without them we have simply scholarship for the sake of scholarship.

The problem deepens in an age of overproduction: because the critic must find something original to say and because major authors have already been richly explored, the critic searches for a new topic, a minor author, a second-tier contemporary writer, a subject beyond the literary sphere, and so chooses the theme not because it grips the soul but because room exists for something new to say. When this is then foisted on students in the classroom, such that they are not introduced to the greater works of a tradition, serious questions of responsibility come into play. Whereas a scholar can ignore a weak dissertation or essay, students cannot escape the works chosen for their seminars.

The literary scholar whose endeavor does not involve a struggle with meaning for life duplicates and perpetuates the logic of *l'art pour l'art,* no less than the reader of literature who voices the sounds but is indifferent to the content. Neither sees that the transformation of the beautiful from that which is whole to that which is partial is indeed a reduction. We would do well to return to the classical wisdom of Horace, that art should both delight and educate, as he elucidates it in the most famous passage of *On the Art of Poetry.* In contemporary literary criticism often neither is at play—neither the joyous reception of beautiful form, its pleasure and delight, nor the idea that what we are reading may change our lives, that we may profit through our encounters by discovering instructive and useful precepts for life.

What I am calling the existential moment is not unrelated to a full understanding of hermeneutics, such that here, too, there is an organic connection between the elements of ideal criticism. An important dimension of hermeneutics beyond the concepts of understanding (*subtilitas intelligendi*) and interpretation (*subtilitas explicandi*) has been the concept of application (*subtilitas applicandi*). Application remains prominent in two other domains where hermeneutics is central: in jurisprudence the meaning of the law is not a dry lesson in interpretation but has consequences for individual cases; in theology the scriptures are not to be explicated simply as historical documents but are to be read for spiritual edification, with an eye to their relevance for life, made apparent in the explication of the homily. Historicism and value-free science have led in philology and now in literary criticism to the neglect of this important hermeneutic principle. The question of what literature tells us about life has disappeared from the forefront of our concerns; in some cases it has receded entirely.

Without this integrative moment, literary criticism cannot overcome a kind of inner emptiness: not to bridge the subject at hand with the existential questions of the day is to open the door to cynicism and disregard for the value of the discipline. However refined the intellectual gymnastics of our interpretive efforts might be, they are complete only when a bridge is drawn to the existential sphere. For the cases when this bridge is drawn, one often turns to interdisciplinary scholars outside literature who, uninhibited by specialization and professionalization, have sought out artworks for their ability to address broader issues in other fields, as, for example, with Coles's teaching of literature to students of business, law, and medicine or Nussbaum's work on literary study and legal education.[8]

My greatest concern about the lack of existential interest in literature is for the students: first, undergraduates who may not grasp, without a good model, why literature is as worthy of study as history or psychology or economics or who, after a course or two, may never again be motivated to turn to great literature for pleasure and edification; second, graduate students who have already made a decision to invest in the enterprise and who are therefore reluctant to leave the discipline even when their vision of the study of literature, which is usually existentially motivated, becomes dismantled as they recognize what is being done with literature in the classroom. As we have seen, the catalysts for this can be many: a focus on mere form at the expense of meaning, a focus on ideology at the expense of literariness, or the concept of a value-free humanities. The love of literature disappears as well when the dominant interpretive strategy in the classroom becomes the relativization of all positions, the all-consuming urge to find irony upon irony and prove that the work recognizes no position as worthy of being embraced. Here, too, the existential component is left empty. Unfortunately, in this last model, the interest can be intellectual to a level that appears engaged, such that one is excited about literature, but the excitement does not transfer to life. Excitement is not yet inspiration.

The existential moment has a special urgency in the study of literature. Literature as an aesthetic object should arouse in the reader a moment of pleasure, but when this moment of pleasure, enthusiasm, excitement, elation, or ecstasy, as Longinus named it, is either smothered by the bulk of scholarly weight or cut off by the ideological ax, the essence of literature disappears, and with it the student's intuitive love for the subject. A good question to ask scholars and teachers of literature is which literary works grabbed them; with which works they had a moving reading experience; or which works changed their perception of the world. If the question draws a blank, one can be suspicious of the critic's existential immersion in the field. A value-free science of literary analysis is no less in balance than is an overvaluation of feeling or absorption. An elevation of the existential should not result in downplaying the rigors of literary insight. The two are not at odds with one another but are mutually reinforcing

All cultures have some form of art, but not all cultures have literary criticism, and in some cultures the literary critic is the artist himself, thus an especially creative person. In European letters we recognize the connection between writer and critic in such figures as Samuel Johnson, Gotthold Ephraim Lessing,

Schiller, Coleridge, Forster, Eliot, or Italo Calvino. Today's literary critics can enhance and enrich our understanding of literature. Even as something is always lost in interpretation, so can something be gained, an attentiveness to diverse structures, images, arguments, and interpretive possibilities. So too does one benefit by way of the moment of evaluation. Through art and literary criticism people learn satisfaction in the enterprise of reading—and not only in activities that overstress the environment or may lack the means to convey transcendence, such as consumption or tourism. One of Benn's greatest poems, "Travel," reminds us of the Stoic wisdom that travel is often an escape from the self, whereas poetry may be a higher path to self-awareness. As I suggest below, one of the issues of the age is how best to configure our free time. The study of literature is not only of intrinsic value but also far more enriching and less demanding on the earth's resources than much of what today constitutes the leisure and tourist industries. A different question is whether the activities of today's literary critics are as meaningful and significant as they might be in a more ideal world.

Chapter 4 Contemporary Models

What aesthetic and hermeneutic principles guide literary criticism to-day? In answering this question, I begin with those characteristics of literary works privileged by contemporary critics and then move on to the dominant principles of exegesis. I provide a cursory evaluation of the two reigning methodologies of the era—the historical and the formalist—and, in slightly more detail, the two more recent schools they have engendered—culture studies and deconstruction. After recognizing the moments of truth in these methodologies, I discuss their weaknesses, including their internal contradictions and their neglect of the aesthetic dimension and unique value of literature. The ethical and political impetus given to much contemporary literary and cultural criticism is worthy; literary criticism should not be pursued in isolation from a broader sphere. However, many of the ethical and political claims that inform contemporary literary and culture studies are undermined by more overarching epistemic considerations, which call into question the idea of normative truth and so undermine the grounding of their own claims.

PRINCIPLES OF AESTHETIC EVALUATION

The question of the standards of good art is rarely addressed today, which is unfortunate, as this neglect does little to support the value of literary criticism. In this relative vacuum of theoretical reflection, we must ask what critics and the general public indirectly value as great art. *Origin* is one principle of aesthetic evaluation. Art viewed in terms of its production context (the author's gender, race, or class, for example) is often deemed valuable simply because of its origins. Elevating origin does indeed have advantages. First, a focus on genesis may uncover works that had been unjustly ignored. Second, even as we recognize that the worth of an idea is determined by its validity, not its genesis, different life experiences may offer lenses for new and interesting ideas; such diversity is welcome. Third, to give female and minority readers, especially aspiring authors, models with whom they may more easily identify is desirable. Nonetheless, to privilege yesterday's underprivileged group—without raising the aesthetic question, by which I mean the value of the work's content and form and the interrelation of the two—is to fall prey to a fallacious standard, and it is counterproductive in terms of enhancing desirable diversity or offering meaningful models.

In an age that elevates subjectivity, *innovation* is sometimes prized as the highest principle of art. The consciousness of belonging to, and contributing to, a tradition appears to have less value than creating something novel. The invention of new forms is said to distinguish good from clichéd art. This elevation of originality and innovation is itself relatively novel, deriving from the post-Christian dissolution of the ideas that art portrays a divine ideal and the artist is the medium through which this ideal becomes visible (Hauser 349). This transition makes possible the idea of intellectual property and is not unrelated to one of the defining features of the technological age, the *verum factum* principle, which I discuss below. Meaningful innovation is indeed desirable and often aesthetically pleasing. Harold Bloom justly elevates this category in his discussion of the canon: "Originality, in the sense of strangeness, is the quality that, more than any other, makes a work canonical" (313).

Certainly, we do not want to read what is merely a derivative repetition of an already greater work—but innovation alone does not guarantee quality. Innovation must be combined with other features of artistic excellence, such as meaning, subtlety, and the justification of parts. When innovation is isolated, a fundamental question is not raised. Does the work say something valuable that could not be said better in more traditional ways? Indeed, in many cases formal innovation arises precisely when artists have little to say. In film, we recognize more rapid cutting and the elevation of suspense and special effects, which often dazzle viewers at the expense of meaningful content. The elevation of form over content is also illustrated by television advertising, which presents us with the most skilled cinema and special effects in the world, and yet at the service of—advertising. The advertising industry, whose ads become sensuously ever more clever, challenges art, especially film, to develop a similar capacity if it is to compete; one danger in this is that the focus on form arises at the cost of content, such that one's experience of a film may function like a two-hour advertisement for the film itself, and no substantial content or meaning emerges. Innovation should be recognized as valuable, perhaps even a necessary, but certainly not a sufficient, condition of great art. Moreover, meaningful innovation can involve as much appropriation and modulation as pure invention. Bach comes immediately to mind.

A category related in a sense to innovation is *eccentricity*. The artwork is deemed great that is beyond its time or stands out against all other works of the same genre. The idiosyncratic and the breaking of taboos become ends in themselves, as often arises in contemporary performance art.[1] Although uniqueness captures one element of great art, mere eccentricity misses the mark. Eccentricity, like the incomprehensible, resists categories of description. But eccentricity is insufficient as the dominant category of evaluation, for what is eccentric may be worthless, meaningless, of no value. Indeed, even as the Dadaists embody a moment of great art, they capture only a moment: the whimsical, the odd, the tasteless do not by definition qualify as art. Art must be infused with a moment of not only particularity but also universality.

Because technology is efficient, much of modern art in response stresses arbitrariness as a form of resistance. Insofar as technical reason cannot be abandoned, art in its arbitrariness appears to be only compensatory. A good technology eliminates chance and contingent factors.[2] Economy of parts and the interconnection of parts are virtues in both spheres. Precisely such parallels between the efficiency of technology and the artwork have given rise to the elevation of the contingent in art, on the part of creators and critics. But to elevate the contingent in order to separate art from technology is to mistake a partial equation for the whole and to fail to recognize that traditional, organic art already differs from technology: the organic has an internal teleology and so evokes the values of autonomy and inner harmony, whereas the mechanical, as we find it in technology, serves external purposes. The arbitrary negates the mechanical, but does so in a philosophically and formally inferior way, creating the sense among the public that art cannot respond meaningfully to the technological age. Precisely, however, and paradoxically, in the autonomy of the organic lies a counterstructure to the age.

Another category of evaluation is *critique*. Much of contemporary criticism views itself as practicing ideology critique, especially since literary criticism, like the humanities generally, likes to associate itself with an ideal of critique, and not unjustly, as the critique of false positions has been one of the strengths of modern arts and letters. Critique motivates not only the interpretations but also in many cases the performances of the classics, resulting in those contemporary productions of classical authors whose primary purpose is to exhibit their distance from present values and beliefs. Within literary criticism the question is often raised whether or not an earlier author had the correct position with regard to gender, class, and race. We should indeed evaluate positions, uncover the biases of an age or a group, but that can hardly be our defining interest as literary critics. Moreover, ideological criticism, which rarely attends to formal elements, is often surprisingly thetic. One assumes as a given the particular ideological measure and thereby risks simply perpetuating established patterns of evaluation. The criteria of measure are dogmatically asserted, not grounded. To ground them would be to fall prey, it is asserted, to foundationalism; criticizing other persons' dogmas, not grounding one's own views, is the raison d'être of this approach, but the consequence is a lack of clarity about the grounds of critique. If there is no foundation, by what measure is the critique valid? The cost of this unresolved contradiction is clear: either dogmatism or immunity to critique or both, an ironic consequence for a theory whose very catchword is critique.

Similar to critique in its negativity is *irony*. Irony can be of at least two kinds. First is the just irony that unravels the untenability of a given position, though the irony is not all-pervasive. Some positions remain intact, if only those that represent the ideal that the ironized position fails to meet. Second is the increasingly common irony that undermines and debases also just positions and so borders on cynicism. The strategy may be evident in the work itself, or it may stem from the critic. We also recognize irony in performances, as in the attempt to make Lessing's or Schiller's characters look foolish or flat. If other ages produced greatness, I look weak in comparison, but if I can show that another age was as mediocre as my own, then my sense of self-worth grows. Indeed, I am superior to those ages, because they thought they were pursuing ideals, whereas I see right through them.

Whereas the previous categories have more to do with production and artwork aesthetics, some critics focus on aspects of reception, for example, *relevance*. Attention to the ways in which art relates to pressing issues of the day is an advantage, and a focus on new insights, aspects of art previously not considered, is important, but these should not overwhelm all others. We cannot call art good or bad based on whether or not it addresses the issues of the day or meets the ideological expectations of a particular group, as, for example, with politicized victim art, which appeals to some persons based solely on its message, not its aesthetic merits. Contemporary approaches that elevate a particular theme or problem may betray a lack of commitment to literature as literature and to literature that is more than merely ephemeral. When we ignore literature as literature, we have difficulties defending the value of literary studies. The issue of relevance sometimes motivates performances of great works; here the shortsightedness of the relevance ideal is particularly visible. One makes a great author relevant not simply by relocating the action to contemporary settings but by showing to what extent the issues integral to an author's dramas, when shown in their integrity, still mark our age.

Another category elevated by contemporary critics is *incomprehensibility*. Justly embracing the complexity and inexhaustibility that characterize many works of great literature, critics isolate and elevate this one moment. The attraction to incomprehensibility is reinforced by aspects of the technological age. The critic seeks a mode that exhibits the chaos and impenetrability of the modern world. Incomprehensibility is seen as a countermoment to the overriding stress in modernity on utility and teleology, including the deceptive use of strategy to manipulate others. In art at least there are no answers, no false directions. Although great art does have a moment of inexhaustibility, art must also be to a degree accessible if it is to have any effect on its audience. Moreover, if incomprehensibility were the most defining characteristic of great literature, we could not distinguish great literature from nonsense.

Less frequently valued among critics but not infrequently elevated among the public is *amusement*. Here, as elsewhere, a valid moment is discovered. Art should not be wearisome; it should give pleasure. But to elevate amusement over substance is folly, especially as amusement by itself becomes boring over time, thereby paradoxically reducing amusement. Great literature is often as demanding as it is superficially pleasurable; its reward requires great effort on the part of the reader. Several factors influence the elevation of amusement. First is the disenchantment common to the age and the understandable but fruitless longing to satisfy disenchantment with amusement. Second is the extraordinary power over our consciousness of television, which, with the obvious exception of documentaries, makes few demands on our minds and influences the way we receive other cultural products. When literature remains preoccupied with insignificant and instantaneous matters, it does not differ from everyday culture, which inundates us with stories of celebrities, sexual intrigue, and trivialities. In this sense Tolstoy draws our attention to a line of argument which says that literature should lead us to a higher reality. Artworks that awaken in us a greater, poetic sense of the world and of nature give us a broader and more meaningful appreciation of that world.

I turn now to several specific movements that have a hold on the academy: two older movements, sociohistoricism, which has remained dominant in its various guises, and formalism, which has yielded much ground in the last decades, and two newer movements, culture studies and deconstruction. In the United States culture studies is highly influential (Marc Weiner states that it is "the predominant paradigm in German Studies" [v]).[3] When taken in its widest sense to include *Trivialliteratur* and the study of television and popular culture, it may have the second strongest hold internationally, after the more traditional sociohistorical paradigm, from which it developed. Deconstruction has never really taken hold in Germany, except in isolated cases, but it remains one of the strongest movements in the United States, with extraordinary prestige and institutional power, if a bit less than it had from the mid-1970s to the mid-1990s. Its nonreception in Germany has the positive dimension that Germany has been spared a good deal of bad theorizing but the unfortunate result that German critics have been very much on the sidelines for the most controversial debates in recent literary theory.[4]

Some methodologies, for example, thematic studies, can be employed under the rubric of one overarching method or another, and they are successful or not to the extent that they integrate the strengths and avoid the weaknesses of the various methods they employ. The reader will recognize that aspects of feminism as well as reception aesthetics will be dealt with only under broader rubrics. These schools have diverse manifestations, but dealing with the conceptual types of criticism in principle has certain advantages over explaining, more empirically, the multiple manifestations of one subschool and another. This broader frame not only allows common principles to emerge, it also unburdens the reader from suffering undue repetition when the merits or weaknesses of one submovement or another overlap, and it is especially appropriate for an overview that encompasses only a limited number of pages. Many critics are eclectic and will justly draw on the strengths of the various methods.

A dominant characteristic of contemporary literary criticism is the emphasis on difference, multiplicity, and plurality, categories that Hegel sees as indicative of an antithetical era. Paradoxically, precisely because the elevation of difference is common, pointing out overarching similarities is valuable. Nonetheless, in response to such a broad overview, this or that critic may justly argue that I have not captured the critic in his or her difference when I criticize certain general characteristics. To the extent that this is true, it speaks for those critics who are able to dodge some of the criticisms I make, and I do not mean to suggest that each critic embodies the strengths and weaknesses of a given paradigm in equal measure. Even some critics who may suffer problems in one study may shine in others. I have tried to emphasize also the virtues of these movements and have attended to them with the thought in mind that a hidden logic lies in the development of literary criticism and that these movements have moments of truth that must be recognized as integral to an ideal literary criticism.[5]

THE SOCIOHISTORIC PARADIGM

The focus on historical context—a dominant feature of literary criticism since the 1960s and indeed the modus operandi that would seem to define the majority of literary critics both in Germany and America today—has at least four advantages. First, it has enlightened us with regard to the extent to which a work must be understood also within its time frame. Much of an artwork is context-bound, and we must understand this context in order to grasp a work's meaning. A knowledge of historical context can help us interpret literary works, comprehend the complex issues and questions they seek to address, and grasp the ways in which literature participates in the wider debates of an age. Precisely this difference is an advance over an interpretive strategy that fails to recognize the past in its specificity and uniqueness.

Second, by linking literature with broader sociohistorical and intellectual-historical developments, the sociohistoric paradigm has increased the use-value of literature for students in the humanities and social sciences. By studying the great literature or films of the Weimar era, for example, the student or scholar of history gathers insight into a variety of topics, ranging from crises of authority to the search for collective identity. As a result literature gains in interdisciplinary value. Related to this, the sociohistorical method works against over-specialization and narrowness. Studies that link literary history with the history of related spheres, both thematically and institutionally, such as education, religion, technology, and publishing, are greatly enriching beyond disciplinary boundaries. Classes that reach beyond literature also appeal to students, especially undergraduates, who in their own liberal-arts curriculum have little interest in disciplinary overspecialization.

Third, the sociohistorical paradigm has led to the discovery of previously neglected works and a greater understanding of the production and reception contexts of literature. We better understand how different contexts of production have led to different kinds of works and to what extent works are received differently under changing historical circumstances. Within reception theory, as articulated, for example, by Wolfgang Iser, we recognize the ways in which literature can transform our previous expectations and categories. In a sense this suggestion allows us to grasp in fuller ways the formative and existential role of literature. We not only read literature in various ways at different times; literature of other times and places also allows us to see differently. The expanse of interest in neglected authors has led to a fuller appreciation of those authors who engaged the political questions of their day.

Fourth, attention to the historicity of individual works helps us recognize the historically conditioned weaknesses of a given work, the ways in which even a great work carries in it traces of the biases and limitations of its age. Particularly in Germany this represents an advance over a tradition of criticism that had been inclined to elevate canonical works as authoritative and ignore their flaws.

Nonetheless, the sociohistorical emphasis has led to an increasing neglect of the specifically aesthetic dimensions of literature. One of the purposes of literary criticism is to discover what is of permanent and what is of transitory value. Another purpose is to deepen our appreciation of great literature, by which I mean our knowledge of works of lasting value in terms of breadth and depth, but both aspects are neglected when works are chosen for extrinsic reasons and when they are analyzed only by way of extrinsic methods or from a historicist mentality that judges a work solely by the terms of its age and seeks to learn only about—and not also from—the past. From the sociohistoric perspective, the predominant questions become how and why literary works developed as they did. In many cases one overlooks the questions of whether the works are worthy of being read or how they are best to be interpreted. Even literary histories written from the sociohistorical perspective sometimes fail as histories of *literature*. Ideological criticism, which is a form of sociohistorical criticism, seeks to uncover the controlling interests behind the apparent meanings of literary works and has, therefore, little interest in literature as literature. Few works of literary criticism—especially among sociologists of literature and ideology critics—attend to aesthetic questions. The texts are studied not as midwives for great insights or as exemplars of creative form; instead, the critic informs the reader of the work's origins and relates these to our current understanding of the age. One seeks to uncover not the power of the work as literature but the ideologies and forces that produced it. As with the reductive uses of psychological criticism, this model is often used to illustrate insights the critic had before even reading the work.

On a metalevel, the newer sociohistorical study of literature has sought to ground its methodology with the argument that in literary history one interpretive strategy has supplanted another, and so no interpretive strategy is superior to another. We must simply rearticulate the positions of the day and understand them as the wake of historical forces. There are several problems with this claim. First, it assumes that if we abandon a theory, rendering it merely historical, then this transcendence is one and the same with logical insight into its lack of validity, though this is not necessarily the case. Second, insofar as the historicist view assumes that each more recent theory refutes the theory it supplants, it presupposes progress, even as its metatheory, historicism, denies progress. Historicism must itself be viewed as a theory with historical origins that has been both supplanted and refuted in the history of criticism. Insufficient reflection has been devoted to the historicity of the very idea of historicity; the historicist idea has surfaced before and has been refuted before. Finally, by considering all positions equally true and equally false, the historicist view fails to take any position seriously.

A contemporary version of the historicist position is offered by Fish, who argues that we indeed have no access to a correct methodology, only to the methodology that we happen to use in a given setting and that is endorsed by our interpretive community. The mark of a good theory is not that it be well grounded but that it be the theory that the majority practices at the moment; not that it give us an accurate reading of a work but instead that it be persuasive and in some sense interesting. Thus, no imperative exists to seek the best theory or to be in any way true to the work. The technology Fish recommends has much in common with a subjectivity that transforms, rather than seeks to understand, the other. Ironically, the critic's subjective impulse is more violent, more expressive of will to power than the paradigm that tries to understand the other as it truly is. This irony is amusing, as the turn away from objectivity in contemporary literary studies appeared originally to have been motivated by the desire to find a sphere free of what the scientific paradigm seemed to offer, with what has been called its "technocratic violence" and "will to mastery" (Hartmann 246).

The historical approach dominant in Germany is, with some exceptions, less ideologically motivated than that in America. Driving it is the penchant for scholarly exactitude. It is not uncommon to read a longer study that gives us reams of data, many parts of which are collected from almost inaccessible sources, but that lack an essential ingredient of literary criticism: a sifting of the data in such a way that their various moments become relevant for a new reading. Such work remains valuable and useful, but when it is presented as the best that literary criticism has to offer or dominates the field, something is amiss.

The final problem with the traditional sociohistorical model is its inability to address certain aspects of literature that have either universal or contemporary importance. In particular I have in mind the preoccupation with national traditions and the neglect of ecological concerns. The importance for literature of both universality and diversity might lead one to question focusing on literature from a primarily national perspective, but the national perspective seems as entrenched as ever. When literature is viewed primarily from a historical angle and for extrinsic reasons, the cultural backdrop becomes foremost. All knowledge becomes local, and so critics want to study only those works whose period and culture they know well. Instead of looking at universal themes or genres, one focuses on the literature of a particular culture, often one's own. This is hardly the best strategy for bringing out the combination of universality and diversity in literature. When it comes to mediating between these two dimensions, whether the focus is philosophical or formal, comparative-literature scholars often do higher-level work than scholars of national literature.

It is ironic, but true, that the sociohistoric paradigm seems in many ways no more attentive to technology and ecology than formalist models, where, because of the lesser interest in content and history, one might expect such neglect. To the extent that scholars emphasize the distinguishing characteristics of capitalist societies, technological and environmental concerns will be neglected. In addition, traditional sociohistorical models flourish as accounts of the past, and technology is very much an issue of the present, such that it is more likely to be grasped by culture-studies scholars who are happy to address contemporary concerns. Precisely this group, however, tends to be driven by issues of particularity, with which the critic can identify as an individual. Technology and ecology, and the related question of intergenerational justice, which is more abstract and therefore not easily recognized as paramount by critics focusing on the personal and the particular, are for the most part not at the center of these scholars' pursuits, however much their focus might be nonformal. The different political landscape in Germany would seem to speak for an easier adoption of an ecological model, but working against such a development is the more traditional orientation of disciplines in Germany, their less frequent appropriation of new impulses.[6] Despite this resistance, the interest in oppression characteristic of many sociohistorically minded critics could in principle be extended to nature. As Lawrence Buell notes, nature is doubly oppressed: instrumentalized in the light of ephemeral human interests and employed symbolically to reinforce the subservience of other oppressed groups, women, nonwhites, and children (*Environmental Imagination* 21). This historical and symbolic connection between oppressed humans and images of nature invites greater attention.

FORMALISM

Formalism has several advantages. First, having reacted against a focus on the biography and psychology of the artist, it attends very closely to the artwork. In addition, it countered a subjective reception of literature, dominated by impressions and the emotive effects of art, with a scientific effort at objectivity, reinforced by a description of literary techniques and close and detailed textual analysis. At the same time, formalism emerged as a reaction to the dry accumulation of facts prominent in the positivistic and philological models it likewise usurped. In a sense formalism sought to integrate the existential concerns of subjective criticism with the scientific focus of the positivistic and philological models, but it turned away from both by rejecting the focus on production and reception contexts at the expense of the artwork. Not surprisingly, we owe to the formalist movement articulations of both the intentionalist fallacy and the affective fallacy (Wimsatt 1–39). In turning its attention to the language, structures, and forces at play in an artwork, formalism advanced the practice of close reading, *explication de texte*. For such critics, the work, once created, has an independent existence. One of the great insights of American New Criticism is "the heresy of paraphrase" (Brooks 192–214) or the argument that any paraphrase of an artwork's content fails to do full justice to the complexity of the poetic work—thus the need for a full explication of diction and rhetoric, of internal tensions and complexities. To put it in the terms of the organic, form and content are so intertwined that any change in one would mean a change in the other, and so the critic must attend to every dimension of each.

Second, because formalists are interested less in the ways in which artworks of various periods differ and more in what they have in common as artworks, the question of an individual work's universal and not merely historical appeal is prominent. As a result, the evaluative question appears more frequently in formalist than in sociohistorical studies, even if, in some cases, the evaluative moment is focused more on form than on meaning.

Third, formalism has cultivated a technical vocabulary that has given us a richer array of categories with which to understand the formal devices of literature. We recognize this advance in Russian Formalism and in the Prague School, which sought to attend to the material qualities of language and elevated as poetic a focus on the patterns of language, their sound, rhythm, and connotations. A strength of these schools is their attention to the literariness of literature, what distinguishes literature from other forms of discourse (e.g., Mukarosvský). The scientific attention to form can provide a frame—as in Roman Jakobson's analyses of the axes of selection and combination—for asking more precise questions of poetic works. Another interesting focus of formalist studies is the logic of genre, which suggests that genres develop as a result of not only extrinsic factors but also the internal dynamics of literary forms. The formalist attention to literature has been especially evident in recent decades in narratological studies by such critics as Franz Stanzel, Gérard Genette, Seymour Chatman, Dorrit Cohn, and Shlomith Rimmon-Kenan. Precise knowledge of narratological techniques is often indispensable for questions of interpretation and meaning, an insight that is not always recognized by critics who view literature primarily from an ideological perspective, but one that is effectively stressed in Cohn's *The Distinction of Fiction.*

Fourth, the attention to form can become a means of addressing content. A characteristic of literature elevated in Russian Formalism and the Prague School is *ostranenie,* or "defamiliarization," the idea that art allows us to perceive in ways that are not familiar to us. Defamiliarization allows us to recognize objects in different and unexpected ways, an important dimension in which form and content overlap. The technique emphasizes the ways in which art undermines our normal expectations and draws our attention to the material of language itself. More broadly speaking, form as expressive of content is prominent in genres like tragedy and comedy, and reflection on the evolution of genres can well be combined with sociohistorical reflections.

In many formalist works, however, a one-sidedness emerges when primarily form, and not equally content, is considered. This is a higher-level criticism than the more frequent sociohistorical criticism of formalism, for whereas sociohistorical critics argue from extrinsic considerations, which they cannot justly elevate over the form of the work, this argument recognizes with formalism the priority of the artwork but argues that the ontology of the work is such that form alone does not exhaust its essence. Inattention to content is inattention to an aspect of its essence and therefore unjustly one-sided. In at least two ways the question of meaning may be left behind: one may elevate form over content in such a way that only form is considered; or one may fail to recognize the way in which form is expressive of content, and vice versa. While both are disadvantageous, the first is worse, for when the teacher focuses only on form, the student is left with a sense of art as mere mechanism, play, and structure. Not to appreciate art in its fullness, the integration of form and content, is one thing; to leave content completely aside is another. Great art always has an intellectual or spiritual component. Different as their styles and ideas are, this dimension is common to authors as diverse as Dante, Shakespeare, Molière, and Goethe.

Two specific dimensions of New Criticism, which have become more pronounced in deconstruction, also evidence insufficient attention to content: the tendency to view all aesthetic meaning as indeterminate (thus the elevation of ambiguity, irony, and paradox, which can indeed be privileged categories, but which are not exhaustive of all literature and can still be related, even in terms of their indeterminacy, to the complexities of the world) and the tendency to view literature as self-contained and self-referential (with a corresponding hesitancy to draw connections to reality). Not surprisingly, we recognize a frequent interest in imagery, language, symbols, and patterns over the more mimetic dimensions of character and action, which also belong to the wholeness of the artwork.

A different intrinsic weakness arises in those formalist studies that, in order to become scientific and precise, seek out discrete parts of a work and engage them on the microlevel, looking at the work linguistically, rhetorically, and stylistically and analyzing its components in finite detail. While the focus on discrete parts can be extraordinarily helpful, it becomes misleading and unprofitable when the critic fails to address the whole of the work, for a basic principle of aesthetics is that the parts receive their full meaning only in the whole. When this overarching dimension is neglected, the work is not captured in its aesthetic meaning; indeed, even the meaning of the parts, which derive from the whole, is shortchanged. A great work is not a mechanical unity, where if one grasps the parts separately, the whole is understood, but an organic unity, in which the parts are transformed in the whole. The best formal critics—Leo Spitzer, to give a prominent example—combine formalism with broader reflections. Not surprisingly, such critics often work in a hermeneutic tradition that seeks to integrate the parts of an artwork—both style and meaning—into a meaningful whole (Spitzer 1–29).

Two other factors have less to do with intrinsic than extrinsic considerations, yet they remain essential for the justification of literary study. First, some formalist studies tend to read works in a historical vacuum, which does not allow us to recognize the interaction of form and historical consciousness, something that critics working in the Hegelian tradition tend to do well. Second, a purely formalist approach has great difficulties tailoring literary criticism to the needs of the age and attending to the historical questions of the day, such as those elicited by transformations in technology. Formalism can be an escape from the historicity of the moment, as was certainly, at least partly, the case with the dominance of immanent textual criticism in early postwar Germany. In conclusion, I would simply note that much of what was said above about the problems of the concept of fully autonomous art, of art for art's sake, manifests itself here as well, in the realm of reception, when formalism becomes the raison d'être of literary study.

CULTURE STUDIES

Culture studies emphasizes the production context and ideological dimensions of literary works, expands the range of subjects analyzed beyond literature, and argues against simplistic historical narratives that overlook subtle conflicts and tensions. Prominent foci in these analyses include historically marginalized groups, resulting in an emphasis on class, gender, ethnicity, sexual orientation, and the concept of the other. Stressing the sphere of production, both of the works analyzed and of our critical enterprise, culture studies tends to argue that the traditional values of literary criticism—its choice of great works and the principles that undergird these choices—are determined by the frameworks that led to the creation of these values; in short, they often replicate values we no longer endorse. The alternative is at least threefold: point out the blind spots in the so-called great works; read texts written by members of the neglected groups; and analyze the ideological connections between the works and their broader contexts.

The advantages of culture studies are multiple. First, by consciously adopting a more critical gaze, we recognize weaker aspects of works that were previously not visible to us. The interest in gender and class relations, the positions of minorities, questions of power, and ideological blind spots is a welcome corrective, first, to a formalism that fails to articulate the connections between literature and life and so capitulates before the justification of literary study and, second, to an undifferentiatedly affirmative model of literature that did not have a lens to uncover the weaknesses of works traditionally considered to be great.[7] Culture studies offers us a sobering perspective that is a needed complement to studies that see literature as building common values. We need to be critical of literary studies that obscure aesthetic weaknesses and seek instead only to elevate the literary works of a tradition or are blind to the untenable or suspect positions that may be openly or surreptitiously assumed in literary works. In this sense culture studies builds on a valid and desirable insight first developed within the sociohistorical paradigm.

Second, power relations, including issues of gender, in literary works and in the surrounding spheres of production and reception, are often fascinating as well as significant, and the claim is not ungrounded that previously not enough attention had been paid to them; this has changed with the emergence of culture studies, including New Historicism. Many intersubjective relations portrayed in literary works can be recognized as determined by arbitrary social conventions, which are neither stable nor grounded. We benefit when a critical lens is adopted toward such relations, especially insofar as gender, race, and sexual orientation have not only been neglected but also have been the locus of great injustices. Often what is taken to be supertemporally valid is simply the result of historical convention; recognizing as much is an important aspect of the reception of literary works. A focus on such issues, both within the works and within descriptions and analyses of the broader context, frees us from the positivism that held sway in many more traditional literary historical studies and enriches our understanding of both work and context. The focus on convention also provides a counterweight to any literary history that draws solely on forms and ideas and not also on broader questions of institutions and related issues arising from the study of production and reception contexts, where questions of power and other factors not directly related to the aesthetic dimension often play significant roles.

Third, we gain through these innovative studies a more broadly conceived concept of history. New Historicism seeks to replace simplified narratives with a multiplicity of often conflicting voices. The emphasis on very specific frames and contexts and the recognition that many broader and more sweeping studies have tended to overlook some of the complexities of an era or a movement, the disunity that sometimes exists within a unity, is a significant achievement. The attention to conflicting voices encourages us to question more simplistic historical accounts and leads us to recognize often overlooked details as well as links and associations across diverse spheres, among them, the social, political, economic, and more broadly cultural. Literary works are embedded in complex contexts, and history needs to be interpreted. In that spirit, Louis Montrose speaks of "the historicity of texts" and "the textuality of history" (20). Our literary histories and concepts too frequently obscure conflicting voices and multiple participants in the narratives that constitute the development of culture. To the extent that we consider the contextual origins of literature, it makes sense to look at the full panorama of history, not simply the coherent narratives we create to grasp multiple factors and not simply the elevated players on the historical stage, whose stories may be more familiar. The emphasis on surprising coincidences, on layers of overlapping meaning in the diverse spheres of a local culture, enriches our concept of a given age and a given work's context. Studying contemporaneous events and issues, including ones not normally integrated into narratives of literary history, may help us approach literary works with new and interesting questions. Indeed, in an approach related to deconstruction, some critics influenced by a culture-studies model are inclined to look for competing voices and unresolved tensions not only in the context of history but in the literary works themselves, which are viewed more as documents of the conflicting tendencies of their age and less as autonomous artworks. This tendency to seek out unresolved tensions, informed by a broader understanding of historical context, can sharpen our interpretations of literary works.

Fourth, culture studies encourages a further sifting of the documents of the past in an effort to explore whether certain works have been undeservedly neglected. Feminism began in literary studies as an effort to study more critically the portrayal of women in works written by men; it then broadened itself, without thereby relinquishing its initial interest, to include the cultivation and interpretation of works by women that had been neglected or arbitrarily ignored.[8] As such these efforts have given us a new and important critical lens in reading great works, and they have brought more outstanding works to our attention.

Related to this idea of sifting neglected works is the interest in diverse cultures, which brings us to the fifth advantage of culture studies, its multiculturalism, including its attention to the works of other cultures. If literary criticism, in Matthew Arnold's phrase, is to study "the best that is known and thought in the world" (283), then we must look not only beyond England, as Arnold already suggests, but also beyond Europe and North America. Through postcolonial studies, non-European cultures are being studied in far more dramatic ways than was ever the case in traditional departments of comparative literature. Multiculturalism is a central facet of the contemporary age. Technology has increased not only knowledge of other cultures but also mobilization, so that we encounter today, more than did most previous cultures, persons of diverse backgrounds. Everyone benefits when the strongest elements of one culture can be recognized and appropriated by another. To become familiar with diverse practices deepens our understanding of the richness of the human community, even when such customs are not integrated into our practices. A fuller sense of the other, in whatever form it may take, widens our horizon of understanding and sympathy. Literature should help us to appreciate the position and complexity of the other, to gain a greater feeling for marginalized groups and persons and neglected or oppressed others, and a virtue of culture studies is to have enhanced this dimension of literature and literary criticism.

The sixth advantage of culture studies in my eyes is that the branch of culture studies that seeks to study the present, which is indeed numerically dominant, has sought to fill a void left vacant by philosophy, which has, with few exceptions, turned increasingly away from the broader analysis of its age to merely historical studies or the abstract conceptual analysis of increasingly finite problems, whose relevance to contemporary culture makes its justification no simpler than that of literary and culture studies. Culture studies seeks to uncover its age in thought, an enterprise that Hegel once called philosophy (7.26). Not surprisingly, therefore, culture studies moves freely across disciplinary boundaries and explores a wide range of subjects. Technology and the environment, for example, are topics that are fully within its scope, even if technology has tended to be a more prominent focus than nature.[9]

The final advantage of culture studies is related to the previous point: culture studies is frequently motivated by existential and moral concerns. Feminism, to cite the most prominent example, strongly desires to draw a connection to life and morality. Culture-studies critics frequently pride themselves on their desire not only to understand the world but also to change it. In this sense, despite certain commonalities with deconstruction, their interest in the concrete aspects of finite reality, including the human body, provides a contrast to the infinite deferment of meaning characteristic of deconstruction.[10]

The first problem with culture studies, however, is that, like many examples of the sociohistorical model, it rarely gives sufficient attention to the formal aspects of literature. It tends to elevate content over form and production and reception over the artwork; its focus is ideology in the context of economic, so-

cial, political, and cultural structures. We often observe what the model of criticism seeks to find instead of the richness of diverse works that allow us to see
the world anew. Discourse analysis offers insight into the various layers of cultural and other discourses that are embedded within a given work, but it rarely
brings these layers back to the artwork and its interpretation. Also its study of
context, which is primarily synchronic and nonaesthetic, rarely integrates the
history of a genre, image, trope, or theme. Often not trained in the social sciences, such critics may not bring the full resources of the social sciences to bear
on a subject, even as they fail as literary critics because they do not attend to the
artwork. We read in the introduction to Grossberg's well-known anthology
that "although there is no prohibition against close textual readings in cultural
studies, they are also not required" (2). From such a framework, the ontological
differences between literary and nonliterary texts or the qualitative differences
among individual literary works are downplayed, if not fully ignored.

The term *culture studies* implies that literature is no longer at the center of
study; when literature is considered (as a part of culture), it is often not addressed as literature. "Studies" is very broad: it no longer implies a concern with
aesthetics, and it no longer suggests criticism as in "literary criticism," which
makes evaluative judgments of the objects under question. When the term *critical* is added, it usually implies ideology criticism and is thus not specifically
aesthetic. To analyze television ads for their strategies and broader messages is
all well and good, but one must recognize that literature has a different ontological status and therefore requires a different approach. This lack of differ-
entiation is a remarkable error in a practice that otherwise seeks to elevate the
category of difference.

The neglect of the aesthetic dimension also affects evaluation, which brings
us to a second problem. Culture studies eschews the evaluation of literary
works as literary works (even within a privileged context, for example, which
novels by workers are better than other novels by workers). The selection of
works is driven by ideology and issues of production and reception. When we
accept the principle that literature is to be analyzed primarily by way of its social function, more attention is given to weaker literature, for whether we analyze literature of greater or lesser aesthetic value makes little difference. Because
culture-studies critics do not bring a distinctively literary approach to their subjects, they may be indifferent to the question of whether their object is literature at all. Because high culture reaches only selected groups and literary study
is really the study of history and society, we must turn to the broader range of
works in popular culture, including magazines, newspapers, diaries, recipes,

advertisements, cartoons, comic books, soap operas, situation comedies, and so forth. Critics distinguish between high culture, which appeals to intellectuals, and popular culture, which addresses the masses.[11] Popular culture, like high culture, is studied not for its aesthetic dimensions but for its ideological and sociological aspects. Certainly understanding the broadest aspects of one's culture, uncovering the underlying ideological components at work in texts viewed by many persons, and relating these to the historical context are valuable. However, when these replace aesthetic analysis and when high culture is viewed through the same lens, much is lost.

I would view the matter differently. High culture is not what appeals to intellectuals. High culture is what appeals to all persons attentive to great art. Popular culture, quantitatively consisting of those works that appeal to large segments of the population, can thus participate in high culture. The two are not mutually exclusive. The first addresses quality, the second quantity. Examples of this combination of high culture and popular culture are evident in literary history. For antiquity one need only mention Homer. In the modern era Shakespeare, Manzoni, and Dickens offer paradigmatic cases. Today film may offer the most striking examples. Artists like John Ford and Alfred Hitchcock have crafted artworks of the highest caliber that appeal to large segments of the population. In this sense we may be especially attracted to study such works, both aesthetically and culturally.

The main problem is not so much the faulty distinction but the abandonment of high culture, however defined, for culture studies likewise dissolves the distinction between high and low culture, though by arguing not that some popular works are great but that all works are to be studied independently of aesthetic criteria. Interest in teaching the masterpieces diminishes, which is disadvantageous for students, as these works tend to have a broader array of interesting features than works by minor authors or works outside the literary sphere altogether. Culture studies frees the faculty member from responsibility to a tradition of great works, and it frees him or her from evaluation as well, since any number of diverse projects have their own value and needn't be related to broader questions of legitimacy. Culture-studies theorists argue that we should not impose the works of one particular group on an entire culture, but this objection is another example of the genetic fallacy and begs the question of evaluation.

A third problem with culture studies is its reduction of literature and literary criticism to critique. Culture studies often operates with a negative model of culture, seeking to uncover and expose the mistaken ideologies that drive the production and reception of cultural artifacts. Insofar as culture studies is capable of criticizing norms, but not of formulating or substantiating new ones, it is parasitic and destabilizing. Moreover, when we do not introduce a relationship to culture that is at least partially positive, we are at a loss in justifying the study of culture to students who aren't already invested in it—and so do not need to be freed from its problems. This negative approach ignores the extent to which culture is also the source of collective identity, which is not only to be despised. An important aspect of aesthetic value, here on a broader scale, is again neglected. The problem becomes especially acute when German studies becomes interchangeable with Holocaust studies. Clearly, one of the accomplishments of culture studies has been to bring this taboo topic to the fore of teaching and research, raising the consciousness of students and investigating the Holocaust in its full complexity. Yet, students who do not also gain a partially positive relationship to German culture will suffer: German students will be locked into an identity crisis, as identity always has a collective component; and foreign students will turn to other literatures and cultures, for one tends to study fields toward which one has not only a negative relationship.

Culture studies suffers a fourth problem: it embroils itself in a number of contradictions. Consider, for example, the topic of diversity. Attention to diversity is a strength, but the embrace of diversity for the sake of diversity carries with it several dangers. If diversity is our highest category, we can make no distinctions of value whatsoever, whether concerning the good, the true, or the beautiful. Indeed, the category of diversity provides no brake to the integration of a position that would do away with diversity; it is as such potentially self-canceling. Diversity must be guided by a normative measure. If embraced without such a measure, diversity leaves us open to arbitrary positions. To the extent that a methodology embraces one structure, namely, diversity, at the expense of another, namely, unity, this elevation of a single structure is everything but an instance of diversity; here, too, the position is self-contradictory. Even as the elevation of diversity or difference may lead us to recognize positions that may have been unjustly neglected, not every such position is more meaningful or preferable than positions from which it differs. In addition, diversity exists within diversity, and when works are selected not for their individual value but because of the author's belonging to a particular group, the level of diversity is diminished.[12]

Culture studies rightly stresses that moral and aesthetic views change through time, and it concludes from this development that these norms are not universally valid; but recognition and validity are not one and the same. Not all valid norms are recognized by every culture, as the history of slavery or torture, for example, makes clear. The contradiction becomes more entangled when culture-studies theorists apply moral norms to their readings despite admitting that such norms cannot be validated: this is a license for dogmatism and arrogance under the veil of relativism and modesty. One might have compassion for a critic who sees no way to ground first principles but keeps searching, knowing that the problem may lie not with the world but with himself. It is difficult, however, to have sympathy for the critic who sees no grounds but then takes this failure as the catalyst for embracing his views over others.

Culture-studies theorists stipulate that we should study and evaluate non-Western cultures on their own terms. The imperative to judge only internally has the following absurd consequence: when a culture has its own critics of a practice that we as outsiders find unjust, we, too, can criticize it; when, however, there are no such critics in that society, we are told not to criticize it—because to do so would be to impose our standards on another culture. The irony and absurdity of this frame is that a culture is morally higher, the fewer internal critics it has. Paradoxically, culture-studies theorists like to apply moral categories in analyses of their own culture and the development of their own culture. They seek to uncover the biased interests and forces that create victims through injustice or misrepresentation, but they have no conceptual frame with which to defend such an appeal to justice or truth. Indeed, the metatheory of culture studies undermines any privileged concept of justice and so serves to imply that prejudice is our only mode of relation. Having eliminated the possibility of a normative frame that is free of power interests and thereby disinterested or just, one cannot articulate what is wrong with the marginalization of the other. The idea that all positions are socially constructed, for example, is not easily compatible with the idea of human rights. The idea that all positions are informed by biased interests is not easily compatible with a critique of bias and an appeal to fairness.

Culture studies presents itself as oppositional to dominant culture, a necessary corrective to a mainstream model that affirms high culture. An irony surfaces when culture studies itself becomes dominant. In what sense, then, does it remain oppositional? The contradictions of a merely negative position become evident. In another aspect culture studies is ironically not oppositional: the preoccupation in culture studies with questions of power relations suggests paradoxically an inability to recognize that questions of value can be answered in other ways, beyond who is in power. A central aspect of the technological age is the reduction of all questions to their function within a larger system, to a complex causality of calculation and power. A preoccupation with such questions, at the expense of other aspects of life that may transcend power, such as wisdom, courage, sacrifice, friendship, and love, reveals culture studies to be consistent with, not oppositional to, the age. For such critics truth is determined by success, not coherence, and so the normative sphere gives way to the descriptive. A position can be exposed as false, however, only on the basis of a theory that transcends the question of power and addresses legitimacy.

Finally, in culture studies a tendency exists to explore the most particular, the most arcane, the most mundane topics without a corresponding sense of obligation to have these topics shed light on broader issues. Critics study the most obscure, the most personal, the most unusual. The connection between culture studies and the critique of authority is not coincidental. Culture studies likes to dismantle hierarchies, proposing thereby that all projects, all interests and needs of the critic, including the most trivial, have legitimacy.[13] While we can recognize the great variety of interests within the humanities, part of education and maturity means recognizing that some questions have more value than others. The greatest problem in this development, beyond its impact on students, who are left without orientation and often uninspired, is that the culture-studies theorist may not even recognize the problem, which is not without its inner logic: a problem arises for a consciousness only when a gap is recognized between descriptive and normative levels, and the culture-studies theorist commonly refuses to recognize a normative sphere. Without such a sphere, the theorist may not see a problem, but those funding the enterprise may well see it, and the culture-studies theorist may see it in his or her unconscious, if nowhere else.

Despite the interest among culture-studies theorists in what is popular, which one would think might lead to a certain breadth, the popular is often not related to what is synchronically or diachronically broad. The projects are new and diverse, but that alone does not suffice. New knowledge is important, but it becomes counterproductive when a measure no longer exists by which to judge its value in relation to other projects or to a whole. Specialization can lead to a loss of the concept of the whole and so to a loss of orientation, which the culture-studies theorist tends to dismiss as unproblematic because he or she believes that the only alternative to particularity is an orientation defined historically by the works of white males instead of an orientation defined systematically by the best ideas, many of which come from non-Western cultures, even if the idea of a universalist ethics emerged in European culture and must be part of this orientation.

In the university we should attempt to address ideas in a disinterested way, to weigh them independently of particular interests. The elevation of disinterested truth is one of our greatest contributions to society. When all discussions are viewed as driven by power and rhetoric alone and when the very idea of disinterested discourse is abandoned, then we are in a serious intellectual crisis, to which the dual movements of deconstruction and culture studies have contributed. That the jargon of culture studies lags only modestly behind the hyperjargon of deconstruction does not speak for culture studies, for deconstruction consistently addresses the futility of communication, whereas culture studies holds to the idea that its analyses may still influence society. Intelligibility is frequently lacking in both models. However, it is a greater irony for culture studies that many enthusiasts write for small groups of colleagues and advanced students—and do so in a form that discourages wider participation in the debate as well as any effect beyond the academy.

DECONSTRUCTION

A deconstructionist approach that focuses on unresolved contradictions has the virtue of attending to texts. Many competing models of literary criticism, including virtually all historically oriented models, are far less attentive to the works themselves. Sociohistorically oriented scholars have criticized deconstruction for not integrating history and politics, and this criticism may have a moment of truth, as all literature has a historical context, and virtually all readings can be culled for their political implications. However, when this criticism stems from a position that fails to study the literary work as a literary work because it is preoccupied with production, ideology, and reception, I should give the nod, however modestly, to deconstruction. Deconstruction recognizes that the meaning of a literary work cannot be reduced to the consciousness that created it; thus, instead of telling us more about the author's biography or era than about the work, the deconstructionist does indeed emphasize artwork aesthetics, and it is, therefore, not surprising that among the few critics addressing the value of literature, we find J. Hillis Miller, who works out of a deconstructionist framework (*On Literature*).

The second advantage of deconstruction is that it attends to the margins of texts, explicating often unrecognized aspects and tensions of much-interpreted works. This is admirable in and of itself and can also give extraordinary impulses to further criticism, forcing it to address previously neglected issues and problems. Related to the interest in margins is attentiveness to contradictions.

Awareness of the internal contradictions of a position is a necessary presupposition of immanent critique: a critique that points out internal contradictions in the position being evaluated is far stronger than a critique that derives from an external measure, which may simply differ in its presuppositions, and so represents one dry assurance against another. Moreover, attentiveness to contradictions usually uncovers aspects of a work that may be unjustly neglected by a criticism that seeks to be overaffirmative of each work's embodiment of classical wholeness and so fails to integrate elements of critique and openness. In this sense deconstruction joins culture studies in balancing an overaffirmative model of literary studies. The desire to delve into the hidden aspects of a work also raises to the fore art's esoteric dimensions. Hermeticism reminds us how difficult, but also how rewarding, it can be to uncover subtleties, complexities, and layers of deep meaning. Esoteric art that hides its most interesting aspects by giving us complex clues and riddles does not insult, it flatters, our intelligence. Experiencing and uncovering such puzzles is part of the pleasure, the fun, the playfulness of art, and deconstruction brings this dimension to the fore.

The third advantage of deconstruction is its emphasis on reflexive structures in literary works. This allows deconstruction to be especially attentive to an important philosophical characteristic of modern literature. Not surprisingly, deconstruction is adept not only at working with obviously self-reflective works but also at teasing out the implicit poetics of many seemingly less self-reflective works. Related to its efforts at dissolving boundaries, deconstruction has been proficient at uncovering not only implicit philosophical positions in literary works but also literary and rhetorical dimensions of philosophical works.

The final advantage of deconstruction is its emphasis on uncovering positions that are falsely taken to be absolute. The deconstructionist has an excellent eye for positions that have been presented as supertemporal but are really historical and contingent. In this sense deconstruction can be connected to one of the primary goals of culture studies: the unraveling of positions falsely taken to be more than mere constructions. The contemporary focus on constructedness has a certain inner logic: because gender roles were falsely seen to be only natural and not also socially constructed, and because certain aspects of human-rights rhetoric were as much limiting toward minorities as they were inclusive, we recognize the great need to point out contingencies and interest-driven claims where previously one had seen only essences and absolutes.

Deconstruction, however, also has several disadvantages. First, although seemingly predestined for a truly aesthetic analysis because of its attention to the work itself, deconstruction ultimately fails to account for the aesthetic aspects of literature, which include the relation of the parts to the whole and our diverse emotive responses to a variety of literary works. The deconstructive approach generally seeks out *only* the margins of the text. Programmatically eschewing any elevation of coherence, center, or wholeness, the critic tends to locate a finite element of a text and to base a reading of the entire work on one or two marginal passages. While all great readings incorporate as much detail as possible, integrating every part into the whole, even the most ancillary, the neglect of one part does not undermine a given reading until a competing reading can explain more of the work and more of its characteristic features by way of that neglected part. Simply to isolate the part is not to attend to the aesthetic laws of the work. In a sense, then, deconstructionists often do not attend to the full complexity, the interwoven fabric, of the artwork. Because deconstructive critics tend to develop one similar reading after another by concentrating on those margins that seemingly support a focus on aporias or that give evidence of "unreadability," one text after another ends up saying something similar to the next. This repetition is a consequence of the critic's lack of interest in treating the text as a whole and in deciphering its many layers, ambiguities, and connections. Deconstruction's embrace of the singular and particular is merely theoretical; in practice it suffers a kind of repetition compulsion that ignores the *differentia specifica* of the work at hand.[14]

Second, deconstruction contradicts itself by seeking to undermine all statements and values as mere constructs, to render them visible as illusions, even as it holds to certain tenets or norms of criticism. The norms cannot be grounded, according to the theory that employs them, and so they lose their status as norms. In addition, the norms have something emotional and unclear about them. Instead of speaking of logic or contradiction, which are at least theoretically verifiable, the deconstructionist tends to speak of rigor or sophistication. A theory is hailed as provocative or disparaged as problematic; these terms do not easily lend themselves to analysis and evaluation. Some literary works do of course embody ambiguities, aporias, or negativity, but to privilege such categories theoretically involves the deconstructionist in contradictions. Even as hierarchies are dismantled, a hierarchy of interpretive strategies remains: those that dismantle hierarchies are ranked higher. Moreover, deconstructionists still elevate certain writers who are more attentive to their own dismantling and so invite privileged analysis. Deconstruction's content of doubt and uncertainty conflicts with its pathos, assurance, and authoritative guise, as has been noted by Gerald Graff (4) and John Ellis (*Against Deconstruction* 151). An additional irony arises when a critical movement like deconstruction, which recognizes only unraveling as a principle, becomes institutionalized, indeed, becomes one of the academy's authoritative methodologies.

Negative positions are generally self-canceling insofar as they presuppose in their argumentation the positive concepts they attempt to negate. Deconstructionists sometimes recognize this tension—Derrida, for example, writes that deconstruction "must borrow its resources from the logic it deconstructs" (*Of Grammatology* 314; cf. 24)—but they fail to draw the consequences. Because positive positions do not suffer this same kind of performative contradiction, the positive has ontological priority over the negative. The ineliminability of certain fundamental principles of discussion renders it not surprising that even Derrida laments that he has been misunderstood or that his intentions were misread ("But, beyond" and *Limited,* esp. 146 and 157–58). However clever one might be in dissimulating, the claim that there are no grounded truths must be taken in one of two ways: either one wants this metaclaim to be understood or taken as a grounded truth (in which case it is contradictory in a performative sense and cancels itself) or one wants it to be taken as something other than a grounded truth, perhaps as a form of play (in which case the affirmation of truth is not seriously challenged). Here is not the place to reflect on the complex issue of *Letztbegründung,* or ultimate justification, as it has been articulated by Apel and Hösle, but the transcendental-pragmatic and objective idealist models of justification offer strong answers to the contradictions of a deconstructionist model that asserts and denies truth and that feels itself both trapped and liberated by the trilemma of the nonfoundationalism of truth, the idea that truth is a fiction because it depends, necessarily, on an arbitrary axiom, a vicious circle, or an infinite regress.[15]

A third deficiency of deconstruction is its having effectively eliminated any referential role for literature. For the deconstructionist, literature undermines the view "that literature is in one way or another referential" (Miller, *Theory* 175; cf. de Man, *Allegories* 152); instead, literature is really only about itself. Because the critic rejects the idea that literature has representational value, the connection between literature and life becomes uninteresting. Without a ground or a connection to life, the deconstructionist circles around in dialogue, with no overarching purpose, which makes the enterprise difficult to defend. One is to focus only on the text.[16] Despite the advantage of returning us to the literary work, this position eliminates one of the arguments for studying the work—its ability to offer engaging discussions of the world. The critic looks ever more closely at the text, with an ever more refined vocabulary, but without a sense of greater purpose. Certain procedures of deconstruction are well equipped to un-pack elements of self-reflective texts, but not all literature is about itself, and not all literature that is about itself draws the conclusion that literature can be exhausted by its self-referentiality. The deconstructionist has a much easier time with modernists who have turned inward and skeptical than, say, with a Dickens or a Tolstoy, whose works speak more directly about the world. Instead of seeking to find relevant insights about the world also in self-reflective mod-ernists, deconstructionists tend to seek out modernists solely for their aestheti-cism and ignore the worldly insights of the realists.

For the deconstructionist, reality and literature are common in their con-structedness. Literature alone does not lie, because it alone admits that it is fic-tion (de Man, *Blindness and Insight* 17–18). What is great about literature is not its ability to uncover the world but its willingness to admit that it cannot do so. In this sense to say that literature is only about literature and not also about the world is unfair; the more accurate claim would be that both literature and the world are indecipherable and without inherent meaning, and so despite the common textuality of literature and world, deconstructionists are at a loss to say something determinate about the world. Like culture-studies critics, they can render problematic other views but must refrain from assuming their own determinate positions. We said earlier that a hermeneutic principle is that the better the categories we bring to a work, the more the work has to say. It does not speak for deconstruction that it turns nature, art, and other persons into empty ciphers without meaning. Not surprisingly, it has difficulties shedding light beyond its own sphere of discourse and justifying its enterprise within the realm of the humanities. The pathos of innovation that animates this theory of the constructedness of the world is amusing to someone already familiar with the *verum factum* principle that is explicated below and has guided modern thinking for centuries. Like culture studies, deconstruction is not as opposi-tional to the zeitgeist as it purports to be. Indeed, by elevating a means (be it cri-tique or negation, subtlety or sophistication) as an end, it mirrors in yet another way the current of the times, for a characteristic of the technological age is the substitution of means for ends.

Although deconstruction appears to have been motivated partly by existen-tial desires, this motivation is weakened by its formalism and negativity. Unsat-isfying as well become the poverty and one-sidedness of its categorical appara-tus, its professed abandonment of the search for a normative value in ethics, and its resulting cynicism, despite its many willful professions of joviality. A characteristic of the modern world is the elevation of function over substance, so it is hardly a countermovement on the part of deconstruction to elevate thereby the sign, which has meaning only in its function and is in its essence arbitrary, and to negate the value of the symbol, which points beyond the world of mere function to a higher substance.

What then remains the ground for the deconstructionist pursuit other than the formal challenge of undoing meaning? Is it the critic's task to demonstrate how clever he or she is, or to enhance our interpretation and evaluation of literary works? Deconstruction is powerless to answer Sextus Empiricus's skepticism concerning the viability of literary criticism. Sextus divides poetry into two kinds, first, gnomic sayings that are clear and useful for life but require no explanation or commentary, and second, obscure passages that literary critics spin around in idle chatter but do not clarify and that are therefore ultimately useless (1.278; cf. 1.318–20). The deconstructionist would do well to tend to the wisdom of one of its skeptical precursors, for unless Sextus can be answered, some literature may remain valuable to us, but no longer literary criticism.

We can recognize in the above movements a pendulum of sorts, which might allow one to speak of a logic inherent in the history of literary criticism. A work of art calls for multiple approaches, and any methodology that isolates one moment at the expense of another will invite the emergence of a competing and alternative model. In this sense a seed of reason is in virtually all new literary-critical developments, as new items are brought to our attention. The emphasis on the authority of tradition is countered by a culture studies that unravels false claims to authority. The emphasis on the coherence of all literary works is countered by the deconstructive attention to contradictions and unresolved ambiguities. Each movement, in its recognition of a moment of truth, pushes our understanding of literature forward, but unless it also incorporates what is of value in countermodels, it likewise represents a regress and a challenge to the next generation. In this displacement of earlier models, much is lost, and so one returns in an almost cyclical fashion to the insights of movements earlier displaced. Each new movement brings to the fore neglected moments that need to be integrated, in their proper place, within a more overarching and more coherent theory and practice of literary criticism.

A valid literary criticism fulfills the following moments: it is drawn to works that merit our attention, because of their universal or contemporary importance or both; it seeks to focus on the aesthetic dimensions of the work, attending thereby to the moment of truth, the sensuous moment, and their interconnections; it seeks to unravel the interrelations also of part and whole, doing justice to each in its full complexity; it does not fail to ask the evaluative question, which presupposes a knowledge of basic aesthetic principles, hermeneutic efforts to grasp the work at hand, and knowledge of other works with which the given text might be compared; it is motivated by both an objective ideal of science and an existential commitment to the value of the subject, which is led by a recognition that literary works have value also for life; it employs a methodology that is chosen after careful consideration and with attention to other options and the idiosyncracies of the work; the interpretation is presented in intelligible, jargon-free terms; it must be free of contradiction, both in its own theory and between itself and the various moments of the text, not only those toward which it is drawn; it must respect the imperative to weigh the valid insights of predecessors and not to contribute needlessly to the overproduction of information, and so it will not seek to disseminate an interpretation that does not say something of value that was not already said from previous angles (in other words, we should not reinterpret simply because we have new theories to apply independently of their heuristic value for particular works).

Part Two **The Technological Age**

When considering the impact of technology on society, we must account for its various phases. The first industrial revolution was powered by the steam engine. Driven by coal and heavily dependent on iron, this revolution led primarily to advances in mechanics, manufacturing, and transportation. The second industrial revolution was powered by electricity; it encompassed the chemical, pharmaceutical, machine-tool, and electrotechnology industries. Even if the steam engine is now obsolete, each of these industries continues to advance and help drive our economies. Nonetheless, we are already in the third industrial revolution, whose defining element is information. The information-driven technologies encompass cybernetics, computing, microelectronics, optoelectronics, telecommunications, robotics, biotechnology, genetic engineering, nanotechnology, and the so-called service and entertainment industries, which technology has increasingly altered.

All three revolutions, as the concept implies, have in common the transformation of the world for given ends, and these transformations change not just the products of industry but all facets of our existence—from the way we spend our time to the way we relate to nature and to others. The pervasiveness is most pronounced in the third industrial revolution. The cumulative effect of inventions means that increasingly more spheres are affected. Moreover, information is such an integral part of human activity that today technology affects virtually every aspect of our existence (Castells 1.61). The pervasiveness of technology in modern life has led Jacques Ellul to speak of "the technological system," in which the whole of technology is greater than the sum of its parts, and Neil Postman to coin the term *technopoly* to designate a worldview that sheds the orienting influence of tradition and assumes instead that all problems are to be addressed via technology.

Technology has a wealth of positive attributes. With the help of technology life expectancy has risen from thirty-five years in 1900 to sixty-six years in 1999 (Brown and Flavin 10); living standards have increased; basic material needs—from food to clothing, water, and health—are more easily met; we enjoy seemingly mundane conveniences that earlier generations did not, such as indoor plumbing, washing machines, and the easy refrigeration of food; more people are able to dwell comfortably than could previously on the same amount of land; we have new resources, such as solar technology and the recycling of waste; we can better diagnose ecological problems and move more efficiently toward solutions; communication has been enhanced, and with this development so has knowledge of the diversity of other cultures and of common problems; technology has freed us from much laborious and repetitive work; and new art forms, such as photography, film, and computer graphics, have emerged. Advances in technology will be more necessary than ever to address the consequences of our uses of technology. To take one example of the positive effects of such advances, incandescent lightbulbs are technically simple but wasteful, whereas flourescent bulbs are technically more sophisticated and also more energy efficient. Like many otherwise welcome developments in modernity, capitalism among them, technology is in need of moderation, critique, and countermeasures. Because my interest is literature as a complement to technology, I focus on those aspects of technology that affect literature positively, as in the creation of more free time that might be devoted to literature, and those negative aspects of technology to which literature can respond as a countermeasure. My goal is not to provide a summation of the greatness and limits of technology.

In a work on literature in the technological age one must ask the following two descriptive questions. First, what are the dominant categories of the technological age, both positive and negative, that must play a role in any reflection on the normative role of literature in this age? Second, what impact does technology have on art, including its themes and forms as well as the conditions of its production and reception? Answers to these questions form the content of the next two chapters.

Chapter 5 Categories
of the Technological Age

This chapter attempts an analysis of some of the overriding categories of the technological age, those that emerged in tandem with the technological age and those that changed dramatically in this age. My concern is less with specific artifacts of technology than with the intellectual-historical presuppositions of technology and the effects of technology on social structures. As Rolf Peter Sieferle has argued, the human reception and evaluation of technology are driven both by the immediate impact of new technologies and the mediated effects of technology on social and intellectual life. Of interest in this context are: the dominance of technical rationality over value rationality; subjectivity, with its elevation of *poiesis* and the *verum factum* principle; the development of ever more discrete subsystems of values, what Broch describes as an "atomizing of value-systems" (483); quantity as a determiner of value and measure of excellence; hubris or the idea that all of life can be controlled and, paradoxically, impuissance or the idea that the web of causality is so complex in modernity, its signs so impenetrable, that no one person can influence it or change it, as was the case in ages past; the loss of a more traditional orientation and the inability via technology to satisfy emotional needs, which results in disenchantment, along with the distrust of all harmony as illusory and the corresponding elevation of dissonance; and the substitution of the particular for the universal together with the direction of means-ends rationality toward the ever more immediate, resulting in shortsightedness, the failure to see oneself embedded within temporal and spatial chains.

Some of these categories are mutually overlapping, which may support the idea that a common and decipherable spirit of the age exists. The interrelatedness of categories is likewise evident in such concepts as speed, acceleration, and progress, which surface throughout my discussion, even though I have not elevated them into their own sections. One could of course have selected other categories, including especially privileged categories like innovation and equality that are justly celebrated in modern culture, but these and other alternatives are in my eyes less central to the question, In what ways can literature help counter some of the deficiencies of the age?

In virtually each section three dimensions are considered: the philosophical or intellectual-historical presuppositions of the category; a variety of examples that illustrate its importance; and its influence on arts and letters. In some cases the philosophical analyses are longer, as with the first two terms, technical rationality and subjectivity. In some cases, as with shortsightedness, whose philosophical prerequisites are for the most part already elaborated under technical rationality, subjectivity, and autonomous value systems, the philosophical reflections are briefer. In reflecting on intellectual-historical presuppositions, one must also consider some thinkers who contribute to the development of certain modern categories, though their work predates even the first industrial revolution. Finally, though this section, in contrast to the first normative part, is more descriptive and phenomenological, it does attempt at appropriate intervals also to weigh the coherence of the categories discussed; in that sense it is not without comments critical of the age. With each category, however, both positive and negative attributes can be applied, and in most cases, the desire is not to transcend the category itself but to temper its one-sidedness. We cannot do without, nor would we want to do without, the means-ends thinking that allows for modern efficiency, the entrepreneurship made possible by the elevation of subjectivity, or the discipline and focus that follow from the emergence of autonomous value systems.

TECHNICAL RATIONALITY

Techne is the craft of making, of skillfully employing tools, of achieving a given end; techne applies to the scientist's application of principles in creating products as well as the writer's use of rhetoric, the athlete's development of the skills of sport, or the debater's mastery of argument as a means to an end. In a sense a strongly instrumental dimension surfaces in every use of techne. As technique, method, or skill, techne encompasses quite simply the way people do things. By defining technique broadly as any means-ends relation, we can say that there is even a technique of prayer, as is implicit in the very name *methodists.* We recognize a technology of production, a technology of organization, and so forth. Technical strategies have become popularized in self-help books: the how-to of influencing people, of making friends, of finding a partner. Much of modern consciousness is guided by the elevation of techne.

Technology's ability to alter the world becomes a problem only when technology becomes autonomous and is no longer guided by valid ends. Today many of our actions do serve trivial ends at odds with the environment and our normative concept of humanity. The consequences are well known: invasions into nature and unsightly constructions; vanishing natural resources; mounting amounts of garbage; hazardous waste; groundwater and air pollution; over-fishing and toxic poisoning of the oceans; deforestation and habitat destruction; soil erosion; loss of wetlands, wildlife, and biodiversity; acid rain; ozone depletion; and global warming. What can keep us from continuing in this vein? Technology may provide us with some assistance, but technology alone cannot provide the brake.

To address this quandary, we must first distinguish several types of rationality within the unity of reason. If we accept a distinction between theoretical and practical knowledge, then within a theoretical frame we might distinguish the philosophical rationality that studies the basic principles of an ideal sphere from the scientific and hermeneutic rationalities that are employed to grasp reality in its manifestation as objectivity, subjectivity, and intersubjectivity, including human interaction, practices, institutions, and cultures. *Philosophical rationality,* as reflection on first principles and the basic structures of being, encompasses metaphysics and ontology. It also includes overarching reflection on the first principles of the individual disciplines, such as the basic principles of aesthetics, and on the unity of knowledge across disciplines. *Scientific rationality* seeks to analyze the phenomena of the object world and explain causal relations; in modernity this encompasses basic scientific research, to the extent that it can be pursued independently of technology, that is, pure as opposed to applied science; the value-free social sciences, insofar as they employ quantitative methodologies to explain causal relations within the spheres of subjectivity and intersubjectivity; and within the humanities, a field like formal logic. *Hermeneutic rationality*, which seeks to understand rather than explain, is essential for grasping texts, institutions, and other cultures.

Within a practical frame, we can distinguish *value rationality* that focuses on the legitimacy of ends from *technical rationality* that reflects on the means to reach a given end. Technical rationality encompasses two forms of means-ends relations: instrumental rationality, which concerns subject-object relations, and strategic rationality, which involves subject-subject relations. Instrumental rationality, in which the subject treats the object as a means, is appropriate for many subject-object relations. It represents the ability of the subject to transform an object for a specific purpose. The more power and means a culture or individual possesses, the greater the capacity for transformation. Means-ends rationality is the most developed form of rationality in modern culture and the one that has remained mostly unaffected in practice by contemporary assaults on reason, even if it has often been targeted for criticism. Strategic rationality arises when the subject relates to another subject or to other subjects in such a way that the other is treated as a means. The person may be reduced to a mere means, or the other subject may be treated both as an end (we recognize the other person's autonomy) and a means (we recognize that we must act strategically toward that other person for our benefit or for the benefit of that other person). Strategic rationality is necessary in order to reach certain ends, though it cannot itself ground those ends. Organizational skills, for example, fall under this rubric.

Within the theoretical frame, we recognize at least four important developments in modernity. First, philosophical rationality has been given less and less attention. The concept of philosophy as a discipline that reflects on first principles and on the presuppositions and ultimate unity of the diverse disciplines has been neglected in favor of views of philosophy that are closer to the scientific paradigms of the other disciplines and subdisciplines. Second, hermeneutic rationality as the lens through which we understand humanity and the creations of humanity, from their artworks to their institutions, has as a result of historicism been increasingly divorced from the spheres of philosophical and value rationality; we seek to interpret cultures and texts without evaluating them. Third, hermeneutic rationality has increasingly adopted the quantitative and analytic techniques that were previously associated with scientific rationality in its study of the object world and were less prominent in the endeavor to understand self and society. Finally, the scientific paradigm is itself less and less interested in simply knowing the world and more and more interested in transforming it. With the partial exceptions of astronomy and mathematics, experimentation, which presupposes instrumental rationality, has become the sine qua non of scientific progress. The scientific model comes increasingly closer to the technical model.

Within the practical sphere one notices, in the wake of the nineteenth-century critique of idealism and the twentieth-century elevation of technology, a neglect of value rationality, which addresses ends, and increased reflection on the means to reach diverse ends. Even Apel, to whom we owe renewed reflection on types of rationality, virtually reduces ethical rationality to a formal process, a kind of technical scheme that neglects the question of the content of ends, which would ideally link value rationality with philosophical rationality.[1] In a broad sense philosophical and value rationality have been usurped by scientific and technical rationality, both of which have increasingly ignored the question of values, although each makes implicit value judgments. A broader humanitarianism slowly gives way to more narrow expertise and the elevation of efficiency and calculation. What matters most is what can be seen and measured, how something can be attained. Positivism and technology have something in common, as has been spelled out by Ernst Cassirer ("Form" 158–59) and Hermann Meyer (234–60, 288–98). Unfortunately, something can be rational in terms of technical rationality but irrational on the scale of value rationality; so, for example, a new invention or methodology that serves less than humane ends. The indisputable importance of technical rationality, however, becomes evident when we consider that something can be rational on the scale of value rationality but irrational on the scale of technical rationality; so, for example, a good end undermined by poor strategic thinking.

A readership that includes also specialists on modern Germany should be especially sensitive to the difference between technical and value rationality, for one unusual dimension of German intellectual history is the way in which during the Weimar Republic these two forms of rationality were severed—and not for Germany's or its neighbors' gain. Jeffrey Herf's overarching argument in *Reactionary Modernism* is that conservative revolutionaries of the 1920s and 1930s harshly criticized enlightenment reason, including value rationality and universalist ethics, at the same time that they fully adopted technical rationality, both technology proper and instrumental strategies toward other human beings. An unfortunate legacy of this complex development is the mistaken equation of national socialism and rationality. From this equation results an unbridled critique of reason. This misreading of German history is possible only on the basis of a reduction of reason to technical rationality. Unfortunately, an undifferentiated critique of reason inadvertently strengthens technical reason by eliminating its most worthy opponent (cf. Hösle, "Foundational Issues" 15–16). Often elevated in place of value rationality is the emotional sphere, which guided the national socialist movement and which, like technical reason itself, can serve both divine and diabolical ends. If contemporary critical discourse is serious about its elevation of difference, then it should attempt to recognize different forms of reason.

The first great philosopher to address the elevation of technical rationality as a dominant characteristic of modernity and as a metaphysical problem was Heidegger, most especially in his essay "The Question Concerning Technology." For Heidegger the age of technology is characterized less by a series of finite inventions than by a worldview: in the technological age all spheres of life are reduced to means-ends relations, the desire on the part of the subject to control the world. The era of what Heidegger calls "enframing" is characterized by the elevation of causality and the question, What can I make? over the questions, What is being? and What is truth? (19). For Heidegger technology is the essence of contemporary culture—not one sphere among others. Moreover, technology is the necessary result of its metaphysical prehistory—the elevation of subjectivity at the expense of being, and of spirit at the expense of nature. In contrast to the Greek relationship to nature (where *poiesis* was very much in harmony with *physis*), modern technology represents a provocation of nature. Heidegger cites as an example the dam that redirects and harnesses the flow of water; it differs from the old wooden bridge that does not itself transform the river (16). The result is a different relationship to the object, not as something neutral but as something instrumentalized, and so Heidegger substitutes for *Gegenstand* (object) the word *Bestand,* usually translated as "standing-reserve" (17). Modern technology has a way of relating to the world, a way of revealing, which Heidegger terms *Gestell* (enframing), with its associations of the orderability of things (command, or *bestellen*), the covering up of essence (deceive, or *verstellen*), and production or construction (produce, or *herstellen*). The age of technology is not so much a series of clever inventions as it is a new worldview. Within such a frame the sacred is reduced to a tool in the hands of those seeking profit.

For Heidegger the danger in this modern world of enframing is not the atom bomb, or any other specific technical apparatus, but the transformation and loss of human essence.[2] Humanity encounters in this age its own products, not its essence, and it responds to this inner emptiness with the creation of newer and newer gadgets. We desire ever more, but often in a throwaway sense. To cite a more recent critic, as a result of "disposable products, rapid obsolescence, unrepairable goods, and mercurial fashions" (Durning 92), our relations with objects lose their reverence, and our respect for what is of lasting value weakens. Our immersion in technology veils us from earlier forms of relating to physis and techne, and so Heidegger proposes we look not at technology (*das Technische*) and not at the particular causes or consequences of technical artifacts but at "the essence of technology" (*das Wesen der Technik*) (3): this is the possibility of enframing as "revealing" (13). Vague as Heidegger's answer may be, we must acknowledge his extraordinary insight into the connections between abstract metaphysics and concrete aspects of industrial culture, including the common thread in both of instrumental thinking.[3]

A related aspect of the technological age is the diminution of individual responsibility, as Hannah Arendt has shown in her study of the banality of evil. A society constructed according to distribution of labor and discrete means-ends obligations awards and invents tasks that certain persons perform. These persons may be attracted to, or repulsed by, the ends in mind; more likely they are indifferent or oblivious; in each of these cases their task is not to question or to judge but simply to execute the requisite tasks. Local efficiency, not ultimate purpose, matters. Precisely this abandonment of holistic thinking, of reflection on overarching purpose and transcendent grounding, defines the connection between technical rationality and the development of autonomous subsystems of culture, to which I return below.

Through technology, Gehlen argues, we gain extraordinary resources. We improve (and extend the power of) our hands and legs, our eyes and ears, our skin, and our minds. Technology serves the purpose of extending our capacities and reaching ever more expansive ends. Gehlen speaks, therefore, of technology as "organ substitution" (e.g., fire and weapons), "organ strengthening" (e.g., the hammer, the microscope, and the telephone), and "organ relief" (e.g., the wheel and crank): technology compensates for weak human organs, facilitates improvements, and satisfies our need for relief (*Man* 3–8, translation modified). Gehlen further recognized, as I have already suggested, that the congruence of modern science, technology, and capitalism sped the emergence of the technological age. Capitalism is a manifestation of technical rationality that in more than one sense forms an allegiance with technology.

In raising concerns about the overvaluation of technical rationality, I do not in the least want to suggest that we can abandon the efficiency of either capitalism or technology, but I do want to ask in which ways they must be tempered by normative reflections. The question, What should we do? cannot be answered by technology alone. The further claim that, because technology cannot tell us what a legitimate end is, this end cannot be answered rationally is one of the greatest dangers of technology's ascendence. If only technical rationality is valid, ethics vanishes from the intellectual landscape. Not all that concerns us as human beings can be addressed via technical rationality, and certainly not ultimate values. Moreover, the balanced self requires not only rationality, analysis, discipline, and creation but also playfulness, feeling, relaxation, and contemplation. When technology becomes the signature force of the age, the paradigm affects the humanities as well. Philosophy, at least its analytical schools, focuses on questions of means, elevating logic and decision theory at the expense of wisdom and contemplation. In literary criticism we see the emergence of new methodologies and reflection on methodologies at the expense of the study of literature itself. Treatises on the *how* of literary analysis outnumber those on the *why* by a remarkable ratio. The means become the end. So, too, do we recognize in contemporary art and literature a common tendency to elevate technique and experimentation, often at the expense of substance.

SUBJECTIVITY

The development of technology with its harnessing of nature and creation of products presupposes a distance to nature and the current order. Not surprisingly, then, subjectivity is a dominant characteristic of modernity and increasingly of the technological age. Indeed, subjectivity has been a characteristic of the modern era ever since the development of early modern science, where the goal of scientific research was mastery of nature, and the scientific enterprise, via its experimental orientation, imitated divinity. The development of subjectivity was likewise aided by, and contributed to, emerging capitalism, according to which the individual's virtues and achievements, no longer his birth or class, determined his position in society, and the Reformation, where the individual's relationship to God was no longer mediated by tradition or the church. Philosophically, the elevation of subjectivity was especially strengthened in the seventeenth century with Descartes' emphasis on the self as the starting principle of philosophical reflection and his distinction between *res cogitans* and *res extensa*. Hobbes combines subjectivity with technical reason in his analysis of the modern state, which is built on calculable self-interest; the state is the creation of humanity, not part of the given order. Social-contract theory, with its elevation of the autonomous subject, dominates in modernity and is far removed from the ancient concept that the state has intrinsic value and is to be seen as part of the wider cosmos, a view that motivates the conclusion of Cicero's *On the Republic* and still echoes in Franz Grillparzer's *A Fraternal Quarrel in the House of Hapsburg*. It might be noted here as an aside that a view of the state as embedded in the cosmos and as having duties to those not currently present is far more compatible with an ecological consciousness than the social-contract view of the state as itself autonomous and serving the rational egoism of those who accept it.

Subjectivity has of course extraordinarily positive dimensions. We admire the value of autonomy in its relation to freedom of thought and expression: without a strong sense of subjectivity, technological inventions and an efficient market economy, which have done so much to address the modern challenges of humanity, would not have been possible. Moreover, only through subjectivity and reflection are we able to grasp the deficiencies of what is given and gain distance from the arbitrary elements of our age. Problems arise, however, when subjectivity is severed from the sphere of value rationality or when subjectivity recognizes nothing of value beyond itself or nothing of value beyond what it itself posits. Apel has rightly recognized in modernity our increasing tendency to instrumentalize the objective sphere and to withdraw into a private subjectivity that recognizes no higher values. In both directions, whether as dominance or as escape, subjectivity is prominent.

Technology is a privileged mode of subjectivity in modernity. Not surprisingly, Faust, one of modernity's greatest mythic figures, lays claim to possessing and transforming nature and to removing those humans who stand in his way. Hösle has effectively argued that in the modern age the concept of *poiesis* has become more dominant than its two complementary forms of relating to the world, *theoria* and *praxis* (*Praktische Philosophie* 96). In theoria subjects observe objects (and are in a sense thereby passive); they comprehend or contemplate something. In the realm of praxis the subject relates to another subject; the subject does something. In poiesis the subject transforms an object (and is thereby strongly active); the subject makes something. The age of technology is characterized by a new asymmetry between these three modes: poiesis takes the upper hand, usurping, with its elevation of making over thinking, the more traditional hierarchy. The urge to transform the world dominates over the desire for contemplation and the development of ethical substance. This mode of relating to the past, to nature, and to other persons arises in tandem with the increasing power of technology.

The elevation of subjectivity is also evident in our concept of nature. Hösle argues in the second chapter of his *Philosophy of the Ecological Crisis* that in the history of humanity several concepts of nature surface, each with increasing subjectivity and culminating in post-Cartesian science, which, with its extreme elevation of subjectivity, leads to a delimiting of God, nature, and intersubjective spirit. We see the constitutive character of the human mind independently of any relation to God. Plants and animals are machines with no inner world (this removes ethical scruples about nature). The human mind creates the empirical world. With Kant and Fichte this development that robs nature of its inner value is completed. The sublime, though triggered by nature, is for Kant ascribed only to human reason. Whereas Plato is often disparaged for his ascendence to the realm of ideas, precisely his objective idealism, which Hegel shares, leads to a more elevated view of nature than the subjective idealism of Kant or Fichte. For the objective idealist, nature is grounded in the ideal and has, because of its relation to the ideal, moral significance. Kant and Fichte, on the other hand, argue that only the will of a rational being has intrinsic value. One consequence of this subjective idealist view is that we no longer have moral duties vis-à-vis nature.

The *verum factum* principle plays a significant role in this process. Deriving from "'verum' et 'factum' . . . convertuntur," or truth and artifice are interchangeable (convertible), and "verum esse ipsum factum," or what is true is what is made, the principle argues that only what is made by humans can claim validity.[4] Humanity assumes the function of God as creator of the world and of truth. The principle recognizes the value of mathematics, which we create, and reveals the importance of experimentation, which was foreign to the Greeks; through our experiments we gain knowledge of nature. The principle also explains the priority of function over substance.[5] Not astronomy, with its more contemplative mode, or traditional biology, with its stress on measure, but modern physics, computer science, and biotechnology become the paradigmatic sciences of the age. With this dominance arises a view of nature as quantifiable and subject to mathematical formula and change, thereby depriving us of our emotional relation to it. Subjectivity demonstrates its sovereignty over nature by dissolving it of subjectivity; sovereignty is also expressed in the re-creation of nature—in technology. Nature yields to the intellectual constructs we fashion in order to analyze it and the inventions and products that either invade or replace it. Unfortunately, however, because humanity is a part of nature, dominion over nature may also mean control over human beings (as in medicine that attends only to the body or organizational structures that treat human beings as objects, not ends).

The verum factum principle proposes—and here we recognize to what extent it has become a cliché of the age—that everything is a construct. Nothing is of value beyond what we ourselves make or will, and so everything that is—or allegedly should be—is easily changed, usurped, and altered. It is revolutionary in two senses: it implies that whatever exists by way of tradition has no intrinsic meaning, and it invites revolution, which by definition seeks to remake and refashion the world. Again, to obliterate subjectivity and return blindly to tradition is not the alternative; instead, we must simply recognize that not everything is subject to manipulation, including our moral obligations. In the context of the verum factum principle, however, technology is increasingly emancipated from ethical and metaphysical constraints. Obsessed with invention as a mode of morality, we are more often than not convinced that whatever we can do, we should do. Ultimately, as subjectivity frees itself ever more from ethical constraints, the conclusion is drawn that only what *I* will has validity. The verum factum principle is thereby shifted from humanity to the individual self.

Heidegger has recognized that our view of the world not as Being or as *ens creatum* but as a construction of subjectivity, "the world conceived and grasped as picture," is characteristic of modernity (*Question* 129). The resulting focus of our attention is not Being but humanity. He continues in his analysis of "The Age of the World Picture": "That the world becomes picture is one and the same event with the event of man's becoming *subjectum* in the midst of that which is" (*Question* 132). We become engaged in a battle of worldviews, in which calculation is the dominant principle. The legacy of what Heidegger analyzes is predominantly visible in the idea that every view, every position, is a construction—and has therefore neither intrinsic value nor a claim on reality objectively stronger than any other. This very un-Heideggerian thought loses sight of Heidegger's critique of subjectivity, including those forms of subjectivity that represent collective subjects but still attempt to exert their will on other persons and on nature. In this extension the only change that occurs is the (increased) power of the (more widely defined) subject.

One aspect of subjectivity is that it recedes from objective reality: this has the positive aspect that it may regenerate a society by projecting new norms, but also the negative side that it may mean, especially in an age that has difficulties finding any anchor, a distancing from all social institutions. Vico analyzed this act of distancing as the "barbarism of reflection," which from the perspective of subjectivity negates the objective order and with it any moment of higher meaning or transcendence (1106). Such distancing is surely a dominant aspect of our age, made ever stronger by technology for at least three reasons. First, technology reinforces the dominant paradigm of the age—that what is of value stems from our selves and is alterable by our selves, not inherent in reality. The genre of the utopia, which emerged in the early modern period, implies a distance from the world and a desire to refashion it; beginning already with Bacon technology is central to the genre. Second, technology elevates certain virtues that revolve around egoistic means-ends thinking and the acquisition of material things, thus severing our attachment to a higher or transcendent sphere. Not surprisingly, the acquisition and distribution of power are dominant categories of modernity from Machiavelli and Hobbes to Nietzsche and Foucault. Third, our relationships to institutions lose much of their warmth in an age when these connections are mediated not directly but by the sophisticated means of technology; thus, we have less and less of an emotional bond to various institutions of objectivity.

The level of subjectivity in the technological age is elevated by the broader percentage of persons with advanced schooling and the release of more and more persons from physical labor. A relatively undereducated person engaged in heavy labor normally has little time, energy, or inclination to reflect on the self. Also contributing to this development is the collapse of traditional models of orientation, such as religion, that embed the individual in a larger order. In its stead we see the ascendency of a pragmatist paradigm, defined for contemporary intellectuals above all by Richard Rorty, who argues that we do not *find* truths, we *make* them. Without a transcendent ground, our self-worth becomes functional, defined by our relations to others, which can elevate envy in an extraordinary way. As one's position can always be greater, an inner dissatisfaction is not unusual, especially when one senses the vulnerability of one's standing in a society that knows not only upward but also downward mobility. And the less one has inner satisfaction, derived from one's connection to transcendent values, the more one is compelled to move up the ladder or to receive recognition from others as compensation for an insufficiency of inner worth.

Subjectivity's link to technology is present even in an everyday sense. Technology provides our homes with water, telephone connections, and entertainment systems; as a result, we needn't leave our enclosed spaces as often as in earlier eras, and when we do, we may drive an automobile rather than walk, or take the bus or train. With this technological arsenal at our disposal, the social dimension diminishes, as we see, for example, in the idea that visiting one's neighbor, in days past a common evening activity, now seems old-fashioned and almost quaint. More significant is the idea of the self-made man, which is foreign to cultures not privy to the technological paradigm; the self-made man is a social analogue of the verum factum principle. The self-made man does not acquire an identity by being part of the cosmos; he gains it by achieving a self-identified end. What is of value is what one has attained on one's own. Capitalism allows us to create our identity anew. While our modern culture justly admires the emphasis the concept of the self-made man places on personal freedom, aspiration, and achievement, a problem arises when our identity is severed from *any* transcendent frame. Carl Sternheim, who is one of the greatest authors to account for this alteration in identity, consistently reflects on the ways in which our modern identities are not rooted in tradition but invented. Though Sternheim admires this Nietzschean creativity, many of his characters suffer from the break with meaningful tradition and relations, though such moments of genuine humanity are quickly suppressed for the sake of survival and upward mobility. So, Christian Maske in *The Snob* forgets his parents and creates a false story of his origins in order to invent, through this fiction, an appealing identity for himself.

Hegel argued that art is past because it has been superseded by philosophy, which is self-reflective and self-grounding and has freed itself from the impurity of the senses (13.23–28). Hegel did not anticipate that modern art would itself become almost philosophical through its integration of self-reflection. In an age in which self-consciousness and the verum factum principle dominate, the harmony of unconscious and conscious creation, which was so elevated by Schelling (e.g., *Philosophie,* par. 19), has given way to the dominance of the conscious. Artistic creation overrides what Schelling called poetic creation and the "unforced favor of nature" (*Schriften* 618).[6] Indeed, reflection on art within the artwork itself has become a dominant feature of modern art from the German romantics to Thomas Mann, Brecht, Pirandello, Fellini, Handke, and Woody Allen. Art turns away from nature and the social fabric of the world and inward toward its own internal reflection, a movement that Silvio Vietta has called "aesthetic constructivism" (*Die vollendete Speculation* 182). The cerebral nature of modern art may be an attempt to rescue art in an age when it no longer seems supreme, but several aspects of this development suggest that it may be less than entirely successful. Self-reflection is often characteristic of lateness—art reflects on art because it no longer has the vitality of simple creation but has become sterile and reflects on its inadequacies. In addition, the self-reflection of modern art is directed primarily at art itself—reflecting on itself, art seems to have lost its connection to the world (and to its audience). The increasing subjectivity of modern art seems to exclude both recognition of substance and a meaningful relation to its recipients.

Moreover, if art is intellectual, like philosophy, but also sensuous, unlike philosophy, an art that is too reflective, too conscious and constructed, may lack that moment of sensuousness that makes art uniquely art. Or, if it is still art, it may be weaker as art. One wonders, to cite an example, whether *Buddenbrooks* has superiority as literature over *The Magic Mountain*. Whereas *The Magic Mountain* is philosophically more complex and demanding, *Buddenbrooks* seems to excel more as a subtle story, which may be truer to the specific potential of art. Some artworks are more graceful than others, conveying an atmosphere and a set of profound insights without becoming unduly reflective. Literature should address the great problems of the age and help orient us toward the ideal; it should regenerate—all this follows from its dependence on truth in the broadest sense of the word. Yet what follows from its sensuous moment is that this regeneration of moral perspective cannot be reduced to the didactic: art conceals its moral purpose by leading us to these insights indirectly. Pseudo-Longinus is right when he argues that the most effective aesthetic forms are those which we receive without reflecting on them as constructs (chs. 17, 22, and 38). Vico, who was the first to recognize the greatness of medieval literature, in particular Dante, argues that Dante matches Homer in imagination and in the range and sublimity of his language and is found wanting only in his learnedness, which for the poet can be but a burden (3.180; cf. *New Science*, pars. 821 and 838). We may or may not want to concur with Vico's evaluation, but it is difficult to argue with the less strong claim that unless the great poet wears his learning lightly, he will easily take us beyond the sensuous and aesthetic sphere and weaken thereby his work. Yet just such overreflection is a dominant aspect of modern art. One thinks of conceptual art, which is less concerned with forms or materials than with ideas and meanings and in some cases consists only of a description of the art object and not the art object itself, or of the increasing tendency to supplement the art object with lengthy theoretical reflections by the artist.[7] The turn to primitive art in the twentieth century can be seen as a partial counterresponse to this dominance of the cerebral.

The subjectivism of the modern world is also mirrored in literary criticism. Both culture-studies theorists and deconstructionists are enamored of the idea that we can only construct reality; in essence they represent the legacy of subjective idealism—without acknowledging the ethical law, as did Kant. This constructivism helps explain the extraordinary attention to new terminology. Theorists create the world through language but must first unburden themselves of the tainted language of the past. The theorist remakes the world in his or her rhetoric and so enacts a form of poiesis. If, for such thinkers, no reality exists independently of our construction, nature and other persons are given rights not because of their substantive or intrinsic value but on the basis of a given thinker's "positionality."

QUANTITY

Like subjectivity, quantity emerged as a dominant category in the early modern era. Science became increasingly quantitative, and function and causality, not essences, formed the primary foci of scientific research. Francis Bacon articulates an ideal of power in his *New Atlantis*: science has as its telos the maximization of strength, speed, and efficiency; normative or qualitative questions begin to recede from view. This shift from essence to function has led to more detailed relational knowledge and extraordinary increases in the quantity of products, which have addressed many of humanity's basic needs. As part of this development, the concept of the infinite was elevated, first in mathematics, then in astronomy and physics.[8] Even the infinitely small, which became the province of physics, has dimensions commensurate with the elevation of quantity, as Heidegger suggests when he discusses the modern phenomenon of the gigantic and illustrates it, paradoxically, with the particles of atomic physics and the ever smaller distances that are a result of modern transportation and communications. Also in the social sciences, we recognize the value and importance of quantitative analyses. The relation of quantity to subjectivity is visible insofar as one considers that the value-free social sciences could emerge only after the subject viewed the world dispassionately as an object.

Above all the economic paradigm, which dominates the technological age, is built on the idea of unlimited growth. In this modern confluence of technology and capitalism, the absolute of quality gives way to the relativism of quantity. The individual may seek to maximize profits and accumulate as much wealth as possible without an internal concept of measure. The Greeks had a word for this preoccupation with always wanting more, *pleonexia,* and unlike its opposite, *sophrosyne,* or temperance, it was not privileged as a virtue (*Republic* 372ff.). The preoccupation with quantity seems directly proportional to the loss of identification with objective values. The success of a nation or culture, for example, is defined not by its cultivation of virtues but by the determining economic figure, the gross national product, or GNP, which is driven by advances in technology. A high per capita GNP, however, is fully compatible with the ruthless exploitation of natural resources and absolute poverty for some persons. Its insufficiency is further evident in the fact that automobile accidents, illnesses triggered by environmental pollution, and immoral, if sometimes legal, businesses can all add to the GNP. The substitution of quantity for quality means that exchange-value replaces use-value: in Oscar Wilde's witty phrase, "People know the price of everything, and the value of nothing" (48). The quantity of money tends to supplant the quality or intrinsic value of a product. Karl Marx is right in recognizing the way in which the capitalistic exchange system allows money to replace any number of traditional values ("Geld"). Money also contributes to the valorization of quantity, for what sets money apart from objects, which are necessarily finite, is that it can refer to anything and everything; money is indeterminate and points toward the infinite.

One consequence of an ever expanding economy is the use of increasing quantities of natural resources: this need for resources affects not only the ecological problem but also the third world, as many of these resources are taken from the third world, first via colonization and then via trade, which permits the third-world economies to grow or at least makes it possible for certain individuals within those countries to form a market for the increasing number of goods being exported from industrialized countries, resulting in economic instead of political dependence. Technology incorporates more and more of the world—more use of natural resources, more covering of nature with asphalt and concrete, more production and distribution centers, more orchestrated activities. In this context a sustainable economy that meets the needs of the present without compromising the ability of future generations to meet their needs is threatened.

The skyscraper and metropolis, the modern world's vertical and horizontal negations of measure, also reflect the contemporary elevation of quantity. Our dwellings and cities are increasingly out of proportion to nature. The economy of scale tends to dictate vast sizes for stores and malls, much as it leads to the emergence of chain restaurants, motels, and shops. The economy of scale is more prominent in the United States, where shopping is usually done by car, than in Europe, where the smaller, neighborhood store continues to survive, though increasingly as part of a chain. Mass production is another aspect of quantity, as are mass markets and increases in buying habits. Marketing becomes more important than production, as the latter becomes automated.

With an increase in products available, the greatest concern of businesses becomes raising the consumer's needs and desires. New technologies make direct
contact by phone and e-mail easier; a competitive economy and an increase in
industries lead to more mailings and more visible advertisements. The result is
informational saturation.

Other spheres are likewise affected by what René Guénon has called "the
reign of quantity." Farming is transformed via machinery, and to pay for the
machinery, one needs a greater quantity of land—whence the transformation
to large-scale agriculture. Whereas this transformation is openly driven by an
economic rationale, its ecological, social, and aesthetic costs are rarely calculated. The overuse of opinion polls is another aspect of the elevation of quantity
over quality; the media tend to be more interested in the percentage of persons
who hold a certain view than in the quality of the arguments for or against a position. And in an age where even universities lose a sense for quality, the number of publications may determine a faculty member's advancement.

When quantity is separated from quality, a perverse logic takes over that
lacks any sense of the organic, any relation to meaning. Consider the production of statistics and information that have no organic connection to our lives
and serve no higher purpose. The computer enables us to search out data almost endlessly, to string and collect information by pressing a series of buttons,
but the questions why these data should be interesting or meaningful and how
they may contribute to an organic sense of self or other are not always asked.
We simply collect facts, figures, dates, and quotes, and we produce the information because we have the technical means to do so. What we say (and what
we read) is as a result often less organically related than the information received by earlier generations. We are assaulted by too much information without meaning, what one contemporary critic calls "data smog" (Shenk). Neil
Postman comments insightfully: "Information has become a form of garbage,
not only incapable of answering the most fundamental human questions but
barely useful in providing coherent direction to the solution of even mundane
problems. To say it still another way: The milieu in which Technopoly flourishes is one in which the tie between information and human purpose has been
severed, i.e., information appears indiscriminately, directed at no one in particular, in enormous volume and at high speeds, and disconnected from theory,
meaning, or purpose" (*Technopoly* 69–70). The dissociation of quantity from
meaning is also evident in the cold-war statistics of how many times one super-
power could blow up another, as if the number of times we could destroy ourselves made a substantive difference: "Nothing more clearly illustrates the in-

sane triumph of quantitative over qualitative thinking than the concept of 'overkill'—as if there were a difference between being dead once or twice, as if death were not an absolutely *qualitative* limit" (Hösle, *Philosophie der ökologischen Krise* 62).

The structure of an economy that is constantly expanding impacts the environment, which is taxed by the use of resources and the energy to process these resources, and it affects persons. First, the expanding economy is built on the presupposition that human desires will continue to grow; so long as one is driven by ever increasing material needs, one can never be truly satisfied, because there is always a better product, which it becomes attractive to own. Second, the expanding economy has traditionally thrived on the increase of material products; such an economy satisfies—to a degree—momentary material urges, but it is less able to address spiritual longing. Certainly the shift toward a service economy suggests that the situation is changing, but here, too, the obvious question arises, Do these services address material or other needs? The elevation of quantity and material goods is manifest in the humbling statistic that 97 million adults in the United States, 55 percent of the population, are overweight (Brown 117). A third factor that could yet come into play would be when expansion comes to an end, either for the individual or for society as a whole, that is, when a person encounters his or her fiscal limits or society reaches its environmental limits: rising material needs could no longer be satisfied—and in a much more radical and recognizable way; one would need to turn elsewhere for satisfaction. For not only intrinsic but in this case also extrinsic reasons, the answer to our needs would no longer lie in quantity.

Quantity is also expressed in possessions. Overconsumption is an aspect of the substitution of quantity for measure.[9] What was once luxurious or superfluous becomes, as a result of technical invention and marketing, a necessity. No longer guided by human ends, technology develops ends of its own that usurp human ends. To say that technology is neutral and that we control it is, as Heidegger suggests, accurate but not true, for it overlooks the ways in which our control and evaluation are already determined by technology. Technology has an interest in its inventions being used: to create profit or to test their effectiveness (for example, military inventions), a point that is central to Alfred Döblin's *Mountains, Oceans, and Giants*.[10] Technology seeks ever newer, ever better inventions—whether for the pure sake of discovery, the overarching interest of profit, or simply greater efficiency. So, for example, computers are constantly updated. Indeed, the very symbol of today's age, the computer, has two overarching principles that determine its value: its quantity of information and

its speed. These two factors can solve only limited problems; more and more information is useless, unless it is of the most essential kind. Not surprising in this
context are the titles of recent books written by two of America's leading entrepreneurs: Bob Davis's *Speed is Life* and Bill Gates's *Business @ the Speed of
Thought.* The contemporary elevation of speed has been described by De-
Grandpre, Gitlin, Gleick, and McKibben, among others. Speed is in a sense
simply another aspect of quantity: the quicker we move, the more we experience in terms of quantity, though not necessarily quality.[11]

Disorientation resulting from a lack of overarching purpose contributes over
time to a transformation of evaluation from quality to quantity. Our confidence in judgment is erased, and we move toward what is new or what is superficially or quantitatively more impressive. Thus arises a passion for novelty: one
is impelled toward ever newer experiences and creations. Technology plays a
role in this dynamic, as each new invention appears to be an antidote to boredom. To answer the emptiness of the self, however, one must address more fundamental aspects, not simply enter into a bond with the new, be it represented
by innovative artistic forms, the results of the acquisitive impulse, or tourism.
Because any appeal to a hierarchy of the soul appears outmoded, to resist fluc-
tuating from one trivial event or screen image to another is difficult. In such a
culture literature rarely provides models. A sense of tradition or of moral authority, of hierarchy or of obligations is not easily regained in this climate. Replacing these spheres is the ever changing horizontal medley of images that surface and disappear too rapidly to have meaning, except in their dissolution of
coherence. In many cases television becomes the clock by which we orchestrate
our lives, contributing further to an erasure of coherent meaning.

As Neil Postman has argued, the dominance of television in contemporary
culture has weakened our capacity for sustained and substantive critical thinking. Postman distinguishes between a "print-based epistemology" and a "televi-
sion-based epistemology" (*Amusing* 24), between a "word-centered culture"
and an "image-centered culture" (*Amusing* 61). In the latter we no longer move
comfortably in the realm of concepts and ideas, in the sphere of reflection and
deductive reasoning. Whereas the written word endures, the spoken word is
ephemeral. Our attention span has shortened, and the level of our political discourse has dropped. Content has in many ways given way to form. The autonomy of form means that style and entertainment, not substance, drive value
judgments. As a culture we are less attentive to the rational thought and analysis that uncover illogic, deception, lies. Instead, we watch as ever more bits of
insignificant information pass through our minds. We are close to Aldous Hux-

ley's vision that technology undoes our capacity to think critically, that what is essential is drowned in a sea of irrelevance.

Every media revolution has its advantages and disadvantages. The printed book freed us from our local culture, widening our grasp, but it also weakened our sense of communal bonds, elevating autonomy at the expense of the social fabric and homogeneity at the expense of local color. This transition also made learning more accessible and contributed to progressive sociopolitical developments. The electronics revolution has given us greater global connections and access to even greater quantities of information, but in such a way that sorting out which information is important becomes increasingly difficult. It has made us more attentive to visual imagery but weakened our skill in serious and abstract reasoning. The electronic revolution has given us more common information, but much of it remains superficial and unimportant.

An important aspect of quantity, and the related temporal category of acceleration, is the reorganization of our lives around the clock rather than according to biological or natural rhythms or around the value of a given experience. The invention of the clock altered our relationship to nature (to the sun, to the shadows, to the seasons), our sense of time (with its devaluation of eternity), and the ordering of our lives (Mumford 12–18). Ellul eloquently captures the significance of this transformation: "Time, which had been the measure of organic sequences, was broken and disassociated. Human life ceased to be an ensemble, a whole, and became a disconnected set of activities having no other bond than the fact that they were performed by the same individual" (*Technological Society* 329). Whereas life and meaning are organic, time is mechanical and intrudes on the former, increasing our sense of disjointedness. Instead of the quality of life's events determining our actions and their intrinsic interrelation, the measurement of time leads to quantity as the determiner of our actions. As David Landes shows in his history of time measurement and its impact on civilization, the disciplined measurement of time is closely tied to "productivity and performance" (7). Not only the clock itself but also technical inventions and eventually social techniques increase the pace of life; with technology the world moves more quickly. Not by chance Campanella's *City of the Sun* of 1623 concludes with a description of a new invention followed by the lack of time to continue more leisurely discussion.

The demands of mechanical time began in emerging capitalism, when wages were calculated by the hour instead of the day. In this initial stage church bells kept people abreast of time. The importance of mechanical time increased with the development of factories and work shifts in the late eighteenth and early nineteenth centuries, which were followed in the nineteenth century by the increased availability of inexpensive clocks and watches, through mass production, thus broadening the rationalization of our sense of time. On a broader scale, as we relinquish natural time, with its emphasis on cyclical and organic structures, and elevate mechanical time, we reinforce the quantitative structure of our age (Wachtel 82–84). The complexity of the modern world, along with its extraordinary advantages, clearly prevents us from relinquishing mechanical time, but one can quickly get a sense for what has been lost in the process by spending a day or two without access to mechanical time and weighing the differences in one's actions, thoughts, and psyche. The rationalization of time is not purely a gain. As Friedrich Georg Jünger suggests, "Not only do we regulate time by our use of clocks—the clocks also regulate our time" (45).

The modern preoccupation with novelty, when it emerges within aesthetics, has a certain inner logic, for if beauty is reduced to the purely sensuous, it attracts us only through infinite variation and incessant novelty. The valuation of quantity in modern aesthetics begins already with romanticism, which elevates what Hegel calls the bad infinite (5.156–66), a constant striving for what lies beyond the present without being able to appreciate what in the present is already of value. This elevation of the bad infinite generates, on the one hand, constant irony toward the present and, on the other hand, a fascination with originality, with what is new for the sake of its being new. Hypercreativity of this kind is ironized in Gottfried Keller's *Zürich Novellas,* where Keller contrasts good and bad originality, the former being what is objectively great, even if it is not strictly new, the latter being an obsession with the new in such a way that it may be useless or even destructive.

The preoccupation with the new has led to a rapid succession of artistic styles. William Barrett draws the suggestive analogy that such art "becomes the ceaseless fabrication of new models. We go to the galleries each season as we go to the salesrooms of the automobile companies—to see what new lines have developed. Art styles become obsolete like the old models of cars. Art and the artist become assimilated to the production lines of the technical order" (217–18). The avant garde becomes absorbed into the novelty that drives capitalism. Ironically, even as the elevation of quantity numbs us to the qualitative question of aesthetic value, precisely the increase in quantity renders qualitative judgments that much more important. In an age of quantity, to distinguish between what is important and what is peripheral is essential; two contemporary literary critical movements, culture studies and deconstruction, however, herald the removal of this distinction as a great innovation, but they are thereby only giving way to a dominant principle of the technological age and under-mining what is needed to counter it.

AUTONOMOUS VALUE SYSTEMS

The categories discussed above—technical rationality, subjectivity, and quan-tity—are related to the development of autonomous value systems. The move-ment from one overarching set of values to the proliferation of more and more discrete autonomous subsystems is part of the modern elevation of quantity. Each sphere has its own autonomous logic: an instrumental-functional reality replaces value reality, and one pursues with an eye to the autonomous logic of each sphere its given end, but without an eye to an overarching purpose, like, for example, the businessman who is scrupulously precise within the rules of business but indifferent to the relation between business and ethics or the why and wherefore of business. Here technical reason gains the upper hand. The extraordinary development and sophistication of each subsystem of modernity would not be possible without the splintering into autonomous spheres. Art, too, has benefited from this liberation and focus. Nonetheless, the process is not without its moral and human costs.

Offering one of the richest analyses of the modern age, Hermann Broch dis-cusses the concept of partial or autonomous value systems in his philosophical trilogy *The Sleepwalkers,* a work in which, not surprisingly, the three main char-acters are each distinguished by a particular relationship to technology, flight (Pasenow), protest (Esch), and embrace (Huguenau). Unlike earlier eras, where one single value provided an overarching framework for the different spheres of life, as did religion in the Middle Ages, the modern world is characterized by a splintering of the spheres of life into autonomous subsystems, each of which has its own inner logic. Broch writes:

> the logic of the soldier demands that he shall throw a hand-grenade between the legs of his enemy;
>   . . . the logic of the businessman demands that all commercial resources shall be exploited with the utmost rigor and efficiency to bring about the destruction of all competition and the sole domination of his own business, whether that be a trading house or a factory or a company or other economic body;
>   the logic of the painter demands that the principles of painting shall be followed to their conclusion with the utmost rigor and thoroughness, at the peril of producing pic-tures that are completely esoteric and comprehensible only to those who produce them;
>   . . . war is war, *l'art pour l'art,* in politics there's no room for compunction, busi-

ness is business,—all these signify the same thing, all these appertain to the same ag-
gressive and radical spirit, informed by that uncanny, I might almost say that metaphysical, lack of concern for consequences, that ruthless logic directed toward the
object and the object alone, which looks neither to the right nor to the left; and this,
all this, is the style of thinking that characterizes our age (445–46, translation modified).

Central aspects of the emergence of autonomous subsystems include the dislo-
cation from tradition, the need to narrow one's focus in order to survive and
compete, the elevation of means over ends, and the sense of unease and restlessness that leads many to seek a transcendence of this compartmentalization
of life.

Technology as an autonomous subsystem has a certain internal coherence.
Each part of the subsystem is linked reciprocally to various others, and the diverse parts function collectively as "an organized whole" (Ellul, *Technological
System* 15).[12] For example, production is related to advertising, which is linked
to the modern media, which depend on the technologies that make the media
all that more pervasive, and to the advances in transportation that allow products to be distributed widely. This internal coherence further means that
progress in one sphere of technology, for example, the space industry, triggers
advances in other areas, ranging from metals to electronics and communications, which affect a range of consumer products. The computer, to take a second example, can be applied to spheres of technology ranging from graphic arts
to spy surveillance. This coherence is value neutral: it can mean the efficiency of
technology to help address crisis situations, such as hunger, or it can mean an
undesirable all-pervasiveness in the sense that to limit the effect of the system or
to abstain from any one of its aspects is difficult, since each element is so intimately connected to the others.

While the autonomous system of technology functions like a whole, it is in
fact severed from a greater whole. One of the distinguishing marks of any autonomous value system is its disengagement from the moral sphere, that is,
from any subservience to a higher logic of values. The autonomous sphere is
primary, not secondary. In the case of technology this means that technology is
independent of moral judgment; it "does not tolerate being halted for a moral
reason" (Ellul, *Technological System* 147).[13] Whereas law can be linked relatively
easily with the overarching concept of justice, technology is in a sense defined
by its independence from any language of ends, any superior values. Technology functions so strongly as the language of means, gaining thereby its own legitimacy as a means, that it is impervious to any effort to evaluate it by way of a

higher end. Inventions and new developments are not to be judged as good or bad but are to be viewed as technologically necessary or inevitable, as a sign of advancement or of achieved causality. Efficiency is transformed from a means to an end. Indeed, this elevation of means has become so powerful that a moral point of view may be deemed inappropriate if one of its potential consequences would involve halting or redirecting some central aspect of technological progress. The technological subsystem gradually displaces the moral as the most overarching system of the age.

In contrast, in classical Greek culture and in Christian culture moral and intellectual values worked in tandem. What was done intellectually served a moral purpose. In the early modern period a shift occurred. In his *New Atlantis* of 1638, for example, Bacon elaborates a utopian scientific program that seeks to push science to the limits of what is possible and that, through its secrecy, has extraordinary autonomy vis-à-vis society. In the wake of this development science is no longer a form of holistic knowledge related to the metaphysical order; instead, a priori knowledge and the search for a system eventually give way to unencumbered empirical research. Later social and economic factors contributed to this increasing autonomy; small-scale skilled labor yielded to the efficiencies of mechanized and impersonal production. Science and technology were guided no longer by religious tradition or social custom but by the love of invention, independent of consequences, and the desire for profit. Moreover, both the development and application of technology presuppose specialization. Its simple complexity renders specialization unavoidable, so, too, the demands for greater efficiency that result from the modernist triad of science, technology, and capitalism. Technical thinking is goal driven, task oriented; its logic is not to reflect on the broader sphere in which it is embedded. Efficiency and productivity, mere formal virtues in other societies, become ends in themselves.

We recognize the atomistic thinking that marks modern culture even within the erotic, as relationships are pursued for their own sake, independently of questions of longevity or higher purpose. Not only do they become thereby autonomous, they also become instrumentalized, such that two dimensions of the technological age overlap: autonomous value systems and the elevation of instrumental reason. In the mutual instrumentalization of libertinage, one succumbs to an activity that lacks love and severs thereby any connection to the transcendent, which alone guarantees dignity. There is a desire to objectify and isolate everything, not to address it in its more holistic context. Statistical and medical concepts increasingly replace traditional and more transcendent categories (cf. Postman, *Technopoly* 90). Sin becomes social deviance, and guilt becomes psychological neurosis. The diverse social sciences isolate, splinter, and destroy the meaning of those aspects of good and evil, truth and falsehood that allow for an overarching and coherent worldview. Kafka unveiled in *The Trial* the dangers of a social bureaucracy that refuses to give an ultimate account of itself, answering only the questions *what* and *how*, and not also the question *why*. Isolation and self-absorption are dangers not only in the humanities and the social sciences but also in various subfields of the natural sciences where one particular issue is pursued without exploring its connection to a broader whole. Even when moral issues are not at stake, science as a whole suffers when scholars investigate only limited questions within their discrete subfields.

The diminution of the organic is not unrelated to the rise of technology. Technology, as Karl Jaspers has explained, favors the inorganic and mechanical over the organic (154–55). The essence of technology is to harness nature by tending to its laws; that is, we adjust antecedent conditions and let the laws of causality engineer the desired result. For this purpose the inorganic is more predictable; by attending to the initial conditions and the various laws that are at work, we can harness it. The organic, because of its vitality and complexity, including the interwoven relation of part and whole, is not as easy to predict, not as easy to harness and redirect through an application of functions and laws. The unforseen consequences of modern technologies have become evident, to cite two examples, in the effects of thalidomide on unborn children and of DDT on wildlife. Not surprisingly, ethical questions become more complex only as we move from the inorganic to the organic.

The idea of developing a technology independently of any higher purpose is behind the concept of the automaton, which plays a major role in E. T. A. Hoffmann's comparison and critique of scientific and poetic impulses that are divorced of moral purposes. In *The Sand-Man* Hoffmann draws similarities between the misguided artist and the immoral scientist, neither of whom respects what is, neither of whom is ethically motivated, both of whom work not for society but out of a preoccupation with originality and creativity and a desire for control. The story satirizes the scientists Spalanzani and Coppola for creating not a whole but a disjointed and partial representation of humanity. In Olimpia is no evidence of organic wholeness, only a collocation of parts. Twenty year's work on Spalanzani's part can bring forth only a disjointed being with "clockwork," "movement," "eyes," and so on, but no human being (211). Only a fragmented individual like Nathanael can respond favorably to the partiality the scientists create. In addition to its satire of scientific optimism, Hoffmann's story makes fun of those one-sided members of society who could be mistaken for puppets, those whose "speaking" does not necessarily presuppose "thinking and feeling" (212, translation modified). The satiric dimension of *The Sand-Man* complements its critique of aesthetic and scientific subjectivity.

The transformation into autonomous subsystems of culture also affects literary criticism. Not only within the microcosm of the artwork is it true that each individual element receives its meaning by being part of the whole. The dissolution of a coherent cosmos means a potential loss in the recognizable value of one's actions as a scholar. Doubts emerge about specializations that no longer appear to serve a larger or overarching purpose. Modernity wavers between, on the one hand, a skepticism or even a cynicism that is unsure of the value of its own enterprise (because it no longer has relevance to an overarching whole) and, on the other hand, an extraordinary overvaluation of its own importance and an overestimation of each discipline (in not being connected to a whole, its partial merit is not recognized; instead, it becomes the whole itself). We oscillate between gross overvaluation of our disciplinary activity and cynicism and insecurity about our endeavors.

HUBRIS AND IMPUISSANCE

Hubris is an aspect of modern life, underscored by our ability to make things and redirect or engineer what already exists. With technology we are able to create anew, and so act out one of the attributes of divinity. With the right technologies, the modern mind believes that it can cure virtually all evils. This unqualified confidence derives from the fact that our gains have been by any measure extraordinary. Despite the need to recognize our advances, the desire to control all is not something admirable, for it is impossible and takes attention away from what we do not and cannot control. What is beyond human control encompasses, first, the sphere of the ideal, including the moral law, which we do not make but discover, and, second, the contingencies of life, which, though rarer in the technological age, still remain. These contingencies allow us to develop a character or habit of mind, sometimes called serenity, sometimes called grace, by which we learn to recognize that we cannot indeed control all, even in an empirical sense, for the world is too complex and humans are too immersed in the finite for this to occur or to be desirable.

Hubris is already implicit in some of what I have said above about subjectivity, but I want to consider it in tandem with another dominant category of the age, impuissance. It may seem paradoxical that in an era where engineering is an everyday facet of life, where we seek and sometimes succeed in controlling one dimension of life after another, we should feel a sense of impuissance, but this is indeed the case. Often though we tempt fate, thinking that everything can be controlled, we are overwhelmed by our impotence—not only in the face of nature but also in response to technology. Consider, for example, the brilliant portrayal of this structure in Buster Keaton's *The Electric House*. Remarkable about such impuissance is that it is not only localized, as in the worker's inability to free himself or herself from the labyrinth of factory life; it is broader, almost universal, and in many cases virtually invisible—by which I mean not only the solution but also the problem.

The dialectic of hubris and impuissance can be said to be symbolized in machines that do not simply act in accordance with our input but are themselves able to learn and acquire new knowledge. The creation of such beings has traditionally been seen as a form of hubris—the human being usurping God as creator. At the same time, the idea of artificial intelligence seemingly renders human beings superfluous and must lead in passing, if not permanently, to a sense of impuissance. The two moments of hubris and impuissance are combined both in this act of creation and in the general impact of technology on the age. Not surprisingly, no previous age has been so strongly defined simultaneously by the extremes of progress and catastrophe.

Two widespread reflections in modernity are, first, that I can't change anything myself as an individual and, second, that no one person is responsible for change; change simply represents the irreversible course of development. Erich Kästner's "Time Drives a Car," which integrates the idea of autonomous value systems, addresses this theme: "Time drives a car. Yet no one can steer. / Life flies by like a homestead . . . / The customers buy. And the vendors solicit. / The money circulates as if it were its duty" (72). Not surprisingly, Kästner's poem was written during the Weimar era, specifically in response to the world financial crisis of 1929, when the theme of impuissance was especially dominant. In Robert Wiene's film *The Cabinet of Dr. Caligari* of 1919 we recognize the individual's lack of control over events in a dark and disjointed world, in which very little, including the legitimacy of authority, remains certain. A sense of desperate impuissance is likewise conveyed in the stories of Kafka, for example, in *A Country Doctor, An Imperial Message,* and *The Bucket Rider.* In Remarque's *All Quiet on the Western Front* of 1929 survival becomes a matter of chance; conscious planning disappears, as does the soldier's concept of the past and future; the soldier is part of a war that he did not will and that seems to serve no higher purpose. The novel's evocation of impuissance—the vacuum of values, the lack of direction, the loss of power over one's destiny, the critique of authority figures, and the sense that one is at the mercy of technology—is not only an account of war but also a metaphor for the postwar world in which the novel appeared.

The sense of a lack of control has only increased since the Weimar era, and it takes on various forms, which are often triggered by technology. With the rapid increase in specialized information and the inflation of technical innovations, we are surrounded by products whose inner workings many persons do not grasp—this lack of knowledge increases the sense of impuissance. In earlier eras educated individuals would understand most of the phenomena around them, including the technology—the basic mechanics of levers, the wheel and axle, gears and belts, cams and cranks, pulleys, springs, and other such phenomena. As engineering becomes more complicated, fueled by the advances of modern science, this level of insight diminishes, such that the generally educated person may not understand the dynamics of the combustion engine, the jet engine, or the rocket engine or even such everyday devices as lasers. Dürrenmatt writes: "People see themselves adjusting in increasingly dramatic ways to objects that they do in fact use but no longer comprehend" (26.63). Not only are we dependent on the experts for our knowledge, the little knowledge we may have is quickly erased by new discoveries, which only exacerbates our sense of unsettling, if equally welcome, advances.

Adding to our sense of impotence is the assessment, more prominent perhaps during the cold war but not trivial at present, that we do not know what might trigger a nuclear war and that if such a war were to take place, it would be immediately out of control. A war that can no longer be controlled—technologically—is a different kind of war. Explosions reducing centers of population to ruins is one thing; nuclear fallout spreading throughout the atmosphere with lethal amounts of radiation is another. The climatic changes, effect on food sources, and resurgence of disease only add to this nightmarish vision of loss of control. Terrorism, which has struck without notice, and the fear of chemical and biological weapons more than compensate for any relaxing of anxiety Americans may have felt at the end of the cold war.

Today our sense of impotence is also driven by rapid developments in information technology. Technical advances arrive at such a pace and with such a complexity that for the most part only the specialist or the interested amateur understands their basic workings. The complexity of the telephone, the radio, television, satellites, and even space probes comes to mind. The harnessing of electricity for information purposes increases the number of complex products:

the photocopier, the quartz clock, the computer. Computers give us ever more complicated processes. We may not ourselves use them, but our life is influenced indirectly by robotics and simulation technology. The use of technology in medicine again surrounds us with machines we don't fully grasp, unless we have made a concerted effort: ultrasound scanners and nuclear magnetic-resonance scanners, for example. Not only do we feel overwhelmed by technology, we do not understand it, and so become dependent on the experts. Indeed, our resulting vulnerability may even lead us to become dependent on professionals for matters that transcend their area of expertise.

Impuissance is ironically enlarged by the wealth of media information available to us. Although we know more about disastrous events around the world, we may be less able to affect the events about which we have knowledge than we were in a culture where our knowledge was restricted to the local and immediate. Further, the layering of ever more information on our daily routines overwhelms us with irrelevance. Our knowledge of the world is clouded by the insignificant details generated by hyperinformation and the persuasive force of modern advertising. We find it difficult to choose between what is important and unimportant. This, too, renders us unsure of ourselves and our relationship to the world. What Postman calls "context-free information" (*Amusing* 65), information that is irrelevant and in an overarching sense incoherent, muddles our sense of what is important. Postman argues not only that much of our information is disconnected to any meaningful context but also that instead of seeking more meaningful information, we invent pseudo-contexts for the contextless information we have: cocktail-party conversations, trivia contests, television game shows (*Amusing* 76).

Whereas postmodern culture sees in this development a welcome dissolution of hierarchy and a reaffirmation of the margins, diversity of this kind does little to help us return to a set of priorities. Underway but not under control, we are inundated with information that does not guide our sense of values or answer questions of existential import. Both objective and subjective limits are at play in our wrestling with overinformation: we lack the time to deal with all the information at our disposal, for human time is limited; and we do not always have the right categories and experience to know how to sort through this overabundance of information as wisely and as efficiently as we would like. Even with the right categories, we lose time simply through the act of sorting, and in the case of information that addresses our more primitive selves, we don't always apply the right categories and move on without distraction. Though we may through subjective strategies be able to limit the overwhelming impact of overinformation, the problem is objective, not simply subjective.

Humans have long lived with disease, have long lived with the vagaries of weather. Today, however, we are less at home with what we cannot control. We are often removed from direct contact with nature and can control and engineer much of life. Technology is our buffer and our salvation, but this very success makes accepting what we cannot control more difficult. Acceptance came easier in an earlier era whose conditions differed from our own in at least three respects. First, earlier cultures had a less complex and less mediated relationship to those aspects of life that tend to be beyond our control, including birth, illness, and death. Second, earlier eras were much more dependent economically on the often harsh vicissitudes of weather. The number of farmers has decreased as our economy has moved toward industry and information, and so has our sense of humility and acceptance. Third, our mode of thinking is driven by the rationale of technology, which suggests that there is always another possibility of solving a problem, another way of adapting to a situation, another way of gaining control over it. While this mentality is advantageous and in many ways admirable, it can also be illusory.

New scientific advances add to our sense of both hubris and impuissance. Biotechnology offers us choices we would never have had to make in earlier eras. Genetic engineering gives us more control over our bodies and those of prospective children and prospective pets, but we do not necessarily have the intellectual and moral apparatus to address the various questions that have arisen or are on the horizon. Our sense of impuissance is deepened when we know that technology will continue to invent, even as our values have continued to destabilize. In this context, Bill Joy notes two aspects of modern technology that give special cause for concern: first, robotics, genetic engineering, and nanotechnology have the potential for self-replication, which may transcend our control and lead to technology's dominance over humanity; second, these technologies are as valuable for the market as they are for the government, which suggests both greater acceleration and greater difficulty in overseeing and restraining their development.

In an age where technology acts as a buffer between human relations, even as it sometimes enhances them, we may feel less control over our intersubjective encounters. Relations are mediated—one step removed from our initiative. As Hugo von Hofmannsthal suggests in *The Difficult Man,* we communicate differently and less successfully over the telephone than in person. And as Fellini's

Ginger and Fred suggests, our relations to events and persons are mediated by images of those persons as much as by the persons themselves. More recently, another layer of mediation has entered our relations: when calling a business, we are often given a recorded message with several options; we select one in order to receive another set of prerecorded options, and so on, until after several minutes we may finally reach a live voice.

In such a complex society ruled by technology one gains the feeling that one has no chance to change things and, therefore, whatever one does will have no serious consequences for the whole. This leads to a feeling of impuissance one might rewrite as indifference, and it is certainly a factor in the ecological crisis. Niklas Luhmann, a systems theorist, takes the extreme position that political administration and technostructure leave no room for individual responsibility or change; one can only work within subsystems, which themselves cannot ultimately be changed. All we can do is describe these systems. The proliferation of autonomous subsystems of culture—law, business, politics, religion, education—makes it difficult to address the ecological problem. Indeed, Luhmann argues that it makes it impossible: the logic of the individual subsystems overrides any logic of values (257). Such a view of autonomous value systems reinforces impuissance and erodes morality. Impuissance also receives support from a dominant strand of structuralism and poststructuralism, the theory that removes subjectivity and agency from the world; subjectivity, as Roland Barthes suggests, "is merely the wake of all the codes which constitute" us (10). The New Historicist view that history is without any meaningful coherence or pattern and just a circulation of systemic forces and a discontinuous conglomeration of coincidences also reinforces this erasure of individual purpose and responsibility.

Another dimension of impuissance arises from the complex dialectic of technology itself: on the one hand, technology allows us to control nature; on the other hand, it services new needs, to which we in turn become enslaved.[14] Our freedom is diminished when we suddenly begin to need what we have, but didn't have or need before. We are determined by external, not internal factors, a structure from which we do not free ourselves with the simple logic of more acquisition (Anders 171–78). Ralph Waldo Emerson inverts the Platonic image of the chariot rider in control of his self and nature, imagining instead technology running wild over man: "Things are in the saddle, / And ride mankind. // There are two laws discrete, / Not reconciled— / Law for man, and law for thing; / The last builds town and fleet, / But it runs wild, / And doth the man unking" (770).

Writers—from Mary Shelley to Friedrich Dürrenmatt—have suggested, not surprisingly, that even scientists may lack control over their insights, inventions, and products. The unintended consequences of our technical ingenuity assume many forms. Edward Tenner analyzes a series of such ironies. Intensive use of drugs against some bacteria and viruses has nurtured the development of resistant strains. The improved transportation that allows us to visit other countries and receive natural resources and other goods from abroad leads to the greater transport of bacteria, pests, and viruses. The introduction of high chimneys on factories to meet local air-pollution standards in the early 1970s led to the long-distance migration of sulfur and nitrogen oxide and resultant worsening of the effects of acid rain. Asbestos promised safe protection from fire and collision until it was identified as a cause of cancer. The pace of innovation and change in the technological age creates countless such experiences that may engender an increased oscillation between overconfidence and crisis. Jonas views this dialectic on a broader scale when reflecting on technology and the future: we know more about the future than any earlier era insofar as science and technology have resulted in considerable advances in our measurements and analyses, but we know less than earlier eras insofar as scientific and technical advances have led to changes and unforeseen effects that were foreign to earlier, less revolutionary cultures (216).

Even in the sphere of literary criticism and culture studies we recognize a dialectic of hubris and impuissance. Art is sometimes elevated in the place of philosophy as the master discipline, for artists are honest enough to recognize that their positions are merely useful illusions. At the same time, art and the humanities become ever more peripheral in a world that elevates technical knowledge and definitive accomplishments. The dialectic is partly colored by a preoccupation with power, both our ability to exercise it and our inability to do so. On the one hand, we recognize the view that all identity, whether individual or collective, is "a social construction," fashioned and invented by us and therefore subject to change and revolution (Greenblatt 209). On the other hand, we are persuaded by the idea, stressed above all by systems theory and the rhetoric of the death of the subject, that each of us is shaped not as an individual but as "the ideological product of the relations of power in a particular society" (Greenblatt 256). This redirection of our will does not take place within the framework of divine providence, as was the case with Vico, or in terms of reason in history, as with Hegel, but without any higher direction. Mark Taylor, for example, speaks of history as "a random sequence of meaningless occurrences" (154). We seem to live in a Kafkaesque world where persons cannot make sense of an impenetrable bureaucracy of claims and counterclaims, where texts, like the patterns of history, are hermetically sealed and inaccessible to even the most eager and skilled interpreter.

DISENCHANTMENT AND DISSONANCE

The term *disenchantment* has been employed by Max Weber to describe the effects of rationalization (250), but we owe an initial recognition of the ambiguities of rationalization to Vico. Both thinkers recognized that we progressively lose our magical or unmediated relationship to the world. Vico argues that historical processes of rationalization dilute the emotional richness and poetic mentality that great art presupposes. Modern science objectifies what was once viewed with wonder and enchantment. In tandem with this, the rational technology of modern bureaucracies leads to depersonalization. We no longer look to great individuals to solve our crises; instead, we turn to the due procedures of rational institutions. On the one hand, this human technology is a great moral advance. The process of rationalization replaces violence, inequality, and unpredictability with security, justice, and stability. Moreover, rationalization develops together with a more reflexive attitude; we are thus able to ground the validity of our institutions and decisions. On the other hand, rationalization necessarily brings with it a loss of unity and emotional richness. The development of the diverse subsystems of culture and the dissolution of a unified consciousness are necessary analogues of the rationalization process. To risk and to sacrifice one's life for a cause are no longer necessary in a world of due process; with this vanishes a great source of morality. The need for fantasy and creativity diminishes as well and is increasingly replaced with the prosaic, the everyday, the common. Rationality renders obsolete the passions that were characteristic of earlier eras. One has fewer connections to tradition, and instead places all positions before the court of reason. The emotional needs of the human soul, though weakened, cannot be fully dissolved and are not satisfied in an age of technical rationality.[15]

According to Weber greater efficiency requires increasing specialization. We as individuals thus enjoy less and less knowledge about more and more complex aspects of modern life, but at the same time we recognize that each sphere of life is calculable and can in principle be known in its many facets: "The increasing intellectualization and rationalization do *not,* therefore, indicate an increasing general knowledge of the conditions under which one lives. It means something else, namely, the knowledge or belief that if one *merely wanted,* one *could* learn it at any time. Hence, it means that in principle no mysterious in-calculable forces come into play, but rather one can, in principle, *master* all things by *calculation*. This means the disenchantment of the world. One no longer needs to grasp for magical means in order to master or implore the spir-its, as did the savage, for whom such mysterious powers existed. Instead, tech-nical means and calculation perform the service" ("Science" 139, translation modified).

The processes of rationalization have become far greater than in the ages known to Vico and Weber. We thus find ourselves in the paradoxical situation that although we have much that previous generations lacked, we nonetheless have a greater sense of emotional unease and disenchantment. Building implic-itly on the claims of Vico and Weber, Ellul argues that technology adds to dis-enchantment by cultivating the idea that one can consciously invent new and different means for virtually anything. Ellul discusses the transition from the modest and discrete "technical operation," whereby an individual means is sought for a given end, to the rationalizing process that leads to what he calls "the technical phenomenon," with its elevation of reason, consciousness, and efficiency at the expense of tradition, chance, and spontaneity (*Technological Society* 19–22). In every sphere of life the most efficient means is consciously calculated and pursued. The overarching result is an expansion of technology into areas that would otherwise have been removed from the elevation of tech-nique, such as friendship and religion. In this process all that seems to tran-scend consciousness and efficiency is weakened or even erased.

At least two additional factors contribute to this process of disenchantment. First, the sphere of the ideal, which constitutes both humanity and nature and which is evoked in the evaporating sphere of the sacred, has diminished in im-portance, and we have turned our attention to lesser pursuits, which, however much action and energy we might put into them, give us less meaning and in-ner fulfillment. Technology frees us from certain tasks (e.g., washing by hand or calculating by hand), thereby saving time for higher endeavors. However, the time we might have invested in higher pursuits is often consumed by lower ones, which become greater temptations in the light of a technologically driven economy that encourages us, through advertising, to address more primitive needs and to accumulate ever more things that are less essential. Television is one such temptation, not only in its sensuous dimensions but also in its eleva-tion of plot and suspense, which also address something primitive in humans, but for the most part without elements of higher meaning or the organic, and it then entices us to the next plot, with its advertisements and teasers. Second, happiness is defined by the relationship between desire and fulfillment: with technology we can increase our capacity to fulfill desires, but happiness results only when our desires do not correspondingly increase; since the outbreak of the industrial revolution, however, our desires have consistently escalated. Moreover, happiness presupposes a connection to a higher sphere. When technology becomes the paradigm of our human relations, such that calculating self-interest and rational egoism determine our actions, a basic human need is absent; happiness tends not to emerge in such a climate. Indeed, happiness, as it turns out, correlates closely with meaningful social relationships, meaningful work, and meaningful leisure, not with levels of income or consumption (Argyle).[16]

Disenchantment is connected to the elevation of quantity: as Heidegger suggests, we encounter in the world our own products, not our essence; this inner emptiness leads to the creation and reception of ever more artifacts, gadgets, and diversions. Advertising creates needs in our subconscious, robbing us of our higher freedom, which is control of our actions through reason and which alone allows us to reach our essence. Not surprisingly, Adalbert Stifter associates the acquisitive impulse with original sin in his *Vienna and the Viennese*. Stifter writes insightfully concerning early store windows "that these displays and advertisements seek to ensure not only that *whoever* wants a product buys it, but even more so and more fundamentally that *whoever* does *not* want a product buys it" (15.167).

Technology engenders leisure time without telling us how best to fill this leisure time. How one spends this time is of concern not only to those whose time it is to spend, for if the time is not spent meaningfully, empty time will intensify disenchantment, which may manifest itself in destructive activities, including crime. One of the central dilemmas of modernity is how to dispose of the free time that has been generated by technology and how to protect meaningful leisure (*otium*) now that technology has not only freed us but also created new requirements, such as the need for constant entertainment and stimulation. From beepers and cell phones to television screens in waiting rooms and airport terminals, meaningful solitude, which is not without its virtues insofar as it allows us to gain distance from the distractions and clichés of the age, is threatened. Indeed, we increasingly fear empty time, time without the television running, without a walkman on our heads, without a computer game in our hands, because we no longer know how to make use of it. Already in the seventeenth century Pascal took note in his *Pensées* of the range of human distractions and the fear of spending quiet time with one's own thoughts (e.g., 70,

165, 168, 515); the developments of technology only exacerbate this universal temptation.

The disenchantment with the true and the good affects beauty as well. The modern artist's desire for autonomy and novelty and fascination with negation reach so far that some artists create no longer art but anti-art. Whether purely ironic artistic expression can sustain anyone, even those who feel clever enough to detect its marks of parody, penetrates to the core of the moral legitimacy of art today. One reflects on one's own enterprise with ironic distance whenever one sees that its inherent value is no longer secure. By their detachment authors or critics show that even as they go through the motions, they have risen above the enterprise. The artist may write exclusively about writing, especially the difficulties of writing, and so become further removed from substantive meaning. But the irony of self-consciousness can be as constraining as any positions it seeks to mock.

In work driven by technology, often only certain elements of humanity are required—perhaps simply our eyes or our hands. The balance of the person may not be employed, and this reduction has consequences for our concept of ourselves and of humanity, as is illustrated in Georg Kaiser's *Gas*. Persons become extensions of machines. When we walk into an office, instead of being greeted, we may listen to the lament of someone working at a terminal screen or watch someone silently lost in another world. We recognize a similar structure already in Arthur Miller's *Death of a Salesman,* where Howard is more interested in his wire recorder than in what Willy Loman wants to say to him. This inattentiveness is part of a broader disengagement from local space, which has been explored by Joshua Meyrowitz. Even as technology allows us to connect globally, making it possible for us to be virtually present anywhere, it encourages disconnection from the local environment. The more we engage with electronic media, the more we see a disassociation of social and physical space. In terms of social technologies, we sometimes meet bureaucrats who deal unthinkingly with only one small part of the larger system in which they operate. Not surprisingly, within a decade of the production of *Gas,* Carl Zuckmayer portrayed partial, reduced, and mechanistic thinking on a broader scale in his comic satire *The Captain of Köpenick.*

The concept of alienation has played a significant role in modern thought, beginning already with Hegel and continuing with Ludwig Feuerbach and the early Marx. Marx recognized in his fragment "Alienated Labor" the importance of harmony with nature. In this early manuscript Marx elaborates a fivefold theory of alienation: workers are alienated from the products of their activities, which are alien objects exercising power over them; from themselves, as the activity of work is not their own but that of their employers; from their humanity, as their work, being one-sided, does not permit their full development; from other persons, as the competitive environment encourages estrangement; and from nature. The labor process is artificial, with little consideration given to aesthetic or environmental concerns; nature, like the worker, is reduced to an object. Marx is correct to see that alienation arises insofar as we are estranged from our ideal fulfillment and from nature, though this alienation, hardly unique to capitalism, is a greater issue of the technological age. Alienation increases in the literal sense of the term when more persons are displaced and more persons travel in order to find work.

Alienation from nature is not unrelated to alienation from others: with the right air-conditioning system, we needn't open our doors and windows; with cars we needn't walk or travel with others. If we live in the city, we may look out onto streets and other buildings. When we walk in urban environments, the sound of traffic accompanies us. Whereas only one in ten people lived in cities in 1900, by 2000 more than half of the world lived in cities (Lowe 5). The size of cities and the separation from nature tend to reduce our emotional attachment to our residences. Impermanent architectural boxes without character force us into a disjunction not only between our homes and nature but also between our homes and our higher selves. Artless and functional norms of architecture are not restricted to factories and office buildings but affect also our places of commerce, our dwellings, and our churches.

Alienation is even greater when we take into account our broader environment, the sounds, smells, congestion of city life, which are especially acute, paradoxically, in a European environment, where one can walk in narrow proximity to the traffic, unlike in the United States, which has more cars but where the congestion of traffic and pedestrians is rarely conflated. In an environment of speed, noise, repetition—an environment of technology—we seek to reduce our sensuous intake, to withdraw, to become indifferent to the stimuli. We may find a metaphorical space of reflection, but this is a triumph of spirit over matter gained at the price of harmony. The spiritual expands only at the expense of the sensuous, which has been negated in order for the self to survive. Or a second alternative arises: the self does not escape into another world but is simply deadened by the stimuli, which weaken the energy needed for the development of one's spiritual self. A curious mixture of the two is the self that withdraws from the random stimuli of city traffic, let's say, by turning to technology in the form of a Walkman; here we have a more complex version of withdrawal, but withdrawal from the environment it remains. At the other end, the mass media, especially in the form of advertising, draw us to their stimuli, addressing primarily the sensuous and not the spiritual self; here, too, we see a disjunction of the sensuous and spiritual, which is no less severe, for its experiential dimensions, than the theoretical schism introduced by Descartes and advanced by Kant. These possibilities—the overcoming of sensuous stimuli, the deadening of all sensibility, or the temptation toward merely sensuous stimuli—increase when advertising becomes part of our daily travels through technology, as, for example, with television-screen advertising in German subway stations or American grocery stores.

Dissonance and alienation are to be not ignored but made conscious and overcome. Alienation drives home to us the importance of a relationship to nature, to other persons, to ourselves, and to an ideal that is not fully manifest in the present—if it is recognized as alienation. A person at home with a boring and lethargic life, at home in a plastic and concrete landscape, at home with whatever is around the person, however loud, however congested, however empty of nature, is not alienated, but that person may not fulfill our greatest potential. A certain level of autonomy is requisite for a meaningful self-relation, but a recognition of one's environment is necessary for a meaningful relationship with others and with nature. Alienation can be both the sign of a problem and the first step toward its resolution, insofar as knowledge of a problem is often the first step toward its overcoming. Precisely in this context we recognize the value of art that helps us recognize alienation as alienation.

Dissonance also arises whenever a person is caught between two historical paradigms. In the age of technology such dissonance is accentuated for at least two reasons. First, in earlier historical transitions, one moved from a traditional role to a new role; this transition was difficult enough, but when a new transition emerges before the last one has had a chance to consolidate, the difficulty increases. Technology brings forth transitions so quickly that we are at a seeming loss for orientation. A symbol of this, if you will, is the frequency with which new models of technology supplant earlier ones, as in computer software. But this is just a symbol: if technology affects social intercourse, entire worlds change with developments in technology—from employment opportunities to the rules of intersubjective relations. Second, earlier transitions were frequently from one encompassing worldview to another integrated concept of the world. If one survived the transition, the various facets of life, though altered, remained interconnected. In a world ruled by autonomous value systems, one has frequent and often conflicting identities, which rarely form a coherent unity. Even if one keeps pace, a coherent worldview is not guaranteed. While this lack of coherence can be viewed on a broader scale in terms of conflicting subsystems of values, it also occurs on a daily basis. Birkerts suggests: "We have stepped into the postmodern swirl of dissociated images and decontextualized data. We are overwhelmed with impressions and bits and are ever more at a loss to integrate the jumble we harvest into any coherent picture" (*Readings* 152).

The conflict of historical paradigms layered with the challenges of discrete subsystems is a theme of much of modern art. Consider, for example, von Sternberg's film *The Blue Angel.* When Professor Immanuel Rath falls in love with Lola Lola, he leaves a caged and sterile world of orderly discipline and clarity, which harks back to the eighteenth century (hence the allusion to Kant in the professor's name). In its place Rath finds a noisy and cluttered but enchanting world, which turns out to be cold and instrumentalizing, driven by economic necessity and the concept of love for love's sake. Rath is at home in neither world: the old world is dying out and was spiritless; the new world, though initially full of allure, is without substance or compassion. The film's circular images reinforce the lack of meaningful options available to Rath. The sense of displacement is symbolized in the mechanical doll with which he awakens after his first night with Lola Lola: in this new world great art, and not only art, has been mechanized and reduced.

All historical ages of significance, as Hegel writes, are categorized by conflict (12.42). Unique about the dissonance of the modern age are the severity of the conflict and the conscious embrace of conflict or contradiction. The increased spread of technology to cultures with still archaic traditions along with the gulf between the so-called first and third worlds, which is fueled by the first world's successful integration of science, technology, and capitalism, illustrate that the contemporary era is one of conflict and that conflicts can be expected to increase in the coming decades. While political and social conflicts are openly embraced by only a minority, a dominant idea of the contemporary age is the theoretical embrace of dissonance: the Nietzschean and postmodern joy of contradiction is viewed as a hidden critique of the traditional search for coherence. Dissonance, not symmetry, is the intellectual slogan of the present—whether one is a student of Adorno or Derrida, of Marquard or Lyotard.

In the wake of this elevation of dissonance, we tend to think of the whole as what is false and not as what is true. Adorno, for example, counters Hegel's sentence "The true is the whole" (3.24) with "The whole is the untrue" (*Minima Moralia* 57). Of value in Adorno's position is its critique of any specious whole that only appears to be such; we must integrate into every whole whatever is left out of the synthesis; in a sense what is needed is an ever richer whole that includes those moments seemingly overridden and ignored. Otherwise three contradictions arise. First, one criticizes the concept of the whole as such, but this critique implicitly rests on the idea that what is of value is what is neglected by the whole; therefore, the ultimate telos of this critique is the embrace of a whole that is able to integrate previously neglected elements. Otherwise one embraces the part, which of necessity means that one neglects other parts; only the whole that integrates all parts is immune to the criticism that it neglects what is of value. Second, in elevating the dissonant as an end in itself, one invites criticism that is dissonant to the original claim; the dissonant position to the embrace of dissonance is, however, critique of dissonance, and so the position cancels itself. Third, in embracing nonidentity in an age of disintegration, in embracing the marginal in an age that lacks a sense of wholeness, one only mirrors what is and suppresses alternatives, whereas the rationale for the embrace of dissonance was apparently the search for alternatives to what is.

Art is influenced by this theoretical elevation of dissonance, even architecture, a form less given over to experimentation, insofar as architecture serves a practical purpose, and its inefficiencies or mistakes are costly. Consider, for example, the Wexner Center for the Visual Arts on the campus of Ohio State University, designed by Peter Eisenman: this structure has no front entrance because the concept of the building presupposes the erasure of hierarchy; the building is fractured, unfunctional, and disorderly, suggesting the critique of both utility and linearity; and it has steps that go nowhere, underscoring the idea that discord is to be elevated above connections (Eisenman). Or consider the Parc de la Villette in Paris, whose architect is Bernard Tschumi and where one of the gardens has been designed by both Eisenman and Derrida: the professed aim is to create a park that has no coherent or shared meaning; it does not seek harmony of function and form; it is intentionally disjunctive, emphasizing collision between the lines, surfaces, and point grid; it parodies conventions and tries to eschew shared significance (Tschumi). Ironically, what it does represent, among other things, is the commonality of dissonance and subjectivity in the technological age.

SHORTSIGHTEDNESS

Our belief that we cannot grasp the past and our subsequent sense of freedom to instrumentalize it are analogous to our disregard for the future. The modern devaluation of the past (as a partner in conversation) and of historical continuity, along with a lack of curiosity about other ages and of concern for the future, is very much tied to the narcissistic impulse, as Christopher Lasch has shown. In this sense the intellectual prerequisite for shortsightedness lies partly in what has been said above about subjectivity, but we also recognize connections to technical rationality, quantity, and autonomous value systems. In economic matters, businesses tend not to invest for the long term but focus instead on quarterly profit-and-loss statements. An economic incentive exists to create products with a short life span, so that replacement products will be purchased soon. Expedient housing and inexpensive products do not age well: they either break or become ugly. Likewise, whenever fashion drives a sphere of the economy, material goods need to be replaced. Shortsightedness is no less evident in the strip-mining that exploits the land and leaves it barren and degraded for the next generation. In some cases, we recognize shortsightedness not only at the level of production and marketing but also among retailers and consumers. One thinks again of energy-inefficient incandescent light bulbs, for example, which cost less in the short term but more in the long term (when length of use and cost of electricity are calculated), but which are far more readily available and more frequently purchased than high-efficiency flourescent bulbs (Howard). Also, the low savings rates in many contemporary societies, partly driven by the consumption habits of technological society, imply our disinterest in sacrifice for the long term.

With few exceptions, politicians do not inspire the populace to sacrifice for long-range goals but check the latest sway in the polls, which through advances in technology become increasingly accurate, and assume their positions accordingly. The goal is less to improve society in the long run than simply to remain in power. Thus support for green taxes, which might steer consumers toward more energy-efficient purchases or cultivate more ecological lifestyles, is rarely articulated beyond those parties that are already identified by their ecological agenda. The technocrat, as we find him in modern organizations, is by definition not interested in the higher realm of justification. Special interest groups pursuing their own subsystems of value and their agendas also contribute to this overarching lack of vision, and the rhetoric of the age, which suggests that there is only particularity, only positionality, and that any gesture to a greater whole is either illusory or regressive, adds fuel to these developments.

Shortsightedness manifests itself in many ways beyond economics and politics. The visual and dynamic culture of television changes our perception of reality, such that our attention span is reduced immeasurably; we tend to think in terms of fragmentary snippets rather than organic wholes. The elevation of the immediate and the instantaneous weakens our bonds to traditional, cumulative wisdom. Today moral intelligence is greatly influenced by the mass media. The media tend to give us a splattering of melodrama, which simplifies complex moral issues; sensationalism, which tends to obviate the need for moral judgment; and less than admirable behavior without distancing elements of irony. Attention to a complex literary work, which rewards continued investment, gives way to the consumption of visual scenes that are discarded as soon as they appear.

Shortsightedness is also evident in the increasing fragility of the institution of marriage. On the macrolevel the endangerment of marriage means that a traditional institution no longer has the long-term validity it once did; on the microlevel it means that divorce and sequential monogamy engender ephemeral commitments. Technology is hardly the primary motor behind divorce, but it does not take a great deal of reflection to see modest connections. First, technology increases mobility, which while offering new opportunities also puts strains on many marriages that would not have been evident in earlier eras. Second, the culture of family and marriage is weakened when meaningful rituals, such as common meals, take place in front of the television; indeed, one need only experience an evening in which the electricity is out for several hours to grasp the differing rhythms of earlier times. Third, whereas in earlier eras all potential partners were persons we encountered first hand, the media increasingly feed us images of ideal partners, at least in terms of sexuality, which seemingly leads many persons to become, through comparison, dissatisfied with their spouses. Fourth, the ideology of subjectivity that is a motor behind technology also allows us to view marriage not as an institution, something sacred beyond our entering into it, but as a contract that can be rewritten and dissolved as our interests dictate. One upgrades a partner as one does an automobile or a television set. Finally, the ideology of technology is one of impatience, which suggests that if something is broken, we should toss it out and find a newer, better, more improved product; instead of adjusting to one's situation, one simply moves on.

A corollary to quantity, which was analyzed above, is speed. Technology produces and transports more goods faster: quantity and speed are thereby inextricably linked. With the pace of technological change, yesterday's knowledge is quickly passé, neither relevant nor transferable. When technological knowledge becomes paradigmatic, our sense of knowledge as wisdom, as what is passed on through generations, is weakened. In such a setting, the stature of older persons, who do not contribute to the sphere of production, is diminished. Moreover, the acceleration of life gives us less time to look back and contemplate what is lost through "progress." Instead, we turn to the superficial, the current, the mere shadows of reality. In this allegiance we may not soar higher than the superficialities of the daily paper. Acceleration becomes an end in itself, no longer a means, such that the idea of reducing speed or momentum to contemplate consequences and higher values sounds as inappropriate and musty as the almost forgotten proverb, "Haste makes waste." Not surprisingly, when some persons get into an automobile they change their personality—their sense of hurriedness increases, and their sense of cordiality decreases. It is also not surprising that the futurists, who in elevating speed and invention gave voice to the obsolescence of the past, were fascinated by the technological paradigm.

In his account of the technological age, Jaspers recognizes situations where the original function of technology slips, "where as a result of the final cause being forgotten, the means themselves become the end, become absolute" (133). Adapting an earlier insight of Ellul's, Langdon Winner develops a similar point, introducing the concept of "reverse adaptation," by which he means "the adjustment of human ends to match the character of the available means" (229). He writes: "Efficiency, speed, precise measurement, rationality, productivity, and technical improvement become ends in themselves applied obsessively to areas of life in which they would previously have been rejected as inappropriate" (229). Here we see the overlap of several spheres: technical reason is elevated, and in this elevation of what is merely partial, shortsightedness is the result. Efficiency or the quest for maximum output per unit of input is applied to every activity, whatever its purpose. Elevated in this equation is not quality but quantity, in short, speed: consider the absurdity of this view with regard to reading and writing, where quality counts far more than quantity. Speed gains autonomy, becomes an end in itself. Technique replaces value. Leisure time is also measured by its level of efficiency, a strategy that would otherwise have been applied only to work. We should spend all our time meaningfully, but not always in the sense of accomplishing much; meaningful activity is not measurable or calculable in terms of quantity or level of immediate output.

When a means becomes an end, we may recognize the veiled intrinsic value of certain means; so, for example, in the secularization of the Protestant ethic, austerity, thrift, and diligence retain their value independently of their role in salvation. Such secondary virtues are not without intrinsic value, especially in an age of ecological crisis. However, to note their status as secondary is important. Though having a certain value as ends, they are not the highest possible ends. The phenomenon of reverse adaptation also affects organizations, where, after technical capabilities are developed, missions are then sought. So, for example, a university bureaucracy develops that may fulfill a certain function; when that task is resolved, the bureaucracy does not dissolve but seeks another project; in this way, the human technology of bureaucracy drives our activities and ideas, and in a bizarre way quantity replaces quality. The worst aspect of this development is the failure to see how the short-term rhetoric of means usurps the long-term rhetoric of values.

In the triad of science, technology, and capitalism, we likewise see at times a lack of consideration for, or recognition of, consequences. The use of technology frequently has its effects on the environment, but an unregulated economy does not account for the externalization of costs. The release of waste into public streams as a result of production and the pollution deriving from transportation affect us, but these costs are not normally calculated in the price of a product. Shortsightedness is an especially ironic structure in the technological age, for our actions in this age will have ever more distant—indeed, unforeseeable—effects. As a result of global warming our behavior today may affect climate conditions in Bangladesh during the next century. The melting of the polar ice caps and the eventual flooding of islands and low lands, in which innocent persons will certainly suffer, will be the effect not simply of natural developments but of changes in nature triggered by human activity. Our nuclear waste will still be an issue for persons in many, many future generations. Yet the level of consciousness and concern is not especially high—as the effects will transcend our localities and our lifetimes.

The humanities are not immune. More and more works of literary criticism are devoted to contemporary authors, who have yet to be the subject of immense quantities of research, making it easier for critics to say something original, and more and more works of metacriticism discuss the scholarly publications of the past few years. With a stress on quantity and originality, the slow effort to write a major work gives way to multiple small efforts that discuss either what has not yet been covered and may therefore be very specialized or what is simply on the immediate horizon in terms of the profession at large. Specialization is a form of shortsightedness. Fewer and fewer works address the broader dimensions of literary history in their overarching scope, much as fewer and fewer works discuss the normative presuppositions and essential principles of the discipline. The postmodern abandonment of the search for metanarratives, as espoused by Lyotard, and postmodernism's embrace of the particular and local at the expense of the universal have given strength to this development, which draws attention away from those elements of the age that are increasingly common and increasingly characterized by technology, including the concept of shortsightedness, and ecological problems, which cannot be solved by an immersion in the particular, whether defined spatially or temporally.

THE INTERRELATEDNESS OF CATEGORIES

Each of the categories sketched above stands in a paradoxical or complementary relationship to another: whereas *autonomous value systems* indicate a constricting view, *quantity* represents, on the one hand, the opposite of constriction but, on the other hand, the infinite vertical extension of each isolated subsystem of modern culture; whereas *technical rationality* and *hubris* underline our power to transform the world, *impuissance* suggests, paradoxically, that the world we have created is so complex that no one person can make a difference; even as the embrace of *dissonance* seems to highlight a dynamic and energized world, its formalism seems to have at its core an emptiness of spirit and lethargy, a *disenchantment* that no longer needs or wants to seek truth; while the level of self-reflection characteristic of modern *subjectivity* would seem to defy blindness or *shortsightedness,* two moments show their hidden identity—first, reflection becomes an instance of blindness, not insight, when truth is not to be grasped, and second, reflection is often self-reflection, a narcissistic circling around one's own particularity.

The overlapping nature of the diverse categories suggests the unity of modern culture. Our immersion in autonomous value systems restricts our vision of the world and so conduces to shortsightedness. Insofar as each autonomous value system follows its own formal rationality without regard to a higher purpose, disenchantment results. Our elevation of quantity and our desire to accumulate more and more also perpetuates our disenchantment, as the question of values cannot be answered quantitatively. The modern elevation of subjectivity is found not only in extreme self-reflection but also in technical rationality, each of which suggests an isolated subject no longer embedded within the cosmos. Our embrace of dissonance may be a hidden reflex of our cynical unwillingness or inability to seek a higher level of symmetry in the world; in short, it may be a reflection of our impuissance.

Chapter 6 Aesthetics
in the Technological Age

Each sphere of aesthetics can be viewed through the lens of technology. The above analysis has already introduced the indirect impact of technology on aesthetics, by way of some of the central categories of the age. Here the focus is on the more direct relationship between technology and aesthetics. Although I break my analysis down into the three areas of production, artwork, and reception aesthetics, each area can have an impact on the other two. Photography, for example, is not simply a new mode of production: photography also influences the subject matter of art (insofar as a new art form is attracted to the subject matter for which it is best suited) and its reception (as Benjamin has argued, we react differently whether we view a unique work, as in a painting, or a mass-produced artifact, as in a photograph or a reproduction of a painting).

PRODUCTION AESTHETICS

Already Vico and Hegel recognized that certain intellectual-historical and sociohistorical conditions are necessary prerequisites for the production of various kinds of artworks. Vico articulates the conditions necessary for the oral tradition of Homer. Hegel recognizes that differing worldviews generate symbolic, classical, and romantic artworks and with these a differing evaluation of the various artforms. Both recognized the appropriateness of epic poetry and tragedy for the age of heroes; with the advent of modern society, in which individuals cannot alter the world as easily as in the age of heroes, the epic disappears and tragedy is transformed. Marx articulates this view with remarkable force: "Is Achilles possible with powder and lead? And is the *Iliad* still possible when the printing press and even printing machines exist? Do not song and saga and muse come to an end with the emergence of the press; hence, do not the conditions necessary for epic poetry vanish?" (*Grundrisse* 111, translation modified). Lukács pursues the connection between history and genre as well, discussing in *The Theory of the Novel* the societal and intellectual conditions that led not only to the dissolution of the epic but also to the emergence of the novel. Technology plays a role in such developments, both literally, as with the emergence and consequences of gunpowder or the printing press, and more loosely, as with the organizational technology of the modern state and the interrelations between technology and the proliferation of subsystems of values, which delimit the extent to which the individual is the motor of change. An illustration of the effects of a single technology is the stirrup, which as a new technology of warfare made possible mounted shock combat and so led to the prominence of the knightly class and with it a new form of social order as well as new forms of artistic expression (White 1–38).

Within production aesthetics we can consider specific modes of creation. Vico's analysis of art as prereflexive gives us new insights into the oral tradition. Vico explains how poetry can develop over time without its aesthetic unity being destroyed. We find in the Homeric epic not the calculated creation of one person but a national poetry that evolved over centuries (873–904).[1] Writing alters this prereflexive and collective enterprise. Instead of a few works collectively developed and preserved, we have a plethora of works, crafted individually by a variety of minds, some greater, some lesser. Technology leads not only to new artforms but also to the dissolution of more traditional forms. Benjamin argues in *The Storyteller* that the development of the printing press helped set the conditions for the novel, which is written by an individual in isolation. The story, in contrast, depends on a lively oral tradition. "Experience that is passed on from mouth to mouth is the source from which all storytellers have drawn" (84, translation modified). As the novel and modern media ascend, the story loses prominence. The mutual exchange of tales and the capacity to tell them in a masterful way, a culture of collective listening, the mystery associated with distant places and activities, a fascination with the richness of one's own past, and the elevation of wisdom, worldly advice, and memory all fall victim to advances in technology. With these developments, the story recedes from prominence.

Marshall McLuhan argues from a complementary angle not that our customs and lifeworld altered our techniques of expression but that our techniques of expression modified our customs and behavior. According to McLuhan, print, being the dominant force of change in modern culture, contributed to a reduction of dialogue and face-to-face contact, thus increasing the context for detachment and self-reflection. The dissemination of printed materials made it easier for people to transcend their spatially and temporally limited horizons (cf. Eisenstein 303–450). Reading, versus the "dialogue of shared discourse" and public life that coincide with orality, also encouraged private, inward-looking individuals (*Gutenberg Galaxy* 164).[2] In turn, both the transformation in levels of self-reflection and the new genre of the novel led to a new content for art, including a greater emphasis on psychology, which engendered new narrative techniques, such as free indirect discourse, in order to convey this new focus more adequately.

Technologies have always influenced modes of creation: one composes differently depending on whether one must memorize one's words, whether one can put them on paper, or whether one can continuously alter them, as with the advent of computers. A text written for computer can be altered effortlessly, whereas a text being prepared for the permanence of the book has a certain finality, which may also affect the writer's level of focus. Also, technology influences the lives of writers and their consciousness. The most common neuroses of a given age, such as hysteria and angst, affect the themes and forms of literature. Different psychological problems and neuroses surface in various ages, as the analyses of Freud and Heidegger, less universal and more historical than is usually assumed, suggest. One of the more distinguishing illnesses or disturbances of the current age is attention-deficit disorder (ADD), a condition of inattention or hyperactivity that may well be effected by intense sensory consumption, leading to a compressed experience of time and heightened sensory expectations (DeGrandpre). Sensory-addicted individuals may be drawn, in reception as well as production, to certain kinds of artworks, just as they are attracted to certain kinds of activities, those characterized by agitation more than contemplation, speed more than slowness.

Artists can also often be understood in the light of their biographical interaction with technology. Lichtenberg's knowledge of experimentation as the new paradigm of science, manifest in his lectures on experimental physics, is mirrored in his linguistic experiments, including his extensive and imaginative use of the subjunctive (Schöne, *Aufklärung*). The involvement of many German romantics, including Novalis, in the theory and practice of mining influenced many of their writings, including the development of plot, theme, and symbol (Ziolkowski, *German Romanticism* 18–63). In response to the early development of photographic images, which Heine criticized as lifeless (6/1.486 and 6/1.665), he and contemporaries like Theodor Mundt elevated, in theory as well as in practice, the ways in which literature could convey motion and the dynamism of life (e.g., *Madonna* 3–6 and 434 and "Bewegungsparteien"). Broch and Musil indirectly integrate into their experimental novels their knowledge of engineering, as they wrestle with the limits of technical knowledge and the need for myth.

Chekhov, Benn, and Döblin have the physician's eye for much of modern life, which is not without influence on their writing. With Benn, for example, we recognize both a methodological dissection of life and a thematic integration of the human body, especially in its decay, along with an innovative use of medical and scientific vocabulary and a continuing fascination with the relationship of mind and body. Not only one's age, occupation, and intellectual biography influence one's writing, but also one's sense of place (Lutwack). Production aesthetics attends to the environmental conditions of the author's work, where an author grew up, matured, and traveled, factors that are increasingly affected by technology's impact on mobility and our sense of place.

In "The Metropolis and Mental Life" Georg Simmel insightfully analyzes the ways in which modern metropolitan life affects consciousness. On the one hand, Simmel recognizes "the *intensification of emotional life* that springs from the swift and continuous exchange of external and internal stimuli" (325, translation modified). Simmel contrasts the pace and impressions of rural life with the overabundant and rapidly changing impressions of urban life, which, he argues, lead to differing valuations of the intellectual and emotional spheres. The city, driven by a market economy and impersonal relations, cultivates a more calculating mentality and a more matter-of-fact attitude toward persons and things, "an unrelenting sobriety" (326, translation modified). The sheer complexity of interwoven relations in a metropolis requires a calculating mind free of emotions: "Punctuality, calculability, and exactness, which are required by the complications and extensiveness of metropolitan life, not only stand in the most intimate connection with its monetary and intellectualistic character, they also color the content of life and promote the exclusion of those irrational, instinctive, sovereign human characteristics and impulses that seek to determine the form of life from within instead of receiving it from the outside in a general, schematically precise way" (328–29, translation modified). A dominant characteristic of such life is a leveling indifference to all things: "The resulting incapacity to react to new stimulations with the requisite amount of energy constitutes in fact that blasé attitude that every child of a large city evinces when compared with children of more peaceful and stable milieus. . . . The essence of the blasé attitude is an indifference toward the distinctions between things. Not in the sense that they are not perceived, as in the case of mental dullness, but rather that the meaning and value of the distinctions between things and thus of the things themselves, are experienced as meaningless. They appear to the blasé person in a homogeneous, flat, and gray tone with no one of them worthy of being preferred to another" (329–30, translation modified).

Uniqueness is not easily compatible with city life, whether in the subject, who must adapt to the calculating intellect and reserve demanded, or in the object, whose unique and incomparable value is not easily recognized in the large flow of impressions and the indifference they trigger. The individual need hardly act to participate in the immense dynamism of city life, but with this increase in impersonal activity, one's uniqueness is easily lost. On the other hand, Simmel recognizes in urban life, precisely because of its anonymity, a freedom from the expectations and prejudices often found in the more closed communities of rural life, which enhances diversity and uniqueness. In both instances, quantity affects quality and character (7.126).

Writers working in the large cities described by Simmel, or almost anywhere in the contemporary world, which has parallels to the early twentieth-century cities described by Simmel, especially in terms of the overabundance of unsolicited stimuli, wrestle with a cynical detachment from emotions and uniqueness, on the one hand, and the freedom of complete unrestraint, on the other. Stream-of-consciousness fiction is one result of this disassociation of sensibility. So, too, can we recognize against this backdrop a cynical streak and a coldness in much of modern art as well as the proliferation of unique styles, driven by the desire to be heard as different, if even at the price of substantial content. In addition, we recognize an increase in discontinuous images along with the related use of montage, which seeks to capture the overloading of heterogeneous impressions characteristic of urban life and increasingly of modern life in general.[3] Although the artwork, unlike the individual technological product, is not always functional and may be irritating or even shocking, its status as an inorganic collocation of parts mirrors the technological age as a whole.

Printing and photography as modes of production influencing aesthetics have received to date the most attention by critics interested in technology and production aesthetics, thanks to the pioneering work of Walter Benjamin. Benjamin points out that although reproduction in the form of copying the works of previous masters had always existed, also as a form of education, the technical reproduction of art is a modern phenomenon practiced with increasing intensity. Whereas previously each artwork was "unique" (218), woodcuts, the printing press, lithography, photography, film, and other forms create multiple products that are increasingly accessible. Photography, to take one example, renders obsolete the question of which is the original; the photograph can be mass produced and loses the uniqueness traditionally associated with painting. Further, the photograph allows us insights into reality that previously did not exist; it deepens our awareness of what is, capturing detail and speed that are invisible to the naked eye. On the one hand, art has always shown us a deeper reality; on the other hand, here it is accomplished via technology and in such a way that the mystery normally attached to great art is absent. In addition, the speed of their production and reproduction invites us to focus on the most current instead of the timeless. The traditional elevation of the original as most genuine and authoritative gives way to the value of modification: an enlarged photograph may be more valuable than the original insofar as it reveals more than the original; the recording of a concert may be more valuable than the original insofar as it extends its range.

This usurpation of the original and unique leads, according to Benjamin, "to a tremendous shattering of tradition" (221). Film, which appeals to the masses, is one of the most visible symbols of this shift from the unique aura of the single artwork to its reproducibility and common accessibility. In this way production affects the content of art (there is greater interest in finding topics that resonate with a broader and more contemporary audience), the form of art (as new forms become available), and the reception of art (art is no longer elevated as something beyond us: it is ever present, easily reproducible and accessible). The transformation of art and our perception of it has its corollaries, argues Benjamin, in the modern experience of human beings in close proximity to one another (the mass) and the theoretical elevation not of the unique and anecdotal but of statistics (16). This aesthetic transformation evolves over time: for example, the photography of human faces, photography as portraiture, especially in the form of the remembrance of persons deceased, still retains vestiges of aura.

The veiled elements of art transform into an open and public accessibility. As unique art dissolves, so, too, does its position within a ritual experience, whether magical or religious. Benjamin sees in this liquidation of tradition the revolutionary potential of technical art, including film. Art is now available for a wider audience and for political purposes: "But the instant the criterion of authenticity ceases to be applicable to artistic production, the total function of art is reversed. Instead of being based on ritual, it begins to be based on another practice—politics" (224). The "cult value" of art, driven by its inaccessibility and autonomy, is replaced by "exhibition value" (224), the simultaneous and collective reception of art. The almost magical aesthetic dimension gives way to political function, "politicizing art" (242), the words with which Benjamin ends his essay and a topic to which I return below.

New modes of perceiving and depicting reality emerge in tandem with the technical transformations Benjamin describes. Our relationship evolves, first, to reality; second, to the artwork; and third, to traditional standards of great art. With this third transformation come eventually a reformulation and dismantling of the traditional canon of great art. Within this context we recognize the reciprocal influence of art and technology and the erasure not only of aura but also of aesthetic standards and expectations, as in Marcel Duchamp's readymades, which consist of industrially manufactured objects that have been signed by the artist and placed in museums. The Dadaists presented a vision of art that was partly motivated by technology, presenting as art the objects of industrial production, a snow shovel, a urinal, a metal plumbing trap. The conceptual moment in art is elevated, which renders the first such art object genial but leaves the viewer with a sense of triviality on its repetition. Disenchantment with such art undoubtedly derives from the fact that the aesthetic dimension is displaced from the work itself to our perception of the work. Benjamin sees in Dada the "relentless destruction of aura" (238, translation modified), which is certainly true, though the further question arises of whether this destruction of aura represents the greatness of Dada or one of its weaknesses.

Experimentation also involves the mixture of artforms. The individual photograph lends itself to technical manipulation. John Heartfield's photomontages, for example, combine the realistic, documentary dimension of photography with caricature, inversion, and ironic captions. Digital photography allows artists to work with photographic images in so creative a fashion, by way of computer technology, that their work has almost as much in common with painting as it does with traditional photography. Also, the new genre of the photographic essay has emerged, along with the photographic autobiography (Rugg). When video dance replaces stage dance, the production context changes, as choreography is created specifically for the camera. New technologies elicit new artforms, as in the radio play, which flourished during the brief period when radio, but not television, was available in most homes, and of course film, which differs from literature in being a collective and collaborative effort.

Film diverges further in being more expensive to create and thus in need of resonance with its public. Whereas literature can afford to be timeless, film's economic imperative is to be timely. This imperative harbors both an advantage (film should be in a position to address the needs of the age) and a disadvantage (film can easily become mere entertainment, rather than art, and it can become time-bound rather than aspiring to a level of universality). Film is potentially more aesthetic than literature, as it plays more fully with space and time and appeals to more senses by integrating the shapes of architecture; the colors of painting; the sounds and tonality of music; the images of photography; and the staging, lighting, words, and performance of theater. Beyond this combination of effects, it has unique aspects, such as framing, camera angles, lenses, focus, color values, and editing. In the case of film, technology has a glorious effect on art; technology signals not the death of art but the creation of a new art form. An obvious advantage for the artist seeking to be creative in a new medium is the freedom from the burdens of tradition, which have sometimes hindered authors of literary works.

Beyond recognizing a legitimate link between artistic production and sensuous perception of reality, Benjamin suffers many errors in his analysis of modern art, as I elaborate below, but I would like to underscore and affirm his general insight into the connection between our view of production and of the value and function of art. Consider briefly the Bauhaus movement, which was revolutionary in several respects. First, in Germany the dominant tradition of the artist was as the lone genius, apart from society and often critical of it. Second, the most recent intellectual and aesthetic model in Germany previous to the Bauhaus, Expressionism, presented vague solutions to difficult problems and was for the most part defiantly critical of technology. The Bauhaus offered both a new concept of the artist and a new relationship to technology. The artist should offer concrete solutions, and technology should be used to solve problems. A parole of the Bauhaus movement was the unity of technology and art. Opposed to the otiose concept of art for art's sake, the Bauhaus sought a more holistic approach, with craftsmen and artists working together for a common goal. Concerned not only with the integration of the intellectual and material elements of art but also with art's economic aspects, the Bauhaus wanted to create products inexpensively, making them available to everyone. Not only should technology be useful for art, but art should reach a large number of people. Good art need not be rare, exclusive, elitist; it can be popular, inexpensive, practical. This new mode of production was intertwined with a new concept of the artwork, which favored the unity of form and function. Too international and too democratic for the National Socialists, it was pushed aside when a new Germanic aesthetic gained ascendancy.

Technology can be applied to generate not only visual but also literary art. Indeed, current technology has made possible moving type, such that we can create poems, whose words change size, font, or colors or even move and disappear on the screen, offering writers new options for creativity.[4] Theo Lutz has created lyric poetry via computer algorithms; the vocabulary on which he bases his computer-generated selections is taken from Kafka. Lutz's specific experiments are not of high quality, which is not surprising, since a computer could create an aesthetically great work only if the result were chance or if the computer were sufficiently developed so as to have a level of subjectivity we do not see in even the most advanced contemporary computers. Nonetheless, it would be a category mistake, the elevation of genesis over validity, to think that such poetry is not in principle capable of beauty on a level with the creations of the human mind. In any case the elevation of artwork over production aesthetics along with the elevation of validity over genesis does not preclude this possibility. The extraordinary value of computer-generated visual art should perhaps encourage us in this area, as another realm of possible confluence between art and technology.

A major reconfiguration of the literary text arises as a result of computer technology and the concept of the hypertext, which represents a distinctive union of art and computer science. A single hypertext, as intimated above, consists of individual blocks of text or nodes of information and the electronic links that join them, which offer the reader a variety of reading and viewing paths.[5] Hypertexts are possible as a result of virtual texts, consisting of information stored in electronic codes, instead of tactile texts comprised of marks on a physical surface. In a hypertext we find connections from one point in the text to other points as well as to other seemingly different texts that form a larger network. In this way we do not have a linear work; one's reading experience can move back and forth between marginal comments or secondary texts, which themselves may have further links and may be viewed as primary. The distinction between primary and secondary may be completely dissolved, leading to disorientation and the erasure of any sense of beginning or end as well as any hierarchy of meaning.

A text originally conceived and developed in the electronic medium, what Moulthrop calls a "native hypertext" ("Traveling" 60), tends to have a nonlinear character. We do not simply progress through the text. We take detours and may or may not return. In many cases one may circle back to certain passages without having read other passages. The possibility of hyperlinks would seem to elevate arbitrariness, discontinuity, and meandering. One may read hyperliterature as one reads the newspaper, but with even less sense of a whole: one starts here, wanders back, glances there, and so forth. The experience of the text is always customized in ways that the reading of a linear literary work is not, as the sequence of reading may differ dramatically from one reader to the next. However, the dissolution of organicism and hierarchy is not obligatory. One could have hyperlinks that are organically and systematically connected in subtle and intricate ways. In addition, one of the writing tools frequently used for hypertexts, Storyspace (Bolter et al.), permits writers to determine that one cannot move from link *a* to link *f* without also having read text *c,* which is viewed as a prerequisite for *f,* so a moment of linearity can be preserved. Finding the reason behind the links is, however, not always simple, and, indeed, a reason is not always present, especially when creators of native hypertexts are attracted to the medium precisely because of its capacity to dissolve hierarchy and order.

Hypertexts invite not only excursive thinking but also multiple voices and perspectives, which Mikhail Bakhtin had already noticed as a distinctive aspect of the novel. Certain artforms invite specific themes, messages, and ideas. Along with the written word, also graphics, data bases, digitized sound, animation, and video can be integrated into hypertexts or hypermedia, which raises the question of whether hypermedia expand or transcend the artform of literature. Hypertexts also seem more conducive to authorial collaboration, which is partly due to the lack of organic connection between parts, not always an advantage and certainly not an advantage in the artwork.

The multiplicity of hypertexts is the result of not only production but also reception. The choices a reader makes while reading will differ from another reader's choices or from the same reader's choices in a second reading, and the result will be a strikingly different text. Moreover, the reader is in many cases forced to struggle in seeking to decipher what can be a very confusing, because unordered, textual experience, and this variety, along with the emphasis on the reader's energy, renders the reader a cocreator of the work's meaning. In this sense the new technology reinforces the theoretical elevation of the reader. Many native hypertexts are demonstrations of these principles, for example, Michael Joyce's *afternoon,* Deena Larson's *Samplers,* or Stuart Moulthrop's *Victory Garden.*

Some hypertexts are not just read-only texts but also read-and-write texts, that is, a reader can read a text, comment on it, add new material, and attach links, and the resulting changes become part of the expanded text for others to see as well. We can call those hypertexts that allow readers to navigate through fixed bodies of connected material, however nonsequential and complex, "exploratory hypertexts" and those hypertexts that no longer have a distinct author, because they are open to constant revision by anyone who interacts with them, "constructive hypertexts" (Joyce 41–43 and 177–80). Constructive hypertexts tend to magnify the pattern of nonorganic writing, as either the reordering of the text, the addition of new material, or the layering of comments in response to other comments often appear arbitrary. *The Columns of Llacaan* [*Die Säulen von Llacaan*] is an example of a hypertext that has been developed through this interactive and collaborative method. Hypertexts, much like many other contemporary artforms, tend to eschew idealization. They give us the chaos and unexpectedness of life, which they tend to mimic, instead of portraying an alternative to the haphazardness of the everyday. However, constructive hypertexts do enhance collective authorship and in their collectivity and variability integrate certain characteristics of the oral tradition. In this sense we may recognize a moment of validity in McLuhan's suggestion that modern media recreate aspects of preprint culture.

The emphasis on form in modern art derives from several factors of production. First, technology gives us new forms, which invite experimentation, so, for example, new discoveries in film technology engender more special effects, and advances in computing and the greater capacity for hyperlinks generate more nonlinear writing as well as artforms that can be created and received only with the new medium of the computer. Second, a society driven by technology and very much under the weight of a tradition that is being ever better preserved because of technology leaves us with a sense of impuissance and derivativeness, such that artists turn more and more to formal innovation instead of substantive themes. At least in terms of novelty of form they can compete.

Third, each artform must, in order to vie successfully with newer media, focus on its own formal capabilities. A development toward the autonomy and isolation of the arts begins independently of the challenges of technology (Sedlmayr, *Verlust* 80–93). Already with J. M. W. Turner we see the diminution of the importance of lines, which are left to the province of sculpture, and with Paul Cézanne the elevation of color, which partly disappears from sculpture and architecture. Technology heightens the autonomy of the arts by creating new possibilities unique to each and fostering challenges that encourage each artform to develop its uniqueness. Architecture, for example, focuses on the new technologies that allow for novel architectural structures, and in many cases the ornamentation of sculpture and the color of painting are left behind. (Color is reintegrated into modern architecture most prominently through glass, which in its various shades makes a strong aesthetic impression.) Also, the increasing specialization and autonomy of spheres lead to works that no longer embody the classical triad of strength, utility, and beauty articulated by Vitruvius (*De architectura,* par. 1.3.2).

Because painting cannot compete with photography, it increasingly focuses on the autonomy of its form and is thereby indirectly influenced by technology, developing techniques unique to itself. Illusionist painting obscures what is unique about painting and is less than photography, so the next steps are, first, a turn toward greater subjectivity, as painting cannot compete with photography, which is in a sense both better at depicting the external world and limited by that external world, and second, a formalist emphasis that allows the painter to explore more fully color, shape, stroke, and texture. The nonrepresentational tendency mirrors another dominant tendency of modern art, self-reflection: in each we recognize that the means and the end are one and the same; in a surprising sense both of these revolutionary tendencies fulfill an aspect of the organic.

The development toward the singular capacities of a given form is not always immediate or smooth. In "The Salon of 1859," Baudelaire criticizes contemporaries who view art as "the exact reproduction of Nature" (152) and who contribute thereby to an impoverishment of the imagination and an erasure of personality in art. While photography should free painting from the tyranny of reproduction, it makes matters worse: "This industry, by invading the territories of art, has become art's most mortal enemy" (154). Photography heightens the painter's desire to become increasingly positivistic: "Each day art further diminishes its self-respect by bowing down before external reality; each day the painter becomes more and more given to painting not what he dreams but what he sees" (154).

Eventually Baudelaire's desire for painting that transcends reproduction is fulfilled, and painting becomes ever more an expression of possibilities, of imagination, of dreams. With the development of photography, literature too experiences a new freedom from the tyranny of reality and feels a greater impulsion toward experimentation with language and linguistic form, as is evident in the modern novel, experimental drama, and concrete poetry. Photography, meanwhile, which is not always viewed as sufficiently artistic, experiments with montage. In the technological age we recognize a renewed fascination with the materials of production often at the expense of a more traditional emphasis on content, which is reinforced by the openness of secular art and the emphasis on autonomy. The titles of paintings, for example, refer less and less to the object portrayed and more and more to the means of production, as, for example, with Piet Mondrian's *Composition with Red, Yellow, and Blue* (1935). The fascination with new modes of production, such as photography, invites a bracketing of moral questions. In Michelangelo Antonioni's masterful film about photography, *Blowup*, the artist's interest in a murder and a corpse is fully one of curiosity and aesthetics, not ethics, even if his art allows him to see what was otherwise veiled.

A process of healthy competition among artforms also affects theater, which tends to emphasize aspects of its particularity in the light of the development of cinema. Like cinema, theater integrates voice and music and the presence of bodies in space and time, but it also differs from cinema: theater is live and therefore unique each time a work is presented, it involves a reciprocal relationship with a collective audience that is also present and live, and it requires in many cases greater imagination on the part of the recipients (unlike film, which can be shot on location, theater almost always simulates its environment). Even as contemporary theater integrates sophisticated technologies, it often accentuates its difference from video and film per se. Not surprisingly, performance studies emerged as a full and separate discipline only after the challenge from cinema and other electronic media arose.

Much as hypertexts focus on aspects of form that differ from the book, such as hyperlinks, and much as painting has developed new resources in its competition with photography, so those forms of literature still available as books may begin to develop more fully what is unique about the book, including, for example, the ways in which it encourages readers to transcend a world of dispersion and focus on another realm, which is created and unified by a single voice; the ways in which it patiently and slowly cultivates a developing narrative and coherence to the lives portrayed; and the way its intrinsic complexity invites new meanings through rereading, even as its form and shape remain ever stable.

Even as the hypertext offers new options, the book will not become obsolete; it will increasingly develop capacities that enhance its distinctive nature and remind us that new artforms may lead less to supersession than to greater variety.

What the Frankfurt School calls the "culture industry" is an aspect of modern society that furthers the role of instrumental reason and its impact on culture, including the production of artworks: the term *culture industry* refers to the commodification and standardization of culture through the entertainment industry. Within the culture industry, the value of a work in production is measured by its capacity for consumption, not its artistic excellence. The appeal to the consumer includes elements of individuality—the association of a film or product with a star—but on the whole the product is standardized. The commodification of art, along with the obsolescence of the patronage model of artistic production, does indeed make it more difficult for artistic culture to have autonomy and critical potential. When art is reduced to the utility of the market, its traditional identity as purposeless is inverted, and intrinsic value gives way to exchange value. However, as I have suggested above, popular culture and high culture are not necessarily in tension with one another. Popular culture is a quantitative term; high culture is a qualitative term. To argue that an artwork which is successful on the market necessarily deviates from whatever standards one might have for high art, deadening the imagination or critical consciousness, is to draw false conclusions in the sphere of artwork aesthetics based on an overvaluation of production and reception and of oneself as critic vis-à-vis the majority.[6]

The media are becoming increasingly global and increasingly pluralistic owing to major changes in the industry, including cable and especially satellite technology. While mergers and consolidation tend to make mass communication more homogeneous, increasing diversification and variety represent an equally strong countertrend, as even larger companies create diverse products in order to reach niche markets. Segmentation and customization are the results. Castells revises McLuhan: "While the media have become indeed globally interconnected, and programs and messages circulate in the global network, *we are not living in a global village, but in customized cottages globally produced and locally distributed*" (1.341). Whether or not the dominant producers will, because of advertising and promotion of their products, increasingly silence the reception of alternative productions remains an open question however. In any case we shall need to attend to the hidden wisdom of the market and of the public, where needs are met by certain artworks and not by others, and to the conscious recommendations of critics, who can educate the public toward certain aesthetic and hermeneutic values and draw our attention to needs that may be overlooked and the merits of artworks that may otherwise not be recognized.

I have pointed above toward some of the ways in which contemporary art is ironically mimetic of the age. Gehlen has shown in his study of modern painting that modern art is influenced by, and in some respects mirrors, the dominance of technology. We see this especially well in abstract art: the release from tradition, the autonomy of means, the importance of experimentation, the elevation of process, the extension of limits, the concern with effects, and of course the moral neutrality of such art are characteristics that, Gehlen argues, mirror technology (16, 189–201). What appears to be revolutionary is indeed revolutionary vis-à-vis tradition, but it is not necessarily revolutionary vis-à-vis the driving forces of the age. Art may mirror technology more than appears to be the case at first glance, a topic we can explore more fully in the context of art's content and form.

ARTWORK AESTHETICS

The original meaning of *techne* encompasses also rhetoric. Not surprisingly, the craft of art often mirrors technological motifs. Modernity's loss of overarching connections is expressed stylistically, for example, in the parataxis and serial style (*Reihungsstil*) of early Expressionist poetry, with its abundance of unconnected and random images, as is evident, for example, in Jakob van Hoddis's "The End of the World" and Alfred Lichtenstein's "Twilight."[7] Certain contemporary poets take this experience of discontinuity to a more radical level. Rolf Dieter Brinkmann creates in his poem "Westward" horizontal and vertical gaps in the presentation of words, so as to form large areas of empty space. These stylistic disjunctures seek to convey the speed and fragmentation of impressions in the technological age. Ironically, the compression of space and time leaves gaps of meaning.

In addressing technology thematically in his play *Gas*, Georg Kaiser also uses language to mirror technological structures and themes: for example, the designation of characters not by individual names but by their previous roles or professions; the single thoughts or sentences that are completed collectively by different persons in sequence, thereby underscoring each person's lack of individuality (35 and 36); the stylized blocking and mechanical repetition of speech patterns in act 4, which mirror in their rhythmic patterns the idea of a machine and which embody both the lack of wholeness in the persons described, who are reduced to the limbs they utilized—a hand, two eyes, and a foot, respectively—and the speakers' own self-destructive lack of vision in wanting simply a scapegoat as a solution (39–42); and the simple repetition of persons who react to a crisis and a challenge by merely reaffirming their roles (45).

Different period styles and diverse historical shifts in form also often mirror a particular relation to technology; paradigmatic in Germany would be Expressionism and New Matter-of-Factness [*Neue Sachlichkeit*]. Or to look at European literature more broadly, we recognize in naturalism the integration of a more scientific perspective on life. Émile Zola approaches his characters with "scientific curiosity" (15). He writes in his preface to *Thérèse Raquin*: "I simply applied to two living bodies the analytical method that surgeons apply to corpses" (14). In his essay *The Experimental Novel* he writes that "the experimental novel is a consequence of the scientific evolution of the century" (23). In such a novel one shows "by experiment in what way a passion acts in a certain social condition" (25). Whereas for Zola and his German admirer Wilhelm Bölsche, who describes the poet as "in his own way an experimentalist, like the chemist" (7), the conflation of poetry and science drives the content and characters of a work, many later authors employ the analogy with science to describe experiments with form (Schwerte). In such experimentation we recognize a revival of the ancient idea that art works with possibilities. For such authors, including Dürrenmatt, such experiments are most meaningful when the results are unpredictable (7.91). No less than scientific experiments, literary experiments help us to understand the world in its increasing complexity.

In tandem with the transformation from print culture to electronic culture, new literary styles gain prominence, so, for example, the nonlinearity of James Joyce and Ezra Pound, even when, as with Joyce, the sources are various and transcend electronic culture. As McLuhan argues, the messages of such works are conveyed by the media themselves. Even montage is partly inspired by the idea of assembly-line technology and needs to be seen as part of this wider frame. Other artists integrate technology by bringing the vocabulary of technology directly into their art, including poetry, as we see, for example, with Gottfried Benn and Volker Braun. As technology gives us new choices, artists attend more fully to the mode of production, so, for example, Stéphane Mallarmé and Stefan George, who view type as essential to the intention, meaning, and impact of their poems. Formalism is driven not only by technical opportunities but also by the disappearance of an overarching worldview. Thus, already in the third century BCE we see a forerunner of concrete poetry. *Technopaegnia* is the modern name for poems whose shapes, via a variety of meters and varying lengths, portray the subjects of the poems. Five such figurative poems have survived: from Simmias of Rhodes, who is credited with inventing the form, we have poems shaped as an ax, a pair of wings, and an egg. Spuriously attributed to Theocritus is one in the shape of a shepherd's pipe, and one in the form of an altar is by Dosiadas of Crete. Such poetry can emerge of course only after poems are created primarily to be read, not heard. Technopaegnia surfaces sporadically in later eras, as, for example, in George Herbert's seventeenth-century poems "The Altar" (23) and "Easter Wings" (40–41) or in the concrete poetry of the modern era.

The sense of quickly shifting paradigms and of disorientation during the technological age is conveyed in modern narratives by rapid shifts in viewpoint, which contrast, for example, with Stifter's attempts to hold on to stability by slowing down narrative progression, as in *Indian Summer,* with its technique of digressing and circling back to the same. So, too, in drama, do we see the ever greater dissolution of the three unities, to the point of the dissolution of the unity of part and whole and of the idea of any coherent meaning, as art reflects the rapid changes of the age and its ever present motion and disorientation. In some cases the formal mirroring of a technological capacity in literature indirectly thematizes the impact of technology on the life portrayed. For example, the use of a specific frame or horizon, of precision and detail, and of darkness and light independently of color, as was commonly associated with photography, is employed in the opening pages of Fontane's *Effi Briest* to convey, through formal association and foreshadowing, a connection to the norms of the technological age, that is, the ways in which these norms will affect Effi's life (Koppen 68–70). In Theodor Storm's *The White Horse Rider* the central conflict arises from the changes brought by technology and its primary representative into a community whose values, whatever limits they may have, are nonetheless not fully respected, and this historical transition is mirrored, textually, in the structure of a frame narrative that moves from oral tradition to written text. Also pronounced in the technological age is the focus on the integration of the patterns and rhythms of nature into literary forms, as in Northrop Frye's *Anatomy of Criticism,* which describes the ways in which literature draws on the mythic associations of the seasons, calling attention, for example, to the importance of spring and renewal for the structure of comedy (163–86)

The greatness of the futurist movement lay in recognizing that transformations in communication and travel affected the modern psyche and that these transformations called for formal changes in art. Marinetti's futuristic manifestos recognize that the world is a disjointed array of information and events, brought to life by newspapers, cinema, telephones, airplanes, phonographs. Such a world calls for new forms, above all, collage. Adjectives and adverbs must disappear, so, too, personal pronouns, finite verbs, and most punctuation. The well-formed Latin sentence is abandoned and replaced by a kind of telegram style, again evocative of technical advances and the speed they represent. Such a style involves the frequent use of infinitives, compound nouns, phonetic spelling, and onomatopoeia, which convey the continuity and rush of life, to be accented by a variety of typographical formats, which allow for emphasis. An example is Marinetti's *Zang Tumb Tuuum,* an account of the Bulgarians' siege of Adrianopolis in the Balkan war, which Marinetti witnessed during his activity as a war reporter in 1912. In Germany the most striking examples occur in the poems of August Stramm, as in "Patrol": "The stones feud / Window grins betrayal / Branches choke / Mountainous bushes rustling flake off / Shriek / Death" (70). The telegram style and collage technique convey fragmentation and depersonalization. Philosophical subordination and individuality tend to disappear in art of this kind, which by way of an imaginative form of mimesis nonetheless seeks a new kind of totality.

The connections between form and function are also visible in the more technically advanced arts. The special effects of cinema depend on continuing advances in technology. The technical capacity of film—camera work and editing, for example—creates an illusion that is able to hide in its presentation the traces of that illusion. Less obvious, film's rapid-fire movement, which—with its action, montage, moving camera, and full scenes—rarely permits quiet contemplation and thus unnerved early viewers more accustomed to literature, mirrors the rapid pace and overfull associations of everyday life, a point that has become truer since Benjamin initially noticed the connection (39). Walter Ruttmann's *Berlin: Symphony of a Great City* employs very rapid cuts to convey the energy of the big city in ways that challenge, if they do not transcend, the capacity of literature to convey the dynamism of modern life.

Genre, too, is related to technology, as is clear from the impact of modern subjectivity on the development of comedy, the popularity of the Western during the American era of conquest, and the disappearance of speculative art from eras of cynicism and despair. In the case of comedy, we recognize the dissolution of the hero who could change the world more easily than in the modern era of rationalization and bureaucracy; Cervantes's *Don Quixote* is a paradigmatic example. Dürrenmatt goes so far as to argue that the web of causality is so complex in the modern world, its signs so impenetrable, that no one person can influence or change it, as was the case in ages past. For Dürrenmatt this impotence means the dissolution of responsibility, guilt, and tragedy (24.62). In comedy we likewise recognize the increasing overvaluation of the self and its private identity, which the comic artist tends to mock. In addition, we recognize, with Henri Bergson, a number of modern comedies that ridicule society's reduction of the self to mechanistic processes (for Bergson laughter is elicited when something vital is reduced to something mechanical), as in Chaplin's *Modern Times*. In this film's elevation of the mechanical as an autonomous structure, we observe the loss of the organic and thus the sacrifice of vital and human elements.

The epistolary novel, to take a more particular example, diminishes in importance with the emergence of newer technologies that make letter writing a less central dimension of culture. (In a hypertext like Carolyn Guyer's *Quibbling* we read instead embedded e-mail messages.) The great philosophical novels of Mann, Musil, and Broch, with their essayistic elements, can be seen as attempts on the part of literature to respond to the challenges of the age, which required a new kind of poetics, of a more cerebral nature, and to offer literary experiments that could be seen as aesthetic equivalents of the modern scientific culture of experiment. We recognize in these works the heroic effort to try to master the quantity of forces at work in modernity by extending artworks beyond traditional forms and a reasonable measure. Even if we may recognize certain weaknesses in such works, we can but admire an elevation of quantity that is driven by the search for quality and comprehension.

With its experimental and material dimensions, concrete poetry might also be seen as reflective of the technological age, even if it has its precursors in earlier ages. Not surprising, Eugen Gomringer consciously speaks of "poetic technique" (19). In his poems the visual placement of words is essential for their meaning. Consider, for example, ideograms, visual texts whereby a concept is given a corresponding visual shape, such that signifier and signified are brought together, so, for example, in one poem the letters constituting the word *wind* themselves form a "windrose" or compass rose (119). In his constellations, named after constellations of stars, the semantic relations of words are defined not by grammar or syntax but solely by physical or spatial relations, as when he writes:

tree
tree child (120).

Brecht's idea of a "theater of the scientific age" (186), which is designed not primarily for pleasure or amusement but as a tool for reflection and an instrument for progress, is likewise related to the technical spirit of the age. In Brecht's eyes a theater appropriate to modernity should be skeptical and critical of the status quo, directed to the audience's rational faculties, and evocative of the possibilities for transforming society. Such a theater integrates contemporary models of science and productivity. Also linked with the modern scientific paradigm, though in different ways, is Dürrenmatt's idea that theater can be a "thought experiment," in which the author creates an alternative to reality, which nonetheless sheds light on reality (27.91).

Technology influences the content of art as well. New topics arise and are integrated as major or minor themes. Many of these involve technology in its broadest dimensions: technology as the embodiment of speed, power, and intensity and as a catalyst of apocalyptic visions, a development strongly sparked by Expressionism and futurism; the complexities and ambiguities of the doctrine of progress, which are central to the theme of displacement in the modern novel; the transference of a religious vocabulary from its original sphere to the realms of technology, production, and urban life, as in the poetry of Georg Heym; technology as the spirit of change, in its positive and negative aspects, a topic that is especially well articulated in the Weimar era and throughout the ages in the genre of big-city poetry (Riha), which thematizes the ambivalence of the metropolis, as both dynamic and chaotic, and in broader novels of the modern era; the embrace of the vital in response to technology as the merely mechanical, which is evident in modern comedy as well as in selected modern poems; the passion of invention, both technical and poetic, which can also, however, be reckless in its disregard for what is, a topic that makes its way into many artworks that thematize, self-reflectively, the limits of poiesis; an increase in literature that integrates the world of the industrial worker, ranging from mines, as in Max von der Grün, to industrial processing, as in Günter Wallraff; the encounters with new machines and objects, from the most massive to the most mundane, which greatly affect our relations to objects and to one another; an increasing sense of angst in modern narratives that is partly related to the wide-ranging effects of technical change; shifts in our sense of identity, as we become less members of an organic community and more part of an anonymous mass, a topic addressed in the Weimar works of such authors as Kaiser and Ernst Toller and reinforced by Heidegger's concept of "the they"; the tension between advances in science and engineering and the loss of orientation in ethics, which has inspired works by Dürrenmatt and Kipphardt, among others, and the related theme of the new responsibilities of the scientist in an age where technology not only transforms, but may also destroy, humanity;[8] and our changing conceptions of perception, altered by new ways of seeing and more mediated ways of relating to the world, a topic that has been prominent above all in modern Austrian literature.

Many works wrestle with specific topics that gain greater relevance with advances in science and technology: the concern with our increasing dependence on machines, as in Samuel Butler's *Erewhon;* the automaton theme, which so haunts humanity, both because it ironically threatens our control of the world and because it appears to make us superfluous, a topic that already informs some of E. T. A. Hoffmann's stories; the geographical (and cultural) tensions between country and city, which develop an ancient topos in new ways; the interest in voluntary simplicity, as with Thoreau, which contrasts with the restlessness of the modern world; the influence of the machine on the psyche and the ways in which, perhaps as a result of our machine-driven world, the human being may act like a machine, a topic that already interested Georg Büchner in *Leonce and Lena* and that gains greater prominence in modern works of literature and film, including Fritz Lang's *Metropolis*; technology's invasion of nature, which may represent not only an aesthetic rupture but also a transformation of the sacred, as, for example, in Nikolaus Lenau's "To Spring 1838"; changing concepts of the sea—from its mysterious vastness to its fragile ecology—in the light of evolving environmental issues; the destructive effects of industrial pollution, a topic explored already by Wilhelm Raabe in his narrative of 1884, *Pfister's Mill,* which stands out as exceptional in its day, though the topic is now prominent, as, for example, in many modern American narratives, including John Cheever's final novella, *Oh What a Paradise It Seems*; the railroad and the automobile as symbols of the technological age, which animate any number of works by writers as diverse as Fontane, Hauptmann, Kästner, and Brecht; the displacement of the worker in the light of new technologies, which informs many socialist-oriented works of the modern era, but whose relevance continues into the present; and the often unexplored tensions between seemingly traditional lives and the effects of technology on those lives, as in Don DeLillo's *White Noise* and Douglas Coupland's *Generation X: Tales for an Accelerated Culture.*[9]

In addition, technology gives rise to a contrasting interest in Eden and Arcadia, wilderness and the frontier. We also recognize, perhaps as a result of the tensions between nature and technical development, extraordinary use of landscape as evocative of human character, as in the writings of Thomas Hardy and Willa Cather. Even in ancient Greece the emergence of landscape as central to the aesthetic location and effect of the temple does not emerge until the third century BCE, only after the cosmic order gives way to a stronger sense of individuality, and a developed urban life and a more reflective consciousness evoke a longing for Arcadia (Gruben 401–2, 414–18). Today's increasingly urban culture also elicits a longing for an encounter with what transcends the continuing domestication of nature. In *Arctic Dreams,* for example, Barry Lopez educates his readers about animals in such a way as to cultivate a sense of wonder and enchantment, if also an appropriate sense of distance.

Inventions and modern developments affect the themes and forms of literature: the extraordinary multiplication of goods and their impact on our sense of self, which was already recognized by the French moralists and which is thematized so well in Stifter's *Vienna and the Viennese,* but which comes to full life only in the twentieth century; the effects of mobility on family and generational relations, which is a subordinate theme in many modern dramas and narratives; technical warfare, which so drives the novels of the lost generation of World War I; the emergence of new professions, such as photographer, that are thematized in works of literature and often have symbolic significance, as in Henrik Ibsen's *The Wild Duck* or Sternheim's *The Strongbox*; the demands that new media place on our attention and time, which have reinforced the tendency toward collage and chaotic structures in modern art and drama; the symbolism of new technologies, such as hidden listening devices, and the transitions from religion to technology and from God to power, as in Miller's *The Archbishop's Ceiling*; the new objects that affect the way we conduct our lives, for example, television, which is increasingly thematized in modern cinema and to a lesser extent in literature; the different relationships to procreation and birth, which, if often for noble reasons, nonetheless become increasingly technical and artificial; the prolongation of natural life, which, though likewise a blessing, nonetheless means that dying and death now take place more frequently in hospitals than at home; and the ways in which telecommunications and advances in travel affect human relationships and our sense of space.

Also driven by the technological age is the thematization of various social and institutional aspects of the age: the effects of specialization on the human psyche and the organization of society, which are recognized by Schiller and Hölderlin already at the end of the eighteenth century; the nineteenth-century tensions between the emerging industrialists and the weakening aristocracy, as in Karl Immermann's *The Epigones*; the entrepreneurs of industry and finance, who play roles in broader novels of the modern age, by authors ranging from Heinrich Mann to Hermann Broch; our being uprooted from tradition and our reflection on a fragmented self no longer embedded in the cosmos, a related theme of identity crisis that is well explored by Kafka, among others; the regimentation of time in modern society and the ways in which the spinning pace of modernity affects the human psyche, evident, for example, in Rilke's *The Notebooks of Malte Laurids Brigge*; the diverse uses of leisure time, especially in an age that appears to be saturated by material well-being and by possibilities for entertainment, which are increasingly recognizable in the modern novel and in modern drama; futuristic dystopias and utopias, from Yevgeny Zamyatin to Ernest Callenbach, defined by threats from technology and potential advances in technology; the specter of nuclear war, which has motivated any number of works in the second half of the twentieth century; and the fear of nuclear waste, which propelled Christa Wolf to write *Accident*. All these topics have become new material for aesthetic reflection.

The technological transformation of our society continues to elicit new issues that will find their way into artworks still on the horizon. In some cases these issues already form aspects of works whose main focus is not technology: new patterns of consumption and the movement from an economy of need to one of acquisition, along with the temptations these patterns elicit, not only for oneself but also on behalf of one's generosity toward others; shifts and complexities in family relations, as children often have more knowledge than parents about new technologies; the ways in which modernization introduces new conflicts into traditional societies, especially in developing countries; the tensions between an increasingly global media and the human need for a sense of place; or the ways in which cyberrelationships affect our identities, including role-playing, which is prominent in anonymous relationships, and the production and reception of online messages, which have their own complex norms, expectations, and effects.[10] Also, the emerging possibility of genetic alteration or germline engineering offers a new theme for literature: its effect on human identity, on our sense of mystery and challenge, and on our idea of human dignity; the extent to which continuing improvements in gene selection would render each past generation, and thus the older persons in our midst, comparatively less effective; and the extent to which gene selection would accentuate over time the gulf between the richer and the poorer. Germline engineering combined with technological innovations, including nanotechnology and cybernetics, also raises the question of the posthuman, with its severing of ties to the previous conditions of humanity, including the elimination of a chain of ancestry, the diminishing of chance and of human frailty, and even the potential eradication of death, a condition that would alter every sense of human meaning.

Especially interesting are the ways in which technology affects thinking about art within artworks, by way of an influence on form or theme or both, for example, the changing roles of author and reader in an age of increased production and mass distribution; the concept of serial production in relationship to the idea of the unique artwork; the tension between rapid changes in technology and the ways in which art adheres to tradition or is dissolved from tradition, thematically and formally; the similarities and differences between the artist and the engineer as inventors; the role of the poetic in an increasingly instrumental world; the emergence of hermetic literature as a response to mass culture, a mode of art elevated by Adorno. Very prominent in the technological age have been the introduction of film techniques, such as montage and jump cuts, in literature and the role of film in engendering stream-of-consciousness narratives. Alfred Döblin openly called for a "cinema style" (121), in which quickness and dynamism would dominate.

Independently of new themes and forms, a shift occurs in valuation. Whereas in classical art stillness is elevated, in much of modernity, as with Döblin, motion is embraced. This transformation begins with the romantics and is given strong articulation in the discussion of art in Büchner's *Lenz.* The futurists, preoccupied with technology, contributed to this development as well through their elevation of energy and "the beauty of speed" (Marinetti 41). The beloved machine embodied for them dynamism and vitalism; speed is the topic of several futurist paintings in the early decades of the twentieth century, for example, by Giacomo Balla ("Velocità d'automobile," 1912; "Plasticità di luci + velocità," 1912/13; "Velocità d'automobile + luci + rumori," 1913) as well as by Luigi Russolo ("Dinamismo di un'automobile," 1912/13) and Gerardo Dottori ("Velocità (Tre tempi)," 1925). The quick transformations of life are also mirrored formally, as, for example, in the notion of art as a happening, which not only permits art to be in complete flux but dissolves the difference between art and life. In antiquity, the focus was on what was permanent and constant; in modernity, especially with the technological transformation of the world, our attention shifts to what changes and what can yet be changed. Modern life has more distractions, more images, more stimuli and competing impressions—as a result of the busyness created by technology—traffic, radio, advertising, television. Much of modern art either mimics this busyness or competes with it on its own terms—with more dramatic repetition, sensationalist images, or special effects.

True to the modern elevation of self-reflection, we see not only the influence of technology on art, both literal and thematic, but also the integration into art of the question of what the role of art is in a technological age, thus, the potential influence of art on technology. We even find works that synthesize both, reflecting on the influence of technology on art and on the potential role of art in the technological age. Such works as Storm's *The White Horse Rider,* Benn's "Lost I," and Tornatore's *Cinema Paradiso* come to mind.

Finally, hypertexts, the most recent technical development in literature, often abandon structures prominent in traditional works. For example, instead of having a beginning, a hypertext narrative normally has several options at the outset, such that the reader can embark on different routes. And a hypertext rarely ends, except insofar as it has been read or reread to the point where the reader loses interest. This new technology affects basic issues of structure and form and may lend itself to theories that are especially complex or that elevate the role of contingency. Not by chance do hypertexts become technically possible at the very time that society itself is increasingly defined by networks of associations. Castells writes: "Networks constitute the new social morphology of our societies, and the diffusion of networking logic substantially modifies the operation and outcomes in processes of production, experience, power, and culture. . . . The topology defined by networks determines that the distance (or intensity and frequence of interaction) between two points (or social positions) is shorter (or more frequent, or more intense) if both points are nodes in a network than if they do not belong to the same network" (1.469–70).[11] Our connection to points in a network is determined less by the traditional constraints of space and time and increasingly by associations mediated by technology. In this sense, the hypertext mirrors the network society, offering great potential for mimesis. In contrast, the traditional literary work may offer a greater resource for resistance.

RECEPTION AESTHETICS

Technology also influences reception. The most obvious example is the shift from an intensive reading experience, where people read and reread a very small number of works, to a more extensive reading experience, driven by the quantity of works made possible by the printing press and improvements in its technology from the eighteenth century onward. What occurred at this time prefigured our increasing sense today that the idea of a heritage of a small number of canonical works, and the accompanying sense of coherence and common discourse, has passed over into ever more diverse reading experiences and reference points even for persons of similar intellectual backgrounds. The lower costs of printing, which allow for a higher number of literary works, influence not only production but also reception; the number and quality of works available affect reading habits. Whereas in 1948, when *Books in Print* first appeared, only 85,000 books from 357 publishers were recorded in the United States, by 2000 more than 66,000 different publishers listed more than 1.6 million works (1.vii–viii). In addition, research suggests that television has led to a decline in reading, which affects recipients in various ways: reading, in contrast to television viewing, better stimulates creativity and fantasy, facilitates greater linguistic mastery, and grants more time for reflection (Van der Voort).

Other obvious examples of a reception altered by technology include the way we react to video in a private setting and on a small screen vis-à-vis film in a common room and projected onto a large screen; the way fax machines allow poetry to be transmitted through an authoritarian state and so permit a briefer genre to reach more readers and affect the political scene; and technically advanced performance spaces in the theater, which influence both performance and interpretation. Our ability to receive a literary work on the computer and to play with the text, as a hypertext or an unfinished work, also creates for us a new relationship to the artwork. In addition, emotions play differing roles in diverse eras, including the era of technology. McLuhan has argued that certain artforms influence consciousness and behavior, so, for example, his claim that film, by way of its immediate evocation of dreams, offered poor persons the magical commodity of identifying with the roles of the rich and powerful and that the press photograph, by way of its documentary nature and resulting public revulsion, discouraged the wealthy from unduly conspicuous consumption (*Understanding Media* 200–01 and 291). Paradoxically, the public's acceptance of the fantasy world of film allowed the entertainment industry to engage in conspicuous consumption in ways that seemed to the public more dreamlike than revolting.

One of the most interesting contemporary reflections on reception aesthetics in the technological age stems not from a literary critic but from a composer, Benjamin Britten. In his Aspen Award Speech of 1964, Britten argues in favor of art that is not primarily intended for prosperity but instead fulfills the particular needs of an age and is directed to a specific audience. In turn, he is especially attentive to the ways in which the initial reception contexts of earlier creative efforts are now past. To hear Bach's *St. Matthew Passion* "on one day of the year only—the day which in the Christian church was the culmination of the year, to which the year's worship was leading" was a remarkably different experience, for example (17). Bach's work was "performed on Good Friday in a church, to a congregation of Christians" (19). This context gave the work an unmistakably significant and distinct reception. As Britten notes, today as a result of technology "this unique work, at the turn of a switch, is at the mercy of any loud roomful of cocktail drinkers—to be listened to or switched off at will, without ceremony or occasion" (17). Hearing such a work in church after fasting through Lent versus hearing it as background music while shaving or entertaining or reading the newspaper represents one of the disadvantages and trivializations of aesthetic reception in the technological age. If questions of suitability and comprehensibility are not addressed, the aesthetic experience is diluted and deluding. Britten continues: "Music demands more from a listener than simply the possession of a tape-machine or a transistor radio. It demands some preparation, some effort, a journey to a special place, saving up for a ticket, some homework on the programme perhaps, some clarification of the ears and sharpening of the instincts. It demands as much effort on the listener's part as the other two corners of the triangle, this holy triangle of composer, performer and listener" (21).

Books on tape also create a different reception context and can influence our reading in several ways. Whereas video now permits, or even encourages, the private reception of film, books on tape seem to encourage a more collective reception of literature. Reading aloud has for the most part disappeared from our culture; a major exception is reading aloud to children. Books on tape, with tone and emphasis transparent in the oral delivery, may lead to a revival of such collective reading experiences, and with them a more communal reception of art and more discussion of literature in smaller circles. We recognized this briefly during the era of the radio, which permitted a broader and more communal reception of literature. Books on tape certainly represent an advantage for the reception of literary works that have a distinctly oral character, such as Storm's *The White Horse Rider.* Since the mid-twentieth century some authors have read their works or parts of their works in recordings. Hearing these can affect not only the recipient's emotional relationship to the work but also the interpretation in cases where moments of irony, perhaps not immediately visible, become more present. Authorial comments have always played a role in the reception process, and readings have been possible without modern technology, but a recording preserves the author's reading for recipients of later generations.

But there are also disadvantages to books on tape, especially as their most widespread use seems to be in automobiles. When hearing a novel, we may find it difficult to tailor the reading to our personal processing of the work. Instead, the work moves forward at a speed defined by the speaker and not at the pace required by our reflections on the work and the moods and thoughts it may evoke. Listening at someone else's pace requires great concentration, something that is generally unavailable when one is driving. The result is a weaker reception of the inexhaustible meaning of the work and a greater tendency to choose works that are more eventful and entertaining and less symbolically resonant or intellectually demanding. Still worse is the tendency to release works in abridged form, which may seem more appropriate for the medium, but which removes much of the nuance, structure, and meaning of the original. Döblin has cogently argued that while essays and lyric poetry lend themselves fairly well to spoken reception, radio broadcasts (and one might add tape versions) of novels are less successful (251–61). Döblin alludes first to the length of such works: "Breadth, expanse, and flow are essential to novels and epic works. For this breadth, expanse, and flow we have available the eyes, which glide over the pages and render it possible for things to happen within a few hours, for which an eventual listener would need many days, if the listener could stand it at all" (258). Whereas the flexibility of the eyes grasp the tension of a work better than the even pace of a recorded voice, Döblin also notes that the spoken word may restrict the recipient's fantasy and imagination: "The actual place of a novel is undeniably the imagination, the spiritual and sensuous fantasizing along, and to this end reading guides us infinitely better; the concentration is deeper, the distractions fewer, the necessary self-hypnosis, which evolves under the direction of the novelist, ensues more easily" (259).

The emergence of television and film has affected the reception of literature in several ways. Most obvious are the film versions of various works of classical and modern literature. The film may interpret and rework the literary work in its own medium, which both honors and develops the original. Often sales of the original will increase as a result of the film, and we recognize the interesting occurrence that our initial reading of the book may be filtered through a film adaptation, although for some recipients the film will substitute for the novel, which remains unread. Nonetheless, film offers a breadth of reception that is rarely achieved by works that must otherwise be read or performed in the theater. Because contemporary authors earn considerable amounts from widely received and successful film versions of literary works, authors increasingly write novels that lend themselves to screenplay adaptations. As a result, one notes a certain length as well as greater emphasis on dialogue, scene, and perspective. In such cases reception influences production and artwork aesthetics. In unusual cases a film, developed from an original screenplay, even gives rise to a novel based on the film.

As we have already seen, to distinguish issues of production and reception is difficult when the creation of new media is concerned. The Internet, for example, allows artists to create texts and place them on a home page for anyone's viewing. This has two advantages: first, everyone has access to the publication; and second, placing texts on the Web is ecologically desirable, as less paper is needed. However, it is harmful insofar as without any editing process or peer review, we again suffer an inflation of information. With an increase in organs of publication and a dissolution of aesthetic evaluation, we encounter more art of lesser quality. At the same time, unedited artistic products may not be easily located on the Web, which has the advantage of diminishing an overabundance of information and the disadvantage of making new art accessible to only a fragmentary audience (cf. Barabási 56–58, 85–86, and 174). The new mode of dissemination makes reception both easier and more difficult.

Literary creations for the Web are more often than not condensed, which derives from elements of reception that influence production. First, most of us are not yet accustomed to reading longer texts on the screen. Second, the Internet is increasingly characterized by imagery, and so we are tempted to roam about from one delightful page to the next, without stopping to read a longer piece of prose. Third, we may be paying per minute for the privilege of browsing; again, this would dissuade many from lingering with a longer prose work, especially if they are not familiar with downloading a text from the Web to their hard drives, thereby discouraging the creation and reception of longer works via the Web. Whether this tendency toward condensation means a greater economy of language or simply a reduction of depth would need to be judged in individual cases, but both possibilities arise. Certainly the elevation of shorter texts and the emphasis on electronic links have the potential to override the importance of the novel, which tends to be slow and durable and requires reflection and imagination. It defers meaning instead of conveying it immediately and encourages contemplation instead of instant gratification.

The inverse occurs with certain hypertexts, whose inexhaustible nature is defined purely quantitatively. Links multiply and crisscross and extend indefinitely. While such links may capture one moment of literature, its inexhaustible meaning, they may do so in a way unrelated to quality. Creating a text that is finite and in its reception inexhaustible at one and the same time is a more challenging task than producing a text that is inexhaustible simply by recourse to technology's capacity for extension. While hypertexts are in some cases long and involved, they tend to have brief individual pages. This mirrors what was said above about literary works on the Web and may derive from the view that readers would not be inclined to read longer texts on any one screen. The result to date seems to be greater effort at lyricism and less evidence of the kind of philosophical prose that characterized many great modernist works of fiction. A concentration on links and other technical facets of the hypertext medium may also detract from more traditional elements of style.

Although hypertexts are often praised for the ways in which they involve the reader, this shift toward the reader may also mean a lack of vision on the part of the author. Traditional books normally aspired to embody coherence and unity, to convey a vision or sense of a world. The reader does not simply receive this vision but works to decipher it and understand it in its otherness. When the reader of a hypertext assumes the author's role, the encounter with another person's grand vision, the experience of a coherent whole, unveiled in often unsuspecting ways, may disappear, which is not necessarily to the reader's advantage. As Birkerts suggests: "The premise behind the textual interchange is that the author possesses wisdom, an insight, a way of looking at experience, that the reader wants" (*The Gutenberg Elegies* 163). Not only might a hypertext involve the erasure of an authorial voice, it may also mean the diminution of the reader. Many persons think that hypertexts are by their nature highly interactive, but by choosing options for more information, the recipient may well be more passive, more of a consumer, than if he or she is actively thinking and imagining while reading a printed book. The hypertext has something of the "culinary" art that Brecht so strongly criticized.[12]

A hypertext, whether on CD-ROM (compact disc read-only memory), DVD (digital video disc), or the Web, may offer us text, pictures, and sound. Traditional works are now being made available in this way, such that one can buy Storm's *The White Horse Rider* or Kafka's *The Metamorphosis,* for example, with the usual prefatory material and appendices, but also with the text, hyperlinks to annotations, the ability to search for key words, and a spoken version of the story. In addition to individual works on CD, one can also gain access via Web sites to the entire corpus of major authors, such as Shakespeare, Goethe, Schiller, and Kafka, or collections of poetry as well as an array of supplementary materials.[13] Moreover, CDs are available that contain the collected works of Lessing, Goethe, Hoffmann, Heine, Fontane, and others as well as CD versions of various reference works. Because of text-searching mechanisms every corpus available on the computer becomes a kind of concordance. The *Thesaurus Lin-*

guae Grecae, which contains virtually all extant Greek literary texts from Homer to the end of the sixth century CE, functions, for example, as a concordance of classical Greek literature.

The electronic medium with its supporting materials affects not only the extent to which the text is intelligible but also the way the mind of the reader or student processes it. Good literary critics will increasingly turn their attention to the production of these potentially influential resources in order to ensure that they are of the highest quality. Such texts will have links to the various kinds of questions one can ask of a work in the realms of production aesthetics (e.g., textual variants and historical and intertextual allusions), artwork aesthetics (e.g., issues of genre, style, and structure as well as leitmotifs and parallel passages), and reception aesthetics (e.g., earlier reviews and information on publishing history). Supporting materials might include etymology, maps, encyclopedia references, and historical information. In addition, such texts will eventually have not simply references to sources but the sources themselves, and not simply descriptions of performances but clips of performances or entire performances. With rapid changes in technology much more will be possible; both the quality of delivery on the screen and the amount of material that can be placed onto a personal computer will be transformed. Also, more scholarly works will be published online, which will make it possible for writers to replace at least some of their footnotes with links to full texts and performances. Publication online will also allow scholars to reach a broader audience, which should increase the demand for more-accessible writing.

Hypertexts consisting of traditional works layered with supporting materials, which we might call "sifted hypertexts," rather than "native hypertexts," are likely to increase the number of foreign-language works we read, since clicking on a word one doesn't understand in order to receive lexical and grammatical assistance is easier and faster than consulting a dictionary and the index of a grammar, if one even knows where to look. Also, older texts, including the works of Shakespeare, benefit from resources of this kind, as is evident at <http://www.chemicool.com/Shakespeare/>. In addition, hypertexts can offer two parallel texts, one in the original language and another in a language accessible to the reader. Further, hypertextual possibilities make it easier to create works that link the diverse spheres of interpretive commentary, social history, linguistic context, and philosophical resonance. The ability to give readers choices of kinds of commentary as they read allows critics to reach students and readers of different backgrounds and with diverse needs simultaneously. An excellent hypermedia edition will have coded annotations not only according to types of information; the best hypertexts will also be coded for the level of reader, with diverse commentaries for the general reader, students of various levels, and scholars.[14]

Similarly, CD-ROM literary histories, such as Baasner and Richard, allow recipients to follow links in effective ways that seem to match the needs that students actually have as they consult a reference work for a quick overview of a period, author, or work or for specific topics and subtopics. The concept of links emphasizes the interconnections between the diverse aspects of an age, from authors and works to issues in poetics, historical concepts, and broader developments. The result for pedagogy is at least threefold. First, autodidacts have more practical resources at their disposal than at any previous point in history. Second, hyperlinks encourage us to see texts within a broader sphere of other texts rather than as isolated objects, an impression that the physical nature of a book may cultivate. By placing a given text in a hypertextual apparatus with links to other texts, including intertextual links, reviews, and so forth, the isolation of the text is almost necessarily transformed into dialogue. Third, because of the useful introductory materials, which can in some ways be individually or collectively tailored, class time can be more easily spent on discussion instead of lecture.

The ability to digitize older texts into a single database can aid dating and attribution and help with stylistic analysis and translation. And via parallel passages it can serve interpretation. Also, one's understanding of context is enhanced. In addition, different versions of a text can be placed in relation to one another. The *Perseus Digital Library* is a database of Greek culture that includes literary works in the original and in translation, lexica, encyclopedia information, histories, maps, and other visual images, including coins, vases, and statues. Hyperlinks make it easier to review historical background information, which could reinforce more positivistic and contextual readings, but the ability to search for words and analyze structures may invite more attention to diction and style.

Hypertexts can be changed readily, unlike printed texts; updating earlier commentaries becomes easier. Traditional and older wisdom need not become lost. The hyperlink possibilities would also seem to make collaborative work easier and more frequent insofar as each collaborator can contribute to a different sphere and insofar as technology makes possible collaboration without the physical presence of others. Hypertexts may also generate not only more group-oriented but also more contrasting criticism, whereby in one hypertext different interpretive strategies could be linked that cover a range of options, a procedure that I elevated above in my discussion of hermeneutic principles. One difference between the reception of a work via hypertext and reception of it via the printed page is that distinctions in the age of a book, including such peripheral matters as typeface, become lost. Reading a rare book or a book that embodies traces of an earlier era has an aesthetic and evocative dimension. One gains a different emotive relationship to the past and a different sense of age, which tend to disappear when one reads a work on the screen.

One difficulty with hypertexts as a model of interpretation is that because they may privilege not only nonsequential but also nonhierarchical and nonorganic writing, links may often be arbitrary, unrelated to one another in any compelling way. McLuhan suggests that all electronic media are organic because of the simultaneity of parts (*Understanding Media* 248), but the concept of the organic implies also a meaningful relation of parts, which is hardly a necessary consequence of electronic media or of the concept of simultaneity, as certain hypertexts all too well demonstrate. Roland Barthes' act of dividing texts into discrete blocks and applying diverse codes is, in Barthes' own words, "arbitrary in the extreme" (13). Inspired by such thinking, critics may create hypertexts that consist of discrete observations, layered alongside one another, without any sense of a meaningful whole or any distinction between more and less important commentary; such a development would not be an advantage in an age of overinformation or in a medium that permits endless commentary. A format of this kind may simply reinforce an already unfortunate tendency of discourse analysis, the collection of contextual references without bringing them to bear on the text's overarching meaning and organic structures. Not only creating associations but also knowing the differing value of these associations is important.

Nonetheless, despite the connections between hypertext and contemporary literary theory that have been described by Landow and others,[15] the idea of nonsequential links is not in principle incompatible with more organically or systematically developed interpretations, especially if we view the traditional footnote as an unsophisticated version of a potential network of meaningful links or if we view any coherent system as being animated not simply by the principle of unity but by a complex multiplicity within an overarching unity, which could also be grasped by a hypertext model. Depending on use, the medium of hypertext could embody either a postmodern model of all knowledge as discontinuous and nonhierarchical or a complex and systematic model of the unity of knowledge across disciplines. To use poststructuralist language, the link between hypertext and poststructural ideology is not natural or inevitable but constructed.

A native hypertext is available only via the computer and is distinctive for its associative links; as I outlined above, one can click on various icons and move to related topics, then return, if one so desires. At least one moment of the organic is here stressed: connections between parts of texts are thereby stretched to the limit. In this hypertextual context, however, at least two disadvantages arise. First, our *forma mentis* may be defined by a kind of consumerist curiosity, where we wander from one enchanted moment to another and lose the capacity to think a thought through to its conclusion or to sustain a concentrated and focused argument. Second, we may recognize only the loose connections between parts, moving from part to part, such that the whole behind the parts, the substance that makes the function worthwhile, becomes veiled or lost altogether. Since we cannot, as with a book, see the work in any sense at once, unity is even symbolically weakened. By no means are these the necessary results of this new technology, but they do arise as potential problems.

Not only hypertexts but also television influence literary criticism. Hubert Winkels has commented on the ways in which television affects our discourse on literature (29–59). To comment in some detail on a literary work in a book or an article differs radically in form and content from the kind of performance that takes place in television discussions of literary works, where one must engage other critics directly and spontaneously and attend to questions of evaluation and not simply interpretation. A book that is announced for discussion on Oprah Winfrey's popular television show instantly sees its sales skyrocket. Professional critics, accustomed to the institutionalization of literary criticism via books and articles and recognizing these avenues as primary for advancement in the profession, have not even begun to recognize the untapped possibilities for literary criticism in the newer media.

One of the traditional effects of art has been its ability to help form a collective identity, a set of common experiences, goals, and ideals. Technology has affected the collective dimension of art in negative as well as positive ways. On the microlevel technology has made it possible for us to experience artworks in less communal settings—listening to symphonic works on CDs, viewing movies via satellite, or watching productions of plays via video. This isolation has weakened an important intersubjective experience: even on the most finite level, our reception of these works is altered; risibility, for example, is a contagious experience. Global technology, however, has made it possible for diverse parts of the world to experience events, aesthetic and otherwise, simultaneously. At the same time, the very technology that permits a global reception also gives us more options, thus potentially reducing the number of experiences that are indeed shared. We can explore this question of global reception still further. On the one hand, various cultures now have greater insight into the works of other cultures, as it becomes ever easier to rent a video from Brazil or India or Russia; on the other hand, beyond this scattered pattern of cross-cultural reception, we recognize the hegemony of certain cultural products. American films continue to dominate worldwide, which gives Hollywood a moral responsibility that transcends its financial goals, as the consciousness of the world is partly formed by those American products that integrate art and technology and have an almost universal reception. Whenever this moral charge is not met and even when it is—as it is undesirable for one culture to supplant other cultures—literature, including world literature, has an important role to play. If literature has moments of opposition to dominant culture, as is sometimes suggested, then it has a special role to play in an age where other artforms are even more dominated by technology.

As I noted above, technology has raised essential aspects of the standard of life: we live longer, we have fewer physical hardships to endure, we enjoy more leisure. These technical advances give us more room to enjoy literature; they bestow on literature not only a greater realm in which to flourish but also a greater mission and responsibility, as literature can become a more central dimension of our lives. Indeed, literature is a wise use of leisure. It offers us something we rarely get in our everyday, fragmented lives and something we would be hard pressed to find in any other way. We shall never move back out of a society of division of labor, as it is simply too efficient, but one way to transcend the feeling that one's profession is one's whole life is to give meaning to one's free time through art. Paradoxically, however, advances in technology have also diminished art, and for at least three reasons. First, technology gives us more opportunities to construct and organize our lives; we have more options, many of which are divorced from art. Second, the mutual development of technology and capitalism leads to ever greater competition and in most cases to highly stressful work environments, such that today's worker may be so exhausted at the end of the day that even the pleasurable demands of great literature may exceed the capacity for concentration, especially when television represents a less exacting alternative. Third, a technologically driven economy strongly depends on advertising, which has moments of art but is not itself art—energies are directed toward such enterprises, which might otherwise be directed to art, from the perspectives of both production and reception. Indeed, leisure becomes viewed as "a consumption opportunity" (Schor 162). Because one does not immediately know how best to use one's leisure time, various options need to be cultivated, which suggests untapped opportunities for the literary critic. In an age when insufficient university positions exist for the number of literary critics produced, a market may exist for such persons to conduct discussion classes for lifelong learners who seek to use their leisure time more meaningfully. This is especially the case with older and retired readers who may not suffer from the more immediate effects of overwork.

Another aspect of reception is the idea that readers of a given culture or era are drawn to works of a particular kind. The extraordinary revival of interest in nature writing, especially on the part of scholars of English and American literature, including a remarkable increase in anthologies of nature writing, is an obvious example of a contemporary interest that is partly motivated by the effects of the technological age, including the desire to immerse oneself in works that cultivate a stronger appreciation of the natural world.[16]

Evaluation of art, which is an aspect of reception, has, beyond its intrinsic difficulties, three obstacles specific to our age. First, the technological transformation of the economy and with it society has virtually eliminated an aristocratic class whose progeny was educated to refined aesthetic sensibilities through its education and travels. Second, the market has replaced this aristocracy, such that persons with no aesthetic sensibility may determine which works are purchased (at auctions or in the publishing houses), and the desire for profit minimizes the willingness to take risks on works that may in fact counter the age, whether in content or form, which in turn influences production. Replacing the cultured patronage system in some countries are government officials, whose positions derive from political appointment or bureaucratic ascendancy and who may be no better informed than others in matters of aesthetic evaluation. Third, the ideology of the age runs counter to an evaluation of art based on intrinsic, rather than extrinsic, criteria. These three factors make the role of the art or literary critic that much more important, and so, too, the application of meaningful categories within the profession.

Part Three **Possibilities for Literature and Literary Criticism in the Technological Age**

Chapter 7 The Value
of Literature Today

In this chapter I discuss to what extent art, both in its transhistorical dimensions as analyzed in Part I and in its specific manifestations today, can address technology and its consequences. I highlight the ways in which aesthetic experience counters some of the defining features of the technological age. In this spirit my analysis incorporates one of Adorno's ideas. I do not endorse Adorno's extreme elevation of the dissonant and the incomprehensible, but I do recognize, with Adorno, art's role as countercultural, a position that he shares, for all their differences, with Schiller, who saw in art's harmony an otherness to the dissonance of the modern world.

INTRINSIC VALUE

We have defined technology in the broader sense as the elevation of technical reason, and we have recognized not only that an overemphasis on the technical and especially the instrumental creates an imbalance in relation to other values but also that the ultimate extension of the instrumental is in our relations toward other human beings. This is a reason to preserve, against all attempts to reduce art to the sociopolitical and ideological, that aspect of art which is purely without purpose. In an age where our use of technology empowers us to control others, we need experience with something that is not purposive in quite the same way. When we appreciate an object of beauty, we do not desire to possess it or transform it, to consume it or use it; we leave it free as it is. Nor do we metamorphose the object into abstract theoretical reflection without retaining further interest in the object. As something aesthetic, the object is a combination of the sensuous and the spiritual, neither just sensuous, as is fit for desire, nor just spiritual, as is fit for thought. Ironically, precisely this preservation of the aesthetic as what is intrinsically valuable, neither to be consumed nor to be left behind, makes it valuable as a counterforce to the instrumental, giving it a privileged position within the organic field of human activity in general and especially today.

Various other aspects of literature address the instrumentalization of life. Consider its relation to play. Play, like the reception of literature, is not a useless activity but highly significant. Indeed, Johan Huizinga argues in his classic study that, along with reason and making, play is central to our being. He thus proposes *homo ludens* as complementary to the more popular *homo sapiens* and *homo faber*. Play serves many hidden purposes: it allows us to take joy in vital inclinations; it expands the imagination; it provides balance to the more instrumental and ordinary sphere of work through its voluntary, disinterested, and extraordinary dimensions; it proffers new modes of seeing and relating; and it offers us an experience of ritual. Schiller reverses the traditional cliché whereby we tend to disparage what is mere play. He counters: "The agreeable, the good, the perfect, with these man is *merely* serious; but with beauty he plays" (105–07, translation modified). Schiller states more fully in the same, fifteenth letter on aesthetic education: "But how can we speak of *mere* play, when we know that it is precisely play and play *alone,* which of all our states and conditions is the one which makes us whole and unfolds both sides of our nature at once?" (105, translation modified). Schiller adds: "Man only plays when he is in the fullest sense of the word a human being, and *he is only fully a human being when he plays*" (107). Play is done for its own sake, as an end in itself, and yet this experience enriches, it does not impoverish. Like the beautiful, play gives us a sense of "rhythm and harmony" (Huizinga 10). Santayana thus speaks of play as not "what is done fruitlessly, but whatever is done spontaneously and for its own sake, whether it have or not an ulterior utility" (19). Play may be a means to an end, but that is incidental. It is primarily an end in itself. As such, it paradoxically serves the purpose of enriching our sense of the value of what is done for its own sake. In this way play may even be said to be an analogue of the Kantian precept that we treat others as ends (and not merely as means).

An irony in the elevation of instrumental reason is that it does not lead to happiness, and for at least three reasons. First, happiness is not something that can be purchased or sought; it comes to one with meaningful values as a kind of gift. Trying to will happiness usually results in the obliteration of the enjoyment we seek. Second, the elements of play, spontaneity, and vitality, which also belong to happiness, are neglected to the very extent that instrumental reason is elevated. Third, when instrumental reason becomes overriding, value rationality, which is essential for happiness, recedes. The erasure of one's potential for happiness at the expense of the instrumental tends to manifest itself either through infinite deferral, whereby immediate value is granted only to the instrumental, or through the dialectic of production and consumption, which Daniel Bell has recognized as one of the cultural contradictions of capitalism. On the one hand, we see the workaholic who labors incessantly, forever deferring material and other goods and never truly enjoying them—partly out of an obsession with the instrumental, partly through a reevaluation of values that disparages rest and enjoyment. On the other hand, we recognize—and increasingly so—a more schizophrenic version of the workaholic, who oscillates between hard work and base pleasure, whether in the form of wild revelry or stupefying entertainment.

In either case, the structure differs radically from the ancient wisdom that recommends less immersion in the instrumental so that one can devote oneself more fully to the enjoyment of what is already available, time spent with nature or in contemplation, for example. We see in this ancient wisdom an elevation of the vital and the intrinsic over the instrumental and thereby the cultivation of a different set of ascetic virtues; higher enjoyment, inner nobility, and a sublime sense of contentment are the result. Modern asceticism preaches instead, as Max Scheler has argued in his study of *ressentiment,* a maximum of technical reason and base pleasure, which leads to a minimum of inner happiness (96–97). The more one works and the more one is entertained by the colorful but vacuous, the sadder one becomes. Quantity does not transform itself into quality. Literature gives greater rewards than work characterized by overexertion and instrumentality or leisure characterized by expense and entertainment. Literature enriches us partly through its intrinsic value, partly as a result of its ability to address neglected values, partly through its simple vitality. The fact that modern man is hardly happier than premodern man suggests that there is something more meaningful than satisfying superfluous material needs; literature is part of this higher meaning and higher contentment.

When we meet people, we tend to be interested more in their profession than their values. Someone contributes to society, we think, if that person produces or sells something. This is what is serious about a person; what lies beyond this utilitarian sphere is relegated to the incidental or the innocuous. One's existence must be justified as a means, and attention is rarely given to the validity of the end served by those means. The worth of someone whose contribution is not defined instrumentally and is oriented more toward the preservation and cultivation of intrinsic values is not as easily recognizable. This elevation of the instrumental leads to a shift in both values and rhetoric. For example, in the classical and medieval worlds, the virtue of self-mastery designated the sovereignty of one's reason over the chaos of sensuous drives, a sense of power over one's inclinations, which was perfectly compatible with a sense of modesty, derived by fusion of one's interests with higher and divine precepts, and a bold indifference to the external utility of one's actions. In the dominant modern paradigm, in contrast, self-mastery is reduced to the means by which one attains whatever ends might be named and so becomes associated with sobriety, solidity, measure, the ability to pursue one's ends without giving way to competing demands, and the ability to outshine and overcome one's opponent (Scheler 98–99). In contrast to this elevation of technical rationality, literature teaches the intrinsic value of human life independently of its articulation in the context of a profession or occupation, an insight increasingly lost in the modern age. Literature, as an embodiment of intrinsic value, may well gain an increasingly meaningful role in a society with an expanding population of retired persons, whose previous identity was very much linked to work and whose leisure options are often reduced to the mundane and the merely sensuous.

Literature is adept not only at embodying but also at thematizing the realm of the noninstrumental. Consider, for example, what I have elsewhere called the comedy of coincidence: the individual character seeks certain finite goals, is thwarted in the process, but in the end reaches a larger goal, which matches truer intentions of which the character was scarcely aware (Roche, *Tragedy and Comedy* 140–50). Such heroes imagine themselves to be significant agents, but their subjectivity is revealed to be illusory; other forces are at play. Works belonging to this genre, such as Shakespeare's *Midsummer Night's Dream,* evoke images of nature to suggest that individuals are not as powerful as they think; external forces, whether fate or providence, nature or other individuals, limit their particular intentions—and all for the good. Art is attracted to the subject matter of nature as escape from the overstimulation of urban life or the artificiality of human convention and as immersion in a realm in which the instrumental is less prominent. Nature is characterized, unlike daily human interaction, by its freedom from conscious purposiveness. We are enchanted by a sphere in which means-ends rationality seems to be suspended.

As technical reason becomes ever more dominant, a desire intensifies for authentic communication, which arises in friendship and love, two of the most common and significant themes of literature, and in the meeting of minds, as takes place between a reader and a work of literature. The greatest friendship is based not on utilitarian or pragmatic grounds but on common values and common experiences. Literature, by eschewing this utilitarian moment, elevates the relationship between reader and book to this idea of shared values and the experience of what is an end in itself, as Wayne Booth suggests in *The Company We Keep*. By transcending the merely utilitarian and the merely particular, art points to a realm that is especially important today. The environment will not be protected if our only motive for action is calculable self-interest, for the consequences to the environment will be distant and will not affect us immediately, which brings us to the second dimension of great art applicable in our age, self transcendence.

SELF-TRANSCENDENCE

Great literature helps us gain a broader perspective on life and enriches our understanding through the stories and language of others. Literature reveals new worlds, stretches our sensibilities, including our sympathies, and draws our attention to alternative frames. One of the best ways to overcome oneself and one's subjectivity is to immerse oneself in another culture, to recognize thereby those aspects of one's culture with only contingent validity, to encounter alternative models, and to free oneself of the narcissistic impulse to reflect constantly on one's own private world. Iris Murdoch rightly suggests that art "transcends selfish and obsessive limitations of personality and can enlarge the sensibility of its consumer" (87). Denis Donoghue suggests that the "pleasure of reading literature arises from the exercise of one's imagination, a going out from one's self toward other lives, other forms of life, past, present, and perhaps future. This denotes its relation to sympathy, fellowship, the spirituality and morality of being human" (*Practice* 73). Encounters with other ages and cultures render literature among the most exotic of artforms, but literature is also among the most accessible, first, because of its language, which has a transparency that many other artforms lack, and, second, because of its combination of availability and economy. Unlike architecture, sculpture, painting, music, dance, or theater, and even to an extent film, literature is accessible independently of one's location or financial resources.

By way of this self-transcendence not only do individuals enlarge their horizons, but cultures integrate the works of other cultures so as to expand their options as well. Hegel elevates the *West-Eastern Divan* as Goethe's greatest work: instead of embodying subjective inwardness, it is a work of "objective cheerfulness" and evokes a readiness "to enjoy also works of foreign and rather distant nations" (unpublished transcription, quoted in Gethmann-Siefert 234). Instead of immersing himself only in his subjective reflexivity or immediate surroundings, Goethe finds a higher form of objectivity in the mediation of cultural alternatives. We overcome tribalism only when we seek both the other and the whole, for a plurality of others without a sense of the whole generates conflict, and a whole without otherness smothers the richness of diversity. The importance of experiencing other cultures derives not only from the idea that we have a moral obligation to search out others. Precisely when a culture reaches a point where its artforms lack the ability to address contemporary concerns satisfactorily, when its art becomes repetitive or narcissistic or unable to gain a grip on the problems of the age, impulses from another culture can regenerate it. An example is the reinvigoration of modern art through its integration of some of the values of primitivism, including its immediacy and spontaneity. Good reason exists to study "modern" authors from countries that have been slower to advance technologically and who may have perspectives, forms of intersubjective experience, and an emotional richness that we may have forgotten.

When literature is conveyed to many, it contributes, as I have suggested, to forming collective identity and common values beyond the multiplicity of private interests. Vico argues that it is not enough to ground philosophically the institutions that give societies and cultures stability; we must also feel strong emotional bonds to these institutions. As we distance ourselves from the institutions of the past, as the modern world becomes increasingly rationalized, art and literature can help bring us closer to tradition and to one another. In a technical age in which collective identity is less and less formed by tradition or community, art may help encourage a warmer attachment to broader cultural institutions. Collective identity tends to be ignored or disparaged by many contemporary critics, but if literature and art do not play roles here, the vacuum will be filled by a collective identity defined by marketing and consumption. The relevance of collective identity in legitimizing support of the arts is an argument in favor of those artworks that meet simultaneously our expectations for high and popular culture. In an age of ecological crisis a meaningful collective identity is especially important, for environmental problems require collective, indeed international, strategies. Above all, good artworks that address the need for a new relationship to nature or for a greater appreciation of intergenerational justice should gain a worldwide audience.

A classic metaphor for literature is the mirror. Through literature we come to see ourselves in ways we did not earlier recognize. So, for example, the hero of Ferdinand Raimund's *The King of the Alps and the Misanthrope,* who sees himself through magic, itself an analogue of the literary enterprise, recognizes his faults and improves. Shakespeare's Timon and Molière's Alceste are not privy to such self-reflection, but their readers are. Zuckmayer's *The Captain of Köpenick* ends with Wilhelm Voigt placing the uniform back on his disheveled body, looking into the mirror, and laughing at the hilarity of the situation. A good performance of this play might well employ a large mirror such that the audience sees itself when Voigt cries out, "Ridiculous!!" (128). This traditional image of art as specular carries with it a twofold idea: first, that we see ourselves more clearly through literature, as we identify with the players in the work; and second, that we draw existentially on this reception as an experience of self-knowledge, overcoming weaknesses in ourselves. The frequent role reversals in literary works, including also reversals of gender or social status, are often designed to help the character gain a fuller sense of other and thereby of self. Through the role-playing of literature—our identification with and distance from the characters on the pages—we are likewise aided in our search for identity. The technological age does not easily lend itself to a sense of coherence, but in reading literature and understanding the unfolding narrative of a human life and the developing whole of an artwork, we are encouraged to gain a deeper sense of coherence that may be transferable to reflection on our selves, on the hidden logic of our own development.

In comedy we often see the negation of a negation or the negation of an untenable position. Comedy undermines protagonists preoccupied with their own particularity, thereby preparing alternative worldviews. The audience is encouraged to recognize itself and its foibles in such heroes, and so the specular experience assumes a moral cast. Literature teaches us the nuances of intersubjective relationships, the strategies, the limits, the possibilities of human interaction. Such insights into intersubjective relations become increasingly important in a culture where technology reduces the number of personal interactions by which we gain experience. We also see in the technological age a delimiting of our sense for rich, layered, and differentiated relations, insofar as television, in its appeal to the masses, tends to transform this complexity into the melodramatic and unnuanced.

The mirror of literature has another aspect: older literature sees in nature a reflection of God, which differs greatly from a modern view that sees in nature not a reflection of the absolute but an object to be manipulated, and in literature a projection of one's ideas as reader. Whereas the mirror model leads to self-transcendence and reverence for what is sacred, the projection model places our values above other spheres. The reductionism of reception aesthetics can be brought home by way of the beauty of nature. Many would argue that the beauty of nature, its value, derives from our ability to perceive it. This anthropocentric view not only misjudges nature, whose being and value belong outside the human sphere even as it also has extrinsic value for us, it reduces the possibility of self-transcendence inherent in our encounters with nature. Nature's difference and independence limit our inflated sense of human subjectivity and elicit a deeper connection to what lies beyond us. This connection can be recognized in our awe at nature's wonder and our instinctive disgust at its destruction. Theodore Roszak speaks of our "ecological unconscious" (13), that is, our intuitive environmental knowledge, as when we wince at the sight of birds or fish being washed ashore in oil or forests being devastated and not replanted. Earlier I discussed the similarities between technical and artistic production by way of the concepts of techne and poiesis. Precisely this connection brings us to another value of art, which encourages a different relationship to nature. The human capacity for creating and forming has intrinsic value and need not be expended in a form that leads to the control of nature. In addition, greater recognition of the beauty of nature as parallel to the beauty of art could elicit in our relationship to nature more cultivation of this beauty, as in the garden, which synthesizes nature and art, and more of a willingness simply to let nature be.[1]

We must reject Hegel's idea that the beauty of nature is necessarily inferior to the art produced by humanity, and for at least two reasons. First, in making his claim, Hegel does not raise ontological questions concerning specific content, appropriateness of form, or level of complexity; his argument is based on the idea of genesis or production—beauty produced by a thinking mind is by definition superior to the beauty of nature (13.14; cf. 13.48–50 and 13.190–202). Here Hegel incorrectly substitutes genesis for validity. Moreover, he seems to presuppose, as he does not elsewhere in his aesthetics, that the human creation of artworks proceeds consciously; if we were to follow this correlation—between the level of spirit in the production of the work and the quality of the work—to its ultimate conclusion, it would follow that the poetic works of a philosopher would be far more valuable than those of a naive genius, independently of questions of form and content and based solely on the level of spirit reached by the creator, which is absurd.

Hegel's claim also overlooks the ultimate cause or principle of such beauty, which brings us to our second criticism. If we accept the objective idealist view that nature is constituted by the ideal sphere, as is humanity, we must reject, as deriving from a constructivist framework, any argument for the necessary superiority of the beauty created by humans. The beauty of nature reveals the patterns of the absolute, as do the creations of human beings. Hegel's claim that a person's "warped fancy" is formally superior to the greatest beauty of nature has to be contested as possible only on the basis of a view that devalues nature, as does Kant or Fichte (13.14). (Interestingly, the power of nature is sometimes so grand that its beauty overrides any theory; Kant fully recognizes the beauty of nature even as his metatheory deprives it of higher value.) One can—with Hegel—justly say that any bad idea of humanity has more spirit, or *Geist,* than the greatest manifestation of nature, but one cannot defend the claim that it is more beautiful. Hegel's mistake reveals his beholdenness to the verum factum principle that dominates modern subjectivity: the premise that only what we make has value leads Hegel to claim mistakenly the absolute superiority of artistic beauty over natural beauty.

In making his argument, Hegel says that in art the human being recognizes "his own self" (13.52). One might counter that in the highest form of beauty we recognize the ideal sphere which gives us dignity but also transcends us. Here, too, one recognizes oneself. In addition, we could argue that where nature is necessarily programmed to reveal the absolute and is necessarily organic, humanity in its freedom and possibility of error can reveal something other than the absolute. Moreover, if we want to argue that one aspect of beauty is the merging of the sensuous and the spiritual, the spiritual development of animals, as is evident to anyone who has developed a strong relationship to an animal, represents a more impressive achievement than many creations of modern art. Even Hegel's claim that human art lasts (13.48), whereas the beauty of nature is passing, cannot be applied universally: the beauty of certain stones may last longer than various human creations, not least of all most happenings.[2] One can and should argue that certain forms of human art are superior to the beauties of nature insofar as they embody those elements that Hegel justly argues elevate spirit over nature; they may, for example, employ language to develop a level of reference, a complexity of ideas, or an element of self-re-flection that is absent or less developed in nature. However, bad architecture is not necessarily superior to beautiful nature, and in its intensity, the sublime of nature can compete with much of human art; it is no less devoid of intrinsic value or symbolic meaning, even if its meaning, like that of works of art, is rendered visible only in the hands of its viewers. This strikes me as an important insight not only theoretically but also in terms of our emotional relationship to nature.

Making inroads into nature has, as we have seen, two dimensions: first, the potential harm done to ecosystems, which have intrinsic value; and second, the potential harm done to human nature, as our own environment becomes increasingly artificial. We can rephrase this analysis by explicating two inverse reasons to value nature: because of its intrinsic value and because of its extrinsic value for humanity. The extrinsic value of nature for humanity involves the natural resources that allow us to satisfy material human needs, but it extends beyond this, satisfying humanity in a spiritual and regenerative sense as well. Nature not only provides human beings with a sense of balance in an overcerebral world, it helps elicit an awareness of essence in an overartificial world. If, as we said above, art exhibits an essence beyond the externality and triviality of everyday life, it is not by chance that art often portrays this essence with images of nature, which may also give us distance from the everyday routines of life. Untainted by civilization, nature frees us from the superficialities and dispersions of life, its constructed and less than meaningful dimensions, revealing something of a higher essence, which is one of the reasons for its having been elevated in literature as a locus of renewal. As examples, consider Shakespeare's *As You Like It,* Hölderlin's *Hyperion,* and Thoreau's *Walden.* In nature and art, as in reflection on death, the superficial is stripped away. Thus, nature has value for us in awakening reflection on essentials and a sense of the natural versus the constructed, that is, simplicity, vitality, passion, spontaneity, and other virtues often neglected in societal settings, where we are more susceptible to artificial rules of behavior.

What nature also often contributes is a sense of wholeness or reconciliation, especially when, as in Schelling, what is evoked is not simply nature in its particularity, nature as an empirical object or a product, created nature, *natura naturata,* but nature as the subject of an ever unfolding process, nature in its entirety, creating nature, *natura naturans* (*Schriften* 284). Whereas the scientific study of nature proceeds via analysis, a fuller experience of nature also involves reception via the emotions and senses, which is increasingly difficult in a land-scape that primarily objectifies nature and is ever more valuable, as only with such a relationship do nature's countercultural moments become available to us. Nature takes us beyond ourselves not just in the empirical sense of removing us from the inessentials of human society, it awakens in us a greater awareness of the value of what is—independently of human invention. Whereas technology reinforces our sense that what is of value is what we create, nature reminds us of what is of value beyond the verum factum principle.

Literature also takes us into a sphere we might call the eternal. Ancient thinkers elevated thought, which has its goal within itself, over action, which has its goal outside itself and is never complete. Literature is a moment of ancient *theoria* in the modern world, insofar as it is whole unto itself. It allows for a moment of leisure, repose, contemplation, which is more responsive to the possible reception of the ideal sphere. When reading good literature, we are so immersed in the work that we forget the external world. We lose ourselves in what we are reading. Literature frees us from action and dispersion for the *vita contemplativa.* Literature teaches patience, a neglected virtue in a culture where time is highly regulated and technology dramatically reduces the distances of space. Through contemplation we abandon the contingent and engage the eternal. Birkerts writes of this concentration and connection: "Through the process of reading we slip out of our customary time orientation, marked by distractedness and surficiality [*sic*], into the realm of duration. Only in the duration state is experience present as meaning. Only in this state are we prepared to consider our lives under what the philosophers used to call 'the aspect of eternity,' to question our origins and destinations, and to conceive of ourselves as souls" (*The Gutenberg Elegies* 32).

Kant's argument that aesthetic judgments are universal gives a final social dimension to art. Kant draws an important distinction between pleasure, which is individual, and beauty, which is universal. Beauty's universality is able to bring us beyond the merely sensuous and private. A concept of art that removes this moment of universality will have a difficult time convincing others of its value. More important, it will not lead us to the paradoxical self-transcendence and self-fulfillment that is part of collective experience and even more so of collective identity. A common human inclination is to share what is beautiful, to tell others about it so that they may experience it as well. The expectation is that others will also find it beautiful. Schiller was one of the first to recognize that this social dimension of beauty has great potential value. Beauty not only harmonizes the parts of the self, it is a prolepsis of a higher harmony among persons and cultures. As an end in itself, beauty appropriately has this connection to the good.

BALANCE

In contrast to one-sidedly materialist impulses, literature offers an embrace of the material sphere in relation to spirit. Literature invites us to embrace not only the finite (the sensuous material of language) but also the infinite (insofar as literature adorns us with a sense of dignity and higher purpose) and the mysterious relation between the two. Great art grants us a sense of what cannot be seen, objectified, or measured, thus opening our eyes to the value of what might superficially be viewed as less. The joy of literature is of a spiritual nature, but also of a sensuous nature compatible with this spirituality. In this way literature is an important counterweight also to modern subjectivity, for the distinguishing characteristic of subjectivity in the technological age is its capacity to render everything, including itself, an object, and so to become split in a way that takes it further from the inner harmony of consciousness and nature, of intellect and body. The reception of beauty requires the mediation not only of understanding, which differentiates, but also of our sensibility for unity. Moreover, by appealing to our senses, art reawakens in us an awareness of our own being as partly nature, which in turn renders more transparent our dependence on the realm of nature beyond us. In short, beauty gives spiritual meaning to the sensuous and brings to the cerebral mind the value of the sensuous. Schiller offers us a significant formulation of this ideal in his eighteenth letter: "By means of beauty sensuous man is led to form and thought; by means of beauty spiritual man is brought back to matter and restored to the world of sense" (123).

A significant factor in the ecological crisis is the distance between human beings and nature; literature can contribute to bridging this difference. Art reintroduces an emphasis on the natural, sensuous part of humans by forming itself partly out of the material world and appealing to our sensuousness; this effects balance in a culture that is no longer intuitive and in many respects too reflective. In a complementary way, art bestows on language and material a richness of meaning and a spiritual value. This is true not only formally but also often thematically; consider the ways in which stained glass elevates the more seemingly prosaic light of day or the manifold ways in which the works of the Dutch masters bestow a spiritual dimension on everyday life. To a culture increasingly tempted by less cerebral activities, literature, being the most cerebral of the arts, may be an especially effective aesthetic antidote. By elevating words, literature counters our tendency to fall victim to an entirely visual culture. As the most intellectual of the arts, it represents a form of sensuousness that raises us to a higher, more abstract level. In this sense it avoids two extremes of modernity: the excessively cerebral and the one-sidedly sensual. Moreover, art can give us any number of stories, taken from earlier eras or from the contemporary imagination, that help us grasp how to bring about a unity of these two spheres, so split in modern technological society. Many fairy tales, for example, both modern and traditional, integrate nature in such a way as to evoke its spiritual dimensions.

A classical paradigm of art elevates symmetry. At its highest level, symmetry indicates a harmony of proportions and a concordance of parts within a greater whole; it is thus intimately connected to the organic and the beautiful. Symmetry evokes rest; it even creates a certain muscular balance in the eye. Certainly a symmetry without sufficient parts to be harmonized is empty. Likewise unappealing is infinite repetition, which can lead to monotony, as with building developments or symmetrical landscaping in a large park. They tire, rather than harmonize, our senses, or we simply no longer notice them and become indifferent to them—in our consciousness at least, as they do not appeal to us. Even the asymmetrical in great art, for example, in what is commonly called the sublime, has as its basis a higher symmetry, that between its essence and the form appropriate to that essence. Just as beauty evokes a privileged calm through symmetry, so does the sublime elicit inspiration on the basis of a symmetry of form and content, even if this takes place on a metalevel. A privileged category in mathematics and science, no less than in art, symmetry may offer a path of connection between two seemingly disparate worlds.[3]

Equally important, the symmetry of beauty has its analogue in truth and justice. According to Plato, justice, whether in the person or the state, is defined by the appropriate relationship of parts to the whole (*Republic* 433a–45e); organic art presupposes an analogous structure. Similarly, we find in Aristotle a parallel between art and virtue. For Aristotle this comparison moves from the idea that the perfect artwork has found the perfect proportion (to take anything away or to add anything would be to miss the right measure) to the idea that virtue is likewise defined by the balance between excess and defect in both passions and actions (1106b). In both models, art as balance relates to virtue as the organic relation of parts or as proper measure. Elaine Scarry has recently returned to the idea that symmetry plays analogous roles in beauty and justice, and she makes the additional claim that our reception of beauty, with its qualities of symmetry, equality, and balance, assists us in recognizing justice as an ideal and motivating us to create it where it is not yet established and to support it where it does exist. "An analogy is inert and at rest only if both terms are present in the world; when one term is absent, the other becomes an active conspirator for the exile's return" (100–101). Even when beauty and justice are both present, "beauty performs a special service because it is available to sensory perception in a way that justice (except in rare places like an assembly) normally is not" (108).

Classical aesthetics, like classical metaphysics and ethics, elevates measure and balance, moderation against the extremes. Of course if all art were simple measure, we would miss richness of variety. François Rabelais, Laurence Stern, and Jean Paul would all fall out of view if measure, and not a wider concept of the organic, were our norm. But I do not want to suggest that all art become measure; instead, I am suggesting that measure is also a valid dimension of art, which, though neglected today, may be especially appropriate for an age that is already given over to imbalance. If we are to counter the societal images that are dominated by the union of technology and capitalism and that equate prestige and happiness with the acquisition of material objects, we need alternative avenues which suggest that human dignity and virtue are attached not to quantity but to measure and that the reverse leads only to a kind of vulgarity and lack of freedom.

Can an aesthetics that embraces infinity, openness, and quantity do justice to the pressing need for a reawakening of the virtues of measure, restraint, and balance, for a sense of contentment with less? Will an art that no longer recognizes balance and the harmony of proportions render us sensitive to our having brought ecospheres out of balance? Artworks that evoke a concept of self-restraint and of embeddedness within the cosmos might better assist us in cultivating the consciousness that would resist overconsumption and limit indefinite expansion. The modern idea of infinity, as it is reflected in infinitely extendable irony, is likewise unsatisfactory. While irony enriches human relationships by bringing to light a person's hidden dimensions, qualities that might otherwise go unnoticed, infinite irony means a dissolution of intersubjective connections. Irony should be used to suggest deeper layers of meaning, not ultimate meaninglessness.

OVERARCHING CONNECTIONS

In his sixth letter on aesthetic education Schiller notes in modernity the dissolution of unity and the proliferation of autonomous value systems: "State and

Church, laws and customs, were now torn asunder; enjoyment was divorced from labor, the means from the end, the effort from the reward" (35). He continues with the lament not only that these broader spheres are dissolved of overarching unity but also that the individual person has become a mere fragment: "Everlastingly chained to a single little fragment of the whole, the human being himself develops into nothing but a fragment; everlastingly in his ear the monotonous sound of the wheel that he turns, he never develops the harmony of his being, and instead of putting the stamp of humanity on his nature, he becomes nothing more than the imprint of his occupation or of his specialized knowledge" (35, translation modified). Hyperion writes on behalf of Hölderlin in his critique of the Germans: "You see artisans, but no human beings, thinkers, but no human beings, priests, but no human beings, masters and servants, but no human beings, minors and adults, but no human beings—is this not like a battlefield on which hacked-off hands and arms and every other member lie pell mell, while the life-blood flows from them to vanish in the sand?" (164, translation modified).

For both these poets art is a privileged means of addressing modern fragmentation. Art conveys dialectical wholeness, encompassing the coherence not only of intellect and sensuousness but also of part and whole. Wholeness is not only an aesthetic but also a human ideal. Schiller, for example, notes the narrowness of the calculating intellect that cannot identify emotionally with the perspectives and needs of others: "The abstract thinker very often has a *cold* heart, since he dissects his impressions, and impressions can move the soul only as long as they remain whole; while the person involved in practical affairs often has a *narrow* heart, since his imagination, confined within the monotonous circle of his profession, cannot expand to appreciate other ways of seeing and knowing" (39, translation modified). Great works of literature think through the insufficiencies of partial positions, evoking thereby the unity that transcends them, for which Hölderlin's *Hyperion* might stand as a model. Moreover, an aesthetic education modeled on such notions of coherence educates without force.

The idea of art as educative toward wholeness seems to have become suspect because of the mistaken equation of the whole and the organic with national socialism. In another publication I have argued that national socialism did not evoke wholeness but instead elevated an autonomous value system (racial nationalism) in the wake of a breakdown of the absolute and the universal ("Nietzsche"). If the absolute is relativized, as in the wake of Nietzsche, then the relative can be absolutized—so the thesis of the leading philosopher of national socialism, Alfred Rosenberg. National socialism was not an elevation of wholeness but a fixation on partiality, a self-contradictory, self-canceling set of unjust claims and desires. The ideal of coherence has also been questioned by those who point out that persons immersed in the aesthetic sphere, lovers of music and literature, have often been brutal toward other persons. In his impressive documentary drama *The Investigation,* Peter Weiss shows how one of the officers in the death camp, Corporal Stark, reads Goethe and discusses him with prisoners, the same prisoners he also beats and kills. This divorce of one sphere from the other does not call Goethe into question as much as it calls into question the reception of Goethe, a view of art as unconnected to one's moral actions and life. We are appalled by such incongruities because we believe that there should be a higher unity of art and morality.

Technology tends to favor the mechanical, whereas art has traditionally aligned itself with the organic. Because of this connection art can reawaken a sense of the organic that may otherwise be lost when technology dominates our worldview. In the technological age we suffer from being in an unduly inorganic environment; our relation to art differs because of its organicism, much as our experience of the intrinsic value of art counters the functionalism of the technological age. In his account of ancient metaphysics, Dmitri Nikulin reminds us that the organic consists of a synthesis of substance and function (35). The organic retains an element of essence, which many contemporary critics want to expunge both from the world and from art, dissolving each into nothing but parts without a concept of the whole. One reason for the common antipathy between technology and nature is that the former is lifeless, whereas the latter is not; the one is for the most part mechanical and predictable, the other is dynamic and seemingly inexhaustible in its complexity. We create technology not only to satisfy material needs, but also to see ourselves reflected in our creations, which then surround us. When we see ourselves in what is lifeless, we are easily discontent.[4]

The organic in art is more than a countermodel to technology. It mirrors the very ecosystems, organic and complex structures, that are endangered by technology. The almost unfathomable coherence and organic complexity of a great artwork, the ways in which its parts relate to one another, serve as an analogue of the inexhaustible richness of interconnectedness that defines an ecosystem. Attentiveness to the one gives us a better eye for the complexity and beauty, the organic structure, of the other. Nature is organic, from its cells to its largest ecosystems. Also humanity is organic both biologically and in the centered self, where part and whole function in harmony. In art, nature, and humanity even the smallest part is connected to every other part and to the whole. The organic demands of its interpreter, whether the focus be nature, an artwork, or the human subject, an extraordinary hermeneutic capacity, including attention to both details and the whole, and a recognition that, for all one's capacity to interpret, certain dimensions elude one's grasp. Through a richer awareness of organic connections, as is cultivated through literature and the study of literature, we are also more likely to recognize the connections between our actions and threats to the environment, which tend to be severed in the splintered frames by which we live. Certainly, many persons who have refined literary sensibilities are indifferent or even hostile to the beauty and complexity of nature; one need only think of Oscar Wilde (970). But a sensibility for wholes is in principle transferable to other realms and so represents a justifiable ideal. Kant was right to link art with organisms.

As already Schiller and Hölderlin recognized, the sense of wholeness symbolized in literature is an important countermoment to the elevation of expertise in the technological age, which is defined by the focus on one particular area with neither knowledge of nor concern for an overarching purpose. Every sphere of life has its experts—from fixing an electrical problem to selling a house. This proliferation derives understandably from the modern overflow of information and elevation of efficiency. Some problems do require a technical solution, yet others require a far-ranging mentality, which builds on values present in literature. Literature seems irrelevant precisely because we think we can control all subspheres of life by way of simple means-ends thinking, but much of life requires the more holistic approach of liberal learning. Italo Calvino articulates the unusual capacity of literature to address the whole in an age of overspecialization when he reflects on the significance of literary values for the new millennium: "Since science has begun to distrust general explanations and solutions that are not sectorial and specialized, the grand challenge for literature is to be capable of weaving together the various branches of knowledge, the various 'codes,' into a manifold and multifaceted vision of the world" (112).

A problem introduced above in the context of autonomous value systems and our increasingly mediated relationship to the world is the lack of coherence that arises in our understanding, or recollection, of how different things relate to one another. The idea that in an age of technology our relationship to the world is increasingly mediated by a hyperreality of self-referential signs, instead of any connection to true reality, gives Jean Baudrillard's concept of the "simulacrum" its moment of truth.[5] This lack of coherence and vacuum of reference have partly to do with the interesting dialectic analyzed by Ortega y Gasset that when technology initially emerged, it was grossly apparent and imposing, but that after some time, it wasn't even noticed: we begin to think that "aspirin and automobiles grow on trees like apples" (311). We can go even further, adding that we begin to think that apples grow in the backroom of the grocery store or that gas comes from a tank at the local station, when in many cases technology transports them over thousands of miles. Indeed, one of the greatest dangers of technology is that because of the complexity of the mediation process we do not see either the sources of our consumption or its consequences. We buy and consume certain products, not thinking where they come from: What animal was slaughtered to create this neatly packaged meat? How much energy was consumed in bringing this fruit to my store? We simply do not reflect on these things because technology grants us distance from the origins and consequences of our action. Our trash is simply taken away, perhaps to another state or country; we needn't think about it further. Our ecological footprint—the area of land and water required on a continuous basis to produce all the goods consumed and assimilate all the waste generated by a given population—far exceeds the territory available (Wackernagel and Rees). We are using the essential products of nature more quickly than they can be renewed and discharging wastes more quickly than they can be absorbed—yet we tend not to see that we are doing so. Technology takes away our knowledge and familiarity with this context. Art can break down the autonomous spheres of our lives and engender an awareness of what has been concealed through habit or mediation.

An irony of the technological age is that at the very time that technology has allowed us to have an impact on the world in so many diverse ways simultaneously, we have, both in practice and in theory, moved increasingly away from a paradigm of knowledge that stresses unity. However, the environmental problem cannot be solved by specialized reflections alone. Particular insights need to be related to a larger whole, much as the insights we gain into the particular elements of a literary work reach their full meaning and relevance only in synthetic relation to one another. The literary critic needs knowledge of a wide array of spheres in order to grasp the phenomenological richness of a literary work. Depending on the work, this could mean, for example, knowledge of science or religion or music or law or distant cultures. Similarly the ecological question invites the collaborative resources of disciplines as divergent as theology, philosophy, biology, chemistry, physics, engineering, anthropology, psychology, economics, and political science. Literature as itself an integrative discipline belongs on this list.

Individual genres can also be viewed in the light of wholeness: tragedy exhibits the inevitable failure of elevating one single position at the expense of another, comedy has as its central structure the negation of finite particularity, and speculative art portrays wholeness as a positive telos that does not refute the idea of further progress. The desire for wholeness increases precisely when one senses its loss. Not surprisingly, therefore, our technological age returns to myth for an overarching narrative that may restore a sense of coherence to our lives, a structuring principle. Modernity longs for myth, an insight that was already present to Nietzsche: "the mythless human being" is prominent in *The Birth of Tragedy* (1.125). Literature gives us insight into the need for regenerating myth, and it grants us symbols by which we can see richer meaning than the cold, calculating gaze of instrumental reason allows. What fills the content of myth is not in any way predetermined. Industry itself or nationalism might serve as myths, though these would hardly satisfy. Heinrich Mann's *Kobes* effectively illustrates the innate desire for myth as an ordering principle, a centering force. Archaic societies centered their world around myth before technology became a powerful mode of relating to the world. Marx recognizes this transition: "All mythology subdues and controls and shapes the forces of nature in the imagination and through the imagination; it therefore vanishes when real control over these forces is established" (*Grundrisse* 110, translation modified). Now with technology, we have in a certain, still to be defined way the need to return to myth, because technology alone cannot satisfy our deeper needs.

One of the great insights of Broch's *The Spell* is precisely this recognition that humans need overarching myths and meanings. For Broch the crisis of Weimar was a crisis of positive values. Any critique of national socialism should not be a simple critique of myth, for the result would be that the only remaining myths stem from unethical hands. Instead, myths must be presented. Humans need symbols and overarching meanings. In order to counter fascism, emotional and religious desiderata must be addressed along with economic needs. Ritual, aura, and meaning have a place in modern society. The idea of sacrifice is present not only in national socialism but also in literary works that criticize instrumental reason, such as Storm's *The White Horse Rider,* or in films that address the nuclear holocaust, such as Andrei Tarkovsky's *The Sacrifice.* In Broch's highly ambiguous novel we see the author's recognition of the need for a more spiritual response to the dangers of technology and the hollowness of modernity. In order to counter the disorientation of the Weimar Republic and the evil of the Third Reich, we need not only a satisfaction of economic needs and a diagnosis of evil; strategies for dealing with the effects of technology on previous, more organic modes of life must be found. At the same time, Broch makes clear the manifold ways in which persons searching for spiritual meaning and regeneration can be taken in by aberrant and immoral developments. An ethical norm is needed to guide one's emotional response, one's invocation of ritual, meaning, and aura, even when this norm is not easily achieved.

A great writer is by definition a creator of meanings. Great literary works are conducive to rich interpretations, with regard to both the layers of the works and their resonance for the reader's reflection on meaning. Such works help the reader grasp the ways in which the various aspects of life can be understood as complex but meaningful narratives. By way of the concreteness of a particular story, image, or drama the writer conveys a broader meaning that is embedded within the artwork but simultaneously transcends it. This combination of the concrete and universal allows the reader to seek overarching values through the particularity of a singular work. Much as Gehlen argues that technology extends our physical and intellectual capacities, so does art allow us to see and recognize more. The technological age, by way of the electronic Web, gives us a superficial sense of being connected, but our processing of this information is instantaneous and often discontinuous and disjointed as well as superficial and flat. This processing differs from the experience of immersing oneself in the unfolding complexities of a literary work, being connected with the world it evokes, its difficulties and variousness, and recognizing over time its often unsuspected internal connections.

Myth, taken in its broadest meaning, is the most significant source of overarching connections in art—not only the myths and narratives of Greek and Christian religion but also modern mythological figures, such as Faust, Don Quixote, and Don Juan, even a contemporary myth of great heuristic value, such as Woody Allen's Zelig. Schelling argues that mythology is "*the necessary condition and first content of all art*" (*Philosophy* 45). For Schelling mythology is nothing other than the universe in its higher manifestation. From this perspective mythology addresses at least three central aesthetic concerns: the need for a substantive and significant story or narrative; the need for heuristically powerful images or symbols; and the need for a connection to the transcendent, to a higher meaning or reality. These elements of art are as timeless as they are timely in the twenty-first century.

PERSPECTIVE

By perspective I do not mean Nietzschean perspectivism, which encourages us to adopt any number of ultimately arbitrary positions with a telos of richness or strength and as a counterstrand to the concepts of unity and truth. Instead, I mean proper perspective, an appropriate lens for the circumstances encountered. In response to the dialectic of hubris and impuissance, I see primarily two perspectives as appropriate, courage and acceptance. Courage is a response to impuissance, but also in a sense to hubris, insofar as one needs courage to challenge reigning thinking and courage to hold back when it is wise. An acceptance of limits would seem to be the measured response to hubris, but also at times to the sense of frustration triggered by impuissance—when in fact events are beyond our control.

Literature counters the claim that individuals can no longer alter the complexity of the world or that no one person can make a difference. First, in many literary works we see in exemplary and ideal fashion the way in which individuals do change the world; what is ideal in art should become reality. In this way literature inspires action. Every individual is part of a chain of causality and can affect the sequence of events of many other persons, if often in unintended ways. Chaos theory reinforces this concept by showing how the actions of minor agents—genes, animals, humans—can lead to major changes in the constellation of events, often unintentionally.

Second, literature introduces not just the general idea of an individual changing the world, it also shows what specific virtues effect change. Two central problems in the modern age are: first, the tragedy of the commons, which Garrett Hardin has elucidated as a particular form of the prisoner's dilemma (in the tragedy of the commons, each self recognizes that he alone is not responsible for a particular problem and is hesitant to act responsibly until others do so as well, for responsible action requires certain sacrifices, thus no one acts responsibly and the common problem only worsens); and second, the fear of expressing unpopular thoughts in an age of conformity. Tragic literature provides ample countermodels, many of which thematize the inspiriting effects of self-sacrifice. One of the greatest obstacles we face in responding appropriately to the ecological crisis is our sense of well-being and convenience, not to say luxury, which would be threatened by changes in our actions. In this context, stories of solidarity and sacrifice, especially across cultures or generations, become ever more important. Equally important are comic works that mock insufficient attempts at change, positions that offer a moment of insight but lack a fuller perspective on the true and the good. Schnitzler's Professor Bernhardi, to take one example, is unwilling to engage with society in order to change it; instead, he retires to a private sphere of self-righteousness. He has insight into truth but hesitates before its realization.

Third, an artwork that exhibits the complex conditions that lead to an individual's inability to change events need not be read as fatalistic. Such art may seek to clarify types of situations or the conditions of failure. By way of sensuous representation, it may have as its goal a reflexive moment: to awaken a critical consciousness of the complex forces of the modern world. Over against the literature that argues we can have no recognition and so cannot change our behavior, we might privilege those works that elevate the virtue Jonas sees as imperative in our age—responsibility. Works of this kind, for example, Miller's *Incident at Vichy,* often predate the cynicism of postmodernism. Perspective may very well be a call to action that is elicited by our reception of a work that agitates us, shakes us, challenges us in our complacency. In this sense Brechtian theater seeks not to pacify the audience but to challenge it to rise to the occasion, to change precisely what can be altered in ways that will improve humanity. To link courage with proper perspective is appropriate, for the traditional definition of courage recognizes the connection between courage and wisdom. Courage, as Plato argues in *Laches,* is not fearlessness or foolish bravado but is linked to, and presupposes, prudence, temperance, and justice.

Courage, then, would seem to be the proper response to a discussion of impuissance, but courage alone does not suffice. Literature may give us a sense of perspective that does not so much motivate us to action as allow us to see the reason in history or allow us to reconcile ourselves to what we cannot control. Through its tales of acceptance, its stories of the role that chance and vicissitude play in the lives of every person, literature can help us reach a more reconciliatory *amor fati.* When technology fails us today, we are much less able to cope than were earlier generations whose lives were less invested in technology. Our advantage reveals itself also as a dependence, a restriction of autonomy. There is much that we cannot control, much that we do not will that happens to us, and our task is, first, to make sense of what does not originate from our actions and, second, to understand in all humility that there will always be factors beyond our control. Literature tells us story after story of what we cannot control, whether in the fate of tragedy or in the fortunes of comedy. Consider the way in which Hölderlin's Hyperion reflects as a narrator on his turbulent life and his act of telling the story of his life, whereby he achieves a differentiated union with his environment and his past, a greater sense of tranquillity. Or consider the fated Abdias of Stifter, who loves his dog immensely, but who shoots it—when it becomes agitated, makes noises, reverses its tracks, looks at him with strange eyes, salivates, and snaps at the feet of his mule—thinking that it has rabies, only to discover afterward that the dog was trying to tell him that he had left his purse of money behind at his last camp.

Besides this moment of acceptance, an element of humility is appropriate to the threat of hubris. We cannot fully comprehend the impact of our actions in a globally interconnected technological world: here, too, we see reason for humility, and reason for a literature that brings this virtue to light. Not only literature but also the act of literary criticism would seem to educate to a proper sense of humility; insofar as the artwork is inexhaustible through finite analysis, and yet full of present richness in the hands of a good interpreter, our interpretations give us an appropriate sense of current meaning and suspension of meaning. Our reading may be very rich, which should be enjoyed, but it may also overlook aspects not yet grasped by us in our finitude. In an age where so much is easily calculable, it is enriching to be aware of a sphere where answers are not necessarily exhaustive and preferences, while grounded, are not always universal. This is a calling to both confidence and humility.

Finally, a corollary to the claim introduced above that one great artwork does not exclude another is the assertion that it is not easy to speak of progress within art. The diversity of art and the possibility of different manifestations of beauty means that some newer works will be different and not necessarily better. In addition, whereas in science we can almost always assume progress, in art many of the more organic and interesting works derive from earlier eras.[6] Indeed, some of the prerequisites of great art —emotional richness, the cultivation of certain virtues, breadth of knowledge—may diminish over time. Recognition of a sphere that has not necessarily reached its peak in the contemporary age is a just antidote to the hubris of the present, rendered visible in technical progress and in the idea, prominent within the humanities, that we have only now freed ourselves from centuries of illusions. Certainly, within art we do recognize the introduction of new forms (new arts, such as film, new techniques, such as free indirect discourse, new technologies for performance) and the introduction of newer, more contemporary themes. However, the greatness of an artwork is measured not by its formal innovations or even the local currency of its theme, but by its organic beauty. In this sense, we have reason to look toward other ages and even other cultures with great humility as we reflect on great artworks. If one of the extraordinary aspects of art is its ability to capture our imagination with what is different, many works of other eras may fulfill this dimension better than works of our era. In addition, newer works may suffer from the sense of being derivative or epigonal, or they may, in seeking to be bold, become one-sided and overlook ideal concepts of wholeness or coherence. The more recent in art is not always superior. Whereas in science the half-life of a new discovery is very short and the authority of tradition weak, in art we recognize or should recognize a great tradition of magnificent works, to which we must try to rise in the present, in our creations and our interpretations. In art, more than in many of the other spheres that dominate the technological age, we are both humbled and inspired by the past and its continuing impact on the present. This non-progressive view of art might encourage us to ask more critical questions of other aspects of contemporary culture, where we may falsely assume that the new is necessarily better.

INEXHAUSTIBLE MEANING

Walter Benjamin, as we saw above, claims that modern technology, especially its modes of reproduction, have not only changed art superficially but also affected its essence. Modern art no longer has aura, which is traditionally associated with uniqueness and inexhaustible meaning. Benjamin's thesis is provoking and suggestive, but it contains at least three problems. First, the dissolution of aura commenced long before modern technology made art mechanically reproducible; it began already with the processes of secularization, which seemed to divest art of its original depth and substance. Second, the loss of aura, if it were such, would not necessarily be welcome. Nor is the alternative model, the politicization of art, anathema to fascism, as Benjamin would have us believe; indeed, Leni Riefenstahl's *The Triumph of the Will* shows us that the collective medium of film can be everything but revolutionary in Benjamin's sense. Moreover, the resistance literature of inner emigration returned to the concept of "eternal value" that Benjamin views as merely regressive (217), and it countered the national socialist leveling of individuality by elevating the "unique existence" Benjamin scorns (220) (Roche, *Gottfried Benn* 39–55). Third, artworks in the technological age are not fully devoid of aura, if we define aura as inexhaustible meaning. Great art remains distant, however close we might come to capturing its essence, and precisely this is Benjamin's definition of aura: "the unique phenomenon of a distance, however close it may be" (222). One cannot claim to exhaust the depth of an artwork's meaning without at the same time reducing it.

No less than Benjamin, though quite differently, Heidegger articulates the concept of art's inexhaustible meaning. In his essay "The Origin of the Work of

Art," he emphasizes two complementary moments: the extent to which art reveals or opens a truth for us, art's *Entbergung*, and the extent to which our attempts to grasp the artwork always meet with a certain resistance or concealment, art's *Verbergung* (53). The artwork cannot be reduced to the categories we apply to objects of mere utility. Heidegger calls this moment of internal resistance or unrecoverable stillness in the artwork *das Insichstehen*, which could be translated as self-subsistence, self-sufficiency, or independence (48). He also terms this moment of irreducible depth, which is beyond what can be recognized, articulated, or mastered, "the earth" (46). The artwork opens a world, makes possible a clearing, and yet does not reveal all: "The earth is the spontaneous forthcoming of that which is continually self-secluding and to that extent sheltering and concealing" (48). Contrary to many contemporary heirs of Heidegger, who have abandoned any notion of truth beyond the particular or pragmatic, Heidegger recovers a concept of the artwork as revealing and concealing a world and a truth that transcend both author and recipient; for Heidegger the artwork partakes of a higher and much richer concept of truth than most contemporaries, preoccupied with the concept of subjectivity, would find acceptable. Also significant in this context is Heidegger's choice of the term *earth*, for he elliptically suggests thereby that art, with its moment of resistance to human will, offers us a countertruth to technology, which he criticizes in other contexts for its "devastation of the earth" ("Überwindung der Metaphysik" 72 and 99).

Recognition of the inexhaustibility of art and beauty does not originate with Benjamin and Heidegger. We need only think of Plato's account of the close proximity of beauty and love (according to Plato's Diotima both the initial catalyst for love and its ultimate telos is beauty) and Plato's insight into love as a form of striving: we love what we lack or do not possess (*Symposium* 200–12). A beautiful work continues to attract and enchant us, even after multiple encounters, because our reflections or analyses do not exhaust its meaning; there are always undiscovered nuances to weigh, new parts to relate to the whole. This inexhaustible richness has two temporal dimensions. First, the artwork brings together layers of meaning in history and reworks them in new ways; to exhaust the work one would have to recognize all of the past that the work contains and sublates, which is not possible in our finite frames. Second, the artwork is open toward the future; it invites readings that will become concrete only when as yet to be formulated perspectives emerge, and it seeks to earn the right to be called a work for the ages, a designation given only to those works that—as a result of their richness, complexity, and beauty—forever merit rereading. The artwork thus condenses in its particularity both the past and the future and for these reasons invites, sustains, and rewards patient elaboration.

Art provides us with a richness of meaning that knows no boredom, only the inexhaustible meaning of truth. Deeper meaning is found in quiet contemplation, not in immersion in things, and the artwork, because of its simultaneous revelation and resistance, invites this continuing and lingering attention. In a sense we can say that the artwork itself is not only inexhaustible but also participates in an ideal sphere and gives light to that sphere without exhausting the ideal: in both senses, then, our reception does not exhaust art's meaning. Goethe alludes to this dimension of great art in his elevation of what he calls the symbolic: "Symbolism transforms the appearance into an idea and the idea into an image—in such a way that the idea always remains infinitely operative and unattainable in the image, and even if it were articulated in every language, it would still remain ineffable" (12.470). The process of rereading cultivates a transcendence of mere speed and linearity, evoking a concept of mythical circularity, which enriches our sense of meaning in time (Calinescu 56). In a culture defined by the quantity and pace of its images, the appreciation of art offers a different experience, defined by intense concentration of attention, a lingering over the complexity of aesthetic structures, patience in exegesis. Such an engagement with the artwork is its own reward, an experience of great value in and of itself. By discussing diverse facets and competing interpretations of a single literary work, we weigh in a sustained way issues and values of both timeless and timely relevance.

By way of its sensuous presentation of concrete figures literature stresses the individual in an age of the mass. As Gehlen notes, the social sciences deal with statistics and models and even psychology must work with abstract types, but history and even more so art, including portraiture and literature, are able to portray "the individual in his uniqueness" (*Man* 151). Indeed, if we accept the idea that literature offers us the uniquely inexhaustible as well as ideal essences, it not only differs from, it also transcends, the social sciences. Literature gives dignity to the person: first, by stressing the individual; second, by focusing on what is essential to the individual, meaningful intersubjective relations and a sense of transcendence; third, by giving the individual noble traits or unveiling the inner emptiness of a loss of such traits; and finally, by setting up an analogy, which is invoked in the work's title, between the work, which is inexhaustible, and the individual, who is also inexhaustible. "Effi Briest," for example, refers both to the novel, in its inexhaustible richness, and the character, whose complexity is likewise irreducible. This as yet unexplored concept of titular reflexivity recognizes the reciprocal depth of both the artwork and the individual human being.

Art awakens in us a sense of irreplaceable and unique beauty. I have already described the potential overlap of art and techne, of artistic and scientific imagination, but differences exist. It may be possible to compare, say, drama or film, with electricity or the telephone, and suggest that if one artist or inventor did not invent any one of these, another would have done so eventually (this applies to the discovery of scientific truths as well), but we cannot say the same of any one single work of literature. A great work of literature participates in universal laws of development and has universal value, but the work's combination of the universal and the particular, unlike a technical invention or a scientific truth, weights the individual more. Inventors of new techniques or products disappear under the objectivity of their inventions, which are reworked and developed by others (Cassirer, "Form" 207–9), whereas an artwork, which is singular, remains tied to its creator. The unique artwork is an especially rich and different product for an age of technology, where so much is simply common. In the technological age we see the standardization and uniformity of life, the similarity of so many aspects of so many otherwise different societies and cultures, which now have common information, common technologies, common products. Already Walter Rathenau recognized "homogeneity" and "homogenization" as the distinguishing characteristics of the age (71). With increasing uniformity in chain stores and standardized products, one loses a sense of character and place. Art counters this monotony with its diversity. Our experience of great art gives us a recognition of what is not only unique and distinctive but also a gift that cannot be willfully manufactured. Great literature turns our attention away from a preoccupation with what is mass-produced and collective, what is easily constructed and replaced.

In response to mass production, the Victorian critic John Ruskin elevated the craftsman ideal, with its integration of intellect and labor and its fine workmanship. According to Ruskin, we should avoid the routine, the imitative, the rigid, the monotonous, and the redundant. Instead we should elevate the inventive, the unique, the irregular, the variable, and the expressive. Ruskin, who inspired the American arts and crafts movement, with its integration of the fine and applied arts, defends his ideal with an appeal to the principle of variety within the organic: "Nothing that lives is, or can be, rigidly perfect; part of it is decaying, part nascent. The foxglove blossom,—a third part bud, a third part past, a third part in full bloom,—is a type of the life of this world. And in all things that live there are certain irregularities and deficiencies which are not only signs of life, but sources of beauty. No human face is exactly the same in its lines on each side, no leaf perfect in its lobes, no branch in its symmetry. All admit irregularity as they imply change; and to banish imperfection is to destroy expression, to check exertion, to paralyze vitality" (10.203–4). In developing his arguments, Ruskin embraces the principle of variation within Gothic architecture and elevates the character and uniqueness of old Venetian glass over against the more accurately cut, but less artistic, and standardized modern glass (10.180–269, esp. 10.199–200).

Two important ingredients of technology, as we have seen, are repetition and external teleology. Efficient technology presupposes repetition; thus, the symmetry in the production of parts, the functioning of the conveyer belt, and the economic imperative to produce multiple instances of the same model. Any piece of technology can be replaced by the same part or a better part; each is interchangeable. Further, the goal of a technical process, if it is not already art, always lies outside itself: each functioning tool is part of a higher-level process that eventually leads to a product of one kind or another. Literary works, which are unique, have a different structure. Already Kant recognized that mere understanding is not capable of exhausting the essence of art or humanity: neither can be reduced to the merely calculable. When we as human beings are treated merely as replaceable parts in a larger system, our dignity is weakened. Too much technology and too little art make the transfer of technical categories to humanity all too dangerous.

Science and technology are universal; their laws are precise and unwavering; literature is diverse, variable, and singular. Technology is primarily oriented toward the general, not the individual, toward mass production, not uniqueness; technology is not especially culturally bound, nor do the laws of efficiency normally allow it to generate unique products. In our reception of literature, on the other hand, we gain greater sensitivity to what is singular, not only the artwork and the human being but also, by analogy, the unrepeatable nature of the world, which is a trust, not something we ultimately own in our private subjectivity or something we can destroy and simply recreate. At the conclusion of *Science and the Modern World,* Alfred North Whitehead speaks of the need to transcend both practical and scholarly knowledge and develop "aesthetic apprehension," by which he means "an appreciation of the infinite variety of vivid values achieved by an organism in its proper environment" (199). Literature, with its moments of particularity and uniqueness, strengthens our sensibility for irreplaceable and unique beauty in a way that philosophy does not. Like nature, literature partakes of a richness and variety that needn't be viewed as exclusive; in each, difference is bountiful and desirable. By way of analogy, then, literature may give us a more differentiated sensibility to the varieties of plant and animal species on earth. In an age of unprecedented loss of plant biodiversity, with one out of every eight plants potentially at risk of extinction, a broad sense of the value of diversity cannot be stressed enough.[7] Through literature we gain a greater appreciation of what is unique, which is essential for a nurturing relationship toward nature.

Art not only awakens, by analogy, awareness of the dignity and beauty of nature, it also helps us to identify with our surroundings and gain a sense of being at home. In earlier cultures persons tended to have a more aesthetic relationship to their environment, for the objects of emotional identification had greater particularity—one identified with a small abode, a community, a trade. To identify with a multinational corporation, a large national bureaucracy, or a society of openly competing perspectives is difficult. Our relations to the world of nature are increasingly colored by abstract scientific theories; our work is increasingly focused on knowledge and information, not tangible goods and objects; and our retirement savings are increasingly abstract, consisting primarily of intangible financial instruments, instead of family estates or land. What is vast, abstract, and diffuse does not invite aesthetic sensibility. This modern condition, while giving us more mobility and greater options, intensifies the need for a more artificially induced aesthetic experience. In earlier cultures, for persons to be at home with themselves, content with their position in life, was easier—as other options were not available to them, or they did not question, as a modern consciousness does, the value of the life to which they were led. Persons had a less complicated relationship to their more immediate surroundings. Today one's sense of happiness may hinge not on one's immediate surroundings or occupation but on more abstract concepts, such as income and success. To invest one's happiness in such terms will mean less engagement with one's immediate surroundings and thus less aesthetic pleasure.

The extraordinary attraction of drugs in contemporary culture says something about the need for alternative modes of thinking and being. Drugs function as an escape, whereas art can give its recipients another perspective that leaves them fulfilled, rather than empty; clear-headed and enriched, rather than confused and clouded. One needn't make a long plea for art over drugs to the readers of this book, but it does seem to me to be an unstudied question, whether precisely some of the needs met by drugs, sensuous enrichment and movement into alternative spheres, aren't needs that art also addresses and has addressed in other cultures. Art can be an alternative: on the formal level of mere play it displaces instrumental thought; on the level of content it offers a window onto different worlds—this moment of alterity is especially the case in art from other ages and cultures and in idealistic art that knows itself to be in conflict with its age. In our discussion of disenchantment, we discussed the emptiness of meaning that leads to stasis and cynicism. Art can counter these dangers not just thematically, but through its very essence. As Plato suggests, art awakens a striving toward something higher, and beauty elicits a sensuous longing that draws us upward toward spirit. Not only in its particular manifestations, but also in its essence, art can perform these functions, which, in bringing us to these higher spheres, renders meaning inexhaustible.

TRANSHISTORICISM

While our everyday routines are of necessity limited in scope, literature opens up new horizons and does so in a variety of ways. First, every great work of literature belongs to a tradition that it invokes, reworks, or overcomes. Studying past literature is an immersion in times that transcend our own. If we recognize the achievements of the past and the possibilities of coming generations, then one of our duties is to sift through the works of the past, to preserve them in their integrity and with the richest possible interpretations, primarily because of their intrinsic value but also with an eye to the past and the future. In meaningfully preserving great works, we exhibit respect for the past, the originators of the works and the tradition that cultivated their interpretation, and for future persons who will likewise participate in the wonder of these works and benefit from the richest interpretations they have garnered. One of the beautiful aspects of a frame narrative, such as Storm's *The White Horse Rider,* that tells a story through several generations is its embrace of continuity, one might even say, its recycling of meaning. Contemporary literature on technology, such as Helga Königsdorf's *Disrespectful Relations,* likewise elevates "longing for a greater continuity" between the past and future (27). Königsdorf reflects—via imaginary conversations between the narrator and the deceased physicist Lise Meitner—on the situation of women in a male-dominated world as well as on the scientist's responsibilities toward the future and the role of imagination and recollection in grappling with questions of values, identity, continuity, and uniqueness. Reading great works of literature is an immersion in times that transcend our own. And the greater value we attach to the past, the more we recognize the importance of preserving a future in which these insights can continue to flourish and to which they can be passed on "from one generation to the next" (48). An encounter with great literature may motivate us to think that there is indeed something worth preserving, that the durable transcends the disposable in value.

Second, the works of earlier eras can teach us specific virtues that have been lost in the present but represent alternatives to contemporary weaknesses. Certain virtues are more prominent in given historical circumstances than in others. Reading older literature reminds us of virtues that are less visible in the technological age but still of great value. Despite the modern elevation of subjectivity, the entertainment industry, led by television, tends to erode self-reliance. The elevation of instrumental reason leads many to think of grace as antiquated. Similarly rare today is an indifference to one's economic position or status within society, an ability to remain autonomous. Loyalty is also less visible—partly because we have become so mobile, partly because our relationships have become increasingly driven by utility. Similar factors contribute to the erosion of generosity and hospitality. The elevation of instrumental rationality over value rationality has led us to replace the concept of vocation, which animates a masterpiece like Tarkovsky's *Andrei Rublev*, with the more superficial concept of career. Physical courage is less tested in an age where relationships are subject to rationalization and codification. Its analogue in the contemporary age is civil courage, but recognizing cowardice when civil, not physical, courage is at stake is not always easy. Similarly lacking in many developed societies that have already institutionalized basic normative values is self-sacrifice. The rights of the individual tend to be valued more than duties toward others or toward an ideal. When self-sacrifice arises, it may involve not physical danger but a sacrifice of one's position or of respect among one's peers. It may also imply changing one's daily routine rather than making a singular and heroic sacrifice; it may mean nonaction rather than common action. In an age, moreover, in which one is hesitant to change because others may not change and where the consequences of one's actions are mingled with the consequences of the actions of countless others, thereby reducing the perception of individual responsibility, self-sacrifice and the leadership associated with it are highly desirable.

Third, the literature of other ages, our knowledge of the past, is the best path to obtain distance from the clichés and biases of the present, especially as the next best alternative often means a kind of subjectivist circling within oneself. Independently of the questions as to which virtues can best counter the prejudices of the present, and where in earlier literature can they be found, arises the very simple idea that on a formal level technology, aided by advertising, encourages us to conform to the standards of the age and to desire whatever others desire. An encounter with literature of other ages gives us different perspectives and alternatives to the present.[8] In that sense it can become contemporary, by which I mean here meaningful for the present, precisely because it is not contemporary, that is, of the present. Familiarity with another culture creates a critical distance toward one's own. The stories of the past free us from the tyranny of the age. Indeed, our relation to the past gives us not only alternatives to motivate critique but also impulses to help us expand our identity. We gain through this process a form of rationality one might call wisdom, which comes with age and experience, including encounters with the past. Wisdom differs from instrumental rationality, even if it is not without its own kind of utility; its greatness lies partly in knowing what is beyond mere utility.

Fourth, great literature, as Chekhov shows in his story *The Student,* addresses themes of universal interest. On a cold, gloomy, and windy Good Friday, a student retells the Gospel story of Peter's anguish at having betrayed Christ. The widows who listen to the story are moved, and the student reflects: "It was evident that what he had just been telling them about, which had happened nineteen centuries ago, had a relation to the present—to both women, to the desolate village, to himself, to all people" (108). He senses that the chain of meaning is not broken between the past and the present. This connection, which is enchanting and full of lofty meaning, gives the student in his desolate material condition a sense of great joy. "He thought that truth and beauty, which had guided human life there in the garden and in the yard of the high priest had continued without interruption to this day, and had evidently always been the chief thing in human life and in all earthly life, indeed" (108). Through art we learn from the past, thus rendering otherness not just an object of curiosity but a partner of existential import. One of the insights of the technological age is that not all forms of progress and technical expansion are desirable. By showing us what is great in the past, art is able to remind us of what is lost with certain forms of progress and to draw our attention to values that might yet be regained. This goal can be attained only if we recognize, beyond obvious historical differences, certain supertemporal constants, so that our engagement with works from earlier eras is not merely antiquarian but an earnest effort to learn from the works of other ages. This constancy is important, yet so is the difference, for studying the past as a genuine partner in conversation gives us alternatives to the passing modes of the present. What becomes valuable is not the newest but the greatest that has ever been thought. To have such an encounter with the past is humbling for the present.

Fifth, literature allows us a vision into the future, as in science fiction, which combines detailed scientific-technical knowledge with imagination, fantasy, and in many cases archetypical structures; science fiction represents, therefore, a privileged synthesis of two spheres normally separated. Moreover, it is capable of addressing the distant consequences and effects of human action in an age of technology and is thus strikingly contemporary; at the same time, it builds on an ancient concept of literature as higher than history, Aristotle's suggestion that what could be is more philosophically interesting than what is; in this sense, science fiction is a privileged combination of the contemporary and the classical. Paradoxically, its embodiment of Aristotle's classical definition of poetry consists in its postcontemporary content, for it is able to raise the ethical questions of the next generation. Not surprisingly, such works resonate very well with the public. Michael Crichton's best-seller *Jurassic Park,* for example, deals with the classical and contemporary theme of scientists irresponsibly creating forces they are unable to control; such a theme is understandably of interest to today's readers, as it was to readers of Mary Shelley's day.

The following table brings into focus the relation between various categories of the technological age and the ways in which great literature can respond to them:

Technical rationality	Intrinsic value
Subjectivity	Self-transcendence
Quantity	Balance
Autonomous value systems	Overarching connections
Hubris and impuissance	Perspective
Disenchantment and dissonance	Inexhaustible meaning
Shortsightedness	Transhistoricism

Chapter 8 Technology, Ethics, and Literature

In his award-winning *Imperative of Responsibility* Hans Jonas offers new insights into the ethical challenges of the technological age. Karl-Otto Apel eleborates in his work on transcendental pragmatics the contemporary threats against humankind and develops an important reformulation of the categorical imperative. Vittorio Hösle, finally, offers a series of systematic reflections on the philosophy of the ecological crisis. Although none of these thinkers focuses on aesthetics, we can develop some of their reflections on technology and ethics in relationship to the question, How can literature and literary criticism respond to the technological age?

Jonas recognizes that previous ethical models presupposed that the consequences of our action were limited—both temporally and spatially. In the technological age, in contrast, our actions have "long-range effects" (27). Many of the effects of our technical activity will not be unveiled for many years and potentially at locations distant from the sources of our actions. Although scientific developments have enhanced our knowledge of future effects, technology has also increased the factors influencing the future; complexity is a corollary of technology. Jonas is especially concerned with the irreversible consequences and cumulative character of our actions. He proposes a categorical imperative that has an extended temporal horizon and a collective, not merely an individual, orientation. According to Jonas, we should not compromise the conditions that are necessary for humanity to continue indefinitely on earth. In current democracies those who do not yet exist have no lobby, and the unborn are themselves powerless, but at least one goal of responsible action should be to ensure the continuation of a species that can act responsibly.[1]

What consequences can we draw for literature from Jonas's analysis? First, we can elevate with Jonas what we might call the "literature of distant effects." Jonas argues that it is easier to perceive evil than good, as the latter is often invisible without its contrary, whereas the perception of evil "is more direct, more compelling, less given to differences of opinion or taste, and, most of all, obtruding itself without our looking for it" (27). The evil that Jonas fears is uniquely threatening: first, because the pace of technical change may prevent self-correction and, second, because in the ultimate matter of the continuation of humanity a second chance is not possible. For these reasons Jonas elevates what he calls "the heuristics of fear" (26). We need to imagine the spatial and temporal, including long-range, effects of our actions. Literature would seem to be uniquely qualified to provide images of such effects. It can succeed in this endeavor by uncovering already contemporary consequences that are not immediately recognized or by portraying future consequences, which require more radical vision and for which literature is an ideal medium: "The creatively imagined *malum* has to take over the role of the experienced *malum,* and this imagination does not arise on its own but must be intentionally induced" (27). While social ills may be more immediately visible to contemporary consciousness, the abstract concept of future threats to humanity requires greater imagination, both for authors and for readers.[2]

Because long-range effects are in the realm of possibility, not actuality, literature is capable of portraying these effects, and to do so is one of its moral obligations, not for every author but certainly for literature taken as a whole in this age. We tend not to change our behavior if the immediate consequences of our action are not visible; therefore, literature has an educative role to play. For Jonas, like Dürrenmatt, the new ethical responsibilities of the technological age are not restricted to scientists. We are all marked existentially by our immersion in, and dependence on, technology and ethically by our use of technology, which contributes indirectly to current and potential problems. The topic of literature in the technological age must, therefore, also engage the problems of our expectations and consumption, the consequences of our everyday action. The value of a heuristics of fear lies not only in helping us recognize our role in the endangerment of nature but also in reinforcing the principle that "the prophecy of doom" is to be given more weight than "the prophecy of bliss" (31). According to Jonas, "One can live without the supreme good but not with the supreme evil" (36). The purpose of the literary prophet is to be proven wrong, that is, to motivate action in the present, such that the worst-case scenario of the future not take place. Huxley's *Brave New World* is an example of just such a motivating dystopia.

In the tradition of Schiller and Scheler, Jonas suggests that though reason alone can ground the good (the objective moment of ethics), many legitimate motivations exist for acting according to the good (the subjective moment of ethics). Literature can play a role in drawing implicit connections, for example, between those nonreciprocal responsibilities and duties we have toward children that are not part of a social contract and our responsibilities toward future human beings. Jonas elevates, as does Hegel, the ancient state, which plays a role as educator, and criticizes the liberal state of free individuals, where rights are elevated over duties ("what is not forbidden is allowed" [173]). The state, by supporting certain kinds of art, can contribute to the moral edification of its population, and when it does not do so, it undermines itself. Through empathy, we can see that, though certain negative consequences may not affect the doer, they will have an impact on coming generations. Because Jonas, unlike Kant, sees ethics as a collective concern, an elevation of the arts, based on Jonas, might affirm the value of those art forms, above all theater and film, that tend to be received communally and cultivate, by the very form of their reception, a sense for what transcends individuality.

Second, not only might we elevate with Jonas a literature concerned with the future consequences of our actions and the need for responsibility, we might also endorse a literature that cultivates a love of existence, what we might call a "literature of the present." Jonas reproves the modern elevation of teleology, which is directed solely toward expansion into the future and fails to appreciate the value of the present. He criticizes Ernst Bloch's elevation of utopia, both his instrumentalization of the present for the future and the emptiness of his utopian paradise. Jonas argues for limits and responsibility, not progress and utopia. In contrast to Bloch, Jonas wants to suspend "the higher aspirations for perfection" (129); simple continuation of existence is what matters for Jonas, and in his eyes asceticism is a virtue. Jonas wants to do away with the external teleology found in Marx, Nietzsche, and Bloch, which argues that "everything past was only a preliminary" (157). He would replace utopia with an ethics of responsibility, so that humanity may simply continue; he would cease to elevate the future at the expense of the present, the ideal at the cost of the real, so that what is, is recognized in its inherent value. Jonas elevates the insight that every present age of humanity is its own end and that this sense of intrinsic value applies to each past age as well: "Genuine man is always already there and was there throughout known history: in his heights and his depths, his greatness and wretchedness, his bliss and torment, his justice and his guilt—in short, in all *ambiguity* that is inseparable from his humanity" (200).

In a rare passage on art Jonas criticizes Bloch's popular theory of art as "prefiguration," a prolepsis of what is to come (200). Jonas narrates his experience of Giovanni Bellini's Madonna triptych: "When I found myself, unexpectedly, standing before Giovanni Bellini's Madonna triptych in the sacristy of St. Zaccaria in Venice, I was overcome by the feeling: here had been a moment of perfection, and I am allowed to see it. Eons had conspired toward that moment, and in eons it would not return if left unseized: the moment when, in a fleeting 'balance of colossal forces' the All seems to pause for the length of a heartbeat to allow a supreme reconciliation of its contradictions in a work of a man. And what this work of man holds fast is absolute *presence* in itself—no past, no future, no promise, no succession, whether better or worse, not a prefiguration [Vor-Schein] of anything, but rather timeless shining [zeitloses Scheinen] in itself" (200). Literature can affirm presentness and show the value of what is; through beautiful moments it can evoke the greatness of the present, stressing not further striving, but contentment, a sense of richness with what is. An aesthetics modeled on Jonas might return us to the idea of art not as prefiguration, or "Vor-Schein," but as a sense of the beauty of the present, as "zeitloses Scheinen."

Literature, then, that criticizes our utopian thinking would fulfill this model, but so, too, would any literature that affirms presentness, that shows the value of what is, that sees greatness and beauty in the present, that evokes timeless appearance. Within this frame, one might elevate sculpture, which has traditionally been viewed as the negation of time. One might even go so far as to suggest that a literary portrait of Jonas's worldview, with its affirmation of being and negation of restlessness, might well involve the creation of a contemporary countermyth to Faust, which so dominates the modern idea of ruthless progress and unfulfilled striving. Such a countermyth might extol the very temptation that Goethe's Faust was to avoid: "Abide a while! You are so fair" (1700). One genre of literature seems especially poised to capture the affirmation of reality that Jonas seeks. Comedy normally results in equilibrium and integrates human beings into their environment. Generally concerned more with survival than with progress or perfection, comic heroes willingly accept limitations; they accommodate and endure. Comedy celebrates the material and biological, and it elevates not the unique and heroic individual but the diversity of the larger group, the whole of the species or even the cosmos; the comic genre embraces the continuity of life. In these ways comedy reaffirms and illustrates a prominent moment in Jonas.[3]

Jonas, however, tends to relinquish in his writings the ideal moment; this is problematic in at least two respects. First, the portrayal of future evil is often less of a motivator than a positive future, with which we can identify. To motivate persons, one must show what should be, not only what should *not* be. Second, the continued existence of what is, has value, but its value is enhanced when we recognize that precisely the ideal gives it meaning. Being is a prerequisite for the ideal, but the ideal gives the present meaning. This second moment is especially drawn by Karl-Otto Apel in the important concluding essay of his *Towards a Transformation of Philosophy*, "The a priori of the Communication Community and the Foundations of Ethics: The Problem of a Rational Foundation of Ethics in the Scientific Age." Apel opens his lengthy essay by pointing to an irony: because of technical transformations the contemporary age needs ethics more than any previous era, yet precisely in this age of acute need we have concluded that a rational grounding of ethics is impossible. Modern science is value-free, and precisely the dominance of this paradigm would seem to argue against an effort to find universal values. Values are not the purview of science, whether in its mathematical-logical form or by way of its empirical studies; values are ultimately subjective and irrational, a position that has many adherents, even among ethicists who try to ground ethics in local traditions or who relegate the question of binding norms to private conscience. Apel counters this dilemma, whereby a universal ethics is viewed as both necessary and impossible, by presenting a series of cogent arguments for a reformulation of Kantian ethics. Like Jonas, Apel recognizes the need to expand Kant in the light of the potentially far-reaching consequences of our actions.

Making use of performative contradictions, Apel develops the transcendental conditions of all rational discourse: that the discussion continue and that it seek higher meaning. From this he draws on behalf of modernity a twofold imperative: that we not destroy ourselves and that we seek always to develop and deepen our discourse (429–31). The first imperative is the necessary condition of the second, and the second gives meaning to the first. With Jonas, Apel ar-

gues for the sober recognition of limits, so that humankind can continue to exist; yet Apel stresses, unlike Jonas, the need not only to preserve the community
of discourse but also to enrich it. The dominant argument in Apel's attempt to
come to terms with Jonas is the need to retain a regulative ideal; without it
Jonas would have difficulties arguing against "a merely social-Darwinistic solution to the problem of preserving the species" (24). Preservation of the human
species should not come at the cost of human dignity and justice. Not only
should there be a real community of discourse, it should seek to approach an
ideal community. This second imperative can be addressed through the spiritual and idealistic dimensions of literature, which reflect on both the dissolution of intersubjectivity in the face of modern crises and the goal of a reawak-
ened intersubjectivity across cultures. With a model of literature based on Apel
we might embrace both the presentness of the beautiful image (*das Sein*) and
the ideal proleptic moment of art (*das Sollen*). This would leave room for an
idealistic art that seeks substantial solutions to contemporary problems and an
enrichment of our current paths and is not escapist, simplistic, naive, or cliché
ridden. If Bloch and Jonas represent two poles, a concept of art based on Apel
might combine the virtues of each, creating a more balanced aesthetic theory.

Not surprisingly, Vittorio Hösle dedicates his *Philosophy of the Ecological
Crisis* to Jonas and his related volume *Practical Philosophy in the Modern World*
to Apel. In a sense Hösle would synthesize the substantive content of Jonas
with the more formal merits of Apel (*Moral und Politik* 21). Jonas tries to
ground our ethical obligations to nature by violating the naturalistic fallacy
and, after showing that nature has a sense of purpose, by trying to derive an
ought from an *is*. Hösle takes a different approach. He argues for an objective
idealist view of nature: nature has value because it is an instantiation of the absolute, not on as high a level as spirit—as it is not conscious of itself like spirit
is and thus not free—but it is a presupposition of spirit, and it contains within
itself the order of the absolute. Nature is not simply a construction of humanity or a tool for humanity. The objective idealist position uncovers the intrinsic
value of nature. Hösle sketches a philosophy of nature that unites the dignity of
nature, so elevated by Jonas, with the autonomy of reason, so strongly embraced by Apel. Hösle's theory explains both why a priori knowledge of nature
is possible (nature is constituted through the ideal sphere) and why humanity
has a special status in the cosmos (humanity is the being that can recognize the
laws of this ideal sphere).

The objective idealist framework not only overcomes the Kantian dualism
that discredits nature (because the will of rational beings is the only entity that

has intrinsic value), it introduces obligations toward nature. Hösle follows Jonas in arguing that not all ethical imperatives are defined by symmetry. Our relations toward nature are not symmetrical with our relations toward other human beings, but humanity nonetheless has obligations toward it. In developing his theory Hösle returns, as did other objective idealists, Leibniz, Schelling, and Hegel, to aspects of antiquity. (Descartes, Kant, and Fichte, who elevate subjectivity, on the other hand, virtually ignore antiquity.) These objective idealists see nature as a manifestation of the absolute. This different mode of viewing nature is perfectly compatible with modern science, as can be recognized in the case of Albert Einstein. By acknowledging ethical obligations in nonsymmetrical relations, Hösle follows a path different from that of Apel, who is limited, first, by a formalism that does not recognize content-filled obligations within individual spheres of life and, second, by a discourse ethics that grounds obligations in our view of others as potential partners in conversation and so leaves no room for obligations toward nature or even toward those human beings who could never contribute meaningfully to our debates. In Apel's scheme, as in much of modernity, intrinsic value gives way to instrumental value.

Unlike both Jonas and Apel, Hösle reflects in some detail on both the economic and political repercussions of his philosophical analyses. Economic and political considerations are clearly more pressing than literary ones, but literature has its role to play as well. In at least four ways we can see through Hösle's various reflections a privileged role for literature or new areas for literature and literary criticism to explore. First, Hösle wisely suggests that we may be more strongly motivated to act in an ecological manner not by hearing of the death of a particular species, in a negative way, but by developing a positive relationship to nature. Hösle recognizes, in implicit contrast to Jonas, that hate and fear do not suffice: new values must be found, and our motivation must be positive (for example, a love of nature), not simply negative (the avoidance of harm). In this spirit we might elevate in our scholarship and in the classroom the nature poetry of the eighteenth century and beyond, which has become less analyzed, as we have moved further and further into political and self-reflective literature.

Brockes, to cite the earliest of the great modern nature lyricists in German, may be less foreign to a contemporary consciousness than he was to readers for much of the twentieth century. One thinks also of the range of nature poems by Albrecht von Haller, Friedrich Klopstock, Goethe, Hölderlin, Joseph Freiherr von Eichendorff, Eduard Mörike, Storm, and others. Also in the modern era are impressive poems about nature by such authors as Marie Luise Kaschnitz, Günter Kunert, Hans Magnus Enzensberger, and Sarah Kirsch, even if many of the more contemporary works embed glimpses of the beauty of nature within a more overarching understanding of the precariousness of nature. The reader of English will find a rich array of nature poetry among such well-known British romantics as Wordsworth, Coleridge, Shelley, and Keats, lesser-known romantic poets like John Clare, early and modern American poets like Ralph Waldo Emerson, Herman Melville, Walt Whitman, and Robert Frost, and not insignificant poems about nature by contemporary English and American writers, such as Ted Hughes, W. S. Merwin, Mary Oliver, Pattiann Rogers, and Alice Walker.[4] Through such poetry one is more likely to feel at home in nature and with nature; the poems awaken a deeper appreciation of nature as *Mitwelt.* The mainstream ecological movement tends to place its emphasis on the need to preserve nature for the sake of humanity's continued existence. An aesthetic relationship to nature goes beyond this in at least two ways: it recognizes the value of nature for us as emotional and sensuous beings, not simply rational beings; and it views nature as something that is of value for its own sake.

Within this context of reflecting on literature as a source of inspiration, we might note the value of the drama of reconciliation, which is scarcely visible in the landscape of contemporary literature, and the utopia. A drama of reconciliation is not easy to compose in an age that elevates negativity and dissonance. For this reason we might be especially attentive to hints in this direction, moments of harmony within a world of contingency, which might represent a nonlinear, nonteleological, almost spatialized version of synthetic literature. Utopian works have for the most part given way in our age to satire and dystopias. No modern utopia can compete with the dystopias of Huxley and Orwell. To write a dystopia is simpler, for to diagnose problems is easier than to propose coherent solutions, especially in an age that is no longer ordered by a coherent worldview and that knows the destructive as well as seductive capacities of modern technology. Moreover, any attempt to propose solutions requires us to cover an array of interrelated issues and to find the appropriate balance between such complex issues as freedom and order and the individual and the collective.

Not surprisingly, one of the greatest utopias of all time, Sir Thomas More's *Utopia,* is embedded within a frame narrative that makes it unclear which positions More ultimately prefers, which he is weighing as possible alternatives, and which he is criticizing. This elasticity gives him more room to experiment, and the reflection required of the reader encourages him to reach a meaningful level of autonomy. A modern utopia would need to deal with certain supertemporal problems thematized in classical utopias, such as gender, education, justice, and the economy, including the production and distribution of resources, as well as various problems that earlier utopias did not explore in detail. Questions of ecology and energy along with the problem of waste, the threat of self-destruction, and the topic of intergenerational justice would have to be addressed. Already in his utopia of 1619, *Christianopolis,* Johann Valentin Andreae lamented the overproduction of books; in a contemporary utopia the topic of overinformation would have to be central. Ernest Callenbach's *Ecotopia* hardly exhausts the potential of the genre.

Second, Hösle suggests the cultivation of ascetic virtues as one mode of overcoming consumerism and pleonasty. He rightly recognizes that the problem of overpopulation is related as much to the level of our needs and consumption as to the simple quantity of persons. Recognizing, on the one hand, the importance of intrinsic values and, on the other hand, the difficulties of imagining distant effects, Hösle suggests that it is better if we can recognize the poor intrinsic value of our actions. Even as he acknowledges the importance of Jonas's analysis of distant effects, Hösle elevates intrinsic value as a stronger motivator than imagined distant effects. Siding with Jonas's elevation of limits, Hösle suggests the recultivation of Stoic virtues. Again literature offers many examples of ascetic life and the different kind of contentment attached to such an existence. Here we might benefit from more attention to the tragedy of self-sacrifice, realistic tales of moderation and restraint, and comic depictions of modern overabundance. Working in harmony with this might be the ironization of those positions assumed to be virtuous and fulfilling in the present, as, for example, the acquisitive impulse. We might also reflect on the elegance, grace, and freedom of a life with fewer modern trappings and a more modest sense of need.

The elevation of the ascetic is especially countercultural if we recognize that one of the dominant goals of modern technology has been to increase living standards and consumption and that both of these factors have contributed to defining social success. As Gehlen notes in *Man in the Age of Technology,* anyone with historical consciousness cannot help but recognize that earlier generations had a much different view of ascetic values: "In any case the individual who renounced the goods of this earth always enjoyed a moral authority, whereas today he would be met with incomprehension" (78, translation modified). Asceticism, according to Gehlen, "adds to the integration and composure of the personality, and at the same time it sharpens the social impulses and increases spiritual awareness" (106, translation modified). Today's danger is less that persons in developed countries will not have enough, but that such persons will have too much: "The system . . . tends . . . to render *the right to renounce the life of high living* impossible, insofar as it itself *produces and automatizes the need to consume*" (108, translation modified). If the tendency is to be broken, recognition of alternative positions will be necessary, which raises the value of countercultural literature and the literature of other ages and cultures.

Third, one of the most startling sentences in Hösle's entire oeuvre is the simple statement that the level of Western consumption, if extended worldwide, would exhaust the earth's resources and is, by virtue of the categorical imperative, therefore immoral (*Philosophie der ökologischen Krise* 24–25). Implicit in this analysis is the need for greater understanding of the conflicts and differences between developed and developing countries, surely one of the most central ethical issues of the twenty-first century; we can view this need as an indirect call for more literary criticism about literature from developing countries and more literature about developing countries. Unlike many adherents of culture studies, Hösle argues that we should engage in dialogue with other cultures not simply because they are other, that is, because of the formal value of otherness; instead and more specifically, we should be motivated by the search for those moral values in other cultures that form a consensus in those cultures and that might also enrich our paradigm (*Philosophie der ökologischen Krise* 138). Beyond the merely formal appeal of encountering otherness, this engagement would give us two substantive moments: it would provide answers to dilemmas we have been unable to resolve within our culture, and it would implicitly raise the self-confidence of the other culture's collective identity.

Fourth, Hösle reflects on the difficulties of any paradigm shift, including the current one, that renders ecology the new paradigm of politics. Ecology, Hösle argues, is on the verge of becoming the driving force in our interrelations and the cause of many struggles—much as economics supplanted nationalism after World War II and nationalism in turn replaced religion as the dominant paradigm in the nineteenth century. Any such shift requires a total conversion of consciousness, and again literature must both work toward this change and help us process it intellectually and emotionally. If ecology represents the new political paradigm, literature can address this transformation thematically. Periods of transition have often provided a context for great aesthetic works, as, for example, with Aeschylus's *Orestia,* Cervantes's *Don Quixote,* and Chekhov's *The Cherry Orchard.*

The normative importance of ecology suggests that literature gains thereby not only an aesthetic opportunity but also an obligation. Literature and literary criticism should not be satisfied with the questions, What new forms can we make? and What new topics can we explore? Instead, we must reflect on the more normative questions, Which forms are most appropriate? and Which topics are most worthy of exploration? In an age of technology, the environment should be central in both literature and literary criticism, but many more topics come to mind, ranging from tragic self-sacrifice motivated by an environmental consciousness, as in the work and fate of Chico Mendes, to the social-justice, including racial, issues that arise as a consequence of the unjust distribution of environmental waste and pollution. Not surprisingly, some writers associate the destruction of nature with human callousness toward other human beings; this link between a lack of ecological consciousness and the violation of social justice is prominent, for example, in Linda Hogan's recent novel *Solar Storms*.

Artists, often ahead of their time, are able to render transparent emerging problems and suggest alternative perspectives. An artist who could thematize environmental issues, as earlier authors did with questions of religious intolerance, war and national injustice, class conflict and poverty, might be heralded as one of the great artists of our age. Literary critics, in turn, might be attentive to the emergence of works that engage issues unique to the technological age. Having said this, I do not want in the least to reduce writers' potential contributions to selected themes, for that would limit the value of a great number of artists from the tradition, from whom we have much to learn independently of the specifics of their age, and it would overstate the importance of theme, which is only one of several strategies that the contemporary artist can employ to address the complex challenges of the technological age. Moreover, one does not want to reduce the richness of literature to ecology any more than one wants to reduce it to race, class, or gender, but attention to this dimension in its specificity would raise new and interesting questions and in its general frame might very well lead us back to the question of literature as literature. The importance of literature in helping us address the ecological question lies not least of all in the fact that values are so often influenced by the broader social and cultural fabric. If we are to change collectively, literature as a factor in forming collective identity will need to play a role. Literature cannot solve our ethical dilemmas; for that we need philosophy and many other disciplines. Nor does good literature or good literary criticism suffice as a response to the problems of the technological age. Nonetheless, literature can help us better grasp our ethical dilemmas and social and ecological problems, and it can aid us in visualizing promising and unpromising directions. Moreover, it can restore some of what is lacking in the technological age, and it can motivate us toward responsible action.

Chapter 9 The Literary Canon and the Literary Critic in the Twenty-First Century

For centuries literary critics did not doubt that some works of litera-ture were greater than others and that one could defend and revise these judgments by an appeal to rational criteria. A consensus about the canon has essentially evaporated.[1] This erosion of the canon has had several catalysts. First, some critics accepted the value of literary works on the basis of tradition and authority alone. These critics were vulnerable in their judgments—on the one hand, because they could not defend them with an appeal to rational criteria, of which they no longer had command, and, on the other hand, because they tended to elevate the works in their totality and were thereby inattentive to often overlooked weaknesses. The inability to articulate reasons for the canon and blind adherence to the canon make one not only dogmatic but also vulnerable to sound criticism.

Second, new methodologies have taught us to ask different ques-tions of the literary works themselves. This innovation has in turn led us to discover previously neglected blind spots in canonical works and to sift them more carefully. In addition, these new methodologies have encouraged us to consider works that previously were neglected, sometimes for less than aesthetic reasons. Both of these moments, the new questions asked of literary works and the newly discovered works that compete with the traditional canon, have led to doubts about the coherence of the established canon.

Third, extra-aesthetic considerations have increasingly come to dominate discussions of the canon, such that the question of literary value has been increasingly displaced by nonaesthetic considerations that have inevitably led to different sets of privileged works. One claims, for example, that one should read in any seminar *x* number of works by a particular group or culture.

Fourth, the crisis within literary criticism is part of a broader crisis of the humanities, which has led to a vacuum of orientation and a lack of confidence concerning any judgments of supertemporal value. Finally, the sheer number of literary works available today makes it impossible for any one person to review them all and to make comparative quality judgments. Separating out the greater from the lesser works becomes more arduous simply as a result of quantity.

None of these arguments is especially persuasive as an absolute barrier to canon formation and evaluation. Certainly, one should not base aesthetic judgment on the consensus of tradition even if one hopes that a certain wisdom may lie hidden in tradition. One must also be in a position to recognize its mistakes and be able to articulate the standards for the inclusion of works in a canon. The number of works competing for our attention today gives one even greater reason to want to have a lens by which to judge which works are worthy of closer reading and study. The most celebrated recent attempt to defend the canon has been undertaken by Harold Bloom, above all in his best-seller *The Western Canon*. Bloom does not seek to defend the canon with systematic or moral categories. His argument is existential: literature offers opportunities for intense experience, hard-won pleasure; it allows us "to enlarge a solitary existence" (484). Bloom writes: "Aesthetic criticism returns us to the autonomy of imaginative literature and the sovereignty of the solitary soul, the reader not as a person in society but as the deep self, our ultimate inwardness" (10).

Since Bloom presupposes, on the one hand, a very individualistic frame and, on the other hand, "universality" as "the fundamental property of poetic value" (71), his interest in the historical dimension is modest. His canon nonetheless relates to history in three respects. First, Bloom uses a modified Vichian paradigm, whereby he divides literature into four ages: the theocratic, from its origins until just before Dante; the aristocratic, from Dante to Goethe; the democratic, from Wordsworth to Tolstoy and Ibsen; and the chaotic, which takes us into the present. Second, drawing on his earlier work on the anxiety of influ-ence, Bloom is fascinated by the ways in which individual authors aspire to be-come distinctive and original by struggling with the influences of their genial predecessors, above all Shakespeare, who is at the very center of Bloom's canon. The dominant category for inclusion in Bloom's canon is strangeness or ori-ginality, which is achieved by transcending the tradition. Third, Bloom oc-casionally notes the ways in which the contemporary age, both its broader tendencies and the writings of professors, works against an elevation of indi-viduality and aesthetic values; in this context, he seeks to elevate great and dis-tinctive literature: "At our present bad moment, we need above all to recover our sense of literary individuality and of poetic autonomy" (98). Without tak-ing anything away from the specific historical elements with which Bloom sup-plements his focus on universality, I have been arguing that we should ask the question, How does literature help us not only enlarge our individual frames of reference but also enhance our understanding of the collective concerns of an era—in our era, technology and ecology?

As aesthetic criteria for inclusion in a canon of great literary works I propose, first, that great works have a substantive idea or concept, which may be devel-oped simply or thoroughly. Works that lack substance, meaning, or a moment of transcendence are hardly worth recommending to others. Second, the work must be crafted in such a way as to be sensuously attractive in terms of its style and rhetoric, its diction and expression, its structure and genre. Again, this sen-suous appeal could range from the simple to the complex, from the beautiful to the sublime and the comic. Third, the work must be organic. The ideal and sensuous moments must cohere with one another and reinforce one another. Content and form must mutually support one another as well and not be in tension, unless such tension is again part of a metaform that reinforces the work's higher meaning. The work must cohere organically also in terms of part and whole. No part can be inexpressive of the whole. Fourth, the work must have a supertemporal dimension. It cannot address a theme that interests one particular age and would be of little or no interest to other eras. At the same time, the best works combine the enduring and the timely and so address the pressing issues of the day even as they contain moments that make them worth-while also for later generations. One cannot isolate any one of these dimensions and call a work great. A grand form enveloping a trivial or ill-conceived idea, a good idea in bad form, a sound idea laid upon a clever form that does not match the idea, and an innovative technique or a tendentious theme without lasting value—each of these instances gives us something less than the collective whole that is demanded of a great work of literature. Whether or not a particular work meets these criteria is a complex hermeneutic question that can be answered only by attending to the particularity of the work and our attempts to interpret it. Evaluation depends on good hermeneutic principles and activity, no less than it does on sound aesthetic principles.

If we accept the idea that not only certain themes but also distinct aesthetic principles resonate especially well in the technological age, then we might note as well those aspects of literature that have both supertemporal value and may be especially attractive in the technological age. The organic, for example, is not only universally necessary, it is especially important today insofar as it counters our dominant experience of information as haphazard, arbitrary, and unconnected. Further, it mirrors the ecosystem of nature and can lead in this way to a fuller recognition of the complexity of the organic in nature. A balance between the ideal and material spheres in art is beneficial for an age that all too often pushes us into one sphere at the expense of the other. Moreover, the concept of inexhaustible meaning may trigger a deeper sense of humility and a greater appreciation of diversity and complexity.

In addition, some works highlight one or the other aspect of literature that is either possible but not necessary or necessary but not always dominant. Some of these are especially significant today. First, in an age that overvalues the instrumental sphere, one of the most ideal forms of artistic expression does not openly criticize the instrumental, which might risk making the artwork itself instrumental, but instead embodies intrinsic value. Art that is enjoyable as art without a specific message for the age already contains a message for the age, the value of what is noninstrumental. In this sense poetry may have a special attraction, as it is often highly self-contained and of value for its pure form. Or one may think of the meandering novel, which takes the reader down paths that are seemingly irrelevant but turn out to have organic meaning, or the comedy of coincidence, whose higher meaning is related to its undermining of the hero's conscious intentions. Indeed, in this context one might note the value of the nonverbal arts, such as painting, which may more easily reach the ideal of embodying vital and intrinsic values. The extraordinary reception of the impressionists even to this day may be understood partly in this light.

Second, we might elevate those works that are especially effective at taking us beyond ourselves. I'm thinking of works that offer us new and unexpected ways of seeing, including works from other cultures and eras that teach us different or neglected virtues, such as restraint or loyalty or courage, and the value of what has survived the test of time. Works of other cultures and eras are timely for us insofar as so much of modern technology leads us into being consumed by the everyday and the present. Literature of other times and places gives distance to local perspectives. But complex works in our own tradition that require great effort, concentration, imagination, and patience to decipher also take us beyond ourselves.

Third, we might elevate those works that teach us the value of what is, that illuminate the ways in which nature and spirit partake of the absolute and embody the ideal sphere. Sacramental art that exhibits a divine presence in the world counters the constructivist spirit that has little reverence for the world and its intrinsic value. Acceptance and appreciation of what is, along with a sense of humility in the face of the divine around us, can be said to be desirable virtues in an age where too much is unnecessarily transformed and too little attention is given to the value of what is. Analogously, our age would benefit from artworks that elevate in theme and form the concept of measure, which is increasingly lost in the technological age's elevation of the infinite.

Fourth, in an era that has increasingly abandoned any sense of coherence or unity, we benefit not only from the organic linkage of part and whole in every artwork but also from holistic artworks that are able to capture a defining idea of an age or a culture or an experience, and even more so integrative artworks that convey the hidden connections between the logic of one subsystem of contemporary reality and another. Art, like philosophy, once had the telos of embodying the unity of an age. The ambitiousness of this goal does not render it any less desirable. Indeed, the greatness of Broch, Mann, and Musil is very much related to their efforts to unify the tendencies of their age.

Finally, much of the best literature in a technological age will deal directly with evil and the ugly, but only in order to show their inadequacies. Certainly, one of the greatest problems in modern art is the split into, on the one hand, kitsch, which fails to deal with evil and with the complexity of the good, and, on the other hand, the arbitrary and the ugly, which are recognized as fully valid realms of art in their own right instead of spheres that must be engaged yet also overcome. One form of ugliness is the degradation of nature. When such ugliness is portrayed in art, as seems desirable and appropriate today, its negativity should be manifest, even if only on a metalevel.

As teachers recommend works and select them for courses, they will also want to reflect, beyond these formal considerations, on specific texts, whether theoretical or literary, that address, directly or indirectly, the technological age or the ecological question. A number of German authors have multiple works, including earlier authors like Schiller, Hölderlin, Hoffmann, and Büchner;

modern authors like Hauptmann, Heinrich Mann, Kaiser, Döblin, Sternheim, Musil, Kafka, Broch, Toller, Ernst Jünger, Zuckmayer, Brecht, and Remarque; and postwar and contemporary authors like Frisch, Borchert, Dürrenmatt, Enzensberger, and Wolf. Also, individual works by authors who only occasionally address technology should be part of our recommendations and seminar lists or need to be read more fully in the light of technological questions.

The canon is partly guided by the works we choose for our classes, and one could imagine a very rich class in German literature that offers students a diachronic survey of central theoretical and literary works addressing literature in the technological age. The works selected for such a class might include Schiller's *On the Aesthetic Education of Man,* selected nature poems from the late eighteenth and early nineteenth centuries, Hoffmann's *The Sand-Man,* Büchner's *Leonce and Lena,* Raabe's *Pfister's Mill,* Storm's *The White Horse Rider,* Kafka's *In the Penal Colony,* Kaiser's *Gas I,* selected technology poems from the twentieth century, Benjamin's *The Work of Art in the Age of Mechanical Reproduction,* Heidegger's *The Question Concerning Technology* and *The Age of the World Picture,* Broch's *The Spell,* Dürrenmatt's *The Physicists,* Jonas's *The Imperative of Responsibility,* and Königsdorf's *Disrespectful Relations.* We should offer both broader and more focused courses on literature and the environment, just as we offer courses on such topics as literature and the other, and we must do so with attention to the full range of aesthetic concerns and not simply for ideological reasons. Film too would be relevant in such courses, not only for its formal integration of technology but also for its thematic portrayal, including such artworks as Lang's *Metropolis,* Ruttmann's *Berlin: Symphony of a Great City,* and Fassbinder's *The Marriage of Maria Braun.*

Students interested in other cultures might turn specifically to works in those cultures that engage technological questions, for example, Thoreau's *Walden* and Zamyatin's *We.* Or they might focus on contemporary efforts to address technology in other cultures, which might mean exploring such works as Gabriel García Márquez's *One Hundred Years of Solitude,* Jorge Amado's *Gabriela, Clove and Cinnamon,* and Isabel Allende's *The House of the Spirits.* Not surprisingly, the *Norton Anthology of Postmodern American Fiction* contains as one of its seven sections "Technoculture," which ranges from works that thematize technology to those that embody hypertextual formats (Geyh).

Also, our recommendations to students from other disciplines should be partly guided by their potential interest in the relation of literature to their disciplines. The student of biology, for example, who seeks a fuller understanding of beauty, might be encouraged to explore Kant's *Critique of Judgment* and Schiller's *On the Aesthetic Education of Man.* Students of sociology and of history who wish to explore the role of technology in culture might be encouraged to read such works as Storm's *The White Horse Rider* and Broch's *The Spell.*

As we move from the literary canon to the literary critic, we can recognize that most of the literary critic's responsibilities can be defined independently of the age in which critics find themselves, and so have already been elaborated in chapter 3. Nonetheless, just as literature ideally addresses not only universal concerns but also those of the age, we can recognize that certain tasks and goals become especially prominent in given periods. Therefore, reflection on the categories elaborated above leads us to some insights that supplement what has already been elaborated in part I concerning the responsibilities of the literary critic.

One aspect of the technological age elaborated above is increasing rationalization, including the elevation of the instrumental and the loss of balance between the sensuous and the rational. Authors, unlike critics, needn't reflect on the rational dimensions of their art; their creativity may well derive from prereflexive and subconscious impulses. The literary critic cannot neglect art's sensuousness, both its materiality and its irreducible moments, but must also attend to the rational dimensions of art in a way that the artist need not. Above all the critic needs value rationality and hermeneutic rationality in an age where these forms have become secondary to instrumental reason. The literary critic endeavors to interpret the work, to elaborate the strengths and weaknesses of diverse interpretations, and so must deal with the work also as a means to an end, the end being a meaningful and significant interpretation. Simultaneously, the critic treats the work as an end in itself. The interpretation is not only geared toward a final product; it is also an activity of intrinsic value, the joyous exercise of the faculties of imagination and reason. In addition to the interpretive activity that presupposes hermeneutic rationality, the critic must attend to aesthetic questions, which presuppose both philosophical and value rationality.

In an age of increased production of literary criticism and ever more sophisticated methodologies, the critic must be able, on the one hand, to recognize which other works of literary criticism are worthy of a full investment of his or her time, which presupposes the ability to decipher the essence of a secondary work quickly and to weigh its merits (both hermeneutic and value rationality), and, on the other hand, to integrate the useful methodologies that surface on a regular basis and so enrich the categories and questions with which we approach literary works. The critic engaged in peer review of others should weigh the value of their contributions with attention primarily to quality, not quantity.

The reception of literature has many levels. Great joy arises in the naive reception of literature. Readers may recall the first time they read a certain book, or even the first time they read any great work of literature or heard any great musical work or were first taken hold by a painting. Irreplaceable value lies in such novel experiences, which are frequently oriented toward the sensuous level. However, the disadvantage of an irreflexive elevation of the sensuous reception of literature is threefold: first, one simply moves on to the next aesthetic experience without benefiting from the previous one in a way that fully transcends the immediacy of the experience; second, because one does not reflect on the literature, one does not have the categories to prevent one's being led astray by bad literature; and third, various dimensions of most works are uncovered only through the complexity of the hermeneutic process. A second stage characterized by the merely rational interpretation of literature is no less desirable. Here the sensuous moment and the joyous, sometimes even disturbing and harrowing, dimensions of aesthetic experience tend to be bracketed. The literary critic must avoid a one-sidedly cerebral reception of literature, especially in an age that seeks balance in art. Ideally, literary critics embody a third mode of reading. They explicate the text but do not leave it broken into parts or view it only from the perspective of reason; instead, they read the parts from the perspective of the whole and attend to all its moments. Works that are truly rich become not less, but more interesting, the more time we spend with them, such that even after giving as full an analysis of an artwork as we can, we are drawn to reread the work, to view the painting or film again. When this is the case, we are not increasingly distant from the work or from the intensity of aesthetic experience but encounter a second naïveté that benefits from each new aesthetic experience—and does so on a level that unites the sensuous and the rational, the momentary and the enduring. In an age of rationalization, this second naïveté is easily lost. The literary critic should demonstrate in his or her engagement with the work not only mastery of evidence and argument but also appreciation of a work's playful and vital dimensions.

By being attentive to what the work has to say and not only to how we manipulate it, we gain a moment of self-transcendence. We might be especially attentive to works that don't simply replicate our feelings and anxieties but give us entirely different perspectives, including works from other ages and cultures. In this spirit the critic may want to question the contemporary aesthetic elevation of the particular, the arbitrary, and the chaotic, which in its emphasis on the mimetic reduces alternatives to the disorientation of the age. In general the literary critic should select works with attention to universal and particular needs. Today such choices may expand the critics' horizons, as they attend to new forms of art triggered by technology as well as neglected realms of beauty, such as that of nature. Despite the imperative to deal with the age, the critic should attend more to substance than to novelty. Works from other eras may say more to us today than the most recent of works. Cervantes, for example, may be in a higher sense more contemporary than Thomas Bernhard.

The literary critic who practices artwork aesthetics will benefit from the balance embodied in good literature and should stress this moment in discussions of art. The literary critic must defend his or her interpretation as coherent within itself and vis-à-vis the artwork, and the critic should seek the overarching connections elicited within the parts of the work and their often hidden coherence and complexity. Because the age is especially attentive to the fascination of the ugly and the allure of evil, the critic must show that whereas a simple unity may be less attractive than multiplicity, a higher unity that integrates multiplicity is richer still. In this spirit the critic will seek to find in all artworks an organic unity, including those that are superficially ugly or disjointed, and will not shy away from such works or from more complex reflections on such works. Nor will the critic hesitate to criticize any form of art that borders on kitsch by failing to engage reality in its complexity, including its deficiencies and moments of nonresolution.

Critics should attend to works that integrate such neglected virtues as courage, acceptance, and humility, and they should attempt to embody for others precisely those virtues that otherwise seem to be neglected. By exhibiting the virtues they discuss in their interpretations with students and others, critics embody the existential worth of literature—not only the value of the existential relationship to literature but also appreciation of literature as an end in itself and recognition of those virtues elicited in aesthetic experience but neglected in modernity. One moment of the critic's ideal perspective is acceptance of his or her interpretation as less than exhaustive of the text's full meaning and resonance.

Much contemporary criticism sees as its goal the uncovering of texts as products of their age and so misses, overlooks, or denies the uniqueness of each artwork. This focus not only elevates production aesthetics over artwork aesthetics, it also clouds the potential meaning of older literature for the present. Insofar as literary critics appreciate the inexhaustible, they must acknowledge the value of those literary works that are not directly pedagogical but that invite us to identify with ambiguous heroes. When the principle of poetic justice was more prevalent, the hermeneutic process was easier. Nonetheless, to recognize the untenability of a character in ways other than via the simplicity of plot or poetic justice is possible. One of the critic's tasks is to render such complexities transparent and to indicate the strategies that make such complex interpretations both possible and coherent.

We have recognized as central to great art its embodiment of principles of both uniqueness and interdependence, principles we recognize in nature and humanity as well. As part of the effort to address the age, the critic would do well to stress connections between literature and those values needed in the present: the literary work as a unique end in itself and therefore an analogue of the human person; the analogy between the organic in literature and the organic in nature, including the importance of the relation of part to whole; the correlation between the value of the heterogeneity of artworks and the variety and multiplicity of cultures; and the importance of balance in the aesthetic experience and the need for such balance in other spheres as well.

The primary tasks of the literary critic are to ascertain the principles for aesthetic evaluation, to recommend good works, to help the student or reader interpret works, and to cultivate an awareness of the intellectual and existential value of hermeneutic activity and aesthetic experience. Ideally, students are brought to the point where they learn not only an interpretation of a given work, but—far more important—also the strategies they must employ to interpret works as yet unread. From the classroom or from the encounter with a good work of secondary criticism, they should bring forth the ability to continue to read meaningfully and in a way that is attentive to the complexities of art. Ideally, the literary critic guides students to the point where they in turn can sharpen the critic's thinking about literature—such that the student, no less than the work under common analysis, becomes the interpreter's partner in conversation.

My study of literature in the technological age has addressed three questions. First, in what ways can artistic, and in particular literary, activity be morally excellent and what are the morally acceptable goals of literary criticism? My response to this twofold question involved a normative discussion of literature and literary criticism, modeled on objective idealism, and it discussed alternative responses, including the intellectual and moral principles that guide literary criticism today. Second, what are the central categories of the age, as they have emerged in the light of technology, and how has technology influenced aesthetics? Third, what should great art and literary criticism be today? My response to this final question stresses the ways in which literature and literary criticism can address some of the central categories and problems of the technological age.

Much as Jonas argues that ethics must be transformed in the age of technology, so have I argued that literature and literary criticism have specific tasks unique to this age. The deficiencies of selected works of contemporary literature can be traced to the failure either to fulfill certain universal conditions of beauty or to address the specific needs of the technological age. Art or literature cannot be reduced to the merely descriptive, with a corresponding elimination of the normative realm. Art is a normative concept, like morality, that may or may not be realized in a given age or in a given work. Literary criticism likewise has certain obligations if it is to continue to earn its place among the disciplines that deserve support. The deficiencies we have noted in contemporary literary criticism derive from inattentiveness to basic aesthetic or philosophical principles or to those issues that have special appeal in an age ruled by technology.

We have seen that among the problems in the technological age is the proliferation of infinite amounts of data—statistics, polls, facts, and figures. Missing in this effort is frequently a measure by which we can determine which data are meaningful and worthy of collection and how they might best be processed and evaluated. This problem is not unrelated to the question of the mission of literary criticism in the twenty-first century, for if literature and literary criticism are no longer anchored in the idea that the object of interpretation and evaluation is to garner a window onto an ideal sphere, why should we continue the enterprise? Instead of addressing the problems of the technological age, literary criticism reproduces them and contributes to them—first, by interpreting works it no longer views as having aesthetic merit or by turning to an infinite number of random topics, often beyond the range of literature, as all topics are now deemed equally worthy of study. Two answers to this crisis are possible: one could simply recognize a senseless, self-serving, and idle enterprise for what it is and draw the consequences; or one could articulate the ways in which literature can be a window onto the absolute and the ways in which literary criticism can make this reflection more layered and accessible, and thereby truer to the absolute. If this can be achieved, authors and critics will help readers reach the fullness of value inherent in them as persons, and both fields will have turned their crises into catalysts for credible and beneficial roles in the technological age.

Notes

CHAPTER 1. INTRODUCTION

1. In May 2002 the Modern Language Association recognized the need to address the neglected question of the value of literature—as a result of pervasive concerns about a crisis of legitimacy. Despite some cogent and eloquent responses, such as that of Berman, the respondents devote as much space to reflection on the emergence of the question today as they do to its answer. See "Why Major in Literature?"

    For recent anthologies on the future of German studies, see McCarthy and Schneider, Van Cleve and Wilson, and Förster. Gerhard Kaiser's slim volume, written after a long and illustrious career, stands out as a partial exception to the rule. His focus is the relevance of literature for life. The specific question of the relevance of literature in the technological age is not part of his deliberations. The opposite strength and weakness are evident in another work written by a senior member of the profession: Jost Hermand admirably concludes his history of Germanics by calling for greater engagement with ecological issues, but his study contains no sustained reflection on the value of literature as literature, which would seem to be a necessary precondition if literature or literary criticism is to contribute meaningfully to this area.

2. On the thematic study of technology in literature, see, for example, Segeberg's *Literatur im technischen Zeitalter,* which is essentially a history of German liter-

ature in the technological age and which, with its eighty-seven pages of notes, contains references to virtually all other literature on the topic through 1997. Of special interest too are Segeberg's earlier work on the topic, with fuller literary analyses, and his anthology as well as the recent anthology of Großklaus and Lämmert. The related issue of literature and the environment has received attention by way of a relatively new organization, the Association for the Study of Literature and Environment <http://www.asle.umn.edu>, and its journal, *ISLE: Interdisciplinary Studies in Literature and Environment.* For an introduction to what is now called ecocriticism, see Glotfelty and Fromm as well as Branch et al., which builds on the earlier volume. Also of interest is a special issue of *New Literary History,* summer 1999, which focuses on ecocriticism (30 [1999]: 505–712). For source materials on teaching environmental literature, see Grumbling and Waage. The first volume on ecofeminist criticism is Gaard and Murphy. Britain's first collective contribution to ecocriticism is Kerridge and Sammells. More international, though focused on the topic of nature, is Murphy. Many studies in the above collections suffer from one of the problems of contemporary criticism I elucidate, the neglect of the aesthetic dimension. In addition, insofar as ecocriticism has tended to focus on nature, it encompasses only one dimension of literature in the technological age. A welcome development is that the most recent contribution to ecocriticism of Lawrence Buell, a leading figure in American literary studies and ecocriticism, addresses both the natural and the human built, including urban, aspects of our environment. For an anthology that extends ecocriticism's range into the urban environment, see Bennett and Teauge.

For anthologies of German literary works on technology, see Bullivant and Ridley, Daniels, Dithmar, Krause, Minaty, Roehler, Sachsse, and Schneider. Each of these anthologies has the merit of drawing our attention to frequently overlooked literary works that thematize aspects of industrialization. The reduction of the truly aesthetic moment, which should not be ignored in such endeavors, comes to the fore, however, when works are selected independently of aesthetic considerations and in the form of brief excerpts, taken out of their organic contexts. A less central concern arises when such anthologies focus on the first and second industrial revolutions at the expense of the third industrial revolution, the transition to the information society; an irony arises, therefore, when they exemplify one of the problems associated with modern information, its frequent lack of organic meaning.

3. Although capitalism is an ideal engine for the development of technology, Gehlen's insight should not lead us to overlook the breadth of technology's impact; communism, too, had its "cult of technology" (Jonas 154), which was reinforced by the Marxist notion that the value of a product is defined by the labor put into it, not by its material basis (i.e., by nature).

4. Sedlmayr speaks, not unjustly, of the need for a third aesthetic category—along with the beauty of nature and the beauty of art—"the beauty of technology" (*Gefahr* 36).

5. On the transcendence of morality vis-à-vis diverse subsystems, see Hösle, *Moral und Politik* 113–15. For an analogous attempt by an analytic philosopher to argue that the moral sphere has a distinctive status and that "moral principles *cannot* be overridden by aesthetic principles," see Beardsmore, esp. 23–30, who carefully shows that such a position is not at all incompatible with the idea that art has intrinsic value. The quotation is from page 23.

6. Useful as a first orientation to objective idealism, especially for those who immediately recognize the foreignness of the position, is Hösle's essay on foundational issues of objective idealism, for it begins with an account and refutation of common perceptions that would make objective idealism seem wrong or musty or both.

CHAPTER 2. THE VALUE OF LITERATURE

1. On the relationship of art and the idea from Plato through the early modern period, see Panofsky.

2. In differentiating the true from the accurate in art, I am abstracting from certain complex cases, such as Rolf Hochhuth's *The Deputy* and *Soldiers,* where the work pretends to be both an artwork, which need not be accurate but only true, and a historical argument or document, which must, therefore, be measured with certain historical and not only aesthetic norms. While the aesthetic dimension is not influenced in such cases, authorial intention affects our discussion of such works as history. Also, the reception context, and with it the question of historical distance, comes into play. Schiller's contemporaries were certainly less concerned with his having Joan of Arc die in battle (note also the adjective in the subtitle, "A Romantic Tragedy in Five Acts," which sets different expectations concerning reality) than we are with Hochhuth's portrayal of Churchill as engineering the death of General Sikorski. What is affected here is again not our evaluation of the artwork as an artwork but our evaluation of the artwork as a historical and political document. In such cases both the aesthetic and historical spheres of evaluation are relevant, but distinct.

3. For an analytic account that seeks to explain and justify our emotional and affective responses to literature, see Feagin.

4. The passage from Remarque also tells us that technology which allows more distant warfare veils the specificity of our actions and makes killing easier, thus changing the face of war.

5. In practice Heidegger is not especially responsive to poetic works as poetic works; instead, he has a tendency to pull lines out of context and reflect on them independently. Ironically, precisely when criticizing subjectivity, Heidegger elevates his own subjectivity and treats poetic works as objects. For a trenchant critique of Heidegger's hermeneutics, see Weimar and Jermann. Although I see in Heidegger's view of truth as unconcealment an enrichment of our understanding of poetic truth, I do not reduce truth to this definition, which carries with it certain deficiencies, especially on the level of sifting competing truth claims, as I suggest more fully below.

6. Peter Zima has demonstrated, not unconvincingly, that modern literary theory tends to be divisible according to a Kantian tradition that elevates form and a Hegelian tradition that elevates content. For a differentiated view of Zima's claims, see my review.

7. On the National Socialist use of the term *organic,* see Denkler. On the resulting hesitancy to employ the category, see, for example, Krieger 36 and 49, who nonetheless seeks to recover a complex sense of the organic that includes, rather than excludes, variety and openness.

8. For a recent criticism of the organic in art, see Dana Phillips, who questions the contemporary scientific relevance of the organic and the related concept of the ecosystem. Certainly, many biologists concentrate on minute aspects of small interactions and never ask

questions about ecology. In addition, the more we know about the complex interactions between all forms of life and this world, the more difficult becomes the question of where to draw lines (James Lovelock's Gaia theory, which views the earth, including its oceans, air, land surface, and living matter, as a complex but single organism, is the clearest example of this difficulty). Nonetheless, virulent research is being conducted on all sorts of interactions within organisms (pharmacology and genetics, for example) as well as between organisms (including microbiology and ecology). Although wholes are difficult to locate in ecology, the relations of parts to other parts remains prominent. Indeed, more persuasive than ever is the concept of a whole that encompasses all seemingly autonomous ecosystems as themselves parts.

9. For a comprehensive study of the connections between Kant's aesthetics and his moral philosophy, see Guyer.

10. For an extensive anthology on the aesthetics of the ugly, see Jauß. Not surprisingly, the contributions are for the most part historical, rather than systematic.

11. Cf. also Plato's claim that inevitably and over time "a man should grow like whatever he enjoys, whether good or bad, even though he may be ashamed to approve it" (*Laws* 656b).

12. For a sampling of Löbach's work, with interviews and commentaries, see Häffele.

13. For a view of tragedy that emphasizes the concept of greatness wasted, see Bradley.

14. The significance of discovering neglected moments in earlier attempts at synthesis is a central dimension of my study *Dynamic Stillness;* see esp. 121–23.

CHAPTER 3. THE VALUE OF LITERARY CRITICISM

1. My discussion focuses on certain systematic aspects of hermeneutics. For a history of modern hermeneutics, see Brenner.

2. Working within an analytic tradition, Palmer likewise argues that "a moral failing in a literary work is at the same time an aesthetic failing" (174).

3. In my own interpretive work, I have often found it useful to adopt just such a proleptic approach, advancing not one reading but several readings of a work and weighing them in relationship to one another; see my readings of Kafka's *The Trial,* Broch's *The Spell,* Benn's "Lost I," Mann's *Doctor Faustus,* Dürrenmatt's *The Physicists* (*Die Moral der Kunst* 174–89), and Woody Allen's *Crimes and Misdemeanors* as well as my discussion of this strategy also in the light of pedagogical principles.

4. A recent comprehensive study of evaluation is von Heydebrand and Winko, whose goal is not to offer a normative theory of evaluation but to describe the motivations, functions, and possibilities of evaluation and to discuss historical changes in evaluation. It is interesting how often they must infer the principles of evaluation when discussing diverse methodological schools, as many critics, even theorists, leave the question of evaluation unaddressed. Indeed, some critics explicitly deny the value of evaluation, for example, Johnson, a culture-studies theorist, who asserts: "Analysts need to abandon once and for all . . . the primarily evaluative reading (is this a good/bad text?)" (74). The composition of a work like Alfred Einstein's *Greatness in Music,* despite the topic's appeal to a broader audience, would be difficult to imagine in today's academic climate. Evaluation

is prominent only in the debate on the canon, which, while triggering many new evaluations, has not led to the regeneration of high-level philosophical debate on the criteria of evaluation.

5. Not least of all, theory would be significant for the developing field of ecocriticism, which is more issue driven than methodology driven and has been described by Phillips, not incorrectly, as suffering from a "rejection of theory" (40).

6. The journal *Philosophy and Literature* has developed an annual competition for poor and opaque writing. The winners are consistently major figures in the field. Jameson was once cited for the above sentence, and Judith Butler was singled out for the following sentence: "The move from a structuralist account in which capital is understood to structure social relations in relatively homologous ways to a view of hegemony in which power relations are subject to repetition, convergence, and rearticulation brought the question of temporality into the thinking of structure, and marked a shift from a form of Althusserian theory that takes structural totalities as theoretical objects to one in which the insights into the contingent possibility of structure inaugurate a renewed conception of hegemony as bound up with the contingent sites and strategies of the rearticulation of power" (13). Honors have also gone to Homi Bhabha for the following: "If, for a while, the ruse of desire is calculable for the uses of discipline soon the repetition of guilt, justification, pseudo-scientific theories, superstition, spurious authorities, and classifications can be seen as the desperate effort to 'normalize' *formally* the disturbance of a discourse of splitting that violates the rational, enlightened claims of its enunciatory modality" (91). The number of leading postmodern critics who write clearly is very small: one thinks above all of Stanley Fish and Richard Rorty.

7. In a discussion of academic language, Marjorie Garber rightly defends the idea that what is sometimes perceived to be jargon is simply the professional vocabulary of a discipline, especially one that is quickly evolving; nonetheless, this claim does not free the critic from the imperative to be as intelligible and lucid as the subject matter and methodology permit.

8. The role of literature in the personal development of students is also central to Rosenblatt's *Literature as Exploration.* Not surprisingly, her work was originally published more than sixty years ago.

CHAPTER 4. CONTEMPORARY MODELS

1. Cf. Carr, for example, 121–31 and 174–76.

2. In hypertexts technology and chance converge, as the reader's choice of links has an element of chance that affects the reading and may erase the possibility of coherent meaning, though not necessarily: chance in the process of discovery need not imply chance at the higher level of meaning.

3. A representative overview of culture-studies positions in American *Germanistik* is available in a symposium entitled "*Germanistik* as German Studies," which is documented in *German Quarterly* 62 (1989): 139–234. In the most recent anthology on the state of the profession, published in *German Quarterly* 73 (2000): 1–44, the pendulum shifts slightly. While culture studies remains vibrant, the value of literature is once again recognized.

Berman, for example, laments the "anti-aesthetic retreat from literature" (3), and Friedrichsmeyer calls for greater attention to "the singularity of literature" (5). An analogous turn in English departments is evident in Donoghue's claim that "the word 'aesthetic' is no longer a term of abuse and contempt" (*Speaking* 8).

4. The reasons for Germany's very modest reception of deconstruction strike me as many, though they remain speculative: perhaps the legacy of historicism in Germany is too strong; perhaps Germany's postwar attitude toward relativism, bolstered by the theories of Apel and Habermas, has made it skeptical toward such movements, especially given Germany's experience with the antirational celebration of particularity and ethnicity; perhaps it stems from the differences between America's and Germany's cultural elevations of individualism; perhaps deconstruction appears to be too playful and unscientific for the German spirit; perhaps Germans, working within a different tradition, including one that elevates text-critical and editorial activity, are more inclined to recognize the value of the literary work over their own interpretive endeavors. Along with arguing that Germans had far stronger intellectual loyalties to Marx and the Frankfurt School and were not attracted to a movement influenced by Nietzsche and Heidegger, who belonged to a suspect political tradition, Robert Holub mentions two institutional factors: the lack of a strong or recognized personality in Germany who advocated the movement or a prestigious institution that embraced it and the small number of teaching positions available during the late 1970s and 1980s for new scholars who might have challenged the established paradigms (39–43).

   An exception to the general tendency, which also involves a connection to the topic of technology, is Kittler, although even Kittler is less of a deconstructionist in the specific sense of the term than a poststructuralist, who is strongly influenced by Foucault, and who, therefore, has much in common with culture studies.

5. In seeking also to highlight the strengths of these schools, my account differs from recent studies that seek solely to criticize contemporary theory, for example, Etlin.

6. An exception in German literary criticism is Jost Hermand, whose sense for the avant-garde has led him to attend to ecology as the most viable new paradigm. His rich works on this subject, for example, his study of green utopias and even more so his collection of essays *Im Wettlauf mit der Zeit,* survey older and recent works as well as historical movements that deal with ecological issues, though, as with earlier sociohistorical studies, we recognize in Hermand a tendency to elevate context and content at the expense of form. On the one hand, it is not surprising that a critic writing in German and publishing in Germany, but teaching in the United States, would be a pioneer in addressing the relationships between ecology and German studies. On the other hand, the transition from a socialist paradigm to an ecological paradigm is by no means common and so speaks for Hermand's unusual ability to break free of traditional categories.

7. An interesting case of a more traditional, formalist critic who rightly insists on fully addressing a literary work's weaknesses is Walter Silz. See his brief theoretical essay. Unfortunately, Silz unintentionally shows in his reading of *Hyperion* that while critique can sometimes involve justified criticism of the weaknesses of an otherwise excellent work, it can in other circumstances reveal the critic's inability to recognize complex patterns that later readers will uncover. Cf. Roche, *Dynamic Stillness* 89.

8. On stages in the development of feminist criticism, see Showalter.

9. Given the number of publications in culture studies, the exceptions are slight: see *Cultural Studies* 8, no. 1 (1994), a special issue devoted to "Culture Studies and the Environment," which discusses this very hesitancy to explore environmental questions, as well as Alexander Wilson's cultural history of nature in North America and Hochman's advocacy of a green cultural studies.

10. As I shall suggest below, culture studies and deconstruction nonetheless share certain common features. Precisely where these two movements intersect, we sometimes find critics working on technology. Ronell, who elevates the destabilizing elements of technology, is an example. However, the intelligibility level of Ronell's book is evident in a passage like the following: "The telephone coils us around its own lack of assumption, if one understands by this the stranglehold by which it affirms the impossibility of acceding to its proper significance. Noise machine, schizo leash, war-zone shots in the dark, lovers' discourse, or phantomic conference call, the telephone as such is, like the phallus, empty but powerful" (265).

11. For a classic study of high and popular culture, see Gans. Whereas Gans focuses on the value of popular art, Schaeffer, who likewise views art from a functional perspective, focuses on the limits of high art. My alternative approach is to evaluate art primarily according to aesthetic, not functional, criteria, but when giving the functional dimension its legitimate due, to elevate great art that can resonate with a larger public. Often art of this kind has both esoteric and exoteric dimensions, e.g., in Shakespeare.

12. For a historical and anthropological study of the concept of diversity, see Wood, whose criticisms are different from (and also harsher than) my own.

13. A problem of culture studies and of contemporary theory in general is that, along with this leveling of areas of interest as well as the elevation of contemporary theory and the movement away from literature, two important prerequisites for the literary critic, knowledge of a large number of literary works from many traditions and knowledge of the classics of literary criticism, have weakened—among students and then professors, as these students move through the system.

14. As an example of this violation of aesthetic integrity and aesthetic complexity, consider Samuel Weber's reading of Hoffmann's *The Sand-Man,* which also involves the widespread deconstructionist effort to draw general conclusions about the impossibility of meaning by focusing on an isolated passage. The elevation of parts without the effort to reconcile them with the whole is evident as well in de Man's reading of Nietzsche's *Birth of Tragedy* (*Allegories* 79–102) and Miller's reading of Goethe's *Elective Affinities* (*Ariadne's Thread* 164–222). On "unreadability," see Miller, *Ariadne's Thread* 224. On the centrality of aporias in deconstruction, cf. Derrida's reference to "that singular aporia called 'deconstruction'" (*Memoires* 137) as well as his *Aporias.*

15. "The absence of the transcendental signified extends the domain and the interplay of signification *ad infinitum*" (Derrida, "Structure" 249)

16. Some deconstructionists would counter that "text" is to be understood in a broader sense and includes also social and political events. Derrida himself writes: "*Text,* as I use the word, is not the book" ("But, beyond" 167). While this comment, an embellishment of his earlier assertion, "*There is nothing outside of the text*" (*Of Grammatology* 158), suggests

a potential link to culture studies, with its emphasis on reading the world, it is not universally shared by deconstructionists, and where it is shared, the different problem arises that the distinctiveness of the literary text is dissolved.

CHAPTER 5. CATEGORIES OF THE TECHNOLOGICAL AGE

1. Apel introduces four types of rationality—scientific, technological, hermeneutic, and ethical—each of which is grounded by the one following it. See *Die Erklären: Verstehen-Kontroverse in transzendentalpragmatischer Sicht* 27. Cf. "Types of Rationality Today" and "Die Vernunftfunktion der kommunikativen Rationalität." Compelling in my eyes is Hösle's critique of Apel's distinctions and the presuppositions behind them in *Praktische Philosophie* 62–70. I would add that in Apel's scheme is no place for reflection on the principles of aesthetics, which I would place under philosophical rationality.

2. The loss of human essence through technology is also the higher meaning of Georg Kaiser's expressionist play *Gas,* which suggests that the danger of technology lies not only in the lethal nature of certain machines but also and even more so in its transformation of our humanity, although Kaiser's play suffers the irony that the solution—at least from the perspective of the Billionaire's son—is more "technology," the creation of a new kind of man.

3. Accurate as Heidegger was in most of his diagnosis of the modern world, his therapy is inadequate for at least three reasons. First, Heidegger elevates objectivity at the expense of autonomy and renders himself immune to criticism by charging that any critique implies that one has fallen into *Seinsvergessenheit,* or forgetfulness of Being. Indeed, the entire theory of Seinsvergessenheit, with its assessment that all arguments are an expression of the will to power and thus invalid, is itself an argument as to why we should not engage in argumentation; it thus presupposes what it criticizes and is as such self-canceling. Second, Heidegger fails to differentiate value rationality from technical rationality. Not only is this insufficiently rigorous thinking, but value rationality is necessary in order to establish norms and so legitimate a coherent critique of technical rationality. Further, one must distinguish between technology and technical reason, which are value free or indifferent to ethics, and certain concrete techniques that negate ethics (techniques of torturing, for example). Third, in order to change anything in the world, we need technical rationality, and so even as we seek to temper it, we cannot forgo it completely. Because Heidegger, having relinquished both autonomy and strategy, has no ethics and no politics, his theory has an emptiness of content. And being uninterested in causality as that which does not capture essence, he is blind to psychology and politics and in effect ends up being manipulated by them, as Hösle suggests. Heidegger's answer is fate (*Geschick*), not responsibility (*Verantwortung*). Moreover, Hösle offers a strong philosophical-historical criticism of Heidegger's diagnosis when he argues that modern metaphysics—with its elevation of subjectivity—is a necessary but not sufficient condition for technology. A further prerequisite is the divorce of science from the philosophical effort to recognize reason in reality. See Hösle, "Heideggers Philosophie der Technik."

4. The verum factum principle was first recognized and articulated by Vico in *De nostri temporis studiorum ratione* (sec. 4), *De antiquissima Italorum sapientia* (book 1, sec. 1), and

Scienza nuova (par. 331). The quoted passages stem from the first section of the first book (*Liber metaphysicus*) of *De antiquissima Italorum sapientia* (1.131). The principle is the subject of short studies by Löwith and Mondolfo. It is a consistent theme in the writings of Hösle, who sees in objective idealism a strong counterposition to this characteristically modern paradigm. See, for example, *Philosophiegeschichte* 13–36.

5. On the concept of substance and function in modernity, see Cassirer, *Substanzbegriff.*

6. In a more traditional aesthetics that sees in art a moment of imitation and transference, we recognize a delimiting of poetic subjectivity, though the acts of imitation and transference could also imply an elevated definition of the poet as vessel. In Hölderlin, for example, the poet does not will his poem; instead he asks to be made a messenger and servant of the gods. The idea that the poet receives and does not invent truth and beauty is especially prominent in the hymn "As on a Holiday." Here the poet is dependent on moments of inspiration that he does not control; he suffers the temptation to emphasize his own role in the process, which can lead to a kind of hubris and blasphemy, followed by self-critical despair.

7. On the topic of conceptual art, see Godfrey.

8. For a classic account of the dissolution of the cosmos (along with such related value concepts as perfection, harmony, meaning, and aim) and the infinitization of the universe, see Koyré.

9. On modern overconsumption, see Durning, who recognizes in consumption one of the three central variables in the global environmental equation, along with population and technology. On the relation of overconsumption and waste, see the older, but still interesting, study by Packard. For a more recent, though less expansive, study of waste, see Hawken.

10. Modern society's tendency to develop and apply technology independently of broader considerations and a fuller rationale is one of the central themes in Ellul's *The Technological Bluff,* which is useful on this topic even though Ellul sometimes overstates his case.

11. Glotz, who recognizes acceleration as a distinguishing characteristic of digital capitalism, could be included here as well, though he emphasizes, as few cultural critics do, the advantages of acceleration.

12. For a fuller discussion of this unity of technology, see Ellul's account of the technological system, esp. 156–68.

13. Ellul's analysis of technology's autonomy from values is rewarding; see esp. his account of the technological system, 145–50; cf. *Technological Society* 97.

14. Verene analyzes the phenomenon of our control of technology and technology's control of us by way of some interesting reflections on Hegel's master-slave dialectic (141–50).

15. For an analysis of an artwork that places at its center the process of rationalization and with it disenchantment, see my essay, written with Vittorio Hösle, on *The Man Who Shot Liberty Valance.*

16. In a more recent study Lane argues that, beyond the satisfaction of basic material needs, what most contributes to happiness cannot be acquired through the market. Modern industrialized societies have tended, however, to substitute income for companionship; not surprisingly, they suffer from "the decline of happiness and the rise of depression" (*The Loss* 35).

CHAPTER 6. AESTHETICS IN THE TECHNOLOGICAL AGE

1. The Homeric question has been much debated in modern classical scholarship. Despite still present controversies concerning authorship, common agreement exists that the works were not composed like modern narratives but evolved out of a powerful oral tradition. Unlike Vico, however, most contemporary classical philologists would recognize Homer as a historical figure who appeared at the end of this long tradition and gave structural unity to the epics.

2. Also helpful on oral culture and the transition to literacy is Ong.

3. On the concept of overloading and its psychological consequences, see Milgram.

4. Examples of moving type in poetry may be found at the SUNY Buffalo Electronic Poetry Center <http://epc.buffalo.edu/>.

5. On the concept of a hypertext, see especially Nielsen, Landow's *Hypertext 2.0,* Joyce's *Of Two Minds,* and McGann (53–74) as well as Landow's anthology. In essence the World Wide Web functions as a hypertext, as is evident from the abbreviations that will be common to many Web browsers: "http" represents "hypertext transfer protocol," and "html," the language used to create Web sites, stands for "hypertext markup language."

6. Adorno, for example, argues for a close relation between the fetishism of music, its commodification and standardization, and a regression of listening, the inability of the masses to understand or desire music beyond what is produced and marketed for them ("Über den Fetischcharakter").

7. For an insightful discussion of the stylistic aspects of Expressionist poetry insofar as they mirror the technological age, see Silvio Vietta, "Großstadtwahrnehmung."

8. For a wide-ranging and perceptive study of the image of the scientist in literature from the Middle Ages to the present, see Haynes, who notes that one of the most prominent modern images is of aloofness and emotional deficiency, characteristics that are related to the ascendency of technical rationality. Also useful for an initial orientation is Ziolkowski, who sees in the portrayal of the modern scientist, since Shelley, the conflation of two diverse myths, that of Prometheus and that of Adam, which epitomizes the modern view of science as involving great technical achievements that have threatening ethical consequences (*Varieties* 175–97).

9. The railroad has received a great deal of attention; see Mahr; Rademacher; Hoeges; and Segeberg, *Literatur;* among others. On the automobile as a poetic symbol, see Reinecke.

10. For a helpful study of the ways in which the Internet affects identity and communication, see Wallace.

11. On the centrality of networks in the contemporary world and in spheres ranging from science to business and society, see Barabási.

12. "Our existing opera is a culinary opera. It was a means of pleasure long before it turned into merchandise" (35).

13. The most ambitious Web project for German literature appears to be *Das Projekt Gutenberg* <http://www.gutenberg.aol.de>, which contained at the time of my writing this the equivalent of more than three hundred thousand pages of text in German by more than four hundred authors and which is growing at a rate of more than two thousand five hundred pages per month; it does not, however, have the kind of interpretive aids one

finds on most CDs. A useful work for the reader seeking literary texts and supplementary materials on the Web is Reinhard Kaiser. For a more comprehensive exploration of practical resources for literary study on the Internet, see Simon-Ritz. Finally, for an excellent handbook of digital resources for humanities scholars, arranged by discipline, see Condron et al.

14. For a symposium on computer-supported text editions, see Kamzelak.

15. Landow sees in the idea of hypertext and contemporary literary theory the common suggestion that "we must abandon conceptual systems founded upon ideas of center, margin, hierarchy, and linearity" (*Hypertext 2.0* 2). The connection between hypertext and poststructuralist theory surfaces in other writers as well, for example, Bolter, 147–68 and Taylor and Saarinen.

16. In the past decade, dozens of anthologies of nature writing have appeared in English. For collections of classic prose, see Finch and Elder as well as Lyon. For more contemporary collections, see Halpern and Anderson, Slovic, and O'Grady. Pack and Parini have anthologized contemporary poems, and Anderson has collected prose and poetry by women. The named volumes only scratch the surface of what is available. In Germany renewed interest in nature is also present (see, for example, Marsch, von Bormann, Kleßman, and Grimm), though it may be less pronounced and directed as much toward the endangerment as the celebration of nature, as in Jürgen Becker's reference to "ruined nature [kaputte Natur]" (62). See also Mayer-Tasch.

CHAPTER 7. THE VALUE OF LITERATURE TODAY

1. Although the beauty of nature has been for the most part neglected since Hegel, precisely the ecological question has once again elevated it to an issue of philosophical reflection; see, for example, Böhme and Seel.

2. As with all artforms, diversity is possible; a happening directed by Josef Beuys once resulted in the planting of some seven thousand trees.

3. For a classic interdisciplinary account of symmetry, see Weyl. For a more recent study of symmetry, in relation to complexity and unpredictability, see Field and Golubitsky.

4. Technology that is so sophisticated as to be not simply mechanical but also complexly dynamic sometimes integrates an element of art.

5. Baudrillard, however, abandons any distinction between object and representation, which would permit him to criticize simulation as simulation. Hyperbole and an indifference to truth are the natural results of this theory.

6. The distinction between science as necessarily progressive and the arts as not participating in progress in quite the same way was a factor in the *Querelle des anciens et modernes* and one of the reasons for the historical separation of the arts and sciences in the seventeenth century (Kristeller 526).

7. For the most recent figures on the risk of extinction, see Tuxill. For a broader study of biological diversity, see Edward Wilson.

8. I agree with Odo Marquard that in the face of the advances of science and modernization, including homogeneity and globalization, literature and the humanities offer us colorful and meaningful lifeworlds and traditions with which we can identify. Against

this compensation thesis of Marquard, however, I would raise at least four objections. First, Marquard elevates the idea that whereas modern science and technology deliver new worlds, the humanities give us what is familiar. The humanities may perform this function, but they also open up new and diverse worlds insofar as they offer us original stories as well as tales from alternative traditions. Second, Marquard elevates as the highest principle of the humanities ambiguity, which, though an important concept, hardly addresses the full range of ethical challenges facing us today. Third, compensation may illuminate one aspect of the arts and humanities in certain finite circumstances, but certainly stronger arguments can be given for their legitimacy, as I suggest in this book. Fourth and related, the compensation thesis reverses the hierarchy of primary and secondary, elevating the technical and instrumental and recognizing values as compensatory to these forces, instead of seeing values as the telos and measuring technical and instrumental reason against these higher ends.

CHAPTER 8. TECHNOLOGY, ETHICS, AND LITERATURE

1. Jonas's evocation of limits has received more attention in Germany, where *The Imperative of Responsibility* won the prestigious Friedenspreis des deutschen Buchhandels, than in America, which is indicative of a wider problem. Leo Marx has articulated the importance in American culture up to the present of a yearning for a harmonious lifestyle closer to nature, the pastoral ideal. Even today advertising for products from beer to cigarettes and automobiles plays on these associations. Nonetheless, the ecological paradigm has met considerable resistance in the United States. First, the vastness of the landscape in relation to human needs keeps the immediacy of the issue at bay. Second, the idea of unlimited progress that has consistently guided the cultural symbols of America works against any conception of limitations. Third, from its origins, as David Nye has demonstrated, the United States has viewed technology as an ally in the development of its various roles in the new world. Fourth, America is an individualistic land that tends to elevate rights over duties, and the ecological paradigm demands a nonindividualistic framework. Finally, because of the modern compartmentalization of life, the United States, not unlike other modern societies, is at one and the same time both a nature-loving and a resource-consuming society that fails to recognize the contradiction between these two tendencies (Buell, *Environmental Imagination* 4).
2. On the difference between visible social problems and abstract future threats, consider the insightful reflections of the narrator in Königsdorf's *Disrespectful Relations:* "But hunger and social destitution are concretely perceivable. The threat to human civilization remains abstract. One can brush aside thoughts about it, much as one does knowledge of one's own mortality" (94).
3. Not surprisingly, one of the earliest works of literary ecology, Meeker, attempts to forge links between comedy and ecology. While I would grant Meeker's argument a great deal of truth, tragedy also has a role to play in a broader reflection on the value of literature in the technological age: first, insofar as tragedy is the genre of responsibility and of taking a strong, courageous, and resolute stand in the face of unrelenting opposition; and second,

insofar as tragedy reveals by way of negation the untenability of false or one-sided positions.

4. Kroeber seeks to analyze selected works by the English Romantics in the light of a model of ecological literary criticism. For the most recent volume of criticism on twentieth-century ecopoetry, with ample references to earlier critics, see Bryson.

CHAPTER 9. THE LITERARY CANON AND THE LITERARY CRITIC IN THE TWENTY-FIRST CENTURY

1. The problem of the canon is more acute in America than in Germany, which is not to say that in Germany the arguments employed to defend the canon are any more coherent than the American arguments against it. When tradition alone is invoked as the argument, the analogy drawn between traditions of aesthetic evaluation and traditions of arbitrary discrimination is not easily countered. Similarly weak is the pragmatic defense that these works have influenced the development of modernist consciousness; not only is this weak in its being only historicist, the critic might well say, so much the worse for the works.

Works Cited

Adorno, Theodor. *Minima Moralia: Reflexionen aus dem beschädigten Leben.* Frankfurt. Suhrkamp, 1969.

———. "Über den Fetischcharakter in der Musik und die Regression des Hörens." *Gesammelte Schriften.* Frankfurt: Suhrkamp, 1973: 14:14–50.

Anders, Günther. *Die Antiquiertheit des Menschen: Über die Seele im Zeitalter der zweiten industriellen Revolution.* Munich: Beck, 1968.

Anderson, Lorraine, ed. *Sisters of the Earth: Women's Prose and Poetry about Nature.* New York: Vintage, 1991.

Anderson, Lorraine, Scott Slovic, and John P. O'Grady, eds. *Literature and the Environment: A Reader on Nature and Culture.* New York: Addison, 1999.

Apel, Karl-Otto. *Die Erklären: Verstehen-Kontroverse in transzendentalpragmatischer Sicht.* Frankfurt: Suhrkamp, 1979.

———. "The Problem of a Macroethic of Responsibility to the Future in the Crisis of Technological Civilization: An Attempt to Come to Terms with Hans Jonas's 'Principle of Responsibility.'" *Man and World* 20 (1987): 3–40.

———. *Towards a Transformation of Philosophy.* Trans. Glyn Adey and David Frisby. London: Routledge, 1980.

———. "Types of Rationality Today: The Continuum of Reason Between Science and Ethics." *Rationality Today.* Ed. Theodore F. Geraets. Ottawa: University of Ottawa Press, 1979: 307–50.

———. "Die Vernunftfunktion der kommunikativen Rationalität: Zum Verhältnis von konsensual-kommunikativer Rationalität, strategischer Rationalität und Systemrationalität." *Die eine Vernunft und die vielen Rationalitäten.* Ed. Karl-Otto Apel and Matthias Kettner. Frankfurt: Suhrkamp, 1996: 17–41.

Arendt, Hannah. *Eichmann in Jerusalem: A Report on the Banality of Evil.* New York: Viking, 1963.

Argyle, Michael. *The Psychology of Happiness.* New York: Methuen, 1987.

Aristotle. *The Basic Works of Aristotle.* Ed. Richard McKeon. New York: Random House, 1941.

Arnold, Matthew. "The Function of Criticism at the Present Time." *The Complete Prose Works of Matthew Arnold.* 11 vols. Ann Arbor: University of Michigan Press, 1962: 3:258–85.

Association for the Study of Literature and Environment. 1 June 2003. <http://www.asle.umn.edu>

Auerbach, Erich. *Mimesis: The Representation of Reality in Western Literature.* Trans. Willard R. Trask. Princeton: Princeton University Press, 1968.

Baasner, Rainer, and Georg Reichard. *Epochen der deutschen Literatur: Aufklärung und Empfindsamkeit. Ein Hypertext-Informationssystem.* Stuttgart: Reclam, 1998.

Bakhtin, Mikhail Mikhailovich. "Discourse in the Novel." *The Dialogic Imagination: Four Essays.* Ed. Michael Holquist. Austin: University of Texas Press, 1981: 259–422.

Barabási, Albert-László. *Linked: The New Science of Networks.* Cambridge: Perseus, 2002.

Barrett, William. *The Illusion of Technique: A Search for Meaning in a Technological Civilization.* Garden City, N.Y.: Anchor Press, 1978.

Barthes, Roland. *S/Z: An Essay.* Trans. Richard Miller. New York: Hill, 1974.

Baudelaire, Charles. *Art in Paris, 1845–1862.* Trans. Jonathan Mayne. London: Phaidon, 1965.

Baudrillard, Jean. *Simulacres et simulation.* Paris: Galilée, 1981.

Beardsmore, R. W. *Art and Morality.* London: Macmillan, 1971.

Becker, Jürgen. *Gedichte, 1965–1980.* Frankfurt: Suhrkamp, 1981.

Bell, Daniel. *The Cultural Contradictions of Capitalism.* New York: Basic, 1976.

Benjamin, Walter. *Illuminations.* Trans. Harry Zohn. New York: Schocken, 1968.

Benn, Gottfried. "Probleme der Lyrik." *Gesammelte Werke.* Ed. Dieter Wellershoff. Wiesbaden: Limes, 1968: 4:1058–1096.

Bennett, Michael, and David Teauge, eds. *The Nature of Cities: Ecocriticism and Urban Environments.* Tucson: University of Arizona Press, 1999.

Berman, Russell A. "Our Predicament, Our Prospects." *German Quarterly* 73 (2000): 1–3.

Bhabha, Homi K. *The Location of Culture.* New York: Routledge, 1994.

Die Bibel: Altes und neues Testament. Einheitsübersetzung. Freiburg: Herder, 1980.

Bienek, Horst. *Werkstattgespräche mit Schriftstellern.* Munich: Hanser, 1962.

Birkerts, Sven. *The Gutenberg Elegies: The Fate of Reading in an Electronic Age.* New York: Fawcett, 1994.

———. *Readings.* Saint Paul: Graywolf, 1999.

Bloom, Harold. *The Western Canon: The Books and School of the Ages.* New York: Riverhead, 1995.

Böhme, Gernot. *Für eine ökologische Naturästhetik.* Frankfurt: Suhrkamp, 1989.

Bölsche, Wilhelm. *Die naturwissenschaftlichen Grundlagen der Poesie: Prolegomena einer realistischen Ästhetik.* 1887. Tübingen: Niemeyer, 1976.

Bolter, Jay David. *Writing Space: The Computer, Hypertext and the History of Writing.* Hillsdale, N.J.: Erlbaum, 1990.

Bolter, Jay David, Michael Joyce, and John B. Smith. *Storyspace: Hypertext Writing Environment for the Macintosh.* Computer software. Cambridge: Eastgate, 1990.

Books in Print. 9 vols. New Providence, N.J.: Bowker, 2000.

Booth, Wayne C. *The Company We Keep: An Ethics of Fiction.* Berkeley: University of California Press, 1988.

Bradley, A. C. "Hegel's Theory of Tragedy." *Oxford Lectures on Poetry.* London: Macmillan, 1909: 69–95.

Branch, Michael P., Rochelle Johnson, Daniel Patterson, and Scott Slovic, eds. *Reading the Earth: New Directions in the Study of Literature and Environment.* Moscow: University of Idaho Press, 1998.

Brecht, Bertolt. *Brecht on Theater: The Development of an Aesthetic.* Trans. John Willet. New York: Hill, 1964.

Brenner, Peter J. *Das Problem der Interpretation: Eine Einführung in die Grundlagen der Literaturwissenschaft.* Tübingen: Niemeyer, 1998.

Brinkmann, Rolf Dieter. *Westwärts 1 & 2: Gedichte.* Reinbek: Rowohlt, 1975.

Britten, Benjamin. *On Receiving the First Aspen Award.* London: Faber, 1964.

Broch, Hermann. *The Sleepwalkers.* Trans. Willa and Edwin Muir. San Francisco: North Point, 1985.

Brooks, Cleanth. *The Well-Wrought Urn: Studies in the Structure of Poetry.* New York: Harcourt, 1947.

Brown, Lester R. "Feeding Nine Billion." *State of the World 1999: A Worldwatch Institute Report on Progress Toward a Sustainable Society.* New York: Norton, 1999: 115–32.

Brown, Lester R., and Christopher Flavin. "A New Economy for a New Century." *State of the World 1999: A Worldwatch Institute Report on Progress Toward a Sustainable Society.* New York: Norton, 1999: 3–21.

Bryson, J. Scott, ed. *Ecopoetry: A Critical Introduction.* Salt Lake City: University of Utah Press, 2002.

Buell, Lawrence. *The Environmental Imagination. Thoreau, Nature Writing, and the Formation of American Culture.* Cambridge: Harvard University Press, 1995.

———. *Writing for an Endangered World: Literature, Culture, and Environment in the U.S. and Beyond.* Cambridge: Harvard University Press, 2001.

Bullivant, Keith, and Hugh Ridley. *Industrie und deutsche Literatur, 1830–1914: Eine Anthologie.* Munich: DTV, 1976.

Butler, Judith. "Further Reflections on the Conversations of Our Time." *Diacritics* 27 (1997): 13–15.

Calinescu, Matei. *Rereading.* New Haven: Yale University Press, 1993.

Calvino, Italo. *Six Memos for the Next Millennium.* New York: Vintage, 1993.

Carr, C. *On Edge: Performance at the End of the Twentieth Century.* Hanover: University Press of New England, 1993.

Carroll, Noël. "Art, Narrative, and Moral Understanding." *Aesthetics and Ethics: Essays at the Intersection.* Ed. Jerrold Levinson. New York: Cambridge University Press, 1998: 126–60.

Cassirer, Ernst. "Form und Technik." *Technikphilosophie.* Ed. Peter Fischer. Leipzig: Reclam, 1996: 157–213.

———. *Substanzbegriff und Funktionsbegriff: Untersuchungen über die Grundfragen der Erkenntniskritik.* 1910. Darmstadt: Wissenschaftliche Buchgesellschaft, 1976

Castells, Manuel. *The Information Age: Economy, Society and Culture.* 3 vols. Oxford: Blackwell, 1996–1998.

Chatman, Seymour. *Story and Discourse: Narrative Structure in Fiction and Film.* Ithaca: Cornell University Press, 1978.

Chekhov, Anton. *Anton Chekhov's Short Stories.* Ed. Ralph E. Matlaw. New York: Norton, 1979.

Cohn, Dorrit. *The Distinction of Fiction.* Baltimore: Johns Hopkins University Press, 1999.

———. *Transparent Minds: Narrative Modes for Presenting Consciousness in Fiction.* Princeton: Princeton University Press, 1978.

Coleridge, Samuel Taylor. *Biographia Literaria or Biographical Sketches of My Literary Life and Opinions.* 2 vols. Ed. James Engell and W. Jackson Bate. Princeton: Princeton University Press, 1983.

Coles, Robert. *The Call of Stories: Teaching and the Moral Imagination.* Boston: Houghton Mifflin, 1989.

Condron, Frances, Michael Fraser, and Stuart Sutherland. *Digital Resources for the Humanities.* Morgantown: West Virginia University Press, 2001.

Culler, Jonathan. *Framing the Sign: Criticism and Its Institutions.* Norman: University of Oklahoma Press, 1988.

Dahlhaus, Carl. *The Idea of Absolute Music.* Trans. Roger Lustig. Chicago: University of Chicago Press, 1989.

Daniels, Karlheinz. *Mensch und Maschine: Literarische Dokumente.* Frankfurt: Diesterweg, 1981.

Davis, Bob. *Speed Is Life: Street Smart Lessons from the Front Lines of Business.* New York: Doubleday, 2001.

DeGrandpre, Richard. *Ritalin Nation: Rapid-Fire Culture and the Transformation of Human Consciousness.* New York: Norton, 1999.

De Man, Paul. *Allegories of Reading: Figural Language in Rousseau, Nietzsche, Rilke, and Proust.* New Haven: Yale University Press, 1979.

———. *Blindness and Insight: Essays in the Rhetoric of Contemporary Criticism.* 2nd ed. Minneapolis: University of Minnesota Press, 1983.

Denkler, Horst. "Organische Konstruktion: Natur und Technik in der Literatur des 'Dritten Reichs.'" *Faszination des Organischen—Konjunkturen einer Kategorie der Moderne.* Ed. Hartmut Eggert, Erhard Schütz, and Peter Sprengel. Munich: Iudicium, 1995: 267–84.

Derrida, Jacques. *Aporias.* Trans. Thomas Dutoit. Stanford: Stanford University Press, 1993.

———. "But, beyond . . . (Open Letter to Anne McClintock and Rob Nixon)." Trans. Peggy Kamuf. *Critical Inquiry* 13 (1986): 155–70.

———. *Limited Inc.* Trans. Samuel Weber and Jeffrey Mehlman. Evanston: Northwestern University Press, 1988.

———. *Memoires for Paul de Man.* Trans. Cecile Lindsay et al. New York: Columbia University Press, 1989.

———. *Of Grammatology.* Trans. Gayatri Chakravorty Spivak. Baltimore: Johns Hopkins University Press, 1976.

———. "Structure, Sign, and Play in the Discourse of the Human Sciences." *The Language of Criticism and the Sciences of Man: The Structuralist Controversy.* Ed. Richard Macksey and Eugenio Donato. Baltimore: Johns Hopkins University Press, 1970: 247–65.

Desmond, William. *Art and the Absolute: A Study of Hegel's Aesthetics.* Albany: State University of New York Press, 1986.

Dithmar, Reinhard. *Industrieliteratur.* Munich: DTV, 1973.

Döblin, Alfred. *Schriften zur Ästhetik, Poetik und Literatur.* Olten: Walter, 1989.

Donoghue, Denis. *The Practice of Reading.* New Haven: Yale University Press, 1998.

———. *Speaking of Beauty.* New Haven: Yale University Press, 2003.

Durning, Alan Thein. *How Much Is Enough? The Consumer Society and the Future of the Earth.* New York: Norton, 1992.

Dürrenmatt, Friedrich. "Ich bin der finsterste Komödienschreiber, den es gibt: Ein *Zeit*-Gespräch mit Friedrich Dürrenmatt." *Die Zeit,* August 16, 1985: 33–34.

———. *Werkausgabe in dreißig Bänden.* Zürich: Diogenes, 1980.

Einstein, Alfred. *Greatness in Music.* 1941. New York: Da Capo, 1976.

Eisenman, Peter. "Wexner Center for the Visual Arts, Ohio." *Deconstruction: Omnibus Volume.* Ed. Andreas Papadakis, Catherine Cooke, and Andrew Benjamin. New York: Rizzoli, 1989: 154–57.

Eisenstein, Elizabeth L. *The Printing Press as an Agent of Change: Communications and Cultural Transformations in Early-Modern Europe.* 2 vols. New York: Cambridge University Press, 1979.

Eliot, T. S. "Tradition and the Individual Talent." *Selected Essays: 1917–1932.* London: Faber, 1932, 13–22.

———. *The Use of Poetry and the Use of Criticism: Studies in the Relation of Criticism to Poetry in England.* London: Faber, 1933.

Ellis, John M. *Against Deconstruction.* Princeton: Princeton University Press, 1989.

———. *Literature Lost: Social Agendas and the Corruption of the Humanities.* New Haven: Yale University Press, 1997.

Ellul, Jacques. *The Technological Bluff.* Trans. Geoffrey W. Bromily. Grand Rapids: Eerdmans, 1990.

———. *The Technological Society.* Trans. John Wilkinson. New York: Knopf, 1964.

———. *The Technological System.* Trans. Joachim Neugroschel. New York: Continuum, 1980.

Emerson, Ralph Waldo. *The Selected Writings of Ralph Waldo Emerson.* Ed. Brooks Atkinson New York: Modern Library, 1950.

Etlin, Richard A. *In Defense of Humanism: Value in the Arts and Letters.* Cambridge: Cambridge University Press, 1996.

Farmelo, Graham. *It Must Be Beautiful: Great Equations of Modern Science*. New York: Granta, 2002.

Feagin, Susan L. *Reading with Feeling: The Aesthetics of Appreciation*. Ithaca: Cornell University Press, 1996.

Feuerbach, Ludwig. *Das Wesen des Christentums*. 1841. Frankfurt: Suhrkamp, 1976.

Field, Michael, and Martin Golubitsky. *Symmetry in Chaos: A Search for Pattern in Mathematics, Art, and Nature*. New York: Oxford University Press, 1992.

Finch, Robert, and John Elder, eds. *The Norton Book of Nature Writing*. New York: Norton, 1990.

Fish, Stanley. "Anti-Foundationalism, Theory Hope, and the Teaching of Composition." *The Current in Criticism: Essays on the Present and Future of Literary Theory*. Ed. Clayton Koelb and Virgil Lokke. West Lafayette, Ind.: Purdue University Press, 1987: 65–79.

———. *Is There a Text in This Class? The Authority of Interpretive Communities*. Cambridge: Harvard University Press, 1980.

Forster, E. M. *Aspects of the Novel*. 1927. London: Arnold, 1974.

Förster, Jürgen, Eva Neuland, and Gerhard Rupp. *Wozu noch Germanistik? Wissenschaft—Beruf—Kulturelle Praxis*. Stuttgart: Metzler, 1989.

Friedrichsmeyer, Sara. "Acknowledging the Beautiful." *German Quarterly* 73 (2000): 4–7.

Frye, Northrop. *Anatomy of Criticism: Four Essays*. Princeton: Princeton University Press, 1957.

Gaard, Greta, and Patrick D. Murphy, eds. *Ecofeminist Literary Criticism: Theory, Interpretation, Pedagogy*. Urbana: University of Illinois Press, 1998.

Gadamer, Hans-Georg. *Wahrheit und Methode: Grundzüge einer philosophischen Hermeneutik*. 6th ed. Tübingen: Mohr, 1990.

Gans, Herbert J. *Popular Culture & High Culture: An Analysis and Evaluation of Taste*. Rev. ed. New York: Basic, 1999.

Garber, Marjorie. *Academic Instincts*. Princeton: Princeton University Press, 2001.

Gardner, John. *On Moral Fiction*. New York: Basic Books, 1978.

Gates, Bill. *Business @ the Speed of Thought: Succeeding in the Digital Economy*. New York: Warner Books, 1999.

Gehlen, Arnold. *Man in the Age of Technology*. Trans. Patricia Lipscomb. New York: Columbia University Press, 1980.

———. *Zeit-Bilder: Zur Soziologie und Ästhetik der modernen Malerei*. 3rd ed. Frankfurt: Klostermann, 1986.

Genette, Gérard. *Nouveau discours du récit*. Paris: Éditions du Seuil, 1983.

Gethmann-Siefert, Annemarie. "Hegel über Kunst und Alltäglichkeit: Zur Rehabilitierung der schönen Kunst und des ästhetischen Genusses." *Hegel-Studien* 28 (1993): 215–65.

Geyh, Paula, Fred G. Leebron, and Andrew Levy, eds. *Postmodern American Fiction: A Norton Anthology*. New York: Norton, 1998.

Gitlin, Todd. *Media Unlimited: How the Torrent of Images and Sounds Overwhelms Our Lives*. New York: Holt, 2001.

Gleick, James. *Faster: The Acceleration of Just About Everything*. New York: Pantheon, 1999.

Glotfelty, Cheryll, and Harold Fromm, eds. *The Ecocriticism Reader: Landmarks in Literary Ecology*. Athens: University of Georgia Press, 1996.

Glotz, Peter. *Die beschleunigte Gesellschaft: Kulturkämpfe im digitalen Kapitalismus.* Munich: Kindler, 1999.

Godfrey, Tony. *Conceptual Art.* London: Phaidon, 1998.

Goethe, Johann Wolfgang von. *Goethes Werke: Hamburger Ausgabe.* 14 vols. 8th ed. Munich: Beck, 1978.

Gomringer, Eugen. *theorie der konkreten poesie.* Vienna: Splitter, 1997.

Graff, Gerald. *Literature Against Itself: Literary Ideas in Modern Society.* Chicago: University of Chicago Press, 1979.

Greenblatt, Stephen. *Renaissance Self-Fashioning.* Chicago: University of Chicago Press, 1980.

Grimm, Gunter E., ed. *Deutsche Naturlyrik: Vom Barock bis zur Gegenwart.* Stuttgart: Reclam, 1995.

Grossberg, Lawrence, Cary Nelson, and Paula A. Treichler, eds. *Cultural Studies.* New York: Routledge, 1992.

Großklaus, Götz, and Eberhard Lämmert, eds. *Literatur in einer industriellen Kultur.* Stuttgart: Cotta, 1989.

Gruben, Gottfried. *Die Tempel der Griechen.* 3rd ed. Munich: Hirmer, 1980.

Grumbling, Vernon Owen. "Literature." *Greening the College Curriculum: A Guide to Environmental Teaching in the Liberal Arts.* Ed. Jonathan Collett and Stephen Karakashian. Washington, D.C.: Island, 1996.

Guénon, René. *The Reign of Quantity and the Signs of the Times.* Trans. Lord Northbourne. Bristol: Burleigh, 1953.

Guyer, Carolyn. *Quibbling.* Computer software. Cambridge: Eastgate, 1993.

Guyer, Paul. *Kant and the Experience of Freedom: Essays on Aesthetics and Morality.* Cambridge: Cambridge University Press, 1993.

Häffele, Claus Dieter. *Kunst + Ökologie: Texte zur "Umweltkritischen Kunst" des Hinweisers Bernd Löbach.* Cremlingen: Designbuch Verlag, 1986.

Halpern, Daniel, ed. *On Nature: Nature, Landscape, and Natural History.* San Francisco: North Point, 1987.

Hardin, Garrett. "The Tragedy of the Commons." *Managing the Commons.* Ed. Garrett Hardin and John Baden. San Francisco: Freeman, 1977: 16–30.

Hartman, Geoffrey. *Criticism in the Wilderness: The Study of Literature Today.* New Haven: Yale University Press, 1980.

Hauser, Arnold. *Sozialgeschichte der Kunst und Literatur.* 1953. Munich: Beck, 1973.

Hawken, Paul. *The Ecology of Commerce: A Declaration of Sustainability.* New York: Harper, 1993.

Haynes, Roslynn D. *From Faust to Strangelove: Representations of the Scientist in Western Literature.* Baltimore: Johns Hopkins University Press, 1994.

Hegel, G. W. F. *Werke in zwanzig Bänden.* Ed. Eva Moldenhauer and Karl Markus Michel. Frankfurt: Suhrkamp, 1978.

Heidegger, Martin. *Being and Time.* Trans. Joan Stambaugh. Albany: State University of New York Press, 1996.

———. "The Origin of the Work of Art." *Poetry, Language, Thought.* Trans. Albert Hofstadter. New York: Harper, 1971.

———. *The Question Concerning Technology and Other Essays.* Trans. William Lovitt. New York: Harper, 1977.

———. "Überwindung der Metaphysik." *Vorträge und Aufsätze.* Pfullingen: Neske, 1954: 71–99.

Heine, Heinrich. *Sämtliche Schriften.* Ed. Klaus Briegleb et al. 6 vols. Munich: Hanser, 1968–1976.

Herbert, George. *The Complete English Works.* Ed. Ann Pasternak Slater. New York: Knopf, 1995.

Herf, Jeffrey. *Reactionary Modernism: Technology, Culture, and Politics in Weimar and the Third Reich.* Cambridge: Cambridge University Press, 1984.

Hermand, Jost. *Geschichte der Germanistik.* Reinbek: Rowohlt, 1994.

———. *Grüne Utopien in Deutschland: Zur Geschichte des ökologischen Bewußtseins.* Frankfurt: Fischer, 1991.

———. *Im Wettlauf mit der Zeit: Anstöße zu einer ökologiebewußten Ästhetik.* Berlin: Sigma, 1991.

Heydebrand, Renate von, and Simon Winko. *Einführung in die Wertung der Literatur: Systematik—Geschichte—Legitimation.* Paderborn: Schöningh, 1996.

Hirsch, E. D. *Validity in Interpretation.* New Haven: Yale University Press, 1967.

Hochman, Jhan. *Green Cultural Studies: Nature in Film, Novel, and Theory.* Moscow: University of Idaho Press, 1998.

Hoeges, Dirk. *Alles veloziferisch: Die Eisenbahn—vom schönen Ungeheuer zur Ästhetik der Geschwindigkeit.* Rheinbach-Merzbach: CMZ-Verlag, 1985.

Hoffmann, E. T. A. *The Best Tales of Hoffmann.* Ed. E. F. Bleiler. New York: Dover, 1967.

Hölderlin, Friedrich. *Hyperion or the Hermit in Greece.* Trans. Willard R. Trask. New York: Ungar, 1984.

Holub, Robert C. *Crossing Borders: Reception Theory, Poststructuralism, Deconstruction.* Madison: University of Wisconsin Press, 1992.

Hösle, Vittorio. "Foundational Issues of Objective Idealism." *Objective Idealism, Ethics, and Politics.* Notre Dame: University of Notre Dame Press, 1998: 1–40.

———. "Heideggers Philosophie der Technik." *Wiener Jahrbuch der Philosophie* 23 (1991): 37–53.

———. *Die Krise der Gegenwart und die Verantwortung der Philosophie: Transzendentalpragmatik, Letztbegründung, Ethik.* 2nd ed. Munich: Beck, 1994.

———. *Moral und Politik: Grundlagen einer politischen Ethik für das 21. Jahrhundert.* Munich: Beck, 1997.

———. *Philosophie der ökologischen Krise: Moskauer Vorträge.* Munich: Beck, 1991.

———. *Philosophiegeschichte und objektiver Idealismus.* Munich: Beck, 1996.

———. *Praktische Philosophie in der modernen Welt.* Munich: Beck, 1992.

———. "Why Do We Laugh at and with Woody Allen?" *Film and Philosophy.* Special issue (2000): 7–50.

Howard, George S. *Ecological Psychology: Creating a More Earth-Friendly Human Nature.* Notre Dame: University of Notre Dame Press, 1997.

Huizinga, Johan. *Homo Ludens: A Study of the Play Element in Culture.* Boston: Beacon, 1950.

Iser, Wolfgang. "Die Appellstruktur der Texte: Unbestimmtheit als Wirkungsbedingung literarischer Prosa." *Rezeptionsästhetik: Theorie und Praxis.* Ed. Rainer Warning. Munich: Fink, 1975: 228–52.

Jakobson, Roman. "Linguistics and Poetics." *Style in Language.* Ed. Thomas A. Sebeok. Cambridge: MIT Press, 1960: 350–77.

Jameson, Fredric. *Signatures of the Visible.* New York: Routledge, 1990.

Jaspers, Karl. *Vom Ursprung und Ziel der Geschichte.* Zürich: Artemis, 1949.

Jauß, Hans Robert, ed. *Die nicht mehr schönen Künste: Grenzphänomene des Ästhetischen. Poetik und Hermeneutik* 3. Munich: Fink, 1968.

Johnson, Richard. "What Is Cultural Studies Anyway?" *Social Text: Theory/Culture/Ideology* 16 (1986/87): 38–80.

Jonas, Hans. *The Imperative of Responsibility: In Search of an Ethics for the Technological Age.* Trans. Hans Jonas with the collaboration of David Herr. Chicago: University of Chicago Press, 1984.

Joy, Bill. "Why the Future Doesn't Need Us." *Wired* (April 2000): 238–62.

Joyce, Michael. *afternoon, a story.* Computer disk. Cambridge: Eastgate, 1987.

———. *Of Two Minds: Hypertext Pedagogy and Poetics.* Ann Arbor: University of Michigan Press, 1995.

Jünger, Friedrich Georg. *Die Perfektion der Technik.* 2nd ed. Frankfurt: Klostermann, 1949.

Kaiser, Georg. *Gas: Schauspiel.* Frankfurt: Ullstein, 1971.

Kaiser, Gerhard. *Wozu noch Literatur? Über Dichtung und Leben.* Munich: Beck, 1996.

Kaiser, Reinhard. *Literarische Spaziergänge im Internet: Bücher und Bibliotheken online.* 2nd ed. Frankfurt: Eichborn, 1997.

Kamzclak, Roland. *Computergestützte Text-Edition.* Tübingen: Niemeyer, 1999.

Kant, Immanuel. *Critique of Judgement.* Trans. Werner S. Pluhar. Indianapolis: Hackett, 1987.

———. *Werkausgabe.* Ed. Wilhelm Weischedel. 12 vols. Frankfurt: Suhrkamp, 1968.

Kästner, Erich. *Gedichte.* Zurich: Atrium, 1959.

Kerridge, Richard, and Neil Sammells. *Writing the Environment: Ecocriticism and Literature.* New York: Zed, 1998.

Kittler, Friedrich. *Aufschreibesysteme, 1800/1900.* 3rd ed. München: Fink, 1995.

Klee, Paul. *Schriften: Rezensionen und Aufsätze.* Ed. Christian Geelhaar. Cologne: DuMont, 1976.

Kleßman, Eckart, ed. *Die vier Jahreszeiten.* Stuttgart: Reclam, 1991.

Königsdorf, Helga. *Respektloser Umgang: Erzählung.* Frankfurt: Luchterhand, 1988.

Koppen, Erwin. *Literatur und Photographie: Über Geschichte und Thematik einer Medienentdeckung.* Stuttgart: Metzler, 1987.

Koyré, Alexandre. *From the Closed World to the Infinite Universe.* Baltimore: Johns Hopkins University Press, 1957.

Krause, Markus, ed. *Poesie & Maschine: Die Technik in der deutschsprachigen Literatur.* Cologne: Kösler, 1989.

Krieger, Murray. *A Reopening of Closure: Organicism Against Itself.* New York: Columbia University Press, 1989.

Kristeller, Paul Oskar. "The Modern System of the Arts: A Study in the History of Aesthetics." *Journal of the History of Ideas* 12 (1951): 496–527 and 13 (1952): 17–46.

Kroeber, Karl. *Ecological Literary Criticism: Romantic Imagining and the Biology of the Mind.* New York: Columbia University Press, 1994.

Landes, David S. *Revolution in Time: Clocks and the Making of the Modern World.* Cambridge: Harvard University Press, 1983.

Landow, George P. *Hypertext 2.0: The Convergence of Contemporary Critical Theory and Technology.* Baltimore: Johns Hopkins University Press, 1997.

Landow, George P., ed. *Hyper/Text/Theory.* Baltimore: Johns Hopkins University Press, 1994.

Lane, Robert E. *The Liberties of Wit: Humanism, Criticism, and the Civic Mind.* New Haven: Yale University Press, 1961.

————. *The Loss of Happiness in Market Democracies.* New Haven: Yale University Press, 2000.

Lasch, Christopher. *The Culture of Narcissism: American Life in an Age of Diminishing Expectations.* New York: Warner, 1979.

Longinus. *On the Sublime.* Ed. W. Hamilton Fyfe and Donald Russell. Cambridge: Harvard University Press, 1995.

Lovelock, James E. *Gaia: A New Look at Life on Earth.* 2nd ed. New York: Oxford University Press, 1987.

Lowe, Marcia D. "Shaping Cities: The Environmental and Human Dimensions." *Worldwatch Paper 105.* October 1991.

Löwith, Karl. "Vicos Grundsatz: verum et factum convertuntur. Seine theologische Prämisse und deren säkulare Konsequenzen." *Sämtliche Schriften.* Stuttgart: Metzler, 1986: 9:195–227.

Luhmann, Niklas. *Ökologische Kommunikation: Kann die moderne Gesellschaft sich auf ökologische Gefährdungen einstellen?* 3rd ed. Opladen: Westdeutscher Verlag, 1990.

Lukács, Georg. *Essays über Realismus.* Berlin: Luchterhand, 1971.

Lutwack, Leonard. *The Role of Place in Literature.* Syracuse: Syracuse University Press, 1984.

Lutz, Theo. "Stochastische Texte." *Augenblick* 4 (1959): 3–9.

Lyon, Thomas J., ed. *This Incomperable Lande: A Book of American Nature Writing.* Boston: Mifflin, 1989.

Lyotard, Jean-François. *The Postmodern Condition: A Report on Knowledge.* Minneapolis: University of Minnesota Press, 1984.

Mahr, Johannes. *Eisenbahnen in der deutschen Dichtung: Der Wandel eines literarischen Motivs im 19. und im beginnenden 20. Jahrhundert.* Munich: Fink, 1982.

Marinetti, Filippo Tommaso. *Selected Writings.* Ed. R. W. Flint. New York: Farrar, 1972.

Marquard, Odo. "On the Unavoidability of the Human Sciences." *In Defense of the Accidental. Philosophical Studies.* Trans. Robert M. Wallace. New York: Oxford University Press, 1991: 91–108.

Marsch, Edgar, ed. *Moderne deutsche Naturlyrik.* Stuttgart: Reclam, 1980.

Marx, Karl. "Die entfremdete Arbeit." *Historisch-kritische Gesamtausgabe.* Berlin: Marx-Engels-Verlag, 1932: section 1, vol. 3, 81–94.

————. "Geld." *Historisch-kritische Gesamtausgabe.* Berlin: Marx-Engels-Verlag, 1932: section 1, vol. 3, 145–49.

————. *Grundrisse: Foundations of the Critique of Political Economy.* Trans. Martin Nicolaus. New York: Random House, 1973.

Marx, Leo. *The Machine in the Garden: Technology and the Pastoral Ideal in America.* New York: Oxford University Press, 1964.

Mayer-Tasch, Peter Cornelius. *Im Gewitter der Geraden: Deutsche Ökolyrik, 1950–1980.* Münich: Beck, 1981.

McCarthy, John A., and Katrin Schneider, eds. *The Future of Germanistik in the USA: Changing Our Prospects.* Nashville: Vanderbilt University Press, 1996.

McGann, Jerome. *Radiant Textuality: Literature after the World Wide Web.* New York: Palgrave, 2001.

McKibben, Bill. *Enough: Staying Human in an Engineered Age.* New York: Holt, 2003.

McLuhan, Marshall. *The Gutenberg Galaxy: The Making of Typographic Man.* Toronto: University of Toronto Press, 1962.

————. *Understanding Media: The Extensions of Man.* Cambridge: MIT Press, 1994.

Meeker, Joseph W. *The Comedy of Survival: Studies in Literary Ecology.* New York: Scribner's, 1974.

Meyer, Hermann J. *Die Technisierung der Welt: Herkunft, Wesen und Gefahren.* Tübingen: Niemeyer, 1961.

Meyrowitz, Joshua. *No Sense of Place: The Impact of Electronic Media on Social Behavior.* Oxford: Oxford University Press, 1985.

Milgram, Stanley. "Das Erleben der Großstadt. Eine psychologische Analyse." *Zeitschrift für Sozialpsychologie* 1 (1970): 142–52.

Mill, John Stuart. *Collected Works.* 33 vols. Toronto: University of Toronto Press, 1963–.

Miller, J. Hillis. *Ariadne's Thread: Story Lines.* New Haven: Yale University Press, 1992.

————. *On Literature.* New York: Routledge, 2002.

————. *Theory Now and Then.* Durham: Duke University Press, 1991.

Minaty, Wolfgang, ed. *Die Eisenbahn: Gedichte. Prosa. Bilder.* Frankfurt: Insel, 1984.

Mondolfo, Rodolfo. *Il "verum-factum" prima di Vico.* Naples: Guida, 1969.

Monro, D. H. *Argument of Laughter.* Notre Dame: University of Notre Dame Press, 1963.

Montrose, Louis A. "Professing the Renaissance: The Poetics and Politics of Culture." *The New Historicism.* Ed. H. Aram Veeser. New York: Routledge, 1989: 15–36.

Moulthrop, Stuart. "Traveling in the Breakdown Lane. A Principle of Resistance for Hypertext." *Mosaic* 28, no. 4 (1995): 55–77.

————. *Victory Garden.* Hyperfiction computer program. Cambridge: Eastgate, 1991.

Mukarovský, Jan. "Standard Language and Poetic Language." *A Prague School Reader on Esthetics, Literary Structure, and Style.* Trans. Paul L. Garvin. Washington, D.C.: Georgetown University Press, 1964: 17–30.

Müller-Seidel, Walter. *Probleme der literarischen Wertung: Über die Wissenschaftlichkeit eines unwissenschaftliches Themas.* 2nd ed. Stuttgart: Metzler, 1969.

Mumford, Lewis. *Technics and Civilization.* New York: Harcourt, 1934.

Mundt, Theodor. *Madonna: Unterhaltungen mit einer Heiligen.* Leipzig: Reichenbach, 1835.

————. "Über Bewegungsparteien in der Literatur." *Literarischer Zodiacus: Journal für Zeit und Leben, Wissenschaft und Kunst* 1 (1835): 1–20. Rpt. Frankfurt: Athenäum, 1971.

Murdoch, Iris. *The Sovereignty of Good.* New York: Routledge, 1970.

Murphy, Patrick D., ed. *Literature of Nature: An International Sourcebook.* Chicago: Fitzroy, 1998.

Nielsen, Jakob. *Hypertext and Hypermedia.* Boston: Academic, 1990.

Nietzsche, Friedrich. *Werke.* Ed. Karl Schlechta. 6th ed. Munich: Hanser, 1969.

Nikulin, Dmitri. *Metaphysik und Ethik: Theoretische und praktische Philosophie in Antike und Neuzeit.* Trans. Martin Pfeiffer. Munich: Beck, 1996.

Nussbaum, Martha. *Poetic Justice: The Literary Imagination and Public Life.* Boston: Beacon, 1995.

Nye, David E. *America as Second Creation: Technology and Narratives of New Beginnings.* Cambridge: MIT Press, 2003.

Ong, Walter J. *Orality and Literacy: The Technologizing of the Word.* New York: Routledge, 1982.

Ortega y Gasset, José. "Thoughts on Technology." Trans. Helene Weyl and Edwin Williams. *Philosophy and Technology: Readings in the Philosophical Problems of Technology.* Ed. Carl Mitcham and Robert Mackey. New York: Free Press, 1972: 290–313.

Pack, Robert, and Jay Parini, eds. *Poems for A Small Planet: Contemporary American Nature Poetry.* Hanover: University Press of New England, 1993.

Packard, Vance. *The Waste Makers.* New York: McKay, 1960.

Palmer, Frank. *Literature and Moral Understanding: A Philosophical Essay on Ethics, Aesthetics, Education, and Culture.* Oxford: Clarendon, 1992.

Panofsky, Erwin. *Idea: Ein Beitrag zur Begriffsgeschichte der älteren Kunsttheorie.* Leipzig: Teubner, 1924.

Pascal, Blaise. *Pensées.* Ed. Philippe Sellier. Paris: Garnier, 1991.

Peacock, Ronald. *Criticism and Personal Taste.* Oxford: Clarendon, 1972.

The Perseus Digital Library. Ed. Gregory Crane. <http://www.perseus.tufts.edu/> (accessed 1 June 2003).

Phillips, Dana. *The Truth of Ecology: Nature, Culture, and Literature in America.* New York: Oxford, 2003.

Plato. *The Collected Dialogues, Including the Letters.* Ed. Edith Hamilton and Huntington Cairns. Princeton: Princeton University Press, 1978.

Plotinus. *The Enneads.* Trans. Stephen MacKenna. New York: Penguin, 1991.

Poe, Edgar Allen. "Philosophy of Composition." *The Complete Works of Edgar Allen Poe.* Ed. Charles F. Richardson. New York: Putnam's, 1902: 287–306.

Pope, Alexander. *The Poems of Alexander Pope.* Ed. John Butt. New Haven: Yale University Press, 1963.

Postman, Neil. *Amusing Ourselves to Death: Public Discourse in the Age of Show Business.* 1985. New York: Penguin, 1986.

———. *Technopoly.* New York: Knopf, 1992.

Das Projekt Gutenberg. <http://www.gutenberg.aol.de> (accessed 1 June 2003).

Rademacher, Gerhard. *Das Technik-Motiv in der Literatur und seine Relevanz: Am Beispiel des Eisenbahngedichts im 19. und 20. Jahrhunderts.* Frankfurt: Lang, 1981.

Rathenau, Walter. "Zur Kritik der Zeit." 1911. *Gesammelte Schriften.* 5 vols. Berlin: Fischer, 1918: 1:7–148.

Reinecke, Siegfried. *Mobile Zeiten: Eine Geschichte der Auto-Dichtung.* Bochum: Germinal, 1986.

Rescher, Nicholas. *The Coherence Theory of Truth.* Oxford: Clarendon, 1973.

Riha, Karl. *Deutsche Großstadtlyrik: Eine Einführung.* Munich: Artemis, 1983.

Rilke, Rainer Maria. *Selected Poems.* Trans. Albert Ernest Flemming. New York: Methuen, 1985.

Rimmon-Kenan, Shlomith. *Narrative Fiction: Contemporary Poetics.* New York: Methuen, 1983.

Roche, Mark W. "Areas of Expertise, Proleptic Interpretation, Penultimate Drafts: Three Ideas for the Graduate Seminar in Literature." *Die Unterrichtspraxis* 20 (1987): 261–68.

———. "Christ as the Lost I: Multiple Interpretations of Gottfried Benn's Poem *Verlorenes Ich.*" *Religion and Literature* 34, no. 3 (2002): 27–56.

———. *Dynamic Stillness: Philosophical Conceptions of Ruhe in Schiller, Hölderlin, Büchner, and Heine.* Tübingen: Niemeyer, 1987.

———. *Gottfried Benn's Static Poetry: Aesthetic and Intellectual-Historical Interpretations.* Chapel Hill: University of North Carolina Press, 1991.

———. "Justice and the Withdrawal of God in Woody Allen's *Crimes and Misdemeanors.*" *Film and Philosophy.* Special issue (2000): 68–83.

———. "Kafka, Pirandello, and the Irony of Ironic Indeterminacy." *Journal of the Kafka Society of America* 18 (1994): 42–47.

———. "Laughter and Truth in *Doktor Faustus:* Nietzschean Structures in Mann's Novel of Self-Cancellations." *Deutsche Vierteljahrsschrift für Literaturwissenschaft und Geistesgeschichte* 60 (1986): 309–32.

———. *Die Moral der Kunst: Über Literatur und Ethik.* Münich: Beck, 2002.

———. "National Socialism and the Disintegration of Values: Reflections on Nietzsche, Rosenberg, and Broch." *Journal of Value Inquiry* 26 (1992): 367–81.

———. Review of *Literarische Ästhetik: Methoden und Modelle der Literaturwissenschaft,* by Peter V. Zima. Tübingen: Francke, 1991. *German Quarterly* 68 (1995): 187–89.

———. "Die Rolle des Erzählers in *Brochs Verzauberung.*" *Brochs Verzauberung.* Ed. Paul Michael Lützeler. Frankfurt: Suhrkamp, 1983: 131–46.

———. *Tragedy and Comedy: A Systematic Study and a Critique of Hegel.* Albany: State University of New York Press, 1998.

Roche, Mark W., and Vittorio Hösle. "Vico's Age of Heroes and the Age of Men in John Ford's *The Man Who Shot Liberty Valance.*" *CLIO* 23 (1994): 131–47.

Roehler, Klaus, and Kalle Giese, eds. *Das Autobuch: Geschichten und Ansichten.* Darmstadt: Luchterhand, 1983.

Ronell, Avital. *The Telephone Book: Technology—Schizophrenia—Electric Speech.* Lincoln: University of Nebraska Press, 1989.

Rorty, Richard. *Philosophy and the Mirror of Nature.* Princeton: Princeton University Press, 1979.

Rosenblatt, Louise M. *Literature as Exploration.* 5th ed. New York: MLA, 1995.

———. *The Reader, the Text, the Poem: The Transactional Theory of the Literary Work.* 2nd ed. Carbondale: Southern Illinois University Press, 1994.

Rosenkranz, Karl. *Ästhetik des Häßlichen.* 1853. Darmstadt: Wissenschaftliche Buchgesellschaft, 1979.

———. *System der Wissenschaft.* Königsberg: Bornträger, 1850.

Roszak, Theodore. *The Voice of the Earth.* New York: Simon, 1992.

Rugg, Linda. *Picturing Ourselves: Photography and Autobiography.* Chicago: University of
Chicago Press, 1997.

Ruskin, John. *The Works of John Ruskin.* Ed. E. T. Cook and Alexander Wedderburn. 39 vols.
London: Allen, 1903–1912.

Sachsse, Hans, ed. *Technik und Gesellschaft.* 3 vols. Munich: UTB, 1976.

Santayana, George. *The Sense of Beauty: Being the Outline of Aesthetic Theory.* 1896. New
York: Dover, 1955.

Die Säulen von Llacaan. <http://netzwerke.textbox.de/llacaan/> (accessed on 1 August
2001).

Scarry, Elaine. *On Beauty and Being Just.* Princeton: Princeton University Press, 1999.

Schaeffer, Jean-Marie. *Art of the Modern Age: Philosophy of Art from Kant to Heidegger.* Trans.
Steven Rendall. Princeton: Princeton University Press, 2000.

Scheler, Max. *Das Ressentiment im Aufbau der Moralen.* 1912. Frankfurt: Klostermann, 1978.

Schelling, Friedrich Wilhelm Joseph. *Philosophie der Kunst.* 1859. Darmstadt: Wissenschaftliche Buchgesellschaft, 1960.

———. *The Philosophy of Art.* Trans. Douglas W. Stott. Minneapolis: University of Minnesota Press, 1989.

———. *Schriften von 1799–1801.* Darmstadt: Wissenschaftliche Buchgesellschaft, 1975.

Schiller, Friedrich. *On the Aesthetic Education of Man in a Series of Letters.* Trans. Elizabeth
M. Wilkinson and L. A. Willoughby. Oxford: Clarendon, 1967.

Schings, Hans-Jürgen. *Die Brüder des Marquis Posa: Schiller und der Geheimbund der Illu-
minaten.* Tübingen: Niemeyer, 1996.

Schneider, Peter-Paul, et al., eds. *Literatur im Industriezeitalter.* 2 vols. Marbach: Deutsche
Schillergesellschaft, 1987.

Schöne, Albrecht. *Aufklärung aus dem Geist der Experimentalphysik: Lichtenbergsche Kon-
junktive.* 2nd ed. Munich: Beck, 1983.

———. *Säkularisation als sprachbildende Kraft: Studien zur Dichtung deutscher Pfarrersöhne.*
Göttingen: Vandenhoeck, 1958.

Schor, Juliet B. *The Overworked American: The Unexpected Decline of Leisure.* New York: Basic, 1991.

Schwerte, Hans. "Der Begriff des Experiments in der Dichtung." *Literatur und Geistesgeschichte: Festgabe für Heinz Otto Burger.* Berlin: Schmidt, 1968: 387–405.

Sedlmayr, Hans. *Gefahr und Hoffnung des technischen Zeitalters.* Salzburg: Müller, 1970.

———. *Verlust der Mitte: Die bildende Kunst des 19. und 20. Jahrhunderts als Symbol der Zeit.*
Salzburg: Müller, 1948.

Seel, Martin. *Eine Ästhetik der Natur.* Frankfurt: Suhrkamp, 1991.

Segeberg, Harro. *Literarische Technik-Bilder: Studien zum Verhältnis von Technik- und Liter-
aturgeschichte im 19. und frühen 20. Jahrhundert.* Tübingen: Niemeyer, 1987.

———. *Literatur im technischen Zeitalter: Von der Frühzeit der deutschen Aufklärung bis zum
Beginn des Ersten Weltkriegs.* Darmstadt: Wissenschaftliche Buchgesellschaft, 1997.

Segeberg, Harro, ed. *Technik in der Literatur: Ein Forschungsüberblick und zwölf Aufsätze.* Frankfurt: Suhrkamp, 1987.

Sextus Empiricus. *Against the Professors.* Trans. R. G. Bury. Cambridge: Harvard University Press, 1949.

Shakespeare, William. *The Complete Works of William Shakespeare.* <http://www.chemicool.com/Shakespeare> (accessed on 1 June 2003).

Shenk, David. *Data Smog: Surviving the Information Glut.* San Francisco: HarperCollins, 1997.

Showalter, Elaine. "Introduction: The Feminist Critical Revolution." *The New Feminist Criticism: Essays on Women, Literature, and Theory.* Ed. Elaine Showalter. New York: Pantheon, 1985: 3–17.

Sieferle, Rolf Peter. *Fortschrittsfeinde? Opposition gegen Technik und Industrie von der Romantik bis zur Gegenwart.* Munich: Beck, 1984.

Silz, Walter. *Hölderlins Hyperion: A Critical Reading.* Philadelphia: University of Pennsylvania Press, 1969.

———. "The Scholar, the Critic, and the Teacher of Literature." *German Quarterly* 37 (1964): 113–19.

Simmel, Georg. "The Metropolis and Mental Life." *On Individuality and Social Forms: Selected Writings.* Ed. Donald N. Levine. Chicago: University of Chicago Press, 1971: 324–39.

Simon-Ritz, Frank, ed. *Germanistik im Internet: Eine Orientierungshilfe.* Berlin: Deutsches Bibliotheksinstitut, 1998. Also available at <http://dbix04.dbi-berlin.de/dbi_pub/einzelpu/ifb-bh8/ifb_00.htm>.

Smith, Barbara Herrnstein. *Contingencies of Value: Alternative Perspectives for Critical Theory.* Cambridge: Harvard University Press, 1988.

Snow, C. P. *The Two Cultures and a Second Look.* 1959. Cambridge: Cambridge University Press, 1965.

Sokal, Alan. "Transgressing the Boundaries: Toward a Transformative Hermeneutics of Quantum Gravity." *Social Text* 46/47 (1996): 217–52.

Sokal, Alan, and Jean Bricmont. *Fashionable Nonsense: Postmodern Intellectuals' Abuse of Science.* New York: Picador, 1998.

Spitzer, Leo. *Linguistics and Literary History: Essays in Stylistics.* Princeton: Princeton University Press, 1948.

Stanzel, Franz. *Typische Formen des Romans.* 8th ed. Göttingen: Vandenhoeck, 1976.

Stifter, Adalbert. *Sämtliche Werke.* Ed. Gustav Wilhelm. 25 vols. Hildesheim: Gerstenberg, 1972.

Stramm, August. *Gedichte Dramen Prosa Briefe.* Ed. Jörg Drews. Stuttgart: Reclam, 1997.

SUNY Buffalo Electronic Poetry Center. <http://epc.buffalo.edu/> (accessed on 1 August 2001).

Taylor, Mark C. *Erring: A Postmodern A/theology.* Chicago: University of Chicago Press, 1984.

Taylor, Mark C., and Esa Saarinen. *Imagologies: Media Philosophy.* New York: Routledge, 1994.

Tenner, Edward. *Why Things Bite Back: Technology and the Revenge of Unintended Consequences.* New York: Vintage, 1997.

Thesaurus Linguae Graecae. <http://www.tlg.uci.edu/> (accessed on 1 June 2003).

Todorov, Tzvetan. *The Fantastic: A Structural Approach to a Literary Genre.* Trans. Richard Howard. Cleveland: Case Western Reserve University Press, 1973.

Tolstoy, Leo. *What Is Art?* Trans. Richard Pevear and Larissa Volokhonsky. New York: Penguin, 1995.

Tschumi, Bernard. "Parc de la Villette, Paris." *Deconstruction: Omnibus Volume.* Ed. Andreas Papadakis, Catherine Cooke, and Andrew Benjamin. New York: Rizzoli, 1989: 175–83.

Tuxill, John. "Appreciating the Benefits of Plant Biodiversity." *State of the World 1999: A Worldwatch Institute Report on Progress Toward a Sustainable Society.* New York: Norton, 1999: 96–114.

Van Cleve, John Walter, and A. Leslie Wilson. *Remarks on the Needed Reform of German Studies in the United States.* Columbia, S.C.: Camden House, 1993.

Van der Voort, Tom H. A. "Television and the Decline of Reading." *Poetics* 20 (1991): 73–89.

Verene, Donald Phillip. *Philosophy and the Return to Self-Knowledge.* New Haven: Yale University Press, 1997.

Vico, Giambattista. *The New Science.* Trans. Thomas Goddard Bergin and Max Harold Fisch. Ithaca: Cornell University Press, 1984.

———. *Opere.* 8 volumes in 11. Bari: Laterza, 1911–1942.

Vietta, Silvio. "Großstadtwahrnehung und ihre literarische Darstellung: Expressionistischer Reihungsstil und Collage." *Deutsche Vierteljahrsschrift für Literaturwissenschaft und Geistesgeschichte* 48 (1974): 354–73.

———. *Die vollendete Speculation führt zur Natur zurück: Natur und Ästhetik.* Leipzig: Reclam, 1995.

von Bormann, Alexander. *Die Erde will ein freies Geleit: Deutsche Naturlyrik aus sechs Jahrhunderten.* Frankfurt: Insel, 1984.

Waage, Frederick O., ed. *Teaching Environmental Literature: Materials, Methods, Resources.* New York: MLA, 1985.

Wachtel, Paul. *The Poverty of Affluence: A Psychological Portrait of the American Way of Life.* New York: Macmillan, 1983.

Wackernagel, Mathis, and William Rees. *Our Ecological Footprint: Reducing Human Impact on the Earth.* Gabriola Island, British Columbia, Canada: New Society, 1996.

Wallace, Patricia. *The Psychology of the Internet.* Cambridge: Cambridge University Press, 1999.

Weber, Max. *Gesammelte Aufsätze zur Wissenschaftslehre.* 2nd ed. Tübingen: Mohr, 1951.

———. "Science as a Vocation." *From Max Weber: Essays in Sociology.* Trans. H. H. Gerth and C. Wright Mills. New York: Oxford University Press, 1946: 129–56.

Weber, Samuel. "The Sideshow, or: Remarks on a Canny Moment." *Modern Language Notes* 88 (1973): 1102–33.

Weimar, Klaus, and Christoph Jermann. "'Zwiesprache' oder Literaturwissenschaft?" *Neue Hefte für Philosophie* 23 (1984): 113–57.

Weiner, Marc. "From the Editor." *German Quarterly* 69 (1996): v–ix.

Weyl, Hermann. *Symmetry.* Princeton: Princeton University Press, 1952.

White, Lynn Jr. *Medieval Technology and Social Change.* Oxford: Clarendon, 1962.

Whitehead, Alfred North. *Science and the Modern World.* 1925. New York: Free Press, 1967.

"Why Major in Literature—What Do We Tell Our Students?" *PMLA* 117 (2002): 487–521.

Wilde, Oscar. *The Complete Works of Oscar Wilde.* New York: Harper, 1989.

Wilson, Alexander. *The Culture of Nature: North American Landscapes from Disney to the Exxon Valdez.* Oxford: Blackwell, 1992.

Wilson, Edward O. *The Diversity of Life.* Cambridge: Harvard University Press, 1992.

Wimsatt, W. K. *The Verbal Icon: Studies in the Meaning of Poetry.* Lexington: University Press of Kentucky, 1954.

Winkels, Hubert. *Leselust und Bildermacht: Über Literatur, Fernsehen, und neue Medien.* Cologne: Kiepenheuer, 1997.

Winner, Langdon. *Autonomous Technology: Technics-out-of-Control as a Theme in Political Thought.* Cambridge: MIT Press, 1977.

Wood, Peter. *Diversity: The Invention of a Concept.* San Francisco: Encounter, 2003.

Wordsworth, William. *A Critical Edition of the Major Works.* Ed. Stephen Gill. Oxford: Oxford University Press, 1984.

Zima, Peter V. *Literarische Aesthetik: Methoden und Modelle der Literaturwissenschaft.* Tübingen: Francke, 1991.

Ziolkowski, Theodore. *German Romanticism and Its Institutions.* Princeton: Princeton University Press, 1990.

———. *Varieties of Literary Thematics.* Princeton: Princeton University Press, 1983.

Zola, Émile. *The Experimental Novel and Other Essays.* Trans. Belle Sherman. New York: Haskell, 1964.

———. *Thérèse Raquin.* Trans. Leonard Tancock. London: Folio, 1969.

Zuckmayer, Carl. *Der Hauptmann von Köpenick.* Frankfurt: Fischer, 1979.

Index

Absolute, the, 45, 110, 136, 244, 253

Absolute music, 5–6, 7

Acceptance, 225, 226–27, 253, 257

Accident (Wolf), 189

ADD (attention deficit disorder), 169

Adorno, Theodor, 160–61, 190, 205, 270n6

Advertising, 26, 89, 104, 144, 155, 156, 159, 190, 201, 236, 272n1

Aeneid (Virgil), 23

Aeschylus, 247

Aesthetic autonomy, 40

Aesthetic constructivism, 134

Aesthetic education, 70. See also *On the Aesthetic Education of Man* (Schiller)

Aesthetic evaluation, 88–93

Aesthetic reading, 29–30, 31

Aesthetics: artwork aesthetics, 33–34, 49, 50–53, 68, 181–91, 257; classical aesthetics, 218; criteria for literary canon, 251–52; and culture studies, 106–7;

and deconstruction, 110–11; different possibilities of, 36; and evaluation, 62; and interconnectedness, 30, 38; Kant on, 12, 21, 26, 27, 37–39; and morality, 27, 262n5; production aesthetics, 33–34, 49–50, 51, 53, 167–81, 195, 257; and quantity, 142; reception aesthetics, 49, 50, 51, 52, 53, 68, 94, 191–202, 212, 256; return to, 266n3; in the technological age, 167–202, 258–59; tradition of aesthetic evaluation, 273n1; and the ugly, 43–44; Wilde on ethics versus, 7

Affective fallacy, 97

Afternoon (Joyce), 177

Aletheia, 29, 60

Alienation, 157–59

All Quiet on the Western Front (Remarque), 26, 148–49

Allen, Woody, 51, 67, 134, 224, 264n3

Allende, Isabel, 254